THE
MARINE
COOKERY
BIBLE

Malcolm Alder-Smith

ISBN – 13: 978-1453846834

ISBN – 10: 1453846832

First published March 2011

Published by Malcolm Alder-Smith
in conjunction with Create Space

Printed by Create Space

Cover design by: aaronbentley.co.uk

Back cover photo by: Joey Collins

THE MARINE
COOKERY BIBLE

Dedicated to the very special people in my life

For my darling wife, Di and my brilliant kids: Chris, Larnz & Ash

CONTENTS

ACKNOWLEDGEMENTS
and special thanks to:

Emma Baggett: My bestest 'yachtie' mate, confidant, mentor, advisor and marine hospitality superstar. Ex-superyacht crew and trainer, Emma and I designed the original Essential Marine Cookery course for the UKSA back in 2006 and have worked together ever since, delivering courses in marine hospitality and cookery to folk wanting to *"Live the Dream"*.

Claire Everard: Claire has always been passionate about food and cookery. The last ten years in the marine industry have given Claire a wealth of experience cooking on yachts all over the world. Her love of cooking good food, passion for healthy eating and creative ability, have enhanced her yachting career. She currently works as chef onboard a privately owned motor yacht based in the Mediterranean along with her husband Mark.

Vanessa Hodgson: Ex-superyacht crew, Ness is one of the special ingredients in the UKSA's four module Marine Hospitality course. She teaches all the fine arts, techniques and skills required for interior crew working on luxury yachts.

The designers: For making the book cover happen, infinite thanks to Aaron, Arlene, Eva and Joey for giving me their valuable time and expertise to produce fabulous visuals.

The hospitality crew: For those who have contributed to the ongoing success of the UKSA EMC course and subsequently this book: Marie Ely (UKSA), Lorenza Savigni (Cucina Italiana), Gemma Cooper (Neilsons), Sarah Churcher (Global Galley), Claire Everard (Global Galley), Gemma Deloud Clark (Marine Hospitality), Debbie Shipley (Food Safety – IW College), Mark Powell (Global Wine – IW College), Paul Buckland (IW College), Richard Baggett (UKSA), Clair Etchell-Johnson (IW College), Rachel Shanks (IW College) and Chris Shirlaw.

UKSA: Some elements of my book are derived from the UKSA Essential Marine Cookery manual, which Emma and I wrote jointly.

My 'Global Research Team'

I send a whole heap of thanks to friends and grad' students, who have helped me out with so much 'today' information, which has contributed to the writing of this book. All these guys managed to find time in their demanding schedules, to support me with the most up to date information available. They are: Anni Hayes, Carly Williams, Clare Marriage, Denzyl Baynes (SA), Elli Rea, Emma McIntyre, Fiona Thomas, Gemma Deloud Clark, John Craven, Justine Murphy, Kate Caughey (NZ), Lizzi Kendall, Matt Speight (Can), Natasha Sunjich (SA), Nicholle Mackenzie, Raiza Rodriguez (Sp), Shelley Butler and Simon Storey. There are others who have asked me not to mention their names – you know who you are, so a special Malcy thanks to you all.

Massive thanks to all the UKSA Essential Marine Cookery graduate students who have trained with us at The Isle of Wight College since 2006. Many of you have challenged us on a daily basis with your passion for cooking and your probing questions about working in the sector. You have provided us with constructive and meaningful feedback, which has enabled us to review and progress our training courses to new levels of excellence. We have always done our best to be honest with you and paint a realistic picture of both the good and less good times working in the industry. Many of you have left us and gone on to work on a range of amazing yachts and superyachts, working and playing hard and visiting every conceivable corner of our beautiful world, sending us Facebook messages, along with some fabulous photos and tales about those exotic locations.

Thank you all, so very much - you have contributed in more ways than you know, to motivate me to write this book and to communicate our shared knowledge and experiences with others who are thinking about "Living the Dream" .....

..... and finally: A very humble thanks to you for buying my book. I sincerely hope that it inspires you to great achievements and maybe, many adventures working on fabulous yachts and superyachts.

INTRODUCTION

Over the last few years, I have trawled websites, crew magazines and book shops, searching for evidence of the existence of books about working and cooking on yachts and superyachts. I have come across a variety of interesting and differentiated publications, some good, certainly some less so and much of what I have read has been targeted at the 'domestic', non professionally crewed yacht market. A fine example of this type of book is Janet Buckingham's excellent Jupiter Moon Cook Book.

I have to say that one of the most entertaining I have read was written by professional superyacht chef Victoria Allman, who wrote: Sea Fare: A Chef's Journey Across the Ocean, which is an Auto-B, incorporating approximately thirty recipes from Victoria's trips around the world. Victoria is well known in the industry and also writes features for Dockwalk magazine.

Jennifer Errico's well researched and brilliantly written book, Working on Yachts and Superyachts, provides the reader with a comprehensive compendium of carefully researched information and guidance, put together by an author with global contacts and first-hand experience of working in the industry.

I am lucky enough to have many good friends out there on the water, working in the most exotic locations that most people can only dream of visiting. These folk are 'living the dream', along with others who have helped me with information, who are now land based and working in education and training for the sector. It was always my intention to provide my readers with information which is as up to date as possible, so my 'Global Research Team' has answered my cry for help and provided me with the information I needed to fill the gaps in my research.

So, are you fed up with "same old, same old," attracted by the lure of the ocean wave or those crystal clear waters off the British Virgin Islands, Aegean or the Maldives? Maybe you are looking for a lifestyle change, want to travel world and get paid for it, or you just love cooking or looking after people and want to transfer your special interpersonal skills to a career of travel and looking after very discerning clients. Living and working on a fabulous yacht, sailing to exotic locations has to be 'the ultimate fix' in the service industry sector. There are many five star hotels across the world which would struggle to complete with the opulence and level of service provided on many superyachts, where the quality status indicator of 'seven star' is increasingly used. Some might describe such yachts as excessively flamboyant, some might even say pretentious, if not down-right ostentatious, but either which way, many are floating luxury and you will have to work hard to become part of that world. So read on my new friend and dream of waking up to cloudless skies and turquoise seas, or spending your early mornings wandering the vibrant food markets of foreign ports with their sparkling fresh fish stalls and unbelievable vegetables of various shapes, sizes, colours and textures. Perfect days spent sailing beautiful coasts or exploring tropical islands and the satisfaction of preparing, cooking, presenting or serving the ultimate in sexy food to your guests. These are all pleasures that you can look forward to.

Whichever way you look at it, as a provider of food and customer service onboard you will be a key member of the crew and an important part of a team responsible for providing your guests with a high-end experience. The quality and enthusiasm of your personal contribution, whether delivering a service for the owner, charter guests or crewed passage, you have the potential to contribute to the overall success of the voyage.

The front end of this book has been designed to help give you the confidence and theoretical 'know how' to pursue a career in marine hospitality; providing you with some of the tools you will need to be an effective and practical crew member. One of the best characteristics a steward/ess, chef, or stew-chef can possess, is the ability to be flexible, especially when you are working at sea where so many different parameters are involved.

For those of you who want to head for the galley, I have one clear message for 'newbies' (new entrants) to the marine hospitality industry and this is echoed by my friends Bucko, Emma and others who have contributed to this book. We all believe in the same philosophy as Jamie Oliver and Rick Stein - *"Keep it simple and let the flavours speak for themselves"*.

The recipes in this book are a selection of tried and tested favourites, their beauty being that many can be served at various times of the day, depending on quantities and style of presentation.

A BIT ABOUT ME

Known to my friends in the yachting industry as Malcy, I was born near Salisbury (UK) and was classically trained as a chef at Highbury College, where I was taught to cook by French, Italian and Swiss master chefs. I was employed in hotel management for about ten years, before buying my own restaurant, which I ran for a few years before taking up a lecturing post in hospitality and catering at The Isle of Wight College.

I have worked for a number of globally acclaimed catering companies and have memorable experiences of working in corporate and event hospitality management during the late 80s and 90s for companies such as Ring & Brymer, Trust House Forte and Forte in the City of London. I also worked in corporate hospitality management for Forte, Gardner Merchant and Sodexho at such events as the Open Golf, Wimbledon, Chelsea Flower Show and the Farnborough Air Show. I guess my most memorable and enjoyable experiences were spent as part of the corporate hospitality management team for Rolls-Royce at the Paris International Air Show at Le Bourget.

I have also worked at various royal palaces, such as Buckingham Palace, Blenheim Palace and Hampton Court. Working at numerous prestigious events over the years, I have, at one time or another, looked after most senior members of the British Royal Family and numerous British Prime Ministers and Foreign Heads of State.

I moved to France a few years back, where I ran a B&B with my wife and youngest son, before returning to work for the newly formed Business Development Unit at The Isle of Wight College

My budding career as an author, food writer and contributor to yachting websites, has seen me write two other specialist books. The first is still on my computer waiting for the right time for me to publish. The second is called 19 - Dix-Neuf, Cuisine du Terroir Correziénne (published by Leonie Press), which is about the fabulous rural food and cooking of Department 19 (Corrèze), where we lived in France until 2005.

I am a big-time Facebook and Twitter fan and find both to be efficient mediums for keeping in touch with my 'yachtie' graduates, tracking their movements all over the world. I get to hear all about the highs and lows, the tears and laughter, or the dream job someone just missed and the wonderful jobs that many manage to find on the most modern superyachts on the water.

My involvement in training new entrants to work in the yachting sector started back in 2006. The first Essential Marine Cookery (EMC) course came about when I was asked by the CEO of UKSA, Jon Ely, to design a five day cookery module as part of the UKSA Marine Hospitality course. The course already included essential marine training, including the RYA Competent Crew, RYA Level 2 Powerboat, RYA Level 2 Shortwave Radio, First Aid and STCW95 and a one week Marine Hospitality module. As you will read later, you will find it virtually impossible to find work in the sector without STCW95 (minimum requirement) and 'owning' the UKSA package above, gives you the competitive advantage over your job-hunting rivals, chasing after that 'live the dream' job on a fabulous superyacht, doing charter work, maybe based in the Mediterranean, British Virgin Islands (BVIs), Caribbean or Pacific.

Emma and I took a blank canvas and designed the first five day EMC course, which we delivered in June 2006. Things have moved a million miles since those early days and although the course has always been a great success, it has now evolved into an intensive six day module, culminating in our students provisioning, preparing, cooking, hosting and serving a three course crew dinner onboard UKSA yachts moored on the River Medina at the world famous yachting mecca that is Cowes, on the Isle of Wight. We now work together for a few weeks each year, to provide high quality marine cookery training at The Isle of Wight College.

Although other marine cookery courses do exist, I firmly believe that we have become the lead trainers of a globally recognised product that will stand the test of time. However, no matter how good our product is, every time we run a course, we do an in depth post-course review, taking onboard graduate comments and feedback, making decisions on what new direction we can take the course or what new dishes or processes are happening 'out there' in the industry that would benefit our students, charter companies, owners and their discerning guests.

Our hospitality graduate to employment ratio has been high and we are extremely proud of our students who initially travelled from around the globe to be trained with us here on the Isle of Wight.

My aims in life are to open a new cookery school operation at The Isle of Wight College and for us to be recognised as the outstanding provider of high quality marine cookery training in the world. I will continue to train new entrants on UKSA's comprehensive marine hospitality courses and write more speciality cookery books. In fact, I already have my next book planned out in my head and can't wait to get started, but I guess I must concentrate on finishing this one first. However, in the short term, as long as I can still manage to get on and off yachts, I will carry on training marine hospitality students for UKSA.

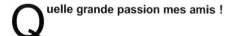

Q uelle grande passion mes amis !

WORKING ON LUXURY YACHTS

The term luxury yacht traditionally refers to a very expensive, privately owned yacht which is professionally crewed. These days, we tend to use the generic term Superyacht, which can either be a sailing yacht or motor yacht. We are now also seeing the increased use of the descriptors such as Megayacht and Gigayacht, whose multi-millionaire and billionaire owners are fabulously wealthy. Put in simple terms, it's all about size, quality and the highest levels of service.

History

The term 'luxury yacht' began to appear at the start of the 20th century, when wealthy individuals had large private yachts built for their personal pleasure. Early luxury motor yachts were epitomised by M/Y Savarona and M/Y Christina O, the latter was owned by the famous Greek shipping magnate Aristotle Onassis, who married Jacqueline Kennedy, the widow of the assassinated US President John. F. Kennedy. Examples of early luxury sailing yachts include Americas Cup classic J Class racers, such as S/Y Endeavour and Sir Thomas Lipton's S/Y Shamrock. The New York Yacht Club hosted many early luxury sailing yacht regattas at Newport, Rhode Island (USA), during what was known as the 'Gilded Age', which refers to the extravagant displays of wealth and excess of America's upper-class during the post-civil war and post-reconstruction years of the late 19th century.

Today

More recently, over the last twenty five years or so, we have seen a big increase in the number and popularity of large, private luxury yachts being designed, under construction or already out there on the water. Luxury yachts typically have no real home port as such, although they must be registered in a port of the country that they fly the flag of. It is not untypical that a yacht has never visited the port in which they are registered.

There are currently said to be around 10,000 registered superyachts of over 24metres in length on the water, requiring professional crew and these yachts are often to be found in the Mediterranean and Caribbean during their regions' respective seasons. These yachts will usually have a base port of choosing, which is usually where crew or contractors undertake maintenance work or where the yachts wait for owners, their guests or charter guests to arrive. Yachts may go back and forth across the Atlantic, between the Caribbean and Mediterranean in the winter and summer; this is known as the 'Milk Run' or 'Crossing'. Some owners will load their yachts onto a yacht transporter and get it delivered to its destination. Some will take passage through the 82km long Panama Canal and head for the Pacific to avoid the long cold European winter months.

Typically ports and destinations in the French and Italian Riviera's are Cannes, Monaco, Antibes, St Tropez, Porto Fino, Porto Cervo, Viareggio, while Palma Majorca has also become a popular port of choice for many. However, luxury yachts are increasingly found cruising in more remote areas of the world. Antigua is one of the main ports in the Windward Islands of the Caribbean, which hosts a Charter Show at the beginning of the winter season. The British Virgin Islands has become a very popular destination for charterers, where people find themselves cruising an abundance of quiet and protected anchorages and breathtaking islands with pristine beaches, where they can find themselves swaying to the rhythm of steel drums at an open air beach bar.

With the relentless demand for luxury yachts during the late 20th and early 21st centuries, we have seen an increase of high quality custom boat building companies and yacht charter brokers, who needed 'beautiful' destinations to display their gleaming white superyachts. Locations such as the Principality of Monaco and Fort Lauderdale come instantly to mind as two of the leading global superyacht shows. The Monaco Yacht Show, usually held at the end of September in the Principality's mythical Port Hercule, typically displays around one hundred superyachts, while nearby nearly one hundred others may be anchored in the bays of St-Jean-Cap-Ferrat and Villefranche. On the other side of 'The Pond' (Atlantic), Fort Lauderdale has recently hosted the

50th Fort Lauderdale International Boat Show (FLIBS), which is typically held at the end of October.

Luxury boat building and yacht charter companies are predominantly based in Western Europe and the United States, but are increasingly to be found in Australia, New Zealand, Asia and Eastern Europe. European manufacturers such as Ferretti, Azimut, Azimut-Benetti, Feadship, Sunseeker and Lürssen dominate the top end of the yacht building market.

Charter

Some luxury yachts are used exclusively by their private owners, while others are operated all year round as charter businesses and a large number are privately owned but available for charter when not being utilised by their owners. The weekly charter rate of luxury yachts around the world ranges across massive monetary values. A fine example of a high-end yacht is M/Y Delma (ex-M/Y Annaliesse), which currently charters out for between €600,000 and €700,000 per week. I know, this is a massive amount of money, however for that money, the charterer will get the boat and its crew only. On top of this sh/e will have to pay for fuel, berthage and anchorage fees and provisioning for all food and drink, for which you can add approximately 25 – 30% of the charter fee. From the perspective of interior crew, there are many wealthy folk out there who have the wherewithal to afford such luxury – oh yes, I forgot to say that they are usually expected to cough up and additional 10% of the charter fee as crew gratuity for exceptional service.

The luxury yacht charter industry functions effectively because private yacht owners mitigate their running costs with charter income as well as keeping their yachts and crew in top running order. On the other hand, private charterers, tend to charter yachts because it is generally considered to be less expensive and less hassle than owning their own yacht. It also provides them with the additional choice related to yacht type, size, location and crew.

Design and layout

Although commentators use the generic term superyacht to cover most large luxury yachts, there are various thoughts about the classification of yacht sizes, so I offer you a guideline for defining the size of professionally crewed luxury yachts:

- Superyacht   from   24 metres (80 feet)

- Megayacht   from   76 metres (250 feet)

- Gigayacht   from   91 metres (300 feet)

Larger yachts, by their very nature require more crew, so to get an idea of the numbers see the table below:

•	21 metres	70 feet	1 – 2 crew
•	24 metres	80 feet	2 – 3 crew
•	30 metres	100 feet	4 – 5 crew
•	36 metres	120 feet	6 – 8 crew
•	45 metres	150 feet	10 – 12 crew
•	61 metres	200 feet	16 – 20 crew
•	91 metres	300 feet	24 – 70 crew

A 50 metre yacht will have one or more luxury tenders and other "toys" which may include a speed boat or sailing boat, jet-skis, windsurfing and diving equipment and a Banana boat. Most new-builds these days have multiple flat screen televisions and state of the art satellite communications. The bridge on many modern yachts would put the interior of the Space Shuttle to shame. They may include:

- Lower deck: exterior swimming platform at the stern; four (sometimes five) guest cabins with en-suite bath or shower rooms aft; engine room amidships; crew quarters forward.

- Main deck: sheltered exterior deck aft leading into the salon; dining room and galley; entrance amidships; owner's suite forward, usually includes either a study or a second twin stateroom.

- Upper deck: exterior deck aft, often used for outdoor dining; second salon (often called the sky lounge); staffed bar inside or outside or both; sixth stateroom will be amidships if it is not on the lower deck or part of the owner's suite; gym (may also be on the lower deck or part of the owner's suite); captain's cabin; bridge.

- Sun deck: on the roof of the upper deck, often features a jacuzzi.

As previously mentioned, the number of very large yachts has risen rapidly since the 1990s and increasingly only yachts above around 65 metres (210ft) stand out among other luxury yachts. Yachts of this size are almost always built to individual commissions and cost tens of millions of dollars (most super-yachts cost far more than their owners' homes on land, even though those homes are likely to be among the largest and most desirable). A yacht of this size usually has four decks above the water line and one or two below. It is likely to have a helicopter landing platform – sometimes two! Apart from additional guest cabins, which are likely to include one or more "VIP suites", besides the owner's suite, extra facilities compared to a 50-metre (160ft) yacht will include some or all of the following: indoor jacuzzi, sauna and steam rooms, a beauty salon, massage and other treatment rooms, medical centre, discotheque, cinema with a film library, plunge pool (possibly with a wave-maker), playroom, and additional living areas such as a separate bar, secondary dining room, private sitting rooms and a library. There will be more tenders and "toys" than there are on a 50 metre (160ft) yacht.

You will find that the industry has become increasingly influenced by the "Mercedes Effect", which has existed for some years in the global automotive industry. New Merc' innovation today, becomes the norm with less expensive or smaller vehicles a couple of years down the line. Similarly, we are increasingly seeing owners of smaller new builds adding some of the value added facilities mentioned above to their new yacht design i.e. we are now seeing a jacuzzi on 120 footers, which previously have not been seen on yachts of that size.

As of 2010, yachts above 100 metres plus (328ft +) are still rare, but increasingly becoming more visible. Most, typically have five decks above the waterline and two below. The very largest yachts, such as Lady Moura, owned by Nasser Al-Rashid, a multi-millionaire businessman from Saudi Arabia, was launched in 1990 and at 344ft, she is an elegant, luxurious vessel, beautifully designed and easily recognisable from her name and escutcheon carved in 24 carat gold. This type of yacht now incorporates such features as helicopter hangars, indoor swimming pools and miniature submarines.

At the time of writing, M/Y Eclipse, owned by the Russian billionaire Roman Abramovich, is the world's largest ever superyacht on the water. Allegedly costing around £300m, measuring in at 162.5mts (533ft), with a crew of around 70, The Eclipse is 36ft longer than the world's previous biggest private yacht, Dubai, owned by Sheikh Mohammed, ruler of the Middle Eastern country of the same name.

The Eclipse has two helicopter pads, 11 guest cabins, two swimming pools, several hot tubs, a disco hall, three launch boats and a mini-submarine capable of submerging up to 165ft. It is fitted with intruder detection alarms and a missile defence system. The yacht has 6,000 sq ft of living space, 600 doors and is also equipped with an 'anti-paparazzi shield' which is activated by flashlight. Lasers fire a bolt of light directly at cameras to obliterate any photographs.

The yacht which has caused the biggest stir in the industry in 2010 has been Derecktor Shipyard's M/Y Cakewalk, which made her debut at the Fort Lauderdale International Boat Show (FLIBS) in October. At 85.6 metres (289ft), she has 7 cabins, catering for 14 guests with a crew of 25. Small, I am sure you will agree, in comparison with M/Y Eclipse. She is a fine example of American workmanship, comprising of six spacious decks, with her beautiful interior design featuring an intricate iron staircase, which reaches from the lobby, right through to the sun deck.

An opulent library with fireplace and grand piano; beautiful dining salon and six spacious guest rooms located on the main deck. Each guest room is designed to be equivalent in size and amenities.

The owner's deck offers generous lounge areas aft deck and dining for up to 14 guests. The owner's full-beam suite boasts panoramic views and has a private sitting area, office and vestibule.

Cakewalk's expansive and uncluttered decks include sunbathing areas forward on the bridge deck and lounge areas on the sun deck, both port and starboard. The aft deck is devoted to utter relaxation with a Jacuzzi, sun-beds and two dining areas.

The toys and tender are housed in Cakewalk's impressive tender bay, nicknamed "The Boathouse", include custom built tenders, commissioned by the owner: a Limited Edition AquaRiva 'Centos'; Vikal Custom Limousine and Intrepid Custom 350 Open.

So tell me - does size really matter?
One decision that you need to make, is whether you intend to actually work on a superyacht with a big crew and a hierarchy where you will be starting at the very bottom of the ladder. So you need to ask yourself the question, "Can I work on a boat that big?". Alternatively you may want to consider working on a much smaller yacht, which can be just as hard, if not harder than working on a big one, where you will initially be a 'jack of all trades' and master of them all. A number of our grads have joined medium and large superyachts and after a couple of seasons, a few are now working their way down, rather than vice-versa. They are now signing up to work sailing charter in the Caribbean or BVIs, where the differences in the sector are huge.

Superyachts attract the mega-rich and celebrity guests, while the smaller charter sailing yachts attract families or groups of friends looking for a relaxed vacation. None of the superyachts airs and graces here, these charterers are after some real fun in the sun, when service is far more casual. They will not be demanding the five or even seven star levels of service; no white gloves here, used when polishing the silver.

The crew (often only two) are expected to be more available, hands-on and relaxed. You will be expected to have a lot more direct contact with your guests, engaging in conversation and generally interacting with them throughout the day. This role requires an ability to multi-skill and multi-task, so it would not be unusual to find yourself pulling sails or the captain pouring the wine. You certainly won't have the usual superyacht 'toys' to play with during downtime on a smaller yacht, however you will have the opportunity to spend time checking out islands, bays, architecture, culture etc. Sure, you are likely to get bigger tips on superyachts and the fringe benefits maybe better, but this has to be balanced off against the fact that as the tips get smaller, there are less people to share them with.

This type of work can be ideal if you have a partner who has a Yacht Masters ticket, so he (or she) is captain and you look after most everything else. We have a number of grads who have been doing this type of work now for two or three seasons and they absolutely love it. The BVIs, Caribbean and the Eastern Med tend to be a popular destinations for this type of work.

Owners

Single owner (sole use) – A yacht, owned by an individual (family), This can be a nice place to be, meaning that, after a period of time, you get to know the wants, needs and expectations of the owner's family and friends.

Single owner (charter) – A yacht, owned by an individual (family). The owner usually cherry picks the days, weeks or months which s/he with family and friends will use their valuable asset. He will also charter out his yacht for pre-determined periods of time, to help off-set the annual running costs.

Multiple owners (sole use) – generally means that you will have more than one 'master', which is not always a nice place to be, meaning that the decision making process is not always straightforward.

Multiple owners (charter) – generally means that you will have a broad mix of onboard guests, which may change from week to week, possibly including one or more of your yacht's owners.

Charter only – generally means that you will have different guests onboard for one or more weeks at a time.

Whichever of the above you find work on, you will find that there are many different onboard dynamics between private, charter, delivery and movement.

WHY WORK ON A YACHT?

So, you're thinking about working in the superyacht industry? OK, let's get right down to the nitty-gritty. To start with, I'm not about to 'big-up' the industry so that you are going to think it's all play and no work; you will have to make up your own mind from what I have written. Read this section through carefully and then read it again, over and over and if you think that working on a yacht or superyacht really is the life for you, then read on. If not, you could give this book to a mate as a late birthday present, or alternatively try flogging it on e.Bay.

What makes ideal superyacht crew?

In no specific order, you need to be or have:
- aged 18+
- a non—smoker
- tolerant of workmates
- prepared to work hard
- an excellent communicator
- no visible tattoos or piercings
- polite and have good manners
- a positive and co-operative attitude
- excellent levels of personal hygiene
- well presented and dressed appropriately
- prepared to wear minimal makeup and perfume
- qualifications, such as the STCW95 (see Training and Qualifications)

Positives about working in the superyacht industry
- Opportunity to travel
- Financially rewarding
- Negotiated annual leave
- Positive work/life balance
- Provision of free uniforms
- Negotiated travel expenses
- Huge variety in what you do
- Always learning something new
- Free lodging and food while onboard
- Visit the most exotic locations in the world
- Working in a team of young, like-minded people
- Free medical care, usually after a qualifying period
- Good opportunities for advancement in the industry
- Live and work on the biggest and most luxurious yachts in the world
- Downtime can mean you exploring places that most folk can only dream of visiting
- You are likely to be paid in Euros or US Dollars and it is unusual for tax to be deducted from your pay
- Working on the 'right' yacht, can mean Atlantic crossings at the end of the Med' season, winter in the Caribbean or BVIs, or a journey through the Panama Canal and the 'off-season' in the Pacific, Thailand, Fiji, Singapore, etc etc etc

Negatives about working in the superyacht industry
- Rough weather
- Lots of cleaning
- Always on the move

- Hard work, with long hours
- Strange countries and strange people
- You need to share living and sleeping space with other people
- You can be away from friends and loved ones for months at a time
- Your work days can, continuously be extremely long and demanding
- Crew accommodation is generally small, offering very limited privacy
- There is no guarantee of a job or re-employment the following season
- If you are used to creature comforts, the change may come as a shock
- The industry, like any other, is open to the impact of global economic boom and bust trends, affecting employment potential, both positively and negatively
- The current trend is to run on skeleton crew for the Med off-season, which means that maybe the chef and a couple of stews get laid off at the end of the season until the following March/April
- Finding initial employment usually requires you to have sufficient funds to enable you to fly to Nice, Palma, or Florida and also to cover the cost of food and crew accommodation for a few weeks or maybe even months
- The length of employment contracts can and do vary. Permanent may have always meant just that in the past, but the talk on the street is that fixed term contracts are likely to become the norm for some crew positions.

Are you made of the right stuff?

The yachting sector really is like no other industry. It's not just about living the dream or even about having a job; it is a lifestyle and you will have to work hard at it 24/7. You will frequently find yourself working extremely long hours that will certainly fall well outside of any European Working Time Directive. It certainly is not for everyone and some don't make it past 'the dockwalk'.

The corporate culture cliché of "work hard, play harder" could have been written specifically for the sector. The notion that hard work and long hours should be balanced with intense, sometime extreme leisure activities, would be described by many experienced crew as an accurate description of the industry.

Many of our graduates work very long shifts, but when they are on downtime and the owner and charter guests have gone, they may have an ad-hoc dockside party with crew from neighbouring yachts, when the chefs get the opportunity to knock up some gastro delights, so that the crew can indulge themselves for a change.

As a 'newbie' (entry level crew), you will be expected to be a team player, who is prepared to work hard and do what it takes, with the rest of the crew, to provide a special vacation for your guests, while they are onboard your yacht.

There is only one thing that you have to consider and that is "customer delight". You will have to be totally focussed, resilient and service-orientated. We have found that once our girls and boys have been in the industry for a season, their careers soon take off; gaining promotion or taking their career in a different direction. To throw in another cliché, "The sky's the limit", as long as you are prepared to work hard and keep your nose clean. Arriving at the opportunity for a successful career on the water can be a mix of networking, good timing, personal attributes, training, qualifications, CV and sometimes, downright good luck! You will have the opportunity to earn good money, meet some wonderful (and not so wonderful) people and see a great deal of this beautiful world which we live in.

Why cook on a yacht?

Being fairly autonomous within the crew, being in charge of what you do best and how you do it; you hold the success of a charter and the happiness and well being of the owner, guests and crew in your hands. The fantastic thing about being a chef, stew-chef or crew cook is that most other crew members don't have the remotest idea about how to do your job; so, they are usually hugely impressed and grateful by your ability to produce great food in all weather conditions.

Galleys on yachts and superyachts, built over the last five to ten years and certainly on some of the new-builds I have seen, are often very well thought out, high-tec food preparation and cooking facilities, which can provide you with the ultimate cooking experience, to indulge your every culinary fantasy.

Yachts or more specifically their owners or charter guests are notorious for changing their plans at a moment's notice, whether because of sea conditions or the owner's whim. Weather conditions can change rapidly, temperatures can soar or plummet and these things, amongst many others, may require a lightening change to carefully planned schedules.

Your guests can be demanding and change their minds or invite guests at short notice. Hospitality crew have been known to be asked to prepare a surprise lunch party at very short notice, only to have the owner's wife change her mind at the last minute and decide to go eat onboard with their friends (who were coming to eat at yours), who just happen to be moored up alongside your gleaming white superyacht.

You need to be able to think calmly and clearly and not stick to rigid routines, to think out of the box. I just hate that cliché, but it fits the context. A sense of humour is vital, as is an ability to laugh in the face of disaster (sometimes metaphorically); gritty resolve does not go amiss either!

Your workplace can be a small, often very hot space that routinely moves in bizarre ways. Yacht galleys are often very badly designed and food does not always stay where you put it and there are occasions when you will find yourself scraping crème brulée off the deck head. You work mainly on your own and unless you are very blessed, you are liable to suffer from sea sickness from time to time. You will never have quite enough stowage. It could be the most beautiful, fastest, hi-tech boat but unless the food is right – forget it.

Living onboard
Remember that you could be living with a few or lots of people while at sea, for days or weeks at a time. You will need to be respectful of other people when you are sharing living quarters. It is a good idea to have hobbies, which can help use your time effectively. A number of friends keep a log or blog and just about everyone appears to use Facebook.

Relationships
Like most jobs, you cannot pick and choose who you are going to work with. The one thing that is pretty well guaranteed is that you will become a member of one large, like minded, global family and you will certainly make many good, if not life-long friends in the industry. The downside is, that you may have to live and work with the odd person, who you just cannot stand, however you still need to be professional and work hard to overcome personal issues. Sexual relationships are usually frowned on, although we are increasingly seeing 'partners' employed, usually on the smaller two man vessels.

Sleeping quarters
You must be prepared to live communally, sharing a cabin with one or more crew members; this may be with the same sex or opposite sex, in very small cabins, so you will need to come to terms with having very limited privacy. A bathroom/shower-room will have to be shared with a number of other crew, so there really is nowhere to hide.

Mobiles, laptops, smoking

Mobiles can be taken onboard, but will have to remain on silent or switched off, when guests are onboard. You will pay considerably more when using 'roaming', while abroad, so buy local SIM cards and let your mates know your number via Facebook or e.mail. With regard to laptops, I cannot think of many of my grad students who do not have a laptop, or i.Pad with them, so take one, as many boats have wireless internet. Smoking is usually a big no-go area on most all professionally crewed yachts; if you are a heavy smoker, then you will need to be sure that you can live without 'the dreaded weed' for days or weeks on end.

Valuables and luggage

Don't take too much baggage with you, as there is usually not much storage space, so take small sized luggage with you or preferably bags which can fold away. Don't take anything of huge value, as there is no need to do so and, at the end of the day, you really don't know who you are sharing with.

Crew mess

Apart from your shared cabin, the crew mess is one of the few places where you will be able to go to relax, when you are off duty. As you might expect, the size and quality of a crew mess and how it is 'kitted out' varies greatly. In a good crew mess (superyachts), you should find a flat-screen HD TV, DVD player and music system, usually these days a docking station for crew iPods. You will also typically find the 'crew fridge/freezer', where drinks and snacks are available. You will need to be respectful of others' living area and be prepared to do your bit to help keep things clean and tidy.

Laundry

It is unusual for crew to do their own laundry, which is often undertaken by a nominated stewardess. There will be a schedule up in the crew mess showing when your laundry should be put out ready for collection. This schedule is built round the priority usage of the onboard laundry systems for laundering guests' bathroom towels, bed-linen, swim towels etc. The assigned member of staff will also be responsible for the laundering of crew uniform, which is often bespoke, therefore expensive and this may be laundered separately for all other clothing to avoid running colours and other potential mishaps.

TRAINING and QUALIFICATIONS

At the time of writing, no written rules exist about what qualifications you need to become a chef or steward/ess on a commercial yacht, be it charter or privately owned. However there are plenty of un-written rules you will need to be aware of, which you will pick up on as you read through this book. The imperative is "Don't underestimate the need for professional crew training and/or job relevant qualifications".

STCW95

Even knowledgeable chefs and hospitality professionals with years of experience behind them, often find the transition from land to sea, one that is difficult to adapt to. There is however something you must know – you will have virtually no chance securing a professional position on a yacht unless you have the STCW95 (Standards of Training, Certification & Watch-keeping for Seafarers), qualification.

The 1978 STCW convention was the first to establish basic requirements on training, certification and watch keeping for seafarers on an international level. It was not until 2002 that the convention had cast its net to encompass the superyacht industry and become law. I always work on the basis that the STCW95 is the pre-requisite for new entry employment in the sector and advise our grad students accordingly.

RYA Competent Crew

I also recommend that you consider taking the RYA Competent Crew course, which is available across a wide range of registered training providers. This is a great 'hands on' practical course, if you are a beginner or fairly new to sailing and have no formal qualifications. The course teaches you the basic principles of sailing, as well as personal safety.

If you have made up your mind, or are seriously thinking about working as interior crew, then (in my mind) there is really only one training provider in the UK, which can offer you a one-stop-shop for a fistful of job-specific training and that is the UKSA. Their four week Essential Marine Hospitality course, although not inexpensive, will provide you with the essential marine training solutions and qualifications, designed to help you gain entry into the marine hospitality sector of the industry. If you cannot afford to undertake the training noted below in one hit, flexible programme options are available, so you can undertake the four modules over timescales which suit your diary and pocket. The UKSA offer a number of open days throughout the year and it is well worth contacting them or checking out their website (www.uksa.org).

UKSA (United Kingdom Sailing Academy)

Location: Cowes, Isle of Wight, England

The UKSA Essential Marine Hospitality (EMH) course covers the following areas and as previously stated, will give you a head start on other newbies seeking to beat you to that dream job:

Hospitality Skills (7 days)
- UKSA Professional Marine Hospitality Certificate

Essential Marine Cookery (6 days)
- IW College Essential Marine Cookery Certificate
- CIEH Level 2 Food Safety in Catering

Core Skills (10 days)
- STCW 95 Basic Training
  - RYA / MCA Personal Survival Techniques
  - MCA Personal Safety and Social Responsibility
  - MCA Fire Prevention and Fire Fighting
  - MCA Elementary First Aid
- RYA Level 2 Powerboat
- RYA Shortwave Radio

Practical Sailing Skills (5 days)
- RYA Competent Crew

UKSA describe the benefits of their EMH training as follows:

- Train to a broad and comprehensive syllabus, delivered by top hospitality and maritime specialists
- Prepares you for a service career with opportunities to live on luxurious yachts and travel to some of the most spectacular areas of the globe
- Train to deliver the level of service to which most 5 star hotels aspire
- Popular with individuals transferring from other hospitality-related careers, as well as couples looking to work together in the industry
- Develop your ability and passion for delivering a level of service beyond first class
- Huge demand for high calibre staff in this sector

UK contact:
+44 (0)1983 203038
www.uksa.org

MAGNUMS & BUTLERS
Location: Antibes (South of France)
                   Queensland (Australia)

Magnums Butlers, run by the inimitable Josephine Ive, who is Principal and owner of Magnums Butlers International. Magnums offer a nine day Luxury Yacht Steward/ess Programme.

The topics covered include:

- Table service, including butler and silver service
- Food and beverage knowledge
- Flower arranging
- Housekeeping
- Etiquette, manners and protocol
- Personal guest care, packing and unpacking suitcases
- Laundry and clothing care
- Interpersonal skills

Australia contact:
+61 7 5476 3022
www.magnumsbutlers.com

BLUE WATER TRAINING
Location: Antibes (South of France) and Palma (Mallorca)

Blue Water offer the following short courses:

- Introductory Stewardess   1 day
- Advanced Stewardess   2 days
- Silver Service   1 day
- MCA STCW95   Range of products

Antibes contact:
+33 (0) 4 93 34 47 73
Email: training@bluewater.com

Palma contact:
+34 971 677 154
Email: bluewateryachtingpalma@telefonica.net
www.training.bluewateryachting.com

YACHT CHEF INTERNATIONAL
Location: Antibes

Yacht Chef International offer the following short courses:
- Master classes   1 day
- Seasoned chef   3 days
- Galley foundation   5 days
- Advanced course planned

Antibes contact:
+33 (0) 6 23 18 44 73
www.yachtchefinternational.com
info@yachtchefinternational.com

AUSTRALIAN SUPERYACHT CREW
Location: Rozelle Bay (NSW - Australia)

Australian Superyacht Crew offer the following short courses:
for new entrants:

- Stewardess / steward interior crew training   6 days
- Chefs Superyacht Cross-training   5 days
- Experienced interior crew training   1 day, 2 day & 3½ days

The majority of their steward and stewardess students are mature-aged or may have already been involved in hospitality (fine-dining, housekeeping etc.) or related customer service industries (nursing, beauty therapy, childcare etc.) and require an intensive, short course that will equip them for a career-change to work on Superyachts.

Their six day Interior Crew courses offer a comprehensive overview of the professional yachting industry, providing you with lots of 'hand-on' training, enabling you to enter the industry; having gained the confidence and pre-requisite knowledge and sills to be able to perform in a steward or stewardess role.

Experienced crew can customise their training according to individual needs:

Stewards and stewardesses who wish to up-skill to progress their careers can do courses from one to three and a half days duration. Training can be delivered onboard your yacht, or at the ASC training facilities.

Senior crew who wish to take the next step up in their career – to become a Chief (Head of Department) and a more effective team leader, can also avail themselves of one-to-one, customised senior training or participate in a group workshop.

Australia contact:
+61 (0)2 9818 2024
www.superyachtcrew.com.au/training
training@superyachtcrew.com.au

IYT (International Yacht Training)
Location: Ft Lauderdale (Florida USA)

IYT offer the following short courses:

- RIB course – Level 2
- STCW95
- Megayacht crew course
- Megayacht interior operations
- Silver service

Contact: +1-954.779.7764
www.yachtmaster.com

Interior jobs available to you

- Chief steward/ess
- 2nd steward/ess
- 3rd steward/ess
- Housekeeper
- Masseuse/stewardess
- Flowers & Detailing
- Laundry
- Head chef
- Sous chef (2nd chef)
- Crew chef
- Stew chef

PASSPORTS, VISAS and CERTIFICATES
PASSPORTS

Passport applications and enquiries (UK) are dealt with by the Identity and Passport Service (IPS). Without stating the obvious, you ain't going nowhere unless you have a current valid passport, preferably with a number of years left on it. The last thing you want, is to be mid-Atlantic and notice that your passport has just run out. In the grand scheme of things, I am guessing that many of my readers are likely to be in their late teens or twenties, so your passport may still have a long shelf-life left on it. If not, splash the cash and get a new ten year Biometric Passport. Some countries insist that your passport is valid for at least six months after the date you enter the country. If you are uncertain about this, ask the country's consulate or embassy in your country of residence.

In March 2006, IPS launched a very important counter-fraud initiative - the Biometric Passport. This type of passport has a new design and improved security features which were not present on previous passports. The new pages have intricate designs, complex watermarks and a chip antenna.

Passport safety
Before and during your journey:

- Check your passport expiry date before you travel.
- Keep a note of your passport number, date and place of issue in a safe place separate from your passport i.e. on your mobile or e.mail to self.
- Carry a photocopy of your passport with you and keep this separate from your passport.
- Take contact details for your next of kin and leave them with your captain, along with your passport.
- If possible, carry another identity document that has your photo on it i.e. driver's licence or identity card.
- Immediately contact the nearest British consulate or embassy (or your nationality) if your passport is lost or stolen overseas.

How much does a passport cost?

At the time of writing, the cost of a First Adult (UK) Passport varies depending on how you apply. At the time of writing a range of charges apply for a 32 page, 10 year British Passport:

- £77.50 basic postal application
- £77.50 check and send service (Post Office)

Renew or amend existing adult passport
- £77.50 basic postal application
- £77.50 check and send service (Post Office)
- £112.50 one week fast track service
- £129.50 one day premium service

Replace lost, stolen or missing passport
- £77.50 basic postal application
- £77.50 check and send service (Post Office)
- £112.50 one week fast track service

Jumbo passport
A 48 page 'Jumbo Passport' is available for First Adult or passport renewals. You can only use the Fast Track or Premium services for this type of passport renewal.

- £90.50 basic postal application
- £90.50 check and send service (Post Office)
- £120.50 one week fast track service
- £138.50 one day premium service

Full details of current passport fees can be found on the IPS website - www.ips.gov.uk or call the Passport Fee Information Line on 0800 056 6654 or the Textphone service on 0808 156 1559.

Applying for a British Passport
The methodology of applying for a passport for the first time in the UK changed from April 2007. Anyone aged 16 or over may have to have an interview as part of the application process. There are four different ways to apply for a UK passport:

- online on the Identity and Passport Service (IPS) website
- through high street partners
- by post using a form (either from the post office or from the IPS)
- in person at a local office

Passport interviews
The interview will confirm that your passport application actually belongs to you and that you are the rightful owner of that identity. If you have previously held a child passport, you will not need to be interviewed to get your first adult passport. You will only need an interview if you have never held a British passport before. You apply in the usual way, but after sending your application form, you will get a letter asking you to arrange an interview. To begin with, not everyone applying for a first passport will be interviewed. If you have not had a letter asking you to arrange an interview within eight working days of your application being received then you do not need to be interviewed.

VISAS

If you are travelling to a place outside British territories you may need to apply for an entry visa from the country's consulate or embassy. The UK Foreign Office website lists contact details of foreign embassies in the UK. Some countries have websites with visa information, for example, the United States Embassy website has details of who needs a visa to travel to the US.

If you are a British dependent territories citizen, British overseas citizen, British subject, British national overseas or a British protected person you may need to apply for a visa even if British citizens do not.

SCHENGEN VISA

The name "Schengen" originates from a small town in Luxembourg where in 1995, seven European Union countries signed a treaty to end internal border checkpoints and controls. More countries have joined the treaty in recent years. There are currently twenty two Schengen countries; most are members of the European Union.

By applying for a Schengen Visa, travelling from one European country to another is simplified. As a 'visitor' to the Schengen area, you will enjoy the many advantages of this unified visa system. Generally speaking, with a Schengen Visa, you may enter one country and travel freely throughout the Schengen region during the validity of the visa. Internal border controls are limited with no or few stops and checks. Your visa will only be valid for the period (dates) stated. If you want to change the dates you will have to apply at the embassy which issued your visa for an extension. Other Schengen countries will not issue you another Schengen visa if you already have a valid one.

Your stay is limited to 90 days within any 6 month period. Please check each countries' requirements before assuming that you only require a Schengen for your European journey. For example, Australians currently require a visa to visit Portugal. The Schengen Visa is particularly useful for South Africans.

The Schengen Office

The Schengen Office can assist with obtaining visas to the following popular Schengen destinations: Austria, France, Hungary, Portugal, Spain and Italy (business visa applications only) and Poland (business visa applications only). There are currently 22 Schengen countries, all in Europe. The Schengen Office also offer an embassy finder link on their website and a visa processing service to over 40 countries. This does not currently include the USA, which has become more difficult to enter since 9/11.

Schengen Countries

Please note that the UK and Ireland are not members of the Schengen Agreement.

The following countries require personal application at the relevant embassy. The Schengen Office does NOT offer a service for these countries: Austria, Belgium, Denmark, Finland, France, Germany, Greece, Iceland, Italy, Luxembourg, Netherlands, Norway, Portugal, Spain and Sweden. You will need to check out the Embassy website of the appropriate country.

The following countries joined the Schengen Agreement on 21st December 2007: Czech Republic, Latvia, Poland, Hungary, Lithuania, Slovakia, Estonia, Malta, Slovenia.

Where to apply for a Schengen Visa

A Schengen Visa is applied for at the Embassy or Consulate of the Schengen country which you will be spending the most nights on your trip. If you are only visiting one country on your trip then you apply for your visa at the Consulate of that country.

Multiple Schengen Visa

A multiple entry visa will allow the holder several entries into the Schengen area, allowing you to return to the UK and then re-enter the Schengen area at a later date. Please note that not all embassies issue multiple entry visas. Some prefer to only issue a single entry visa to cover you for the specific trip you are going on.

When to apply for a Schengen Visa

You need to apply before travelling.

Do I need travel insurance?

You will need to have arranged your travel insurance, which needs to include medical cover and repatriation when you apply for your Schengen Visa (the actual repatriation clause needs to be presented to the Consulate). It must cover the duration of the requested visa. Annual insurance may be required if you are requesting a multi-entry visa.

UK residency requirements

When applying for a Schengen Visa, generally you need to have at least three months left on your UK immigration visa at the time you return from your trip. If for example your visa expires on 12 December 2011, you can only apply for a visa up to 12 September 2011.

Applying within the UK

If you are applying for your Schengen visa within the UK, you need to bear in mind:

- you need a minimum of 3-6 months left on both your passport and your UK visa
- not many embassies will issue visas to people who are in the UK on tourist visas of 6 months duration or less

Cost

Prices vary between countries and start from £36 (at the time of writing), depending on where you are applying for your visa. There may be a small surcharge if you pay by credit card. Prices include VAT (UK), but exclude embassy fees and postage back to clients.

Suspensions

It is important to be aware that Governments who are tied into the Schengen Treaty can, at their will, suspend their involvement in the Treaty for a period of time. A good example of this was when the Italian government suspended their involvement in the Schengen Treaty for several weeks from June 28 to July 15 2009, in order to restore border control and increase security for the G8 Summit, which was held from 08 – 10 July in L'Aquila. A similar measure was adopted back in 2001, when the G8 summit was held in Genoa.

Specialist Visa clearing Agencies:

These agencies are one of the more simple ways of accessing accurate and up-to-date information, however this comes with a cost.

The Schengen Office
Room 5a to 6, Level 2
9-15 Neal Street, Covent Garden,
London, WC2H 9PU.
UK - Phone 020 7240 3535
Website: www.theschengenoffice.com
Email: info@theschengenoffice.com

Alternatively, you can contact the Immigration Work Visa and Naturalization Services:
Websites: www.workpermit.co.uk or www.workpermit.com

AMERICAN VISAS

The United States of America automatically assume that every person entering their country is an immigrant.

From a yachting perspective, as the summer season ends in the Mediterranean, the new season in the Caribbean kicks in and the appropriate American Visa/s are an essential pre-requisite for all crew. Unless your yacht is only going to be based in the Caribbean area, you may be in and out of American waters on a fairly regular basis, meaning you will need a B1/B2 Visa.

Visas for the United States are issued by a U.S. Embassy or Consulate. A visa entitles the holder to travel to the United States and apply for admission; it does not guarantee entry. An immigration inspector at the port of entry determines the visa holder's eligibility for admission into the United States.

Who needs a visa to enter USA

Anyone who is not eligible to enter the United States visa-free under the Visa Waiver Program (VWP), or, is not exempt from the visa requirement. Please note: Travellers born in the United States and those who hold dual citizenship with the United States must enter and depart the United States on U.S. passports.

Method of Application

With limited exceptions, non-immigrant visa applications aged between 14 and 79 are required to arrange an appointment for an interview with a U.S. Consular Officer. Interviews are by appointment only. The Embassy does not accept walk-in applications. An interview in London can cost around £130 and there is no guarantee of a successful outcome.

Covering Letter

At the time of writing, it is virtually impossible to get your BI/B2 in London without a covering letter from your employer, owner, captain or crew agent, on official headed note paper, with full contact details. The letter must indicate that you are either currently employed or have been interviewed and are in receipt of a written job offer, name of yacht, with a confirmed start date. This may ease in time and in fact my Global Research Team tell me that they have found it easier to get their B1/B2 in either Paris or Lisbon, but some pre-emptive ground-work is essential and wherever you go, you must have arranged an appointment in advance.

Embassy Security

It is unlikely that you will be allowed to take any valuables into the interview with you, so if you can take a friend along to look after them, so much the better. Valuables include, but are not restricted to mobile phones, digital cameras, laptops, i.Pads etc etc. If you are uncertain, then check this out before you go. Talk to friends who have already got their visas and see what advice they can give.

Processing Times

The average visa processing time for successful applicants is five business days, during which time the applicant's passport must remain with the U.S. Embassy.

Applicants who are advised at the visa interview that their application requires additional processing, should allow at least 8 weeks for this stage of the application process. Once processing is completed, the applicant will be contacted for his/her passport, then a further four weeks should be allowed for the visa to be issued and the passport to be returned.

Applicants who are advised at the time of their interview that action on their application has been suspended under Section 221(g) of the Immigration and Nationality Act should allow a minimum of ten to fifteen business days for their application to be processed once they submit the missing documents to the Embassy.

Private Yacht
If you will be working on a private yacht out of a foreign port and cruising in U.S. waters for more than 29 days, you will require a B1 visa.

Holiday
If you wish to remain in the United States for a holiday after your period of employment, you will be required to apply for admission as a visitor on a B2 visa.

Visa Waiver Program
Most visitors to the U.S. enter the country as tourists. With the introduction of visa free travel to citizens of 27 countries, it is now possible for many travellers, including British citizens, to enter the United States without a visa under the Visa Waiver Program (VWP). Visa free travel is also available to 'qualified travellers' who enter the U.S. on business or in transit.

Citizens of the following countries; the United Kingdom, Andorra, Australia, Austria, Belgium Brunei, Denmark, Finland, France, Germany, Iceland, Ireland, Italy, Japan, Liechtenstein, Luxembourg, Monaco, the Netherlands, New Zealand, Norway, Portugal, San Marino, Singapore, Slovenia, Spain, Sweden, and Switzerland may be eligible to travel to the United States visa free under the Visa Waiver Program if they are travelling for business, pleasure or are in transit, and they meet all of the following requirements.

Citizens of the following countries; the Czech Republic, Estonia, Hungary, Latvia, Lithuania, Malta, Slovakia and the Republic of Korea may be eligible to travel to the United States visa free under the Visa Waiver Program if they are travelling for business, pleasure or are in transit, are in possession of an electronic passport, have obtained travel authorization and they meet all of the following requirements.

Requirements
The traveller is a citizen of one of the countries named above, travelling on a valid, machine readable or e-passport with an electronic chip. Failure to determine that your passport qualifies for the VWP may result in you being denied boarding by the airline.

It is important to note that, a passport indicating that the bearer is a British Subject, British Dependent Territories Citizen, British Overseas Citizen, British National (Overseas) Citizen, or British Protected Person does not qualify for travel without a visa. A passport which states holder has Right of Abode or indefinite leave to remain in the United Kingdom does not qualify the bearer for visa free travel.

Some travellers may not be eligible to enter the United States visa free under the VWP. These include people who have been arrested, even if the arrest did not result in a criminal conviction, those with criminal records, (the Rehabilitation of Offenders Act does not apply to U.S. visa law), certain serious communicable illnesses, those who have been refused admission into, or have been deported from the United States, or have previously overstayed on the VWP. Such travellers must apply for special restricted visas. If they attempt to travel without a visa, they may be refused entry into the United States.

Visa-free travel does not include those who plan to study, work or remain more than 90 days. Such travellers need visas. If an immigration official has reason to believe that a visa-free traveller is going to study, work or stay longer than 90 days, the officer will refuse to admit the traveller.

815 - 406 - 2209

ENG 1
Valid Medical Fitness Certificate
This certificate is required under The Merchant Shipping (Medical Examination) Regulations 2002.

If you are likely to be working on yachts over 24mts in length, then you must take a medical with an Approved Medical Practitioner and be able to provide your employer with a current, valid certificate. The MCA (Maritime and Coastguard Agency) website provides a list of approved medical practitioners around the world, who have been approved to carry out seafarer medical examinations. At the time of writing, the maximum statutory fee for a medical examination is £80 (UK). You will also need to be aware that, should additional tests be required i.e. referral for a Physical Fitness Test, additional fees may be incurred. You will need to check the MCA website for non UK based medical practitioners and related information.

There is no statutory fee for the completion of an ML5 Medical Report. The doctor will generally make a charge in line with British Medical Association rates. As previously mentioned with the STCW95, you are unlikely to gain meaningful employment in the sector (over 24mts) unless you have a current ENG 1 Medical Fitness Certificate.

Copy your critical documents
If you have ever lost your passport, or had it stolen while on vacation in a foreign country, you will already know the sort of nightmare this can create. My advice is to take photocopies of all important documentation prior to departure from your home country. Make at least two copies, leaving one set at home with your family or someone you can trust, and know will be easily contactable and has the ability to act quickly in an emergency. You should take another spare set with you, however do make sure that this set is kept in a separate place to the originals. Be sensible, your official documents can be critical to your continued employment on a yacht, so make sure that you keep your spare copies together in one easily accessible location. Having a set of clearly copied back-up documents can prove to authorities/ airlines/consulates/embassies that you have been in possession of the requisite documents prior their loss. Copies are naturally a big bonus, when it comes to needing to access replacements, maybe at short notice. I usually keep a note of serial numbers, passport number etc on my mobile phone and in my filo-fax. Another favourite of mine, is to e.mail scanned copies to myself of the 'critical' passport pages, paper driving licence and card. I suggest that you keep this e.mail in a separate folder. You can also upload the files and keep them in a folder on your laptop or save them to a flash-drive or separate hard-drive. This way, you are not reliant on hard-copy of anything, as you can access it anywhere in the world (within reason!).

By the way, do not be surprised when the captain requires you to surrender your passport to him/her when you join your new yacht – be assured, this is normal practice and done for fairly obvious reasons.

Immunisation
Don't just head off into the wide blue yonder, without having thought about where you may travel to in your new world of five star plus marine employment. OK, you will be working and spending most of your time on a yacht or superyacht, mostly in exotic parts of the world, however you will have the opportunity for trips ashore and you will no doubt be tempted by off-season backpacking trips to areas of the world where you might find yourself vulnerable to disease. You can minimize the risk to your health by taking sensible precautions; especially if you intend to spend any length of time in developing parts of the world.

Check with your doctor before you depart to your chosen destination to find that new job. Most developed countries have comprehensive public immunization programmes and these will cover many conditions, usually including: mumps, measles, rubella, polio, tetanus, diphtheria, whooping cough, pneumonia, tuberculosis and some forms of meningitis.

If you have (as a minor) been through a programme of immunisation, it is still worth checking things out, to see if you need any boosters. Your doctor should be able to provide you with a record card of immunizations which you will need to keep up-to-date as your life as a yachtie progresses.

You need to be aware however, that you are likely to require some additional immunizations, especially if you think you might take in that off-season backpacking I mentioned earlier, where you may come into contact with viral infections or other unwanted infections noted below:

- Hepatitis A
- Hepatitis B
- Typhoid
- Yellow fever
- Rabies
- Malaria

STDs

Without stating the glaringly obvious, if you are going to have sexual relationships, where ever you are, then using 'protection' is an absolute must.

I am sure most of you know this already, but I feel it's worth mentioning some of the most common STDs and their symptoms. It's important to remember that you can get and pass on many of these diseases through different forms of sex (vaginal, anal and oral).

It is essential that you see a doctor right away for STD testing, if you think that you might have an STD and be sure to mention that you are worried about an STD. I appreciate that you are unlikely to be in the same place when your test results come through, so arranging to have them relayed to you via e.mail or txt is sensible.

Your doctor may think that some common symptoms of an STD, especially non-specific symptoms, like burning during urination, could be caused by a simple urinary tract infection and not something like Chlamydia, especially if your doctor doesn't know that you are sexually active.

Most people have none of the symptoms such as abdominal discharge (male/female), pain in the testicles and burning during urination. Long term irritation may cause lower abdominal pain, inflammation of the eyes and skin lesions. In women, it can cause inflammation of the pelvic organs; Pelvic Inflammatory Disease (PID). Chlamydia can be completely cured, but can be caught again, especially if both partners aren't treated.

I am not about to go into much more detail, however I will note a number of different STDs, which you should be aware of and can easily find more detail on the www.:

- Genital herpes
- Gonorrhoea
- Hepatitis B
- HIV Infection and Aids
- Syphilis

CREW HOUSES

OK folks, now we're moving along and you've got your biometric passport, ENG 1 and maybe a B1/B2 visa. Yeh, all sorted and you've spent some fairly serious pennies doing your STCW95, or a whole load of serious pennies doing a more comprehensive crew training package, as mentioned earlier in the book. You've got what you think is a pretty hot CV (resumé), your training centre has given you some really useful contacts and you've touched base with a number of crew agents and made arrangements for interviews. So, "Your starter for 10", what next? It's mid-February and this is the time of year when aspirational crew start thinking about heading south (depending on where you live), to find interior work for the next Med Season. So folks, unless you are one of the fortunate minority who manage to secure crew work before you leave your home country, there really is only one place to head for now – Antibes, the global superyacht mecca on the beautiful Côtes d'Azur in the South of France.

ANTIBES ..... is a busy historic port town, situated very roughly, half way between Cannes and Nice and now you are going to need somewhere to stay while you find that all important first job. Antibes is the centre of Mediterranean yachting, therefore you might expect to find some good (or not so good) crew houses in this beautiful part of the Eurozone. There are some really good ones here, but don't just book a flight to Nice and expect to jump on the bus (Bus 200), train or grab a taxi into Antibes and be able to just roll up and check into a room. If you are a total virgin yachtie, you need thorough advanced planning for this part of your new life, which very importantly, includes some sound financial planning, networking and dockwalking. You need to be near to, or at least not too far away from the action, such as crew bars like the Irish Pub, The Hop Store, crew agencies, training centres and of course the port or marina.

It is very important for you to understand at this stage that, regardless of what some folk might tell you, your chances of walking straight into that dream job during week one, with a fat paycheck at the end of the first month, is so rare, that it's almost "bleu". You should be able to pick up some day work (great experience), but even this type of work, which looks good for your CV, usually means that you stilll need a bed to sleep in when you get back ashore. The average length of stay in crew houses for newbies is around three weeks and much less for experienced crew, who will already have great network contacts from previous seasons and will already know captains, first mates, chief stews and crew, who are in the know about crew vacancies. Many experienced crew who have taken time out of the industry during the winter season, may have secured new positions before they arrive. So guys, be prepared to dig in for the long haul, as you can spend anything from a couple of weeks, up to three months of networking, dockwalking, dayworking chasing up crew agents, turning up for endless interviews until you find that first 'dream job'.

I know that you are serious about getting yourself a great job in the industry, however it is important you understand and take onboard the following advice from day one. When you are out and about around Antibes (or your base of choice), just remember that as in many small communities, you will get noticed and not always for the right reasons. When you are sat in a crew bar sinking your seventh half of strong lager, feeling slightly worse for wear, just remember that the tall, good looking blond guy you've been chatting up all night, might be the captain of the yacht, which you are being interviewed for the next day. *"Big mistake, big, huge!"* (Pretty Woman 1990).

I have so many good friends in the industry, both male and female and they have got themselves fabulous jobs on some of the most beautiful yachts in the world and have managed this by doing things the right way from day one. So folks, when you are 'networking', just remember to stay focused, because this will, sooner or later pay-off and once you secure that first job, the world is literally your oyster. You will be the envy of your friends at home, who will see you turning up on Facebook in yet another exotic location, maybe travelling through the Panama Canal or rubbing shoulders with the stars and celebrities at the Cannes Film Festival or Monaco Grand Prix.

Antibes has a good offering of competitively priced crew accommodation, which mainly consists of hostel standard accommodation in either shared rooms or apartments. Several have bars, internet cafés, job boards and they are great for networking. I have provided you with a few random ideas below, which will hopefully give you an idea of what to expect:

THE CREW HOUSE

So, where do you stay, when you arrive in Antibes? Some think about camping, some will rent apartments, but many head for crew houses and the original and I guess most well known in the yachting world is the aptly named 'The Crew House', run by Martin Loveridge and his French wife, Virginie. Most say it's a very friendly hostel, with no curfews or lockouts and that it is ideally situated in the heart of Antibes, just a short walk from all amenities, such as the shops, beach, port, crew agencies, public transport, etc. The bedrooms are cleaned three times a week, where linen is provided and changed once a week and each guest has a locker in their bedroom. You are also provided with the free use of the washing machine and tumble dryer.

Crew houses are often where your initial (often long lasting) yacht crew friendships and networking experiences will happen. At The Crew House, most rooms overlook a large courtyard, where guests can sit, chat and socialise in the sun. It is mainly frequented by like-minded "boat people" looking for jobs in the industry and, as with most crew houses, you will find a very cosmopolitan/eclectic bunch of folk from all over the world.

Internet is provided free through Wi-Fi with your own computer or if you require use of a computer, then you will be charged for this service. However, if you are used to five star everything at home and on your holidays, then sorry to disappoint guys, but you are just not going to get "all-singing, all-dancing" in a crew house. What you will get here is single beds, which are provided in mixed dorms; this is very much a "muck in, make friends and make it happen" kinda place, so get used to the idea or check out some of the alternatives.

THE GLAMORGAN

The Glamorgan, a relatively new entrant to crew accommodation, has quickly become well known in the industry. It is run by Welshman, Chris Browne, a captain with years of experience, who decided to convert his lovely townhouse into crew accommodation back in 2004. The Glamorgan is approximately a two minute walk from the bus and train stations, and Port Vauban Marina is only a short walk away.

Chris provides some good space in his communal crew lounge, where you can relax on comfy sofas and watch Satellite, English Sky TV or choose a DVD from the library. The sitting area leads off into a modern, fully equipped kitchen, where you are able to cook your own meals. There are also free laundry facilities, which include two modern washing machines, two tumble dryers, irons and ironing boards.

The bedrooms are comfortable and the modern en-suite shower-rooms definitely create big-time added value for your stay. The bedrooms have air-con for the summer and heating for the colder months and I am told that, all bedrooms will have Satellite and Sky by the end of 2010. Chris does not like to overcrowd his bedrooms unlike some crew houses, so the bedrooms only sleep two or three, which is great if you have paired up with a buddy to find work. Two of the bedrooms are adjoining, so this would suit wonderfully if you are heading to Antibes in a small group, which we find is something that many of our students like to do.

Chis has a couple of computers in the house, which you can use and he also offers you the use of a printer (unlimited printing), copier and scanner; ideal if you need to tweek your CV (resumé). The house is also equipped with a Wi-Fi network for those who have their own laptops or i.Pads.

So, why not try out a bit of "Glamorgan Chic", where you can sit out in the large shaded garden, relaxing under parasols during the daytime, or using The Glamorgan's Wi-Fi to chat to your FB Friends. In the hot summer months, you can also cook on the barbecue and eat al fresco or you can just sit and catch the beautiful Mediterranean fresh air.

As you might have guessed, The Glamorgan, which comes highly recommended by yacht crew agencies, training schools and my 'Global Research Team', is not the cheapest crew accommodation in town, however if you need any more convincing, check out Chris's website at www.theglamorgan.com

DEBBIE'S CREW HOUSE

If you are looking for a less central location, then you might want to check out Debbie's Crew House, which is about five minutes by train from Antibes station and twenty minutes by train from Nice. You will have realised by now that most of the well known crew houses are run by ex-crew, who all know the sort of anxieties that you are going to experience trying to find work. This crew house is no exception and is run by Debbie Stiano, an ex-Chief Stewardess and her chief engineer husband, the brilliant Franco.

This clean, homely and friendly house is located on the outskirts of Antibes, in a secure, gated (PIN coded) yard. There are no more than two people in each of the seven spacious bedrooms, which are cleaned twice a week and include towels and linen. This crew house offers generous accommodation, free laundry facilities, kitchen and a relaxed atmosphere, where you are able to use the Sky HD package, including films, sport channels and Wi-Fi.

As with some other houses, a computer and printer are also available for your use, free of charge. The large sitting room cum dining room has a large open fire for the colder off-season months. Debbie's is renowned for their summer fun pizza parties, when their outdoor pizza oven is manned by Italian Pizza Chef extraordinaire Franco. You should note that there is a three night minimum stay, with 24 hours notice before your departure.

As this is also Debbie and Franco's home, you will have to put up with a swimming pool, garden, table tennis, badminton, table football, bicycles and the odd domestic pet, which all sounds pretty good to me! Debbie has been cute and placed Debbie's Crew House on Facebook and she also has a cracking website www.debbiescrewhouse.com which is certainly worth a look before you travel.

THE CREW GRAPEVINE

The last of my suggestions and a recent entrant to the crew house scene (2009) is The Crew Grapevine, run by an Australian and American couple; ex-chef Jennifer (USA) and her husband Jason (Capt Downes). My 'Global Research Team' tell me that they are extremely helpful and will try hard to help you find work, using their many connections in the industry. You can also arrange an airport or station pick-up on your arrival (depending on availability) which can be a big bonus; taking you direct to this comfortable crew house.

The 400 year old house offers five bedrooms, including air-con and heating, which sleep up to four people. The Downes' also provide individual lockers, for which you will need your own padlock. You will also find that towels, linen and laundry facilities are supplied and that all the rooms have an en-suite shower and loo, which is always a big plus. There is an open-plan sitting room/dining room/kitchen, which features an open working fireplace, so you will always get a warm welcome the year through. As with The Glamorgan, there is an area fitted with computers, a printer and fax, which come free of charge along with Wi-Fi throughout. Your relaxation time can be enhanced by utilising The Crew Grapevine's DVD library and my spies tell me that a roof terrace will be available for guests in the near future. Jennifer and Jason also regularly update a blackboard, which displays useful contacts for day work.

The minimum stay is three nights and this has to be paid for in cash, plus a 50€ returnable deposit. So if you have budgeted for a six week stay, then I strongly recommend that you use your credit card to withdraw cash as you need it, rather than having large amounts of euros on tap to tempt the nearest 'tea leaf'. The Crew Grapevine also offer apartments and studios to rent.

Many of my grad students have stayed at The Glamorgan, a few have stayed in The Crew Grapevine (as it only opened recently) and Debbie's Crew House and they have all been impressed with the standard of accommodation, cleanliness and client comfort of the public areas, and especially the help they have been given by the owners. So guys, if you are looking for budget accommodation and are prepared to muck-in, then The Crew House may be right for you. If a bit more space and additional comfort is more your thing and you can afford the extra Euros, then maybe think about heading for The Glamorgan, The Crew Grapevine or Debbie's Crew House.

My apologies to the many other crew house owners, who will make you very welcome in Antibes, for not providing a write up for them. I only have limited space and I have taken a random selection, in an attempt to cut across a range of priorities i.e. location, cost, comfort, amenities, value for money, personal feedback etc and I hope that the ones I have included will give you a feel for what you might expect to find on arrival.

CREW HOUSE CONTACT DETAILS
ANTIBES

Amma's Crew House	+33 (0) 6 19 63 82 50
Antibes Youth Hostel Caravelle	+33 (0) 4 93 61 34 40
Chrys Hotel	+33 (0)4 92 91 70 20
Crew Grapevine info@crewgrapevine.com	+33 (0) 6 16 66 28 43 www.crewgrapevine.com
Debbie's Crew House deborah.banks@wanadoo.fr	+33 (0) 6 32 38 75 28 www.debbiescrewhouse.com
Hotel Etoile	+33 (0)4 93 34 26 30
Hotel Josse	+33 (0)4 92 93 38 38
Hotel Le collier	+33 (0)4 93 74 56 40
Hotel Trianon	+33 (0)4 93 61 18 11
Le Resideal	+33 (0)4 92 90 76 00
Stella's Crew House	+33 (0)4 93 34 12 14
The Crew House	+33 (0) 4 92 90 49 39

The Glamorgan
glamorgan@wanadoo.fr

+33 (0) 4 93 34 42 71
www.theglamorgan.com

PALMA

Cotoner 31a Sta Catalina
info@accommodationpalma.com

+34 (0) 971 284828
www.accommodationpalma.com

Hostel Apuntadores
apuntadores@ctv.es

+34 (0) 971 713491
www.palma-hostales.com

Hostel Colon
colon@amic-hotels.com

+34 (0) 971 750245

Hostel Brondo
hostal.brondo@terra.es

+34 (0) 669 197168

The Boat House
theboathouse@hotmail.com

+34 (0) 696 907676

The Crew House
info@crewhouse.net

+34 (0) 600 726050

FORT LAUDERDALE

The Beach Hostel
info@fortlauderdalehostel.com

001 954 567 7275
www.fortlauderdalehostel.com

The Bridge @ Cordova
info@thebridgeatcordova.com

001 954 525 2323
www.thebridgeatcordova.com

The Bridge II @ 16th Street
info@thebridgehotelfortlauderdale.com

001 954 522 6350
www.thebridgehotelfortlauderdale.com

Captain's Quarters

001 954.764.7828

Colonial Crew Apartments
floridafloyd@mac.com

001 954.764.0686
www.picturesandmaps.com

Crew Castal
guiltfree@earthlink.net

001 954 931 8945
americancrewhouses.webs.com

Crew Quarters
beverly@crewquarters.com

001 954 522 1631
www.crewquarters.com

Floyds Hostel
info@floydshostel.com

001 954 462 0631
www.floydshostel.com

Mary's Crew House
maryscrwhouse@yahoo.com

001 954.242.1109
www.maryscrewhouse.com

Palm Place
lcooksey@bellsouth.net

001 954 655 8526
www.palmplaceres.com/

IMPORTANT TO REMEMBER

Subsistence money

You will need to be in full control of your finances, therefore it is essential that you have sufficient savings available before you set off and that you set yourself a budget to enable you to subsist for your planned timescale. Options to help stretch your budget may include day-work or offering to cook or crew for free, so a captain can assess your ability.

Photographs

It is sensible to take a number of recent passport sized photos with you; you never know when you might need them. It makes sense to import a digital photo onto your CV (resumé), this prevents the perennial problem of your photo getting separated from your CV. It also helps to keep a number of different 'portrait' style photos on your social networking account. Another good idea is to e.mail digital images to your e.mail account and save them in a folder, ready to access whenever and wherever you might need them. Wear a plain polo shirt, preferably white or blue for a head and shoulders, portrait shot. Girls should be photographed sporting a 'sensible' hair style and wear no jewellery. Boys should have short, tidy hair and be clean shaven.

Some good advice worth budgeting for, is to go and have some photo's taken by a professional photographer. Always dress smartly, without over-doing it and always look professional. A professional photographer will advise you about using a suitable, neutral background, or if you are using a machine, then select a neutral colour, such as cream or off-white.

Crew agents are likely to bin CVs (resumés) that do not include photos and the same thing applies if your photo is of poor quality, or you just don't look the part. Wearing heavy make-up girls is a big no-no and must be avoided; something more subtle and pleasing to the eye is more likely to initiate a positive response. You might think that showing too much cleavage will land you that dream job, however it may well have the opposite effect and in the bin goes your hopes in the short term. Photos must always be current and make sure you take a selection or colour and black and white ones with you.

Personal attributes

Interior crew must attain and maintain certain standards. It is essential that you create a positive impression to your guests at all times. When in uniform, even when onshore, you must remember that you still represent your yacht and will be identified as such. Any unbecoming behaviour (in uniform), is likely to have a negative impact on the image of your yacht, crew, captain and of course – the owner.

Personal hygiene: Male interior staff should be clean shaven, hands should be immaculately clean and finger nails clean and trimmed. Hair should be short and well groomed. Female interior staff, should have immaculately manicured finger nails, short hair or have their hair tied back and wear no excessive make-up or jewellery. Identified crew footwear should be clean and well presented. Uniforms (provided) must always be clean, well pressed and worn correctly. Interior staff should not have any visible tattoos or piercings.

Product knowledge: Dependant on your job role, It is important that you are familiar with each day's menus and are able to describe the ingredients, cooking method, garnishes etc to your guests. You should also know what menu alternatives are available from the galley for vegetarian guests or guests with allergies or intolerances. You should know how to serve each dish on the menu, which side to serve and clear from and the symmetry of the plate, when placed on the table in front of the guest. Over time, you will attain a working knowledge of different types of wine from around the world, which food they match with and their service temperature (See Food and Wine Combinations – Page 252). You will also learn about aperitifs, cocktails, port and brandy (Cognac and Armagnac).

Punctuality: Although the concept of punctuality onboard a yacht is somewhat different to work on dry land i.e. there's no place to hide, the old doctor or dentist blag is a definite no-no and pulling a 'sicky' is less easy to get away with. You are still expected to be where you are supposed to be at pre-determined times. Just remember that you are a member of a supportive team and your crew rely on your ability to pull your weight at all times.

Personality: When guests are onboard, you must always be tactful, courteous, good humoured and don't overdo the perma-smile. Depending on the type and size of yacht you are working on, you will be advised of when you can or can't talk to guests. In the more informal environment of a two-man charter, you will be in close contact with your guests for much of the day and as such, be expected to be approachable, flexible and be able to chat with guests in a pleasing and well spoken manner. Always having a positive attitude and smiling at the right time can pay big dividends, as I hope you will find out.

Attitude to guests: Having spent much of my working life looking after people in the hospitality industry, I have always found that anticipating customer (guest) wants and needs is high on the list of customer delight. This is something that will come to you as time goes on and will help you get recognition and hopefully promotion. One of the reasons why you will get a job is your personality, however it is important that you are not overly familiar with guests. If you get work on a large yacht, a good chief stew will soon let you know your working limitations/parameters. Keeping an eye on guests, especially when they are dining, must be done without staring. Ask yourself, is someone's wine glass empty, might they want another bread roll, offer the pepper mill etc etc…Your guests' onboard experience should be totally seamless from the date they arrive, to when they depart. You will need to go out of your way to be the best of the best.

INSURANCE
Personal & yacht
Esther Barney wrote in The Crew Report (September 2009) *"The global financial crisis may have pushed owners to reduce running costs, including the insurance level for crewmembers; in some cases it has been cancelled altogether. While you may feel you are too busy to sort it out, or that your yacht should provide full coverage, it is important to take ownership of your insurance situation. If you do not know what your vessel's policy covers or have not read the documentation, then put this at the top of your "to do" list."*

If you are uncomfortable about the perceived level of cover on your yacht, you would be advised to contact one of the specialist crew insurance companies below, or be advised by crewmates who may have already addressed their own personal insurance cover. It is essential that your cover includes repatriation costs to your home country.

- **AXA PPP Healthcare**
  www.axappphealthcare.co.uk
- **Crew Insurance Services**
  www.crewinsuranceservices.com
- **MHG Marine Benefits**
  www.mhgmarine.com
- **Pantaenius Yacht Insurance**
  www.pantaenius.com
- **Seven Seas Health**
  www.sevenseashealth.com
- **Worldwide Yacht Crew Cover**
  www.wycc-insurance.com

INTERNET CAFÉS

Although many crew houses now have a Wi-Fi internet connection, you may find yourself in one that doesn't, so an Internet Café will be really useful, when you need to make appointments to see crew agents. Check out the following ones:

The Office
8 Boulegard Aguillon
Antibes, Juan les Pins 06600
+33 (0)4 93 34 09 96

The Office is very friendly, helpful and is often used by captains, yacht owners, crew and job seekers to have post delivered, use their fax (still a very popular method of communication in France), computers, internet etc.

Workstation
1 avenue St Roche
Antibes, Juan les Pins 06600

This internet café is part of The Crew House (see page 25) and is very helpful. English computers, notice board for day work, as well as long term positions.

Xtreme Cyber
16-22 at 6 rue Aubernon

Xtreme Cyber is the newest Internet Café in Antibes. They offer a really fast connection to the internet, plus scanner, colour printer, web cam and all the support you need to work on the www. You are also welcome to take your own laptop and connect on-site. They will also help you write up your C.V. (although you really should have this done before you arrive). They offer a translation service from English to Italian and French and can help you with your PC problems. They also offer coffee, tea, cold drinks and sweet or savoury snacks.

MARINAS
Port Vauban
The main marina, is acknowledged throughout the yachting world as a superyacht hub, offering some forty berths in the 25 metre plus range, with lengths of up to 165 meters accommodated. The harbour is surrounded by boating facilities of every kind. Berthing is alongside and stern-to and there is also an on-site heliport.
Antibes: +33 (0)4 92 91 60 00
www.port-vauban-antibes.com

International Yacht Club
Otherwise known as "Billionaires Row", the deepest marina in Europe and where you will find some of the largest superyachts in the world.
Antibes: +33 (0)4 93 34 30 30
iyca@iycantibes.com

Port Camille Rayon
Yachts from 25 meters to 75 meters, mainly devoted to luxury yachting.
Golfe Juan: +33 (0)4 93 63 30 30
www.portcamillerayon.net

Port Golfe Juan
Located between Antibes and Cannes, with only limited facilities at the time of writing. However it is very busy during the many events that take place during the year, such as the Cannes Film Festival and the Monaco Grand Prix. Initial improvements have been carried out during 2010 and there are future planned investments.
Golfe Juan: +33 (0)4 93 63 96 25
www.riviera-ports.com

Port Gallice
Mainly berths for 25 metre to 30 metre range, in one of the most up-market ports in the very chic town of Juan les Pins.
Juan les Pins: +33 (0)4 92 93 74 40

Ports of Cannes and Nice
A single telephone number: 0820 425 555 (€0.12/min)
From abroad: +33 (0)4 898 898 28
Service open 7 days a week, from 07:00 to midnight.

Port de Villefranche sur Mer
+33 (0)4 93 01 78 05
+33 (0)4 93 01 70 70

BANKS
Banks in Antibes include: HSBC, Barclays, as well as the prominent French Banks: Crédit Lyonnais, Crédit Mutual, Société Générale. I have found that BNP Parisbas are very helpful. Also, CA Britline is the English speaking bank of Crédit Agricole.

You may also want to investigate the advantages/benefits of opening an off-shore bank account i.e. in the Channel Islands (Jersey) or the Isle of Man. Check with your own bank, asking for Offshore Banking Services, which most of the 'big' banks are able to help you with.

TOURIST OFFICE
The Office de Tourisme is great place to pick up a map of Antibes and local information. The maps are free, all you will need is a quick *"Je voudrais un plan de la ville, s'il vous plait – c'est libre?"*

TRANSPORT SOUTH
I recently saw a blog on Dockwalk.com from, what I can only guess had to be a fairly 'green' newbie, who needed to find out if there was long term car parking in Antibes. Now it took me only seconds to find this out on the www, and I now know that the open air car parks by the Antibes beaches at Ponteil and Salis are free of charge apart from the peak summer months (i.e. Med Season) and the open air car park behind La Post (Post Office) is free of charge overnight.

Now although I applaud the idea of planning and driving what can be a fabulous, interesting and scenic route from Calais down to the Côte d'Azur, I found myself wondering big-time, WHY? There are far easier transport solutions available and when there is the possibility that you might find yourself in Fort Lauderdale in the middle of January, with a week off, the last place you are going to head for is Antibes to recover your voiture. By the way and for your added IAG; parking near the ramparts in Antibes is around 33€ per day (ouch!), so if you think you may find yourself in the middle of the ocean, heading in the wrong direction, while your car is parked up in Antibes, then it might be prudent to leave it back in Blighty!

FLIGHTS

There are a large number of carriers who fly into the Nice International Airport, so you can pick up relatively inexpensive flights from many countries in Europe. EasyJet one way flights are usually less expensive and competitively priced, even compared with the French high-speed train, the TGV (Train à Grande Vitesse).

Aéroport Nice Côte d'Azur
+33 820 423 333
From abroad (if the above number does not work):
+33 (0)4 89 88 98 28
www.nice.aeroport.fr

The following are examples of some airlines, which currently fly into Nice Airport:

Air France, Air Lingus, Air Transat, Baboo, BMI Baby, Blu Express, BMI British Midland, Britsh Airways, Easy Jet, Flybe, Iberia, Ryanair. Here are a few useful links you might want to check out:

- www.ba.com
- www.klm.com
- www.flybe.com
- www.ryanair.com
- www.flybaboo.ch
- www.easyjet.com
- www.expedia.co.uk
- www.skyscanner.net
- www.blu-express.com
- www.cheapflights.co.uk

When you arrive at the airport, you have a choice of transport to take you to your destination in Antibes. However, try to avoid booking a late evening flight (inbound), as you are likely to arrive after the last train and bus services have departed and then your only option will be a taxi, which can make a bad impression on your carefully planned budget.

BUS 200 - direction Cannes, will drop you at Antibes train station (approx 40min). The local buses provide a very affordable transport option along the coast.

TRAIN - a free shuttle will take you from the airport to Nice St Augustin train station, the train then takes approx' 20 minutes to Antibes. Trains run from here, East and west and this is by far the easiest way to access the whole stretch of coastline from Cannes to Monaco and beyond to St Remo and the Italian Riviera. A trip to Italy or over to St Tropez only takes around an hour and will cost your around €20. In the summer months, it is possible to purchase a daily travel card, which will give you unlimited travel along the Riviera for €15.

TAXI - will cost you about 50€, but make sure you fix a price before you depart from the airport.

BIKE HIRE – when you have arrived in Antibes, is available from:
Holiday Bikes, 122 Boulevard Wilson, Juan les Pins
+33 (0)4 93 61 51 51

TRAIN – SNCF (French National Railway)

Travelling by train in France can be a challenging, interesting and enjoyable experience. On long-haul journeys, booking a ticket in advance is essential, as is sitting in the seat allocated to you on your ticket, or you will soon be told to move. Buying something to eat, on the station prior to your departure is also a good idea.

French train schedules and fares
You can check train times and fares for any journey in France, using either www.raileurope.co.uk (for UK residents) or the French Railways (SNCF) website: www.voyages-sncf.com. The latter can be a little quirky, so I suggest that you check out the advice below.

HOW TO BUY TRAIN TICKETS IN FRANCE
Buying tickets at the station
It can be easy to buy tickets at the station, even if you don't speak French. For local journeys, such as Nice-Cannes, you just turn up, buy a ticket and hop on, no reservation necessary. Tickets can be purchased from the self-service machines at main stations, which usually have an English language facility.

Long distance trains in France are however a completely different ball game and this includes the TGV (Train à Grande Vitesse – High Speed Train); Corail Lunéa train (Night train) from Paris to Nice and Corail Téoz trains from Paris to Nice. For these services it's compulsory to make a seat reservation and I have found it helpful to book seats in advance, as just turning up hoping to buy a ticket on a busy day (Religious Holiday), you may find yourself without a seat. However, seats are usually available, even on the day of travel and you can buy a ticket immediately before the train departs. However, on the day of travel, you'll pay the full normal fare, which is a bit daft, when you can buy the same ticket, much cheaper if you pre-book. It is definitely a good idea to pre-book during busy holiday periods.

A very important thing to remember is to *'validate your ticket'*, by putting it into the small orange machine marked *'Compstez votre billet'*, at the entrance to your platform – there's a fine if you don't do this!

Buying tickets on-line
- If you book well in advance on a 'no refunds, no changes to your travel plans' basis, you can find some amazing advance purchase fares called 'Prems'. Prems fares start at just 19€, even for a long-distance journey such as Paris to Nice.

- French train bookings open 90 days before the train's departure. You can't book before reservations open.

- You can buy French train tickets online direct from SNCF website www.voyages-sncf.com, which as mentioned previously, can be a little quirky.

- If you live in the UK, it's far easier to buy French train tickets at www.raileurope.co.uk, which is much more simple to use that the SNCF site. It is also backed-up by a UK call centre 0844 848 5 848 (lines open 09:00-21:00 Mon-Fri, 09:00-18:00 Sat & 10:00-17:00 Sun). It offers exactly the same fares and availability as voyages-sncf.com, including the amazingly cheap advance purchase Prems fares, but prices are converted into sterling for your convenience. You can save a few percent by buying in Euros at www.voyages-sncf.com but if anything goes wrong, you'll be dealing with a French call centre, not a UK one, so be warned! www.raileurope.co.uk now charges a £1.95 postage fee and 2% credit card fee, but you can avoid both charges by collecting tickets at the station, using a debit card.

- If you live in the USA, Canada, Australia or New Zealand, you can buy train tickets for France online at:

- ○ www.raileurope.com (USA),
- ○ www.raileurope.ca (Canada)
- ○ www.raileurope.com.au (Australia & NZ).

Rail Europe is a direct subsidiary of SNCF, but you might save a bit by buying direct from voyages-sncf.com.

Which station from Paris?

Gare de Lyon - serves TGV trains to the south-east: Lyon, Avignon, Marseille, Cannes, Nice, Monte-Carlo, Nîmes, Montpellier, Narbonne & Perpignan.

Gare d'Austerlitz - serves Téon trains to Limoges and Toulouse & Lunéa over night trains to Cannes, Nice, Monte Carlo, Toulouse, Perpignan, Narbonne, Lourdes, Biarritz, Madrid and Barcelona.

DOCKWALKING

So, you've arrived, found yourself some comfortable and hopefully affordable crew accommodation, got a few interviews lined up, so what do you do now? No point sitting around kicking your heals, so there is only one thing for it – THE DOCKWALK.

One of the most important factors for getting work is to be positive and pro-active. You are not going to be the only person out there looking for work, so you need to make yourself stand out from the crowd. Conventionally, doing the dockwalk on the coast at the start (or end) of the Med Season presents the opportunity of accessing day-work, which could end up with a job offer, as long as you are able to prove your credentials. It is possible to find temporary and full-time work this way, especially if you are looking for work on smaller yachts. It has been called both character building and sole destroying, but either which way, dockwalking is still the most effective tool in your bag. It can also provide you with an income to keep you going until you find something more permanent.

There are of course advantages to doing the dockwalk. You certainly get 'the feel' for the environment and have an opportunity to bump into like-minded folks, so this is another good way to network. Depending on accessibility to the marina, you will be able to take a good look, in real time, at the range of vessels moored-up and can assess what you think might be right for you. The big advantage is, that you may just be in the right place at the right time – cliché I know, but true! The downside, especially if you lack self-confidence, is plucking up the courage to approach complete strangers on a multi-million pound yacht to ask for a job. If you are the sort of person who finds it hard to handle rejection, then maybe the dockwalk won't be right for you. You will find that these days some marinas are out-of-bounds to 'Joe Public', which means you will find it difficult to get near the yachts, let alone step your unclad foot onboard to talk to the crew.

Don't leave it too late to get down to Antibes in the Spring. Last season (2010) saw more crew looking for work than positions available. There are often big numbers chasing entry-level stew, positions on the bigger yachts, so you may need to consider biting the bullet and work your way up from a smaller yacht. There are more small yachts than bigger ones, so potentially a greater opportunity of employment.

Many owners and captains have become more conscious of the bottom line and are being cautious about employing additional crew until charters are booked, so watch out in the future for more day work and short-term contracts until the financial climate improves.

How do I Dockwalk?

- Check out the crew clothing shops near the Blue Lady Bar (Boulevard Aguillon – Antibes).
- Get up early in the morning, look the part. Dress in smart shorts and T-shirt (no scruffy deckies or flip-flops) and take a back-pack with you, with a set of overalls or working clothes.
- You should aim to be on the docks or pontoon for around seven in the morning, as most boats start work at eight and will have recruited by then.
- Usually you will find the skipper or mate of a boat will be in the cockpit having a coffee at this time. Call the name of the boat, if you don't know what to say to get their attention. Larger boats will have a door bell system (honest!).
- Be cheerful and keen. Ask if they have any day work and if not, would they like a copy of your CV or business card for future reference. Make sure it has clear contact details; a mobile (cell phone) is an essential piece of kit. Buying yourself a local SIM card helps to keep costs down.

FYI: United States Immigration are getting very tough on people entering the USA on tourist visas and then being caught dockwalking. As a foreign national working in the USA, you either need an official work visa or be signed onto a vessel to work under the B1/B2 Visa. Casual day working is illegal using the BI/B2 Visa.

There was a lot of chat on blogs in November 2010, where the talk was about the high number of hopefuls being deported from the United States for dockwalking without the appropriate documentation. I also understand that an increasing number of marinas in the Caribbean do not allow dockwalking at all, so do take this advice seriously.

DAY WORK

Although it's great to have company, flying solo is the best way to find day work. One person is more likely to be employed that two, so dockwalking on your own makes a lot of sense.

Don't turn up with any pre-conceived ideas; it does not help to start getting "sniffy" about what day work might involve. Sanding, varnishing, cleaning, engine room work etc could all be on the agenda. This all adds up to experience and making those essential first contacts. If you show enthusiasm, a skipper may well keep employing you and this could lead to a permanent job, or a great reference that could be the deciding factor of you gaining a position on another boat, above other candidates.

- Read any notices displayed on the passerelle (gangway), before ringing the bell.
- If the owner is onboard don't even approach the boat. Check out for tell-tale indicators such as: cushions or flower arrangements on the aft-deck, these are the usual giveaways.
- Most of the larger motor yachts based on International Quay tend to have permanent day workers, so Y Quay is a better option.
- Spend time walking the docks of Antibes, Cannes (Port Canto and Old Port), Golfe Juan, Port Galic, Monaco (Le port Hercule & Le port de Fontvieille), Nice, St Tropez, St Remo (Italy) etc
- There is a good coast train that stops at most all the ports. Do a different port each day, looking smart and fresh and armed with plenty of CVs. It is also a good idea to get yourself some business cards printed. For a relatively small cost, this can be a good investment.
- You must be clean shaven, with a sensible hair cut and no visible tattoos or body piercings and above all be smartly dressed and ready to work.

It is unlikely that you will strike gold on day one! If you don't get an instant return on your efforts, my advice is to hang-in there as long as your finances allow. The jobs are out there, so have a plan and set yourself realistic targets to achieve your ultimate goal – sector employment!

As I have already mentioned, the current economic climate has many yachts in the sector looking for ways of making savings. Some captains think this means they can get free work out of newbies in exchange for 'experience'. However, when you work for experience or lunch, you're sending out the message that your time isn't valuable. You may be new to the industry, but you want there to be some tangible, financial return on your hard work. Even if you're temporary crew (non-day work), it's a good idea to have a contract to avoid getting shafted on your pay and conditions. I noted in the forum, *Pay Recovery* on Dockwalk.com, Cindy Smith mentions a friend who worked for three months on board a boat and did not realize s/he was not being paid. The best advice I can give is that for any type of employment, other than day work, which should be paid in cash at the end of the day, should be undertaken on the basis of a written employment contract. Day workers aren't usually contracted to a yacht, they are casual workers, often employed on demand and not classed as official crew members.

Finally, if you feel your day work has gone well, always ask for a reference. You may not be a permanent crew member, but being able to prove that you are a reliable, hard worker and can show some yacht time on your C.V. will be a big advantage for future employment prospects. Ask your day supervisor if s/he is comfortable being added to your C.V. as a referee is a cute way of building a picture for future employers.

If you done good, it is quite likely that you will become more and more in demand and as you are not contracted to any specific vessel, you are a free agent. This way, you can get the vibe across a number of yachts, which is great to help your decision making about the size of yacht you would prefer to work on.

As noted above, you must make sure that you are legal. Casual day work in the USA is not legal using a B1/B2 Visa. If you try to blag it, you may find yourself in trouble with the local police/immigration if you get caught. Working illegally can lead to deportation.

WHEN NOT TO HEAD SOUTH (from UK)
The main Med season has traditionally run from March/April through to October and you will usually find that May, June and July are fairly quiet on the job-front, with most yachts fully operational and crewed. Many yachts stay in the Med all the year round, however we are seeing an increasing number crossing the Atlantic for the winter to extend charter opportunities, so be prepared for the possibility of heading off to the Caribbean, BVIs or Pacific, where the season runs from October/November to March/April. If Florida-bound, then a B1/B2 Visa is necessary.

The end of the Med season in 2010 appeared to arrive prematurely for some yachts, with many colleagues telling me about end of season crew parties kicking off as early as the back end of August, increasing in number through September. This year's shrinkage in the length of the charter season, I believe has come about due to continued concerns and uncertainty regarding the global recession, with owners risk assessing the viability of running a fully crewed yacht for longer than was absolutely necessary.

I have a particular acquaintance, I'll call her Stephanie, who headed off to Antibes in October 2010, expecting to find work on a yacht heading for a warmer winter on the other side of the Atlantic. Unfortunately in her case, things did not work out in Antibes. She tells me that the crew agents were a tad surprised to see a newbie looking for work at that time of the year; although, two or three years back, it would have been the norm to get off-Med-season employment opportunities at this time of year. She was advised that had she arrived in August, there would have been plenty of day work experience that they could have put her way, advising that this would most likely have enabled her (with her background) to get on a yacht crossing to the Caribbean for the season. They explained that most all of the yachts staying out in the Med for the winter would be downsizing to a skeleton crew and therefore unlikely to take on new crew, especially newbies, for the off-season. Stephanie was unlucky, as we had a number of grads who found day work and others who have joined yachts and have done 'the crossing'.

The other side of the Euro coin is another newbie, who I'll call Ali, who went down to Antibes around the same time as 'Stephanie'. After three weeks of dockwalking and agencies and not a single interview in sight, Ali was ready to head for home when the call came through and she was offered (and accepted) day work on a 47m superyacht out of Cannes as a trial for a stewardess position. Ali said the experience was great, but the vibe with the crew just wasn't right.

In the meantime she was offered three days work on a fabulous 57m superyacht out of Monaco and loved it. The vibe was right this time, with a completely different atmosphere and group dynamic with the crew; even though (as she proudly told me) she did spend eight hours on her hands and knees cleaning the dirt out from the floorboards with a toothbrush! They liked Ali as well and offered her a more day work for the following week.

While she was busy day working on this fabulous yacht, she was contacted again for a solo stew/cook role for a 24m M/Y, which was headed for the shipyard for a month, which meant she could book her flight home in time for Christmas, before heading back in time for a New Year start as a crew/cook - her first full-time job on a luxury yacht. Basically, Ali finished up with three job offers within days of each other and this was in the middle of November; not traditionally the best time to find superyacht work on the Côte d'Azur.

Heading off across the Atlantic with Virgin or BA, in the direction of Fort Lauderdale, Caribbean or BVIs, to find work is an attractive option to some at the end of the Med season, but there is obviously a higher financial outlay to be considered if your post-training budget does not stretch to crossing the Atlantic.

If after evaluating the merits and de-merits of your options, you decide that the US East Coast is for you, then before heading off, check out the info' above on Fort Lauderdale crew house accommodation and definitely talk to as many people as you can to find the best deals for a comfortable, friendly, well located crew house and 'talk to' as many crew agents as you can before you head off.

I would advise newbies with ambitions of getting onto a yacht out of the South of France at the end of the Med Season, hoping to make 'the crossing', that you are more likely to get work if you have the 'essential qualifications' (see Training & Qualifications), and a background in hospitality, leisure or tourism or related services. Captains are taking a huge risk, by employing a newbie with little or no experience in customer facing hospitality services, when they are unlikely to be able to evaluate their return on investment until they reach their charter destination. I understand that, in recent years, captains have been disappointed with the number of newbies they have taken on in the Med to make the crossing, who have just not worked out. Agents are also telling me that many of the yachts this year (2010) have made 'the crossing', with the intention of taking on any new crew they needed for the season out of Fort Lauderdale or the Caribbean.

So, unless you have previous experience working on yachts and/or connections within the industry or a relevant skill set required i.e. chef, housekeeper, florist, masseuse, cabin-crew (airline), dive-master etc and already hold a B1/B2 visa, you may want to consider working in the hospitality sector for the winter months, before heading off to Antibes in March with a healthy bank balance, ready for the next Med season. You can also spend some of this time keeping a close eye on potential employment opportunities through your developing network connections, friends and most importantly – crew agencies.

Networking

This can be one of the most rewarding methods of finding work on the yacht of your dreams. If you have attended professional crew training, you will have already made some good, sometimes lifelong friendships and they will form the foundation stone of your networking for the future. As they gain employment, so your network of contacts has the potential to grow. Many crew and 'newbies' use social networks like Facebook, so it can be fairly easy to keep in touch with them. You will be at a big advantage if you already have friends who are currently employed in the sector, as they are likely to be the first to know when jobs are coming up.

OK – so your day of dockwalking did not come up with the goods and now all you want to do is sit down and have a nice cold beer; this, you have decided, is the last and most enjoyable way of looking for crew work. But don't just drop into any old bar, definitely not, you my friend have got to be cute and up there with the front runners; what you need is to spend some time (and Euros) in Antibe's "Crew Bars" i.e. The Gaffe, Lincoln, Blue Lady, The Extreme Bar, The Hop Store etc. Order yourself a coke or beer and start talking to likely looking targets. Many of the bars are regular haunts for captains and crew, so once people get to know you, they will often tell you about jobs going on their (or other) boats. Many of the bars (and crew houses) have notice boards, where jobs are listed and where you can always place an advert for work wanted. Be warned though, you are not going to make the right impression by drinking too much and drawing unwanted attention to yourself, so drinking in moderation is essential.

Finding work

One of the big advantages of splashing the cash and undertaking professional crew training is that, as part of the package you buy into, professional training organisations will (in some cases) be able to help you write up a C.V. of the expected style and standard and put you in touch with some good employment contacts i.e. crew agents. You should arm yourself with a range of qualifications and that will indicate to the crew agent that you have invested a lot of time and money in getting the very best training available, enabling you to work in the sector, and hopefully making you eminently employable.

Having spent a lot of time and money on your training, the last thing you want to do is to waste time and money utilising an inappropriate or less effective method of finding work. Owners and captains are more likely to employ experienced crew, rather than 'newbies', so you need to be totally on the ball and use the most effective methods available to you. Before you make a start, you will want to give some consideration to a range of issues, not least – what type of boat would you like to work on. Small, medium or large; old, classic new, re-furb'; motor or sail. A recent trip to Manoel Island Marina in Malta provided a classic snap shot of a broad range of yacht types available on a relatively small dock, the largest being the 95 metre Indian Empress, owned by Indian business baron Vijay Mallya.

Looking for a new job can be both an exciting and frustrating experience and the prospect of finding the right yacht for you is seldom a straightforward process. There are a number of job-finding methods available to you and as with anything in life, some require more hard work and application than others if you are going to be successful. The primary ones (in no particular order) are: crew agents, dock-walking, internet and networking. The secondary ones (in no particular order) are: crew bars/restaurants, crew house notice boards, magazine adverts.

Employment trends

As previously mentioned, there are many pros and cons to finding work as the sector continues to feel the effects of the global recession (2008/11) and predicting employment trends has become as accurate as gazing into a gypsy's crystal ball.

When I started researching this book, I noted sector media were reporting how a large number of experienced crew (global) were out of work during the winter of 2008/09 and we saw a similar trend as the Med season closed in 2009. I managed to catch up with two of my good friends, Nichole and Shelley in October 2009, who confirmed emerging off-season employment issues. Both girls had two solid seasons experience behind them working as interior crew, when at the end of the Med season (working on separate boats), they suddenly both found themselves, for no apparent reason, unemployed. Although they both checked out their network of friends, contacts and crew agents, they found there was little chance of employment on the European side of the Atlantic until maybe March/April 2010. So, rather than kicking their heals back in 'Dear Old Blighty' for the winter months, they headed off to OZ, Thailand, Cambodia and Vietnam to do some travelling for a few months. It is important to stress that both girls were very focused on getting back to Europe in good time to get down to Antibes for the 2010 season, before other experienced crew and the batch of 'newbies' arrive on the scene looking for placements. They knew full well that one or two weeks can make the difference between a good boat or bad boat, full-time employment or day-work. They also knew that they would be challenged for crew positions by potentially cash rich, vibrant, self-confident youngsters, who, after evaluating their continued land-based employment potential would cash in their highly paid city jobs, undertaken professional crew training and headed for the 'dream'. Yes, they may lack experience, but many are likely to come onto the scene armed with a raft of job relevant qualifications; OK, not always sufficient for many agents, captains or owners, but it may make some employers sit up and think that there are different ways of managing HR efficiencies on their yachts.

Experience, experience, experience is great (and preferred by most), but it sometimes comes with large egos and at a high price. Utilising a crew-mix of experience and well 'paper qualified', inexperience is something that more captains are going to have to consider, as their own salaries are being threatened. It is interesting to check out yachtie forum posts and see how crew are reacting to the changing job market. It has been very hard for some to adjust to the new reality that most crew cannot currently cherry pick their jobs. It's getting back to where it used to be and you have to work your way up. You have to earn your money by proving that you are willing and able to learn and showing that you can be loyal. This is how it used to be and now it's getting back to some kind of reality.

These young friends of mine are possibly a prime example of the emerging employment trend in the sector; employers looking for multi-taskers, who have the willingness to assume multiple responsibilities. Owners have had to cut costs drastically across their commercial corporations and as I am sure you are already aware, 'downsizing', 'HR efficiencies' or whatever you want to call it, is often the first and easiest step in protecting the bottom line. So, if downsizing is good enough for owners' corporations, which create the wealth to pay for the yacht and its running costs, then why not apply the same criteria to their yachts as well, which can haemorrhage money at an alarming rate.

I have noticed from reports in sector media, that the role of the freelance chef is getting stronger. Boats are having a multi-tasker take care of feeding the crew when there are no owner or charter guests onboard and a chef is brought in a few days before the charter and departs the vessel, sometimes the same day as the charter guests.

I had first-hand experience of the multi-tasker syndrome recently when I received a phone call from a good friend working interior crew on a superyacht, who contacted me one Friday afternoon as I was driving home from work and asked if I could do a two week galley gig out of Greece. The package was brilliant; expenses for everything, collect at the airport, straight to the yacht, all provisioning and menu planning done, all I have to do was show up the following Tuesday and cook – my kind of galley heaven! "The owner eats everything except garlic" I was told, Jesus, even I (a garlic lover extraordinaire) could live with that! Unfortunately I had to turn the deal down for personal reasons. This opportunity was dangled in front of me for exactly the reason mentioned in the previous paragraph. My friend was looking after the crew-cooking and multitasking and the only time the captain needed a 'qualified' chef onboard was when the owner was there.

Crew placement specialist Debbie Blazy at Camper & Nicholsons' Antibes offices says in Dockwalk (June 2009) *"My advice to crew seeking work, is that salary should not be your main priority. Yachts where the long-term prospects are good, where there is the possibility of career progression, should be much higher on your wish list than the one paying top dollar."*

Crew agents (at that time) were in the enviable position of being able to put forward a choice of names of experienced and professional candidates for every job available, submitting some top-notch candidates. Those newly qualified to the industry sometimes found themselves struggling to make an impact with the crew agents and some found it difficult to get interviews and money started to run out along with the opportunities.

Owners and captains will utilise tried and tested methodologies for employing new crew. If they have a good working relationship with a particular crew agent, then that is who they are likely to use in the future. At the end of the day, it boils down to basic risk assessment for an employer – high risk versus low risk – you know the answer!

Crew Agents – a few thoughts

You may be wondering why you need to use a crew agent to find the job of your dreams. Well, it is possible to get yourself employment in the sector by being based in the UK or elsewhere in the world, however this ranges from being extremely difficult to darn-well nearly impossible and there are many disadvantages in taking this route. At the time of writing we are (hopefully) easing our way out of a global recession and you really do need to be where the action is if you are looking for 'an in' to your first position in the sector. Although the situation is likely to ease as we come out of recession, just remember that an increasing number of experienced crew are being laid off for the European winter and they will be chasing the same jobs as you when owners or captains are looking to employ new crew for the next Med' season, in time for the Cannes Film Festival and the Monaco Grand Prix.

A crew agent can save you time and money, when both are of the essence. It is down to the agent to facilitate the recruitment procedure, by undertaking all the groundwork and providing you with one or more opportunities for an interview, trial or both. It is important to remember that it is unlikely to be just you they are sending for interview, so it is important to make sure that you are adequately prepared and have got everything right before your interview.

You, as the key stakeholder, who can benefit a great deal from this help, should not necessarily expect to get this service free of charge. Many of the agencies charge a signing-on fee and to get around current maritime legislation, pass it off as an administration fee, which when you think about it, is exactly what it is. Over recent years, agents tended to be inundated with 'newbies' wanting to get on their books. Many went with high expectations and having done no (or limited) research, were unprepared about what to expect, had no plan and in many cases a very limited budget. Subsequently, with money running out, they did not hang around for very long, leaving the agents with names of potential crew on their books, who, by this time had already given up and headed out of town penniless and more to the point – jobless. The agents were, on occasion, embarrassed to find that they had put CVs forward for jobs, only to find that candidates were no longer around or even contactable. Under the circumstances, you can hardly be surprised that they charge for the professional service that many provide.

A good agent knows the market well and he/she will know the key players. They should have an established network of contacts and a good working knowledge of boats, owners and captains. They will come to know you as you progress up the ladder and will help to position you onto a boat that will enhance your career. To state the obvious; there are good and not so good crew agents out there people, so be advised by those who know. Talk to experienced crew if you are unsure of the vibe you get.

At the time of writing and after nearly three years of global recession, it sometimes appears that there are fewer jobs available in the sector and owners, captains and agents can cherry pick the very best experienced crew. This means that, where a year or so back, you might have walked into a job with two Med' seasons and a couple of Trans-Atlantic crossings behind you, some agents are looking for three Med' seasons or more. 'Crew think' in early 2010 was to manage the boat more efficiently and effectively. So for some (out of season), it was down to finding less expensive dockage, run on a skeleton crew and stop spending money in the wake of the economic downturn. So, make sure you have your CV is up to scratch, a covering letter, good references to back up your C.V. and most of all; be confident and prepared to impress!

If you are lucky enough to hit it off with a particular agent and manage to impress with your qualifications, C.V. and personality, then that agent can make the difference when it comes to recommending you to a potential employer. I make no bones about that fact that this is a very sexist and ageist industry and yes, you may well find that additional attributes may help you land that first job.

There are of course other issues that you will need to think about. It helps to be able to check out the boat, crew or meet the owner. You are likely to be interviewed by the captain (depending on boat size) and he (or she) is the decision maker, who will ultimately decide whether to give you the offer of day-work, a trial period or full-time employment.

YACHT CREW AGENCIES
useful contacts

As already mentioned, some agencies charge - many are free; some have on-line jobs to view, others don't. If it's an agent you need, then you must try to visit them or they're unlikely to put you forward for a job, as they haven't met you and therefore don't know you. An agent will know more about you as soon as you walk through the door, so face-to-face is best. Remember that registering with agents can be a very time consuming process, so it is best not to leave it until the last minute. Try to be selective. Chat to friends who are already in the industry for up-to-the-minute advice on which ones are likely to make an effort on your behalf.

There are many brilliant agents out there; however some, unfortunately, do not have such a good reputation in the industry. Those, which I am unable to mention in this publication, can be extremely unhelpful, obstructive and others have been known to be downright rude. In mitigation, however, they do have to put up with a lot of nonsense from ill prepared new entrants, who arrive on their doorstep with not a clue about what they need to do to get a job on a yacht. So hopefully, by the time you get down to Antibes, Palma, Fort Lauderdale (or where ever) you will be fully armed with everything you need to make the toughest agent and captain smile and recognise you as great crew potential.

CREW AGENTS – MEDITERRANEAN

ALM Yacht Management
www.tonylovec.com
miha@tonylovec.com

Nice
+33 (0)3 86 41 229017
e.mail CV

AMPM Crew Solutions
www.ampmcrew.com
info@ampm.com

Antibes
+33 (0)4 93 34 06 14
register online

BCN Yacht Services
www.bcnyacht.com

Barcelona
+34 (0)6 67 44 00 59

Bluewater
www.bluewateryachting.com
crew@bluewateryachting.com
crewpalma@bluewateryachting.com

Antibes & Palma
+33 (0)4 93 34 34 13
online check-in

Burgess
www.burgessyachts.com
recruitment@burgessyachts.com

Monaco
+377 97 97 81 21
e.mail CV to Lucy or via website

Camper and Nicholson Int
www.cnconnect.com
crew-assist@cnyachts.com

Antibes & Palma
+33 (0)4 92 91 29 12
online check-in

Cosmopolitan Crew
www.cosmo-crew.com
cv@cosmo-crew.com

Villeneuve-Loubet
+33 (0) 953 91 68 48
e.mail CV

Crew Network
www.crewnetwork.com
antibes@crewnetwork.com

Antibes, Palma & Ft Laud
+33 (0)4 97 21 13 13
online check-in

Cyd Mansell
www.cydmansell.com
cydmansell@wanadoo.fr

Antibes
+33 (0)6 03 29 04 07
e.mail check-in

Dovaston Crew
www.dovaston.com
fred@dovaston.com

Palma
+34 (0)9 71 67 73 75
register on line - online jobs list

Hill Robinson
www.hillrobinson.com
info@hillrobinson.com

Antibes
+33 (0)4 92 90 59 59

International Crew Recruitment
www.intl-crewrecruitment.com

Antibes
+33 (0)4 93 34 27 93

Jobseekers International
www.jobseekersint.com
admin@jobseekersint.com

Palma
+34 (0)6 49 6957 68
fill in Pdf form & post

Leticia Van Allen Crew
www.leticiayachtcrew.com
info@leticiayachtcrew.com

Palma
+34 (0)8 71 96 06 94
on-line registration

Luxury Yacht Group
www.luxyachts.com
info@luxyachts.com

Antibes
+33 (0)4 97 21 11 97
online registration

Monaco Equipage
www.monacoequipage.com
info@monacoequipage.com

Monaco
+377 97 77 81 77
e.mail check-in

Nakhimov Crew
nakhimovcrew.com

Monaco
+377 97 98 57 89

Peter Insull Yacht Crew Agency
www.insull.com
64crew@insull.com

Antibes
+33 (0)4 93 34 64
e.mail check-in

ReCrewt
www.recrewt.com
crew@recrewt.com

Antibes
+33 (0)4 93 34 22 97
online registration

SAF Recruitment
www.sallyfinbow.com
sally@sallyfinbow.com

Antibes
+33 (0)4 93 65 75 24
e.mail check-in

Sunseeker Superyacht Management
www.sunseekersym.com

Golfe Juan
+33 (0)4 93 34 13 94

Superyachtjobs.com
info@superyachtjobs.com

+44 207 924 4004

Yacht Help Group
www.yachthelpgroup.com
+34 971 40 51 42   (Palma)

Barcelona
+34 932 25 42 05

YCO Crew
www.ycocrew.com
info@ycocrew.com

Antibes & Palma
+33 (0)4 92 90 92 90
+34 (0)9 71 402 878

YPI Crew
www.ypicrew.com
info@ypicrew.com

Antibes
+33 (0)4 92 90 46 10

CREW AGENTS – INTERNATIONAL

Antigua Yacht Services
www.caribbeancruisingvacation.com
info@caribbeancruisingvacation.com
not agency but worth sending CV

Antigua (English Harbour)
888 615 4006

Jane's Yacht Services
www.yachtservices.ag
antyacht@candw.ag

Antigua (English Harbour)
1 268 460 2711
on line registration

Select Crew
antsails@candw.ag

Antigua (English Harbour)
1 268 460 1527

St Barts Yachts
www.st-barts.com

Charleston (US)
843 577-737

CREW AGENTS – AUSTRALIA

Australian Yacht Crew
www.ayc.com.au
info@ayc.com.au

Australia
+61 419 924 799

Australian Superyacht Crew
www.superyachtcrew.com.au
training@superychtcrew.com.au

Sydney
+61 (0) 2 9818 2024

Superyacht Crew Academy
www.superyacht-crew-academy

Sydney
+ 61 2 9979 9669

Superyacht Stewardess Training
donna@superyachts.com.au

Sydney
+61 (0) 41068 9288

Yacht Crew Australia
www.yachtcrewaustralia.com
info@yachtcrewaustralia.com

Queensland
+61 (0) 7 5563 9891

CREW AGENTS – UNITED KINGDOM

Global Crew Network
www.globalcrewnetwork.com
info@gloablcrewnetwork.com

UK
+44 (0)870 9101 888
online registration & fee to pay

Sea Gem International
www.seageminternational.com
rod@seageminternational.com

UK
+30 28 420 24337
jobs on line

Viking Recruitment Ltd
www.vikingrecruitment.com
info@vikingrecruitment.com

UK (more hospitality crew)
+44 (0) 1304 240 881
register online

Wilson Halligan
www.wilsonhalligancom
terry@wilsonhalligan.com

Hamble (UK)
+44 (0) 2380 458 652
register online

YPI Crew
www.ypicrew.com
ypi@ypi.co.uk

UK
+44 (0) 1273 571722
register on-line

CREW AGENTS – UNITED STATES

Camper and Nicholson Int
www.cnconnect.com
onfo@ftl.cnyachts.com

651 Seabreeze BLVD, FL
954 524 4250

Crewfinders
www.crewfinders.com
crew@crewfinders.com

404-408 SE17th St FL
954 522 2739
online registration

Crew Head Hunter
www.crewheadhunter.com
info@crewheadhunter.com

1217 Ahlrich Ave.
619.972.8100

Crew Network
www.crewnetwork.com

1800 SE 10th Ave, FL
954 467 9777

Crew Unlimited
www.crewunlimited.com
info@crewunlimited.com

2067 S. Federal Highway FL
954-462-4624
jobs online & online registration

Culinary Fusion
www.culinaryfusion.com
www.culinaryfusion@earthlink.net

842 SW 9th St FL
954 764 2725
for trained chefs

Dependable Crew
www.dependablecrew.com

237 16th Place Costa Mesa, CA
949-514-0430

Elite Crew International
www.elitecrewintl.com
online registration – Megayachts

714 SE 17th St FL
954 522 4840

International Yacht Collection
www.yachtcollection.com
info@yachtcollection.com

1850 SE 17th St FL
954 522 2323
online registration

International Yacht Crew
www.internationalyachtcrew.com

Jamestown, Rhode Island
online log-in

La Casse Maritime
www.lacasseservices.com
info@lacassemaritime.com

1551 Shelter Island Dr. San Diego
619.523.2318
online registration

Luxury Yacht Group
www.luxyachts.com
info@luxyachts.com

1362 SE 17th St, FL
954 525 9959
online registration

Merrill Stephens
www.merrillstevens.com
yachtinginfo@merrillsteves.com

1800 SE 10th Ave, FL
954 791 2600
online registration

Moran Yachts
www.moranyachts.com
crew@moranyachts.com

1300 SE 17th Street, FL
954.768.0707
use crew agents but can email CV

Palm Beach Yachts Int
www.yachtcrew.com
donna@yachtcrew.com

4200 Nth Flagler Drv, West P. Beach
561.863.0082
on line registration

Yacht Crew Register
www.yachtcrewregister.com
info@yachtcrew.ca

Canada
registration fee
online jobs

Northrop + Johnson

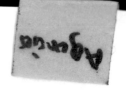

WEB BASED AGENCIES

Using crew agents via the internet is an option that you may want to consider and it is a good idea to seek advice as to which ones are most likely to provide a return on your investment in time and money. Yes – there is a cost involved with many of these sites, so there is no point just picking sites at random.

- www.7knots.com
- www.crewbay.com
- www.crewfile.com
- www.findacrew.net
- www.crew4crew.net
- www.hasslefree.com
- www.jobs-at-sea.com
- www.yachtcrews.com
- www.crewseekers.net
- www.crewsearcher.net

- www.yacht-services.com
- www.reliance-yachts.com
- www.worldofyachting.com
- www.echoyachtdelivery.com
- www.bluewateryachting.com
- www.blueoceanyachting.com
- www.superyachtsydney.com
- www.yachtcrewregister.com
- www.exclusivecharterservice.com

Internet Scams

The old saying goes – *'if a job sounds too good to be true, it probably is'.* A recent forum on Dockwalk.com was dedicated to the various scams that circulate crew inboxes. Most experienced crew are aware of such scams, some do not heed the warning when the temptation of making 'mucho dinero' is too great to resist. One such scam offered one hundred pounds (sterling) an hour and the option to select any position you liked from a tempting list of crew jobs. Too good to be true – damn right it was!

I have attempted to provide you with some sound advice about finding work in the industry, but don't just listen to me, talk to friends, network, check out websites (Dockwalk and TheCrewReport.com are both excellent), use reputable agents and most of all follow your head and not your heart or more particularly your bank account.

Being vigilant about which companies are trustworthy is an absolute must. One final warning here; if recruiters ask for your bank details to facilitate immigration paperwork, don't even think about going there – yep, it's another scam.

COMMUNICATION

Websites

Dockwalk, the monthly American publication for Captains and Crew will be found on the www, Facebook and Twitter. Their FB traffic is mainly one way, with Dockwalk highlighting topics in their latest publication, which is often really useful information. We are also increasingly seeing some really useful Blogs, which lots of crew are buying into. Although informative, this is not a proved method for finding employment. While on the subject of this publication, I do find their website (www.dockwalk.com) very useful; especially the Digital Dockwalk section, which provides you with free access to current and past Dockwalk publications.

Mobiles

OK, so everyone has got a mobile and with the acceleration of new innovations in information technology and communication systems, it never ceases to surprise end users what the next new 'mobi' can do for us. The simple secret of mobile use when abroad, is to buy yourself a local SIM card for local calls. Alternative methods of communication, such as Facebook, e.mail and Skype provide the user with alternate cost effective options.

You may want to give serious consideration about how and more particularly, where, you use your latest, very expensive to replace i.Phone. The back end of the 2010 season saw an increased incidence of mobile phone theft on 'the coast' and I personally know of half a dozen friends who had their new i.Phones stolen. Now am I being cynical, or did this just happen to tie in with the launch earlier in the year of the latest i.Phone?

Sorry to say this, but I know you girlies (in particular) a very keen to flash your new phone, but most forget that it is not just crew who frequent the crew bars. If a group of banditos decide to target crew bars and you leave your communication instrument lying unattended for a few seconds, you just got to know that it ain't gonna be there when you next want to txt your roomie!

A great investment is a SIM Card copier, which you can buy from Amazon for around £6.50 (€8). Copy your SIM card and keep the copier separate from your phone at all times. Also, why not take a spare 'old' mobile and SIM with you, which operate on your network.

Facebook

Most of the folk I know in the industry are great users of social networking sites, in particular Facebook. It is (if used sensibly) a great way for folks to keep in touch with each other and is often used to arrange downtime meetings if friends are heading for the same destination. I get lots of traffic from our UKSA grad students who have kept in touch over the years.

Something I haven't mentioned so far, is that yachties do get home sick, just like anyone or anywhere else, yachties are usually no different. I have known some youngsters who have headed off to Antibes, full of the joys of spring and with great aspirations of working in the industry for years to come, only to return to the UK a few weeks later because they miss their family and friends so much. This is one of the reasons that you need to think seriously about how you are going to keep in touch with home and friends when abroad. Many crew agencies and training academies are on Facebook and form groups, attracting a great deal of 'FB Friends' from the industry. A few suggestions are:

- UKSA EMC
- Galley Help
- Yacht network
- The Crew Circle
- Yachting insider
- Yacht Steward/ess
- Superyacht Sydney
- Sydney Superyachts
- Yacht Crew Register
- Superyacht jobs.com
- The megayacht industry
- Superyacht Stewardess Training
- How many yacht crew are there in the world

FACEBOOK GROUPS

- Yachting
- Galley Help
- Yacht network
- Yachting crews
- Superyacht jobs
- The Crew Circle
- Yacht Steward/ess
- Superyacht Sydney
- Sydney Superyachts
- Yacht Owners and Crew
- The Mega Yacht Industry
- International yacht training
- Blue Ocean Yacht Charters
- Superyacht Stewardess Training
- Cro yachting – Yacht charter Croatia
- How many yacht crew are there in the world?

SKYPE

My experienced pro-yachting buddy Elli says: *"We use it; it's brilliant for keeping in touch with people back home and also friends around the world. We leave ours logged on a lot of the day when we are 'off charter', so people can call us whenever they see us on-line. The video is really good, especially for keeping up with friends' kids who are growing up at scary rates! It's free, which is great, but you can also put credit on it, so we ring friends and family on their landlines and mobiles, which costs next to nothing. It is also really useful for calling the bank back at home, which would normally cost us a fortune from our mobiles, since they put you on hold for hours!*

On the negative side, the connection can be very broken at times. We really struggled with it when we were working in the BVI's, so it can make for a very frustrating phone call and there is often a time delay. Overall, it's really good, we've had two job interviews via Skype and the video means it's more personal and we were given both jobs without ever actually meeting the owners."
Elli Rea (UK)

Simon says: *"Skype is good. Free calls anywhere in the world and very easy to set up; all you need is an internet connection. It is not always easy when onboard though, as I know that some boats do not allow you internet connection if you have the boss on, as it slows down their connection speed."*
Simon Storey (UK)

Kate from New Zealand says: *"The first boat I worked on had Skype and it was a god-send. We had a laptop set up in the crew mess and we always had a great connection, as we were based in Port Gallice (Juan-les-Pins). It was amazing to have free video contact with my family and friends so far away across the world in New Zealand whenever I wanted out of working hours – it's as if they were right there with me. The second boat I worked on, Skype was not allowed. This was a much different set up, where guests were onboard the majority of the time and if crew were talking on Skype, that meant the guests' laptop connection speed would slow down considerably. Facebook wasn't allowed either – just e.mail. So I guess it really depends what the rules of the boat are, but when it's allowed, Skype is BRILLIANT!"*
Kate Caughey (NZ)

Fiona has spent a lot of crew time working the Pacific, which provides a different Skype story, saying that life in the Pacific is not quite so easy. *"Our set-up is that we have a satellite system, which enables us to get on-line or telephone when at sea. This system however is prohibitively expensive, so I would only use it for example for wishing 'Happy Christmas or Happy Birthday' to loved ones or heaven-forbid if an emergency took place.*

We prepare e.mails off-line and then literally log on once a day to send and download received e.mails, which we usually respond to the following day. Skype is not an option with satellite as it is far too costly, so I am told. So that is how it is when we are at sea, which can be for two weeks or more at a time.

When In port, things tend to be a bit easier. In Darwin, Singapore or here in Palua, we have access to the Marina wireless network and Skype works as reliably as the network allows. It is a bit 'iffy' here in Palau, but not too bad, it just takes patience and tolerance when the connection 'drops' and you have to try again. If the speech gets broken up, then I just use the text function to communicate.

In the Adaman Islands, we bought an internet stick (dongle) from the local telecommunications company and that, for the most part, worked a treat. I could not survive without being able to Skype my son, family and friends. You can also Skype from your laptop to mobiles at a fraction of the cost of mobile to mobile – this too, gives me a freedom which otherwise I would not have, due to the prohibitive costs. Monthly mobile bills of £500 or more are just not feasible for me!"
Fiona Thomas (UK)

DOWNTIME

Just so you don't get the impression that employment in the hospitality yacht sector is all work, work, work, I asked some of my grads to give me their thoughts on 'down time'. I selected the one below from my buddy Den, just to give you a balanced gender view on what perceptions are of downtime or a crew night out. This is a very important and often memorable (or in many cases – less memorable) aspects of crew life, so I felt I should provide you with some up-to-date info on this social phenomenon.

CREW NIGHT OUT
from a guys point of view

You might think that the first thing that runs through a "Yachtie's" mind when docking in a new port is, *"I wonder where the closest bar is?"* This could be because of the dry boat rule when underway or when guests are onboard. Den writes:

"There's always high spirits amongst crew when they get ready to explore the shores of a new port after docking, which always starts out with a few crew beers in the mess. Almost always, at least one or two crew members would have been to the port on a previous occasion, which eliminates having to ask the age old question of where can we find a party. Although, don't let that stop you if you want to find a particular party, which may only be thumping on that particular evening, for instance.

Going out to a social gathering after days or even weeks at sea, or with owners aboard, is really only about two things. The first is seeing how quickly a beverage can be consumed and who you can convince to join you in this quest.

Generally most popular ports have a "Yachtie's" local or favourite watering hole, such as the famous Waxy O'Connor's in Fort Lauderdale or The Hop Store in Antibes. This is a toss-up in being both a good thing and a bad thing. The norm is to meet at these locals and then groups will gradually split up and explore other bars, restaurants and clubs, depending on the preference or mood of each group. On many occasions your crew will meet up with crew from other boats, who they have met in a previous port and this is reason enough to start a dock party as soon as everyone knocks off for the day. This consists of an "ESKI" commonly known as a cool box with ice and beverages which are consumed to music, laughter and familiar faces – dependant on there being no guests onboard of course. The dock party will move to a bar when the beverages are done and then the real fun starts. It's certainly not uncommon for casual flings to stem from these nights out both with crew onboard their own vessel or with crew from others.

The life of a "yachtie" revolves around hard work and that is why the most common motto amongst crew is "work hard, play harder" and from my experience I can vouch that we "yachties" certainly know how to have a good time!"
Denzil Baynes (S.A.)

GIRLIE DOWNTIME

Stew's are known to work eighteen hour days when there are guests onboard, so it is hardly surprising that when the owner and/or guests depart that the opportunity to chill moves to the top of the agenda. Maybe surprisingly, it's not just 'pardy-pardy', although the odd glass or three has been known to be consumed following the demanding work schedule of a challenging charter! Depending on location and availability, this may also be an opportunity to play with some of the aquatic toys onboard.

Dock parties are a familiar site, when single or multiple crews get together with the chefs doing their thing on a make shift BBQ, with everyone pulling together to enjoy ice cold beer or diet coke and some random food, mostly prepared by top class chefs.

Most of the girlies sure like to bend the plastic and as mentioned in the section Deal or No Deal, tangible indulgences are there in plenty, just waiting to be indulged. An increasingly popular way to pass some downtime, is to book into a five star spar hotel and pamper yourself in a little therapy for a day or two.

With yachts hitting on destinations that are out of the reach of many tourists, it is not unusual to see crew hiring scooters or 4x4s and head off to explore some weird and wonderful locations.

If there is a week's break between charters, some may think nothing of flying hundreds of air miles to meet up with that someone special in their life.

Problems, situations & politics

I have to be honest with you folks, life onboard is certainly not without the potential for disagreements. The industry is usually very hard work, long hours, mega-demanding guests, last minute changes to itinerary, unexpected guests arriving for lunch or dinner and the odd one, or more, that might appear out of the blue for breakfast. Many will have personal likes and dislikes that will no doubt clash with carefully made plans. There are of course issues and conflicts which will surface between crew members, which if not resolved quickly, have the potential to find you or someone else out of a job. The likelihood for bitchiness, clash of personalities, invasion of personal space (inevitable) etc is massive. One of our grads, John, has provided me with an insight into working on a large superyacht, with a big crew from when he first joined the industry back in 2008. John's thoughts below are written from experience of working as a steward on a 60m+ Private/Charter Motor Yacht, with a full-time, multi-national crew of 19 (sometimes more!).

"Working on a large superyacht, will always come with situations that you have to deal with or overcome, often on a daily basis. The main problem that seems to arise is that not everyone can get on with each other. There can be too many personalities that may not match your own and opinions of other crew members which you may not agree with. If such issues are not dealt with correctly, either by you, or a superior, problems will most certainly arise.

When you join a large super yacht, on the surface, it may seem that everyone gets on with everyone, if this actually turns out the be the case, then you will be very lucky! If not, problems will usually arise due to "boat politics". This may be down to one or more reasons, and or influenced by differences in the crew hierarchy. On every boat there will be a dominant person (or more than one), whether they're the Captain, a deck or interior crew member. If your problem is with that one person in particular, then you are stuck with nowhere to run. If a group of crew have the same problem as you, and you start to talk about it, you will start to hear everyone else's issues which may turn out to be the same, or even add to your own.

If you were to challenge this person and should any of your own personal opinions or ethics be breached in the work environment, this may be seen as a challenge to their status or authority. Should you make this mistake, an unfortunate chain of events can occur, which may result in the suffering of yourself and fellow crew or worse still, you can end up without a job.

The best advice I can give, is to stay away from the 'goss' as much as possible. Although this will be hard, try not to take anyone else's word against another person, make up your own mind and do all you can to stay on the right side of that crew member. It may be as simple as knowing that they had one too many the night before, or just keeping your distance first thing in the morning, until they have had their first cigarette (usually not allowed) or coffee – remember, problems can, and usually are amplified by alcohol. Try to find common ground and take a submissive approach, so as to not provoke confrontation.

If you can get around these minor down points, I promise the good times will always outweigh the bad. There are many positive aspects of working with a large crew, such as; more people to socialize with, in and out of work, and you will form strong relationships or even loves, which you will remember for years to come. You may find that you form small pockets of friends, probably within the department you are working, but don't restrict yourself to a small group, try to get to know as many crew as you can, in all departments. Yachting is an extremely sociable profession and downtime, when possible, is usually spent off the boat, where you want to leave any bad points behind, but be aware, gossip can be even more dangerous off the boat, than on it, so don't do it, keep your nose clean and make the effort to get on with everyone. If you are not careful, you could end up burning some very valuable bridges, which you may need in the future. Even when you have a job, which you are really happy with, keep the thought of "where do I want to be next year" in your head at all time and create contacts in the form of networking, email, phone numbers, business cards and even Facebook may land you your next dream job.

Lastly, you have heard it before, so here it is again "There's no 'I' in team". Remember, although your job may be in the interior, it is very important to work as a team with all departments. Be aware of the things that need to be replaced or repaired, like a light bulb or the gas supply to your hob and oven, which you will need first thing in the morning. If you can't fix it – maybe the person you upset last night can!
John Craven (UK)

DEAL or NO DEAL?
Or should I say, to spend or don't spend? The luxury yacht crew sector is renowned for its excessive and often reckless consumerism, where it's sure as hell easy to dispose of a huge wad of your monthly salary on designer (read 'very expensive') 'Jimmy's', clothes, jewellery, watches, sun glasses, the very latest mobile phone, luxury holidays, hotels & restaurants, spars, cars etc, which most only every dreamed of being able to afford. The most gullible are, and it should come as no surprise: YOU - the 'newbies', who really don't know any better and are easily seduced into a false sense of "I've earned it, so I'm damn well gonna spend it".

I know of a number of mid-twenty year old 'stewies', who avoided the gross extravagancies of their peers (except for the odd splurge of course) and set themselves realistic and achieveable targets for saving a healthy percentage of their monthly income over a fixed number of years. One such 25 year old, has just put down a sizeable deposit on her first house and how many 25 year olds can say that these days?

Once you've got your deckies (deck shoes) firmly planted under the galley table and a fairly sizeable (usually tax free) wage packet goes into your bank account every month, it can be very difficult to avoid the temptation of spend, spend, spend.

Some folk hit the industry with pre-determined 'retirement' timescales in mind; others will plan to make yachting employment more long term. Eventually, maturity and a profound sense of monetary value kicks in and sinking your savings into something more tangible becomes more appealing.

STANDING ORDERS
I guess these are what on dry land we would call 'House Rules', however they are a critical ingredient to the safe, efficient and effective management of a yacht, its guests and crew. Each yacht will have its own Standing Orders and they may differ from vessel to vessel.

These are the rules and regulations which are to be adhered to by all crew members and are written by the captain. Standing Orders usually fall under a range of key headings, which provide a structure for the efficient and effective running of the boat; each heading will usually consist of a number of sub-headings. A copy of a boat's SOs will be made available to all crew members, who will be expected to read them and become familiar with the content. Headings are likely to include: Individual responsibilities, Work routines, Watch-keeping, Dress, Discipline, Safety and emergency procedures, Check lists and forms.

YOUR VERY FIRST JOB

Once you have secured a position on your first yacht, you will be so full excitement and anticipation, about so many different things, your head will spin. I asked my friend Natasha to give me her thoughts on getting that prized first job (in her case) on a fabulous, brand new superyacht. This is what she had to say about her first job in the extreme world of yachting:

"Oh the nerves and the excitement! Where do I start? The who, how, what, when, where - the thousands of questions, all leading to me joining my first yacht. Breaking into this mega-diverse industry was not as easy as I had hoped or expected. I endlessly applied to over thirty different crew agents, did some serious networking in crew houses and crew bars and got myself totally psyched-up and prepared to do "the dock walk", until I received that one golden phone call. Finally I got my big break. The details were blurry, because all I could think about was, finally, I have got myself a job on a yacht and who the hell cares about the rest. However in time, little did I know, the rest does count – big time!

You have to start somewhere, right? I was extremely fortunate to join my 47m superyacht in the shipyard. Being there from the beginning was fruitful. I was in awe of it all, arriving with an over packed bag; I have now mastered the art of packing less and shopping more, this skill takes a little time to acquire. Butterflies in my tummy and a couple of sleepless nights were expected, as so much was happening around me. There is so much to take on board in a short period of time, that you can be thrown in at the deep end, and left to sink or swim. There are new crew to live with, in an ohhh so small environment, you get to become 'family' very, very quickly. The beauty of it all is meeting people of different ages from all over the world, with their diverse cultures, traits and personalities, some stronger than others. All these factors become irrelevant when it comes to the first crew meeting –"Just as a reminder, we are here to perform our duties to the highest standards possible".

As the first charter begins, everyone is "big smiles", the owner arrives and all that runs through my head is "Please don't spill the wine, hope they like me, please don't spill the wine, hope they like me". Yes, yes, yes – RESULT!

Welcome to the world of "the yachtie". Indeed you do travel the world, different ports, countries and cultures, yet you may only get to enjoy them through your porthole window (if you're lucky enough to have one), while doing the ironing or trying to soak the delicate, white, make-up stained, Versace blouse. Long hours, endless cleaning and sleep deprivation, the reality hits you fast, but yes, this is my dream job.

The day does finally arrive when the charter is over! As you wave goodbye to the owner and his guests, you manage to muster the last perma-smile you have left in you; the crew is already planning cocktails and snacks. This is definitely the ultimate work hard, play hard culture. It may not be for everyone, but it is addictive. The priority is to know what you want out of the industry, whether your objectives are long or short term. It is important to try to resist temptation. Some "yachties" I know (myself included) have fallen prey to the culture of getting carried away with shopping and spending, like I am totally loaded, wining and dining like a superstar or partying like a pro, these are the perks of the job, which you work so hard for. Put it into perspective and remember that circumstances beyond your control could mean that you may not have a job come the end of the Med' season!

We are all human and there is bound to be romance in the air, either with a yachtie on the boat moored-up alongside, or holding onto a loved one at home. There are even those times when members of your own crew start looking attractive after a two week Atlantic crossing, but do be aware of on board relationships, if they go sour, you make your bed and you got to sleep in it and must take the consequences.
Natasha Sunjich (SA)

WORKING COUPLES

I know a number of working couples, most of them working on two man yachts in the Pacific, Med, Caribbean, Belize and the BVIs and they do a very good, professional job; having to manage a totally different yachting environment to those working on much larger superyachts. I have also known some couples to work together on much larger vessels while keeping their private and professional lives at a distance. Others are not so discreet and risk losing their jobs if they become too distracted from their core purpose. If one partner is a senior member of the crew, then nepotism can and often does kick in, sometimes putting junior crew in a potentially untenable situation.

Walking away from employment, due to what may be perceived (on land) as unfair dismissal, just won't wash on a yacht and moving from one boat to another because you can't or won't feel easy within the hierarchy, has the potential to damage your employment potential. Problems can (and do) arise when the working couple is for instance: the Captain and Chief Stewardess or Stewardess and Chef. Egos have been known to hit new heights and getting your problems resolved can prove very difficult and stressful, if not nigh impossible.

From an employer's point of view, there are obviously positives and negatives with employing a couple and the obvious negative is that if one goes, so (usually) does the other. Whatever you do – as newbies, never expect to be able to easily find employment on a superyacht for you and your partner, it just does not work that way, unless you and yours have the qualifications, experience and ability to run a two man sailing yacht charter.

One couple I know, manage to plan their downtime, so that they can periodically get to see each other for a few days or more; even if this does take a Phd in Effective Transport Logistics. Two of my female grad's made the conscious decision to work solo for a couple of years, while they worked their way up the crew-ladder, gaining invaluable experience. However, they had been looking for 'couple' work on a superyacht for some time and found it exceptionally difficult. As I complete this book, I am happy to report that these two friends and their partners have recently found dream jobs as working couples. Both downsizing after spending over two years working on large motor yachts, they now find themselves out in the Caribbean on fabulous sailing yachts.

A DAY IN THE LIFE ON A 2 CREW YACHT (BVIs)
You may decide that working as a couple is right for you. My friend Elli and her partner Andy did a couple of seasons out in the BVIs. Elli has provided me with a useful insight into what her average day was like doing this type of charter work.

- 06:30 – both of us get up.
- 06:45 – Andy (Captain) chamois down the cockpit and puts out all the cockpit cushions.
- I (stew/chef) put coffee machine on and prepare the fruit platter ready for breakfast.
- As soon as guests are up we offer them coffee and tea.
- When everybody is up, I give them the cooked option for breakfast.
- 07:45 – Andy sets the table.

- I cook the breakfast and serve.
- Whilst guests are eating, Andy clears up in the galley and looks after the guests, I go round the cabins and make the beds and clean down the heads.
- 08:30 – Guests often go for a swim or snorkel. Andy washes up breakfast pots and I dry and put them away (Always this way around because the chef will know where everything lives in her galley, the captain will not!) then I clean down the galley whilst Andy does his engine checks.
- I check the lunch and dinner menu and take anything out of the freezer to defrost if needed.
- 09:00 – Andy will discuss with the guests the plan for the day, their ideas may well have changed from the night before. Up the anchor and sail to a snorkel spot for a mid morning swim.
- Whilst underway, check if guests need drinks, snacks, remind them to apply sun cream.
- En-route to the snorkel spot, arrange all the snorkel gear so it's quick and easy for the guests on arrival.
- Drop the sails, pick up a mooring ball or anchor.
- Help guests with their snorkel gear and remind them to stay with a buddy, if people are unsure or nervous either Andy or I will go and snorkel with them as a guide.
- 11:30 – Up anchor or drop mooring ball, sail to lunch stop, again remembering to offer drinks/snacks etc whilst underway.
- 12:30 – Anchor at the lunch spot. Andy will chat with guests and make sure that everyone has drinks.
- I'll prepare lunch.
- 12:50 – Andy sets the table with a jug of iced water and glasses and ask guests if they would like wine/ beer/ soda
- I plate up lunch.
- 13:00 – Serve lunch, check that everyone has everything they need, leave them for 5 minutes then check again, if everyone's ok go and eat lunch.
- 13:30 – Clear the table and wash up, Andy washes, I dry.
- 14:00 – In the afternoon there are often several options which Andy will have discussed with the guests in the morning, maybe a good 3 hour sail to the evening stop, or a short sail to a snorkel spot then another short sail on to the evening spot, or staying at the lunch spot all afternoon to do water sports and spending the night there.

Assuming we're moving straight to the evening spot:
- Up the anchor/drop the mooring ball.
- Whilst underway prepare the evening dessert if it needs to set for a few hours.
- Make sure everyone has everything they need, if they are interested in the sailing get them involved, let them helm, or winch.
- 17:00 – Arrive at evening spot, drop the anchor or pick up the mooring ball. If there is a bar in the anchorage now is a good time to encourage the guests to go and get a cocktail ashore. If Andy takes them ashore, I read through my evening menu and plan how I am going to organise my time. When Andy returns he cleans down the cockpit whilst I vacuum inside.
- 17:30 – Prepare the hors d'oeuvres, put on some music.
- 18:00 – Andy picks the guests up from the bar, they return to hors d'oeuvres and another cocktail to watch the sun go down.
- 18:30 – Prepare dinner using the plan I made earlier to ensure everything comes together at the right time. For my first few charters I wrote this plan down or if it is a particularly complex meal I still do, otherwise it's just in my head! I wash up as I go along and clear down my work surface after each little job so that the galley is easy to work in and looks neat, tidy and efficient.

- Whilst I am preparing dinner Andy is entertaining the guests, getting them drinks and discussing the plan for the following day.
- 19:30 – I select the place mats and napkins for the evening and fold the napkins, trying to have a different fold each evening.
- 19:45 – Andy sets the table and arranges wine or other drinks.
- 19:55 – I plate up the evening meal.
- 20:00 - Andy and I serve together, I present the last plate and tell the guests what the dish is. As with lunch time we check that everyone has everything they need, then go out again 5 minutes later to check before we eat our dinner.
- 20:15 – Andy washes any pots and pans left over from the dinner preparation and I dry and put away or start to prepare dessert if it is not pre-prepared.
- 20:30 – Andy clears the plates when the last guest has finished eating and also removes the salt and pepper and any cutlery not used.
- 20:35 – Serve dessert, again I present the last dish and tell them what it is.
- Andy washes the dinner plates whilst I go round the cabins and clean the heads and turn down the beds.
- Once I have finished the cabins I dry and put the pots away whilst Andy clears the dessert dishes and removes all the mats and napkins from the table and offers coffee or another drink.
- Andy arranges the after dinner drinks whilst I clean down the galley and write the menu for the next day on the blackboard which we display in the galley.
- 21:15 – Either go and join the guests for a drink if we are invited or take a drink to the bow to cool down and unwind for 10 minutes once the guests are all comfortable.
- Wait for the last guest to go to bed, 22:00 if we're lucky or 02:00 if we're not! Wash the glasses, put all the cockpit cushions way, check that the saloon is clean and tidy and head to bed ready to start it all again in the morning!!!

Elli Rea (UK)

FOOD SAFETY

The hospitality services on luxury yachts are similar in many ways to those found in the high-end hotels. However, they are nothing like static commercial catering businesses in a number of ways. They will be built in one country, sold to an owner from another and they are constantly on the move from one country or continent to another, passing through international waters to reach their destinations.

Galleys can be designed to suit every whim and fancy of their mega-rich owners and may well be fitted out to a much higher standard than most commercial kitchens on dry land – some of the galleys on recent new-builds are absolutely fabulous. In legal terms, their design does not have to conform to Food Safety Laws of one particular country.

It is, therefore, very important that strict food safety standards are introduced and followed by everyone involved in food production and service onboard. The same sort of high standards expected in a land based kitchen should be exceeded onboard a yacht. Whether you are working as a chef, sous-chef or crew-chef on a superyacht or as a stew/cook on a charter yacht, it is essential that food is stored correctly; that you clear-up as you go and your galley is kept spotlessly clean and pristine, ready for inspection at any time.

When your guests eat the food that you have lovingly prepared for them, there is a natural expectation that it is safe to eat. This expectation places important responsibilities on you and others onboard who are working with food. If you are working on a two-man charter, then this will be down to you as stew-cook, or if you are the chef on superyacht, then you will have overall responsibility for food safety standards and the training of your staff to ensure a hygienically safe food production area at any time of day or night. Food contamination onboard can wreck a charter, so you need to be aware of some of the basics.

Food contamination can be any of the following:

- Bacterial contamination – when there are pathogenic micro-organisms present in food, including: bacteria, viruses and moulds.
- Cross-contamination – when the same equipment or surfaces are used for raw and high risk food and are not properly cleaned and sanitized between usages.
- Physical contamination – when foreign items i.e. glass, plastic, plasters, fingernails, hair, metal items from equipment enter the food product
- Chemical contamination – when cleaning chemicals are misused.

Personal hygiene
The first law of food safety is the personal hygiene of all food handlers onboard, who must ensure that food does not become contaminated through poor personal hygiene standards.

Hand hygiene
Food handlers must wash their hands regularly with anti-bacterial hand wash, to help reduce the number of bacteria on their skin and to prevent cross-contamination. Hands must be washed:

- upon entering the galley
- between handling raw and high risk foods
- after going to the toilet
- after handling waste food or refuse
- after eating or smoking (usually not allowed onboard)
- after blowing or touching your nose or other parts of your body.

Clothing
Outstanding personal presentation is not a 'given', it is simply essential that your 'whites' will be kept spotlessly clean, well laundered and ironed and that you 'look the part' at all times. One set of 'whites' is definitely not an option, and if you are a chef worth your weight in Beluga you will already own a number of sets. You may find that the owner will provide you with sets of bespoke, branded chef's 'whites', if not you will need to check out what is acceptable as your uniform. Tasteless, bright shellfish and seafood patterned chef's pants are maybe not what your owner or captain will find palatable. Your clean 'whites' are worn to protect you, however, this is an aside to their main purpose – the protection of food from contamination. There are a couple of excellent suppliers in the UK (Nisbets & Denys). I have checked out a range of suppliers in the USA, however they appear to be light years behind in their ideas of contemporary chef's clothing and tend to be very traditionalist in their thinking and design.

FOOD POISONING
An outbreak of food poisoning on board can be even more problematical than an allergic reaction, as it is likely that the former will effect most people who have eaten contaminated food, whereas, the latter is only likely to affect one person, however both can be fatal.

Most food poisoning is caused by carelessness or lack of knowledge of people involved in the food chain. This may not mean you, so it is important, if not essential to source your provisions from reputable suppliers – the harbour or marina office are usually happy to point you in the right direction.

Bacteria are the main cause of food poisoning (Bacterial Food Poisoning), however illness can also be caused by chemicals, metals, poisonous plants, fish, viruses and mycotoxins (toxins produced by some moulds) or through non-bacterial food Poisoning and neurotoxins (toxins that attack the nervous system).

Bacterial food poisoning
This is caused by an acute disturbance of the gastro-intestinal tract, which results in abdominal pain, which can be with or without vomiting or diarrhoea. The illness results from the eating of food which has been contaminated by specific pathogenic bacteria or their toxins.

Common food poisoning bacteria
There are three pathogenic bacteria which are responsible for the majority of cases of bacterial food poisoning in the UK:

- Salmonella species
- Clostridium perfringens
- Staphylococcus aureus

The most common cause of diarrhoea is Campylobacter Jejuni, which causes a food-borne disease - not food poisoning.

Many instances of bacterial food poisoning can be avoided by all food handlers on board observing strict food safety practices i.e. personal hygiene, safe systems of work which includes a strict regime of cleaning and sanitizing work surfaces, equipment and contact surfaces (i.e. handles) after use. Certain foods are susceptible to bacterial contamination and are known as "High Risk Food"; foods which, under certain conditions will support the rapid multiplication of bacteria. These foods are often ready-to-eat, high protein, moist foods that require refrigeration, such as:

- Cooked meats and cooked meat products
- Meat stock and meat gravies
- Shellfish and other seafood
- Milk, cream and custards
- Egg and dairy products
- Cooked poultry
- Cooked eggs
- Cooked rice

Temperature Control

A lack of knowledge or ignorance of temperature control of food, whether raw, cooked or on display can leave food susceptible to contamination. Correct temperature control during storage is essential, as the rate of food spoilage is affected by temperature, humidity, stock rotation and the integrity of packaging.

NON BACTERIAL FOOD POISONING

Chemical food poisoning – is rare and the most likely examples onboard would be caused by the storage of chemicals near food, chemicals stored in an unlabelled food containers or the misuse of cleaning chemicals in the galley.

Food poisoning from metals – is even rarer than chemical food poisoning and the incidence of this on modern marine vessels is likely to be minimal.

Poisonous plants – problems are usually caused via incorrectly processed beans, such as red kidney or haricot beans, so again the incidence is likely to minimal.

Poisonous fish – are the most likely source of non-bacterial, onboard, food poisoning. As many of your guests will want to try their hand at fishing, there will be an expectation that you have the knowledge and ability to prepare and cook their prize catch safely. So be aware, there are three main types of fish poisoning:

- **Scombrotoxic fish poisoning** – dark-fleshed fish such as tuna, mackerel and sardines can produce toxins during storage. Making sure that you refrigerate the fish as soon as you can after it is caught reduces the risk, however once the spoilage has occurred the toxin cannot be destroyed.
  Onset time: The typical average onset of symptoms is ten minutes to three hours. The symptoms, which can last up to eight hours, include diarrhoea, nausea, vomiting, abdominal pain, rashes and a burning sensation in the mouth.

- **Ciguatera poisoning** - this is a life-threatening illness, which can arise from eating reef-dwelling fish i.e. sea bass, grouper, barracudas and eels, which have fed on types of marine algae that produce a toxin. There are approximately 300 varieties of fish, which are caught in the Pacific and Caribbean, which can poison humans.
  Onset time: One to six hours. The symptoms include sickness, diarrhoea, throat and respiratory problems and can be fatal.

- **Paralytic shellfish poisoning and diarrhetic shellfish poisoning** - these types of food poisoning are potentially fatal and can be caused by mussels and other bi-valve molluscs which have fed on plankton that produce neurotoxins. The toxins can survive cooking.
  Onset time: Symptoms of Paralytic shellfish poisoning appear immediately and progress within 4 to 12 hours from numbness in the mouth, then the neck, arms and legs; followed by respiratory paralysis which often leads to death. Diarrhetic shellfish

poisoning may occur in a similar way, however, symptoms include diarrhoea and vomiting which last only a few days.

Shellfish - Enteric fever (typhoid and paratyphoid) and viral infection can be caused by eating contaminated shellfish caught in polluted water, so try to be vigilant, take local advice and buy from reputable suppliers.

FOODBORNE DISEASES
Food-borne disease can be caused by contaminated food or water and are responsible for outbreaks of serious illness. Unlike bacterial food poisoning, the pathogen multiplies in the person who has eaten the food and not in the food causing the illness.

Food-borne diseases, in the main, tend to have rather nasty symptoms ranging from stomach cramps to death; however they may or may not include diarrhoea and vomiting.

Food-borne diseases and their sources include:
- **Bacillary dysentery** – caused by faeces from infected people
- **Typhoid** – caused by faeces from infected people, contaminated water, milk or food
- **Paratyphoid** – caused by faeces from infected people
- **Campylocbacter enteritis** – caused by animals, wild animals, untreated water, raw meat, offal and poultry
- **Listeriosis** – found in soil, water, vegetation, human and animal faeces. Foods include: pâtés, soft cheeses, prepared salads, dairy products and salami. ***Soft cheese should be avoided by pregnant women.***
- **E.coli** – found in contaminated beef burgers, dairy products, raw meat, water and barbecued food. The spread maybe by food, water, sewage or person to person and can be lethal.

When you shouldn't be handling food
You should not be handling or preparing food if you are suffering from sickness or diarrhoea resulting from a common cause of gastro-intestinal infection. You can usually return to work when you have been free from vomiting or diarrhoea for 48 hours after any treatment has ceased.

Training and staff induction
I strongly recommend that when employing interior crew, that owners/captains and charter companies ensure that applicants have an up-to-date food safety qualification (see below). The chef must find time to induct the new member of his team and train him/her on onboard routines, safe systems, provisioning, storage and food safety.

In the UK, there are three well known awarding bodies which provide nationally recognised training and qualifications for food safety (hygiene): The Chartered Institute of Environmental Health (CIEH), The Royal Society for Public Health (RSPH) and Highfield. Recent legislation change in the UK brought a raft of new food safety qualifications onto the scene and the word 'hygiene' disappeared from UK course titles to be replaced by 'food safety'. Most owners, captains and charter companies now look to employ chefs, sous-chefs, crew-chefs, stew/cooks and stewards/esses with a minimum Level 2 Award in Food Safety in Catering qualification (UK). This one day training course is available from you local college or private training provider, at a cost of approx £75 at the time of writing. It is also becoming more freely available via e.learning (computer). If you intend to work as a head chef on superyachts, then I strongly advise that you take the Level 3 Supervising Food Safety in Catering qualification (UK) – a three day training course at a cost of approx £250. This will contribute towards your competitive edge over other job applicants.

FOOD ALLERGIES

What is a food allergy?

When someone eats a type of food that the body mistakenly believes is harmful, there is an immune system response. Once this happens, the person's immune system creates specific antibodies to it. The next time the individual eats that food, the immune system releases massive amounts of chemicals, including histamine, in order to protect the body. These chemicals trigger a surge of allergic symptoms that can affect the respiratory system (breathing), gastrointestinal tract, skin, or cardiovascular system.

People and their allergies

Modern eating trends dictate that many voyage and charter guests will be focused on healthy eating options and the 'girls', in particular, may want to concentrate your cooking skills on complimenting their waste-line for the duration of their time onboard. Whoever you have onboard, you may find yourself cooking for one or more in the party, who are allergic (or think they are allergic) or intolerant to certain types of food. You will of course, also get those who proclaim (often very loudly) that they have an allergy to this or that, just so they become the centre of attention!

Your knowledge of allergies is essential and you would expect to be informed during discussions with the owner or on your guest information sheet about allergies, dietary restrictions etc. If you don't know, don't make assumptions – ask the owner, or party leader. Double checking before you start provisioning or cooking is a wise move and can save everyone problems and help avoid potential disruption to the voyage/charter after you have left the marina. It is important to remember that some allergic reaction symptoms are similar to food poisoning and it is possible for guests to think that it may have been your cooking and not an allergy that has caused the problem.

When at sea; having a guest on board, who has an allergic reaction to food is vastly different to being on dry land, where you can usually access professional medical care or advice within a short period of time. So some essential tips and guidance, may help to save someone's life!

Allergy foods

Although an individual may be allergic to a particular food that their body might think is harmful, such as fruit, vegetables and meats, there are only eight foods that account for approximately 90% of all food-allergic reactions. These are: milk, egg, peanut, tree nut (walnut, cashew etc), fish, shellfish, soy and wheat.

European food labelling

New European Union labelling rules were introduced in 2005. These require that all pre-packed food (including alcoholic drinks), sold in the European Union (EU) must clearly show on the label if it contains one of the following foods – or if one of its ingredients contains, or is made from:

- Milk
- Fish
- Eggs
- Soya
- Peanuts
- Mustard
- Sesame seeds
- Crustaceans (including prawns, crab and lobster)
- Cereals containing gluten (including wheat, rye, barley and oats)
- Tree nuts i.e. almonds, hazelnuts, walnuts, Brazil nuts, cashews, pecans, pistachios and macadamia nuts (including nut oils)

Even if you have bought a branded product before, you should still check the label. The ability to read and understand the ingredients identified on labels is essential – if a product doesn't have a label, or there are unfamiliar terms, then avoid buying that product if you know you have a guest onboard who has an allergy. Foods that aren't pre-packed don't have to be labeled with the same information as pre-packed foods, so you might not always be able to check the ingredients. These foods include ones from a butcher, fishmonger, baker, deli and foods that are weighed loose.

ALLERGY or INTOLERANCE?
Many people believe that food allergy and food intolerance mean the same thing – they do not. Food intolerance, is an adverse food-induced reaction that does not involve the immune system. Lactose intolerance is one example, when a person is unable to digest significant amounts of lactose; the major milk sugar. When a person consumes milk products, symptoms such as gas (wind), bloating of the stomach and abdominal pain may occur.

Coeliac disease (pronounced 'see-lee-ac') is not an allergy or a simple food intolerance. It is an autoimmune disease, which is triggered by eating gluten from the cereals such as: wheat, rye and barley. Some coeliacs are also sensitive to oats.

Prevention – what you can do
You can help by taking certain precautions to help control contamination of food:

- Check ingredients (labels etc)
- Train all food handlers on board
- Introduce safe systems of work
- Store foods separately in sealed containers
- Follow recommended safe food handling procedures
- Take a nationally recognised First Aid at Work course
- Use separate knives and colour coded chopping boards
- Use recommended or reliable food suppliers or supermarkets
- Use anti-bacterial spray (sanitizer) on work surfaces and equipment – frequently

Symptoms of an allergic reaction
The most common symptoms of an allergic reaction include:

- diarrhoea
- coughing
- itchy skin or rash
- nausea / vomiting
- abdominal cramps
- drop in blood pressure
- faintness and collapse
- dry, itchy throat and tongue
- swelling of the lips and throat
- hives (red, blotchy, itchy skin)
- tingling sensation in the mouth
- loss of consciousness or death
- breathing difficulties (wheezing or shortness of breath)

Typically, the symptoms will appear within a very short period of time i.e. within minutes to two hours after the person has eaten the food to which he or she is allergic.

Anaphylaxis (pronounced 'anna-fill-axis')
This is a serious allergic reaction, which has a rapid onset and can be life-threatening. Common causes include:

- Food
- Latex
- Medication
- Insect stings (wasp, bee, hornet etc)

A less common cause is food-dependent exercise-induced anaphylaxis, which occurs when a person eats specific food and exercises within three to four hours after eating.

A visit to the Ashburton Cookery School (Devon) in early 2010, enabled me to meet some wonderful people on a two day, weekend Gastro Plus course – all part of my book research! One lady, who I will not name, told us about her almost unheard of cause of Anaphylaxis and that is alcohol, a very rare, but equally life-threatening condition.

Treatment
Anaphylaxis is an emergency condition, which requires immediate professional medical attention (if available). Assessment of the patient's airway, breathing and circulation should be done in all suspected anaphylactic reactions.

- CPR should be undertaken, if needed, by a competent person. People with known severe allergic reactions are likely to carry an Epi-Pen or other allergy kit and should be assisted to administer the treatment if necessary. Emergency intervention by paramedics or ambulance (if available) may include placing a tube through the nose or mouth into the airway or emergency surgery to place a tube directly into the trachea (airway), via an external incision in the throat (tracheostomy). Epinephrine (Adrenalin) should be given by injection immediately. This opens the airways and raises the blood pressure.

Treatment for shock includes intravenous fluids and medications that support the actions of the heart and circulatory system. Antihistamines, corticosteroids, may be given to further reduce symptoms (after lifesaving measures and adrenalin have been administered).

Anaphylaxis is a severe disorder, which has a poor prognosis without prompt treatment. Symptoms, however usually resolve with appropriate treatment.

Treating a Food Allergy
People are usually already aware that they have a food allergy, so strict avoidance of the allergy causing food is the only way to avoid a reaction (cause and affect).

Medical treatment, such as Epinephrine (adrenaline), is the medication of choice for controlling (stabilising) a severe reaction. It is available by prescription as a self-injectable device (EpiPen).

If one of your guests has a food allergy, they should have their medication with them. If during a meal, they think they are having a reaction, get them to stop eating and take their medication. You may find that people who have a severe food allergy, wear a bracelet or necklace, giving details of their allergy, so medical staff (if available) will know about it in an emergency.

Cure
There are currently no medications available that cure food allergies. Strict avoidance is the only way to prevent an allergic reaction. Many people outgrow food allergies, in a similar way as

youngsters do with asthma. However, allergies such as peanuts, nuts, fish and shellfish are often considered lifelong allergies.

Coping in a foreign country
It is a good idea to find out before you travel, how you can explain about an allergic reaction in the appropriate foreign language. Nobody expects you to be multi-lingual, and you may find that your owner or certainly on charter, that you spend a lot of time in only a handful of countries that speak different languages. The Allergy Action website has an informative section on the names of common allergies and useful expressions in various languages, which can be helpful when ordering or buying food abroad.

DIETS
The word diet comes from the medieval Latin word 'dieta' meaning "a daily food allowance".

You have only limited or no control over the personal eating habits or food preferences of individual guests who you are catering for. However, it is expected that the yacht chef will have a high level of involvement in menu design through consultation with the owner/captain/charter guests.

For charter work, you will receive guidelines from the charter company and or party leader, so menu design can be influenced by the use of preference sheets. Guests will ask for, and expect you to prepare almost anything at very short notice, so knowledge of a range of popular diets can be as useful to you as your favorite chef's knife. It is also useful to know that any diet which restricts or eliminates a major food group for more than a short period of time will inevitably deprive the body of essential vitamins and minerals, which can be detrimental to a person's health in the long term. Most all diets do this.

I usually talk about a diet meaning a strict food and drink regime, which has the aim to either lose weight, prevent weight gain, or promote a lifestyle and philosophy - or maybe, just maybe to impress our employer, colleagues and friends. It is important that I provide you with some information on vegetarian and vegan eating, so that you start to understand some of the thinking behind them.

Vegan
Veganism is more of a way of life and a philosophy than a diet. A vegan does not eat anything that is animal based, including eggs, dairy, and honey. Vegans do not generally adopt veganism just for health reasons, but also for environmental and ethical/compassionate reasons. Vegans believe that modern intensive farming methods are bad for our environment and unsustainable in the long term. Vegans usually say that, if all our food were plant based our environment would benefit, animals would suffer less, more food would be produced, and people would generally enjoy better physical and mental health.

Vegetarian
Vegetarianism is the practice of following a diet that excludes meat, game, slaughter by-products, fish, shellfish, other sea animals and poultry. There are several variants of the diet, some of which also exclude eggs and/or some products produced from animal labour such as dairy products and honey. Examples include: lacto vegetarian, fruitarian vegetarian, lacto-ovo-vegetarian, living food diet vegetarian, ovo-vegetarian, pescovegetarian, and semi-vegetarian.

The majority of vegetarians are lacto-ovo-vegetarians, in other words, they do not eat animal-based foods, except for eggs, dairy, and honey. Several studies over the last few years have shown that vegetarians have a lower body weight, suffer less from diseases, and generally have a longer life expectancy than people who eat meat.

The reasons for choosing vegetarianism may be related to one or more of the following: morality, religion, culture, ethics, aesthetics, environment, society, economy, politics, taste, or health.

To check out what is happening out there on the water, I sent out a Facebook SOS to my 'global research team' to see what is *de rigeur* right now. Another good friend, who works charter with her husband down in the Med told me that *"Most of the girls and women onboard go for anything that is fashionable at the time, low fat seems to be the current en vogue one, for instance egg white omelettes are what the skinny girls always order. I have also found over the past year that more healthy food such as fresh fruit smoothies have become increasingly popular in the mornings. Grains are also popular and the recently discovered ancient grain, Quinoa** has really taken off.*

Over the past year, I have found a really fine balance of about 50/50 of charter guests who want plated meals and buffet style in the middle of the table. Our chef played around a lot with flavoured butters and sauces, to go with the bread, which was very popular. It will come as no surprise that fish dishes are extremely popular, with the healthy options being poached or steamed, also cooking them whole, the bigger the better. Our owner is Greek-Cypriot and it's a 'pride thing' to have the biggest and best fish to offer your guests – the Russians love that too. I also find that many guests say that they don't want deserts, but then when you offer it, they always accept, so the healthier desserts are always big winners, as they feel they are being naughty, but then it's not that bad!"

Elli told me: *"Low fat is the biggest one, little oil, no butter, no desserts, well at least not until they get on the boat and realise that they really do like desserts, so you have to make them every night so that they can say "oh well just a taste" and finish the whole lot – does this sound familiar? I've just done a fully vegan charter but that was the first one I've ever done, veggie is more common and there is a big demand from people with various allergies or intolerances - gluten free is a common one, along with nut and dairy".*

Fiona agrees, saying *"Elli's right, definitely low fat - except for afternoon tea and desserts in the evening! I did a week with someone who could not eat dairy and eggs which actually can be pretty limiting but I still managed a full and varied menu. I referred to a publication I found on the net called 'Go Dairy Free'. I found it incredibly useful and I have used some great recipes from this."*
www.godairyfree.org

** QUINOA

A recently rediscovered ancient "grain" native to South America, Quinoa was once called "the gold of the Incas", who recognized its value in increasing the stamina of their warriors. Not only is quinoa high in protein, but the protein it supplies is complete protein, meaning that it includes all nine essential amino acids. Not only is quinoa's amino acid profile well balanced, making it a good choice for vegans concerned about adequate protein intake, but quinoa is especially well-endowed with the amino acid lysine, which is essential for tissue growth and repair. In addition to protein, quinoa features a host of other health-building nutrients. Because quinoa is a very good source of manganese as well as a good source of magnesium, iron, copper and phosphorus, this "grain" may be especially valuable for people with migraine headaches, diabetes and atherosclerosis.

Graduate Clare Marriage says, *"Same here, there are lots of low cholesterol requests, asking for desserts only once or twice, and then they wonder where the dessert is the rest of time! I have had dairy free too but then they decided half way through that it didn't matter……. It seems to me that most diets go out the window once they're on holiday! Sugar free diets are also common along with the usual diabetics and low cholesteral. Would you believe it – I haven't had any 'veggies' or vegans over my two years of chartering".*

Low Cholesterol

A low cholesterol diet is not hard to follow, given the variety of foods available.

Fruit and Vegetables

Include plenty of fruit and vegetables, they are low in calories and fat. There are many ways of preparing and cooking these foods, which are delicious and will not raise cholesterol levels.

Fats and Oils

Try to reduce the amounts of saturated fats in your food preparation, since eating food with these fats is likely to raise cholesterol levels and increase the percentage risk of heart disease. Avoid using food items which state that they contain "partially hydrogenated" vegetable oils, such as those used in margarines, spread and shortenings, which contain a particular form of saturated fat, know as "trans fats". These can raise blood cholesterol levels (including LDL, the 'bad' cholesterol), just like saturated fat and can promote the formation of waxy, cholesterol plaques on arteries.

When cooking with oils, you should use olive or canola oils, which are particularly high in monounsaturated fats or vegetable oils such as sunflower or corn oil, which are high in polyunsaturated fats. Unlike saturated and trans fats, unsaturated fats can help lower your cholesterol and the heart healthy.

Breads and Grains

Use whole grain foods instead of foods containing white flour. Recent studies have indicated that ingesting high amounts of carbohydrates can also raise cholesterol levels and increase the risk of heart disease – especially for those with diabetes.

Dairy

Use low fat or skimmed dairy products instead of regular or full-fat ones. This helps to reduce the risk of heart disease and it is also more user-friendly for the waistline.

Kosher

Kosher rules follow Jewish law, in that only certain animals can be eaten. A kosher diet is strict, but you can stick to the rules by adjusting where and how you shop.

Meat and Fish

Cook with lean meats, such as chicken, pork or turkey instead of red meat. Leaner meats will not raise cholesterol levels as much as red meat. If a guest is dying for a steak, that isn't a total no-no, you can trim off any fat and brush with an appropriate oil before cooking.

Eating fresh fish provides a very healthy option and provides big pluses all round as a healthy food. 'Oily' fish is acknowledged as helping to aid a healthy diet, as it provides Omega 3 fatty acids, which are recognised as being good for the brain, heart and immune systems. Examples of oily fish are: mackerel, tuna, salmon, trout, shark and swordfish.

Rather than give you further, unnecessary detail on specific diets, here are some that you may (or may not) have heard of:

- Atkins
- Raw Food
- Mediterranean

- South Beach Diet
- The Grapefruit Diet
- The Hamptons Diet
- The Beverly Hills Diet

MENU PLANNING

The whole menu planning concept for a yacht is somewhat different to the well noted methodologies taught to generations of hospitality and catering students throughout the world. The Theory of Catering and Practical Cookery books were the bibles for catering students for a couple of generations in the UK. The former devoted some forty plus pages to Menu Planning, over 10% of the total content of the student's guide to customer satisfaction and profitability.

The golden rule of menu planning, and it may seem obvious, is to only include dishes that you are confident and capable of preparing. If you are just starting out in the industry, maybe working on a two crew yacht in the Caribbean for instance, you are likely to be working on a one or two week menu plan on a charter for 4 – 8 guests. No matter how good your planning and taking note of everything you have been told on your guests' preference sheets, you are always going to get guests who say, "You know that fabulous chicken dish you cooked a couple of nights back, we'd love that again tomorrow night". This is a 'can do' industry and as long as you can source the ingredients (of course you can!), you will then have to change your menu plan for the next day, but this might also mean you checking that the starter and dessert on your menu plan still 'fit'.

Be imaginative and make lists of breakfast, lunch and dinner options, look through cookery books, periodicals and the internet to make sure that you have a really good variety of ideas for breakfast, lunch, hors d'oeuvres, dinner - starters, main, and desserts. Remember my friend, you are likely to be the only crew onboard who can cook, so only design menus that can realistically be sourced, prepared, cooked, presented and served in pre-determined timescales.

There are a range of issues to take into consideration when planning your menus, so to help you along, I have included a list of things that you might need to take into consideration.

- Space
- Budget
- Colour
- Climate
- Texture
- Balance
- Location
- Language
- Garnishes
- Capability
- Seasonality
- Vegetarians
- Balanced diet
- Size of galley
- Size of yacht
- Local produce
- Themed menus
- Nutritional value

- Number of crew
- Profile of guests
- Cookery methods
- Preference sheets
- Number of guests
- Speciality produce
- Duration of voyage
- Temperature (local)
- Crockery and cutlery
- Nationality (customers)
- Stowage space available
- Galley equipment available
- Availability of fresh produce
- Special dietary requirements
- Availability of meat, poultry and fish
- Repetitiveness of ingredients, colours & texture
- Refrigeration (including freezers & ice machines)

You will also want to consider your back up plan. The 'what if', that frequently happens when working on yachts? It is important to keep a good larder, which can provide you with some flexibility should an emergency arise.

The best place to start your planning, is by drawing up a table by hand on a piece of paper or even better on your 'lappy', allowing eight rows, one as your header and the rest for the seven days of the week. Allow an appropriate number of columns and title them up from left to right: Days, breakfast, lunch, hors d'oeuvres, cocktail, dinner: starter, main and dessert. Depending on the size of your yacht, preferences etc, you may want to add more columns for things like Sundowners, Afternoon tea etc. Now start to fill in the columns with dishes.

I have included an overview below of the types of dishes which you may want to consider for your menu plan.

Breakfast
This could consist of basic English, Continental or American options:

English: Fruit compote, porridge, cereals, homemade muesli, etc. Followed by a 'Full English' (grilled is best), offering – bacon, tomatoes, sausages and choice of cooked eggs: boiled, poached, fried, scrambled, omelettes, plus homemade bread, jams etc.

Continental: Fresh fruit platter, local cheese platter, cold cuts, salami, ham platter. Homemade warm bread, rolls, or bought croissants, pain au chocolate, baguettes, brioches, Danish pastries, German black bread, rye bread. Jams and conserves, Greek or natural yoghurt and honey. Eggs scrambled with smoked salmon, en cocotte, crepes, etc.

American: Bacon/sausages with pancakes and maple syrup, eggs fried, eggs Benedict, scrambled with peppers and cheese, homemade bread/rolls, sweet and savoury muffins, cinnamon toast. Bagels, tea breads, sweet strudels, fruit, cereals and homemade muesli etc.

Lunch
Needs to be varied and reasonably light, unless otherwise requested. Be prepared to add warm ingredients if the weather is changeable. Consider dishes such as:

- Pasta
- Soup or chowder
- All types of salads
- Gougère or soufflé
- Seafood – fish or shellfish
- Rice i.e. risotto or pilaff (pilau)
- Pizza, quiche, savoury tarts or tartlettes

Lunches are often served with fresh bread; desert, if offered at luch would be fairly basic something like ice cream and or fruit, followed by fresh coffee or a selection of teas.

Canapés & hor d'oeuvres
Depending on the type of charter or the clients that you are dealing with it is often popular to have casual snacks, hors d'oeuvres, or canapés at around five o'clock. Often eaten with "Sundowners" (alcoholic cocktail or blender) they are usually served when the boat has arrived at its destination for the day, whether you are tied up in port or laying at anchor. This is a really nice way to round off the main part of the day. The possibilities are endless, classic French canapés, Greek style meze, Spanish tapas, Mexican nachos, dips, crudités, or even a bowl of peanuts!

Dinner
Should in most cases consist of three courses; which should be well balanced and not too heavy; being careful not to repeat ingredients from the preceding lunch or evening. 'Proper' desserts are popular, particularly with male guests. It helps to visualise your week, so draw up a simple table. Once you have filled in the columns simple mistakes can be seen more clearly, making sure that you have a good distribution of ingredients

Getting started
To help you get started, I have included a number of sample menus from page 267, which are currently in use on the water, so take a look – I hope they give you some inspiration.

Preference sheets
If you are completely new to the industry, then the term "preference sheet" may also be new to you. Preference sheets come in various formats, but in general are a survey of your guests' wishes, which are identified prior to their arrival onboard. This helps to customise/personalise every aspect of their charter.

Maybe the only thing more varied that the range of yachts available for charter, is the eclectic cross-section of people who charter them. Charters are marketed as the ultimate experience of high quality, personalised service, making every charter unique. The preference sheet is there as the primary tool, which is designed to make it possible for the crew to provide guests with a faultlessly personalised vacation.

Usually the charter broker (if used) will send out a preference sheet to the group leader some weeks prior to their charter commencing. Some preference sheets ask the group leader to list the tastes, wishes, likes and dislikes of every guest in the party, while in other cases, each guest will be asked to fill out an individual preference sheet. The types of questions you would expect to find on the 'Food Preference' section of a preference sheet includes, but are not exclusive to the following:

- Do you have major food dislikes?
- Will you be having dinner ashore?
- Do you have dietary requirements?
- Do you prefer large or small breakfast?
- Are any of your charter party vegetarians?
- What types of wine and liqueur do you prefer?
- Are there any food allergies in your charter party?
- What time do you normally get up in the morning?
- What non-alcoholic beverages do you enjoy during the day?
- Are there any special occasions i.e. birthdays, during the charter?
- Are there medical conditions i.e. diabetes, the chef should be aware of?

Many preference sheets focus heavily on food, as the yacht's chef will use the sheets to stock the galley with everything requested before the charterers arrive onboard. Some charter brokers use more extensive preference sheets, which ask a whole range of questions about sleeping habits, exercise regimes, which 'toys' they want to use etc.

Remember, a yacht is smaller than a hotel or cruise ship and as such, they cannot store everything in the world in such a relatively small space. Unfortunately, charter guests often fail to fill out their preference sheets accurately or completely. Many guests, for instance, will write "I'll eat anything" on their preference sheet and then step onboard and tell the chef they can't eat fish, or are allergic to shellfish. This may, of course, be a challenge for the chef and crew.

For guests arriving for a week-long charter on a superyacht, one of the most important things for the captain and chef to know before they arrive is the level and kind of service they expect to receive. Are they expecting 'white-glove', tip-top, five star plus service, or is there intention to have a fun packed, informal, activity week.

It is worth remembering that there is no perfect preference sheet. They are meant as a starting point; a methodology to facilitate discussions between the charterers, captain and importantly with the chef, creating a critical rapport before the guests arrive.

An example preference sheet from Barrington Hall on:
www.yacht-charters.tv/charter-guide/terms/prefsheet

Getting to know your yacht
First things first - get to grips with your boat; thoroughly inspect the galley space and any available stowage throughout the vessel. Check what type of refrigeration and freezer space is available. Whilst the top super yachts have the luxury of walk in fridges and freezers, temperature controlled wine storage and air conditioned galleys, the reality for most yacht chefs is not quite so luxurious.

Look closely at any appliances that you may have and check that they are fully functional. If the galley has been left stocked by the previous chef then make a thorough inventory of its contents, make sure that everything is in date and properly stowed, even if a galley has been left clean and tidy it does no harm whatsoever to clean as you sort. If spare refrigeration and/or freezer space is available, empty them out completely, defrost if necessary and check all the food as above. Once you have established exactly what space is available make a plan of the yacht and its stowage areas, from this plan and the dimensions of your stowage you can start to plan where and how you are going to stow all your provisions and ultimately how much you can buy.

PROVISIONING
There are many names for it, but what it all boils down to is the fine art of buying a lot of food and attempting to squash it into what can be a particularly unsuitable space i.e. the interior of a yacht. The yacht chef/cook has the added challenge of shopping in different countries most weeks where challenges include locating the market or supermarket, trying to find ingredients that you can actually identify and working out how to ask *"Do you sell Branston Pickle?"* in Serbo-Croatian.

A recent poll on TheCrewReport.com showed that over sixty percent of superyachts have a provisioning budget either for crew or both guests and crew. It is very important that a chef knows how to budget and keep his/her costs within the constraints of their identified spend. There are a number of guidelines which will help with your provisioning and budgeting.

- Always plan your menus well in advance of a charter/voyage, so that you can provide this information to guests or the owner prior to departure. If you are working on a private yacht, life tends to become a little easier, as you should quickly get used to the wants, needs and expectations of your owner and his/her family.

- You will find it beneficial to be able to use a spreadsheet on your 'lappy' i.e. Microsoft Excel, which will provide you with the soft-option to produce a professional looking expense report for your owner, captain or charter company.

- You will need to find out about all your guests' eating habits before they get onboard, so that you can be fully prepared for individual likes, dislikes, diets, allergies, intolerances etc.

- Depending on your work environment, it helps to be as strict as you can be, about sticking to your menus and your budget. You do need to be aware, that some superyachts do not operate a budget i.e. your guests get what they want, when they want it – literally. Read 'The Crab Trap' by Victoria Allman in Dockwalk, February 2011.

- I am a firm believer in buying the freshest possible (preferably local) food produce, which is exactly what we always did when we lived in France a few years back. This often means cutting out the middle-man. You will be in the enviable position of buying fresh produce from some of the most amazing indoor and outdoor markets in the world. If you are looking for speciality produce, check at the marina manager's office, they really can be extremely helpful.

- Depending on circumstances, you may want, or even need to use a provisioning company. If you are going to utilise the services of a 'provisoner', it is essential that they are aware of your budget limitations or expectations. I have known colleagues and friends, whose owner or captain will pay to have food products flown out to the Caribbean or wherever, to maintain continuity of specialised and sometimes non-specialised food provisions. The cost often being totally irrelevant.

- It is always preferable to buy seasonal, local produce, whenever possible. Utilise the local meat and fish markets and buy the freshest produce available. You will quickly get used to identifying critical quality purchasing points for meat, poultry, fish, shellfish and vegetables.

- Buying frozen produce may, on occasion, be a necessity, however your guests will always expect the best and in my mind, this does not necessarily mean frozen. However, some 'shock-frozen' produce, once de-frosted can be virtually indistinguishable from fresh to many pallets.

- Remember, wherever your home country, the method by which meat is butchered or jointed, is likely to be totally different in a 'foreign' country.

- There are times when, if you are on a tight budget, that looking for and buying substitute products will actually be beneficial for both the guest and your bottom line. Less expensive cuts of meat, may not cook as quickly, but their slow cooking can produce fabulous flavours and melt-in-the-mouth textures. A good example of this is the ubiquitous Braised Lamb Shanks, which we have seen on many gastro-pub menus in the UK over recent years.

- Menu variation is essential. Keep an electronic copy of every menu you write. As a good friend of mine says "Be cute" – and break your menus down into files and folders by product type i.e. Fish, Poultry, Meat, Pudding etc or by location i.e. Caribbean, French, Greek, Italian etc etc........ It is also important to make or note of, or even delete, menus or recipes which are not well received by owners or guests, or ones which simply do not work in your own mind. Whatever you do, don't risk making the same mistake twice.

- Buying something extravagant can give you a real buzz. You know what I mean; something that you would never, ever dream of buying for yourself. But hang on for a second, this is not your money and you are usually working to a budget. You may have got the vibe from a guest about an 'about to happen' special celebration and feel the need to spend over budget. It can be a useful tactic to have an agreement with the owner/captain, as to whether or not they wish to inspect your shopping lists.

- Buying produce in quantity can make significant savings, especially for produce which is tolerant of ambient temperature storage.

- Purchasing whole chickens, whole fish etc yourself is great and can save you money, especially if you know how to butcher meat or scale, gut, fillet and skin fish. However, you need to seriously consider what you will do with the product waste i.e. bones, skin, guts etc. My thinking is, if you are buying it – keep it simple, buy individual well prepared portions, which are ready to cook. This is especially true if you work in a small galley.

- Think portion sizes. Think genders, Think waste. Think creativity. Think presentation.

- I always work on the 'three day rule' for refrigerated produce. Use 'day dots' or labels on raw and cooked high protein foods, such as fresh meat, fish, poultry and game. Once a high protein food item has been in your chiller for three days, whether raw or previously cooked, it becomes a danger to consumers, regardless of how low a temperature it has been stored at. Cured food products have a longer 'fridge life'.

- Ensure that once food has been defrosted, that the food is suitable for use before including it on your menu.

- As most of you will be working in tropical, sub-tropical or Mediterranean temperature zones, you will need to become well disciplined about food storage efficiencies. Leaving 'high risk' food out on a work surface for any length of time, will provide a high level risk of bacterial contamination (See Food Safety – Page 57).

TIPS FROM EXPERIENCED CREW

WORKING IN THE TROPICS

Fiona has worked out of Darwin (Australia), visiting Singapore, the Andaman Islands, Maldives, Sri Lanka and Palau to name a few locations and the last time I spoke to her, she was about to head off for a few weeks cruising and fishing the Micronesian waters (North, North-East of New Guinea). Fiona cooks on a 24m motor catamaran and works with a fairly small crew. She has sent me her thoughts on menu planning:

"There are several menu plans I have to draw up and provisioning may be split according to each of these plans or it may be necessary to do one provisioning exercise to encompass all. This depends very much on my findings when ascertaining provision availability. When we are based in a port or anchorage for some time, then I plan crew menus on a week by week basis as we will always be somewhere where there is some provisioning, even if it is relatively limited.

Crew Menu: Crossing
It is important for me to ensure that the preparation of most of the meals for a crossing is done in advance so that if there are any adverse weather/sea conditions or problems arising, there is always food available with little to no work involved for myself or any other member of the crew. I do this by doubling up on quantities of meals prior to the crossing, which are suitable to be frozen. The best dishes for this purpose are 'one pot' dishes served with pasta, rice or noodles. This also allows me to have some down-time on the crossing instead of fighting my way through the day. I take the opportunity to scan in recipes and I also buy the latest cookery magazines and scrutinize these for days on end, selecting recipes suitable for the trips and those suitable for the crew. All frozen meals are labeled: dish name, number of portions and date of freezing and are logged in my freezer inventory. I also prepare a few days worth of dishes that can be kept in the refrigerator.

I always ensure that there is fresh fruit cut up and stored in a container for breakfast or snacks as well as salad, such as tomatoes, radishes, peppers, cucumber, carrot and cabbage which will not spoil. I take every opportunity to top these up if we have a calm run and stocks are dwindling. I bake a cake or delve into frozen stocks if sea conditions are bad, so that the Captain and Engineer have something to snack on during the day or night. They also have dry snacks such as nuts, trail mix, pot noodles and cup-a-soups available to them. I like to try out new bread recipes, but ensure that I always have some frozen sliced bread just in case I am not able to use the bread making machine.

Yachting takes place in a dynamic environment with so many variables that it is always wise to keep a stock of meals made-up and frozen in case any of these variables make cooking uncomfortable or worse still, a danger. Such variables are: wind direction and speed (weather conditions), current direction and speed (sea state) as well as generator malfunctioning so as to render kitchen equipment useless."
Fiona Thomas (UK)

THE CARIBBEAN
Anni Hayes used to run flotilla holidays in Croatia and went on to work running skippered charters in the Caribbean for the "Moorings". From a recent conversation I had with Anni, she told me that she has since been catering on private and charter vessels in the Med, Caribbean, Dubai, India and pretty much everywhere in-between! At the time of writing she is about to head off across the pond via Tenerife. The following are Anni's thoughts and tips from when she worked charter in the Caribbean a few years back.

"I really only knew about US guests and the Caribbean, although I was fairly sure it would not be that much different to the Med and certainly in Croatia you could get pretty much whatever food you needed, usually minus good wine, it's the same in Greece.

Depending on the boat etc., budgets in those days were usually around $30 plus per person per day - this was for both crew and guests. A lot of the bigger boats don't have a budget, but expensive wines, spirits etc are paid for outside the budget by guests. Otherwise this $30ish amount covered all food, wine, beer and house liquor. It is not hard to stay in budget once you have your stores up and running. However, there were a few things that I struggled with when I first came out here - namely:

- *Sauces*
- *Bar-B-Q Marinades*
- *Presentation of food*
- *Organising the galley*
- *Working out what stores I needed*
- *Quantity of produce required for 7 days with 8 guests.*

The Caribbean has become much better for provisioning. Certainly the British Virgin Islands (BVIs) and Lesser Antilles are well provided with wide ranging shops. Down Island, the ABC islands (Lesser Antilles) and Belize etc are still pretty basic and limited, so one solution is to catch lots of fish but make sure you know how to gut, scale and fillet!

Fresh produce is easy to come by 95% of the time. The more populated islands, particularly those frequented by the super yachts have got provisioning services and you can order most stuff straight to your yacht. This goes for the wine and spirits too, and more recently they have got much better with cheeses and deli produce. Fresh fish is difficult unless caught by yourself, but frozen fish mongers are very good and at least you know you're not going to poison anyone!

Some of the things which are difficult to get hold of are fresh herbs; the BVIs are good but not anywhere else. Also things like natural yogurt, (most chefs make their own) and various types of salad are in short supply, so you get very into Romanian lettuce as there is no other choice. In the more populated areas, most islands offer some pre-cooking service. Obviously this is not cheap but great if you are in a pickle, i.e. for "veggie" guests. I sometimes buy a few frozen meals just in case.

Becoming annoyingly popular (some say) are gluten and lactose intolerant diets, plus no or low carb' and Kosher. Most boats do not offer Kosher as an option as is virtually impossible to do properly but we have had a lot of no pork or shellfish and some no meat and dairy mixed. Never going to be able to do it all but it is worth knowing alternatives to wheat and dairy products and knowing at least what Kosher means.

I would suggest also that you have some knowledge of sushi and that you can make some basic bits for "sundowners", as this is becoming more and more in demand. What some boats like is bread baking. I personally refused to bake as I could visit a bakery first thing in the morning, alternatively that's what Pillsbury is for but it may be worth learning how to make a basic bread dough (see Bread Making – Page 88).

Presentation is probably the main thing that I didn't know a lot about when I got here, also table laying and napkin folding etc. I would seriously suggest you pick up a garnish/presentation book for ideas. On the book subject, you can get all the "Ship to Shore" stuff and local books out here. I would definitely recommend getting a good basic book that shows a table with US and European measurements and includes recipes for gravy, sauces, stocks etc, as I found these very helpful.

Americans are big on shrimp and scallop type meals and also luuuurve BBQ food. So do some BBQ dishes - you can often get the men to do it and it saves washing up too!

One easy mistake when you first start is to over complicate things. I find more than 5 ingredients then I don't bother. The presentation makes up for most things. Cake decorating for birthdays, anniversaries and celebrations is pretty handy, although it's not exactly my strong point!

As a generalisation the kids from the States have no pallet for anything but cheeseburgers, pasta and white bread, so always have peanut butter and jam stuff ready to go for when they don't like the exotic chicken you have spent ages preparing and cooking.

For most boats, cheeseburger (in paradise) with all the trimmings and salad etc is a perfectly good lunch. As mentioned the key is to not go too crazy. If you are on a budget, pricy things out here (other than fillet steak and lobster) are berries, fresh herbs and other imports that don't keep long – so bear this in mind when writing your menu plan."

Tips for Working in the Caribbean

- Always have dried grated parmesan (never fresh – far too sophisticated) as guests will want it on everything.
- Learn a bit about wines to baffle and impress (make sure they are Californian!).
- The hardest part is trying to have the organisational skills to have everything done pre-charter. This is not totally needed as more and more islands are getting small stores but they don't stock a lot.
- It depends on the boat, but some food i.e. ice creams, will not keep in boat freezers.
- When starting a job, I'd recommend bringing your own good quality knives and a vegetable peeler as this can save hours of work that could be spent in the water or at a bar! Pack your knife set in your 'hold' luggage and declare it at check-in.
- Almost all boats insist on STCW95 for cook/chef jobs, including small yachts.

- Know a few cocktails, especially some blended ones i.e. margaritas, daiquiris – its worth getting a book or check out www.cocktail.uk.com.

The BVIs (British Virgin Islands)

EMC graduate Eli Rea's partner, Andy, qualified for his Yacht Masters at the same time that she graduated from the UKSA Marine Hospitality course. They soon got a position working charter in the BVIs for their first Caribbean season.

Elli writes:

"A lot of boats cruise in and out of different areas over the season, but I was lucky enough to spend the whole of the winter season in the British Virgin Islands. An amazing, beautiful place with a fantastic charter market; it is also well set up for crews. My boyfriend and I ran the boat together as the only crew members, so my job was not only Chef, but Stew, First Mate and everything else as well! Consequently I got to know where and how to shop, to make my life easier and, hopefully, if you cruise into the BVIs or spend a whole season there, this information will make your life easier as well.

Food: Almost all your provisioning will be done on Tortola, in Road Town. There are three supermarkets on Tortola; Rightway, Bobby's and One Mart, and a cash and carry called RTW. The best way to provision is undoubtedly ordering from One Mart. Simply fill in a copy of their Excel spreadsheet, listing the produce you want, email it off to One Mart and it will be delivered to the boat on the day and time you ask for it. Although One Mart is great for getting most of your food, I find myself visiting the other supermarkets to complete my provisioning for charter. Between One Mart and Rightway you can get pretty much everything you need. RTW is great for bulk buying coffee, cereals etc, and for stocking the snack basket! Bobby's is the only supermarket within walking distance from Village Cay Marina, in the centre of Road Town and is a bit more expensive than the others, but is great for picking up last minute bits and bobs before charter. Other places to shop in Road Town include the health food store, where you can pick up, amongst other things, gluten free pasta and speciality breads. Best of British is a fantastic shop, selling all the things you miss from home like Marmite, Oxo Cubes, Eggs for Easter and Mince Pies for Christmas. For all your fish, I would suggest that you order direct from Sailors Ketch, again they will deliver to the boat on the dock and have a fantastic range of fish and fish products, like brilliant crab cakes and seaweed salad. For directions to all these places and more information, just pop into Village Cay Marina office or CYM (Caribbean Yacht Management). The marina office will point you in their direction, where you will find very helpful ex-charter crew, who will be happy to help you out.

Alcohol: You can order your alcohol from One Mart or buy it in RTW but there are two other companies which import and supply crewed yachts and have a great range of drinks available. The first of these is TICO which supplies not only crewed yachts but also most the restaurants in the area. In the same way as ordering from One Mart, you simply send them an email with your order and they will deliver to the dock on the day and time you want. The other fantastic place to get your booze is CYM (Caribbean Yacht Management). Run by South African ex-crew, they import all sorts of alcohol including South African cider and a great range of wine. Incidentally CYM also stocks a range of South African food goodies and mini shampoos and shower gels.

Both TICO and One Mart will deliver to your boat on the dock however, for the other shopping you may need some transport. There are loads of taxis around but you can also hire a car cheaply at ITGO car rental, just two minutes walk from Village Cay Marina, again ask in the Marina office and they'll point you in the right direction.

If you are missing any information when you arrive, you will always find a crewed yacht in Village Cay Marina and the crews out there are amazingly helpful. Enjoy and hopefully I'll see you in the BVIs real soon!

YOUR BVI CONTACT LIST

One Mart Crewed Yacht Provisioning
Tel: (+1) 284 494 4649 x 249
Fax: (+1) 284 494 1012
Cel: (+1) 284 496 7167
Email: orders@onemartfoods.com

CYM (Caribbean Yacht Management)
Tel: (+1) 284 499 1899
Fax: (+1) 284 494 8718
Website:
www.caribbeanyachtmanagement.com

TICO
Tel: (+1) 284 494 2211
Fax: (+1) 284 494 4888
Email: orders@ticobvi.com
Website: www.ticobvi.com

ITGO Car Rental
Tel: (+1) 284 494 5150
Fax: (+1) 284 494 4975
Email: info@itgobvi.com
Website: www.itgobvi.com

Sailors Ketch
Tel/ fax: (+1) 284 495 1100
or (+1) 284 495 2125
Email: sailorsketch@aol.com
Website: www.sailorsketch.com
(online price list)

Village Cay Marina
Tel: (+1) 284 494 2771
Website: www.igy-villagecay.com

FOOD BUDGETS

It is important that you can cook to a budget and that you are totally clear on how much per person, per day you have to spend. This should be made clear to you from the start, so if you have any queries sort them out straight away. A few years back, budgets were virtually unheard of on superyachts, however today many chefs must, when requested, be able to account for everything purchased. A recent poll in TheCrewReport.com indicated that over sixty percent of superyachts have a provisioning budget for either crew or crew and guests. Careful budgeting on dry land can make the difference between the survival of a business and the road to ruin, similarly it is important that yacht chefs understand how to use these skills.

Here are a few tips, which I hope will help with budgeting, some are obvious, others less so:

- Accurately cost your menus (advice below).

- Purchasing large volumes can be cost effective. Shopping in bulk from warehouse stores can lead to significant discounts, however you need to purchase in a logical way. You must be sure that you have adequate storage/stowage/refrigeration space available.

- These days, meat and four veg' are not high on most guests' agenda, so limit portion sizes, therefore limiting waste. A cost conscious land based restaurant will closely monitor what comes back from the restaurant on guests' plates.

- Keep food refrigerated at all times. Leaving out for any length of time increases the risk of bacterial contamination and therefore spoilage.

- If your budget is getting tight, then substitute more expensive cuts of meat, fish or shellfish, with less expensive ones. You can create wonderful, tasty dishes with less expensive products, which is what a great deal of traditional rural cooking was based on around the world.

- When you store food in your refrigerator or freezer, it is good practice to wrap food securely in cling film or zip-lock bags and use a labeling system. Write the name of the food item and the date it was cooked. Stick strictly to a rigid three day rule for refrigerated food, as after this period of time, the food will have started to go off and should be thrown away.

- Ensure that when using defrosted produce that it is suitable for use before including it on your menu. The texture of high risk protein food is altered by the speed with which the food item has been frozen. Slow freezing creates large ice particles between the fibres and can leave a spongy texture when it is defrosted. IQF (individual quick freezing) is a process used commercially, as it does what is says on the tin and has a limited negative impact on the quality of the product. Shock freezing is also a relatively new commercial process and it is often hard to differentiate between fresh and what has been frozen.

- Design your menus so they reflect your boat's location. Your guests and crew will enjoy eating 'local', especially on themed nights.

How to cost a recipe

This really is a fairly simplistic process. You are not having to worry yourself about gross-profit, net-profit, selling price etc, as you would do on dry land. It is really essential that when provisioning, you keep all receipts for reference and obviously for accounting purposes. Creating a simple spreadsheet and imputing simple formulas can make your budgeting quite straightforward.

To help your budgeting, you will need to find the unit cost of each item purchased.

- Cost per unit = total price / number of units

To calculate the cost for the amount of each ingredient in your recipe, multiply the unit price by the amount used. A simple example of this would be a pack of 6 chicken suprèmes cost you 6 euros, therefore the cost per unit is 1 euro.

Recipe costs

- Ascertain the cost for the quantity of each recipe ingredient, utilising the cost per unit process above.

- Total all the recipe ingredient costs together, to acquire the total recipe cost.

- You can now break down the total recipe cost further into the cost price per portion. This is the most important figure to know for budgeting purposes.

- Cost per portion = total cost of recipe / number of portions.

I used to work for a large hotel group, which had their food costings calculated down to a tee and woe betide the head chef if his weekly figures did not fit the company food cost per person profile.

Quantities

If you are unsure about how much food will be enough, take a very unsophisticated approach. Literally sit down and work out how much you will need per person, per meal - most recipes recommend how many people they will serve. So, simply multiply or divide amounts for the number of people that you are catering for. It is usually best to have too much rather than too little, so don't be mean on portion sizes unless guests have requested small portions. You find through trial and error that, over time, you develop the ability to "guestimate" quite accurately.

Writing your shopping list

There are two ways of approaching this, either draw up your menus and then write-up your shopping list accordingly or simply write a list that, for instance, allows for seven breakfasts, lunches and dinners. The latter option would probably be more suitable when you have gained experience and feel more confident, or for long ocean passages. It can be quite liberating being able to decide on a daily basis what the menu will be.

Before venturing out, it is sensible to purchase a phrase book, especially if your language skills do not stretch much further than *"Dos cervezas por favor"*. Most skippers will be very busy themselves before a charter and often have a completely misguided belief that you will be absolutely fine; therefore do not be surprised if you find yourself dropped off on the pontoon of an entirely strange port with a large wad of cash thrust into your hand and a cheery wave. A trip to the harbor office will usually result in directions to the centre of town and maybe even a map; try asking them to mark where all the shops are on the map. Think about what you need and the best order in which to purchase it, perhaps an early morning visit to the fish market and bakery and then back to the boat, followed by a general shop later.

If doing a large Supermarket shop that may involve several trolleys, ask to see the supermarket manager and with some pigeon French/Spanish/Italian and many charades, you should be able to get some help. If they can provide you with an assistant to push the extra trolleys or an area to store them whilst you carry on shopping, life is made much easier. Always make a point of really looking at all the products available, you may discover some new exciting ingredients which inspire you to try creating new dishes, or even save you time.

You are then left with the problem of transporting it all back to the boat - some shops will deliver; otherwise it generally means a taxi or a hire car. It can be quite astonishing just how much you can cram into a small car if you are really determined. As a general rule of thumb, seven trolleys of shopping will usually fit into a Fiat Panda – but only just!

General tips for stowage

When cooking on a small boat, stowage will be limited and challenging and whilst many of the big super yachts have walk in fridges and freezers and built in herb gardens the reality is that you are likely to be equally challenged for space no matter how large the yacht. Crew who are extremely experienced and have been in the industry for many years, now find themselves involved as 'consultants' for their owners, who are having new yachts built, who find that the designers lack foresight about the necessity for adequate onboard interior storage facilities.

Think carefully about how you are going to stow your provisions. It can be a good idea to arrange the cupboards around your normal preparation area as ergonomically as possible, so plan where you will put your most frequently used ingredients so that they are easily to hand. If your storage is spread widely over the boat it can also be useful to have a day locker where you can gather all the non refrigerated ingredients that you need for that day's service. In competition with you will be the entire crew who will also have earmarked that hidden away locker for engine spares or a medical kit.

It is likely that beyond the confines of the galley you will find that available storage space is often in inconvenient and inaccessible places. A 'can do' attitude at these moments is a must.

Tins

When stowing tins, keep each product grouped together i.e. tinned plum tomatoes, cannellini beans, artichoke hearts etc. This not only saves time but makes life much easier if you have to grope around in a dark locker under a sofa cushion. If you are provisioning for a long ocean passage and there is any likelihood of water ingress, bear in mind that paper labels can deteriorate or come off completely, so it's a good idea to write on the lids with permanent marker. This avoids a Russian roulette guessing game of opening tins until you get lucky!

Crew cooking

There are few things that affect crew moral more than food. Whilst for many the thought of a skilled cook preparing all their meals would seem like a great perk - the reality can be problematic. From the crew's point of view, they want someone who takes cooking for them as seriously as cooking for the owner or charter guests. Although it is lovely to be catered for, it can be frustrating not being able to decide for yourself what you would like to eat. It is very important for everyone on board that good chef/crew relations are maintained. A good chef should be intuitive and be aware of the "mood" of the crew. Sometimes an amazing Cordon Bleu meal will be just the thing to lift their spirits, whilst another day they just want something simple and filling. For the busy chef, it can sometimes feel like cooking for the crew is just an extra chore that s/he could do without, but it is essential to take this part of the job seriously. Make sure that the crew have a cupboard or locker that they can help themselves from during the day, or when on night watch. Depending on your budget or healthiness of your crew this could be stocked with fruit, cake, biscuits, crackers, nuts, dried fruit, crisps, chocolate, trail mix etc. They will also need access to a kettle for hot drinks and plenty of cold water, squash and juice. By doing this you will prevent crew helping themselves to some vital ingredient purchased for that evening's meal and hence avoiding, onboard friction. On larger yachts, the crew mess is likely to have a fridge for perishable snacks, which will need to be kept stocked-up. Some simple tips might include:

- Listening to your crew.
- Having regular "request" nights or days where crew get to choose the menu.
- Making it clear which cupboards or fridges the crew can help themselves from.

Cooking for different nationalities

Although for most yachts, other than the top super yachts, you will probably have a fairly standard menu guided by: budget, seasonality, location, availability and preference sheets. It is worth bearing in mind that different nationalities do have different tastes and whilst your menu may be entirely suitable for your American guests one week, it may be a bit wide of the mark for your German guests the next. It can also be quite intimidating cooking pasta for Italians or a perfect Bouillabaisse for the French. Never be afraid to discuss the menu on a daily basis with your guests, sometimes they will delight in being invited into the galley to show you just how their "mama" cooks spaghetti or prepares the perfect zabaglione.

As a general tip, it is wise to make sure that your repertoire can cover most eventualities; this may start with you having a fairly standard, broadly European menu that you feel confident preparing, cooking and presenting. Then arm yourself with some good books on, for instance basic Italian/Thai/Classic French cookery and keep challenging yourself with acquiring new skills. Putting it simply, the more you can do, the more employable you will become. If you get to the stage where your skills range from a great Shepherd's Pie and an English Sherry trifle to Pacific Rim Fusion, you've cracked it and should be on your way to bigger and better things.

Disposal of rubbish and packaging

Years ago nearly all rubbish from yachts and ships was simply thrown overboard, these days this is not the case with perhaps the exception of some biodegradable food scraps. Expect to see a clause in the yacht's standard Standing Orders: "All crew, especially the engineers shall take care to abide by all international and local regulations regarding pollution of the sea."

The best approach is to aim to get rid of most packaging materials before you leave the port, as you unpack your shopping, remove any unnecessary plastic/cardboard or styro-foam. As a general rule, most yachts employ a strict no cardboard rule; this basically means that absolutely nothing in cardboard boxes or paper packaging comes onboard; even if this involves transferring it to plastic bags or plastic boxes on the dock. Whilst this may seem like a complete palaver when you are already short of time, the pay-off is a huge reduction in the chances of a cockroach infestation. All it takes is one insect onboard that has eggs and you have a huge problem. Once you have turned on the galley light in the evening to find that the kitchen surfaces crawling with cockroaches or you find them in your bunk it will not be an experience that you will wish to repeat. The only way to get rid of an infestation is to fumigate the boat which is a time consuming and expensive process.

Once you are at sea, try to separate your waste/rubbish into biodegradable scraps and non degradable items. Large yachts often have the luxury of a trash compacter and if you don't have one, then simply squash all cans and any remaining rubbish as flat as possible before putting in a rubbish sack. Try to rinse out any cans or plastic containers first and keep pushing everything down in the bin so that you end up with a very full bag of dry flat rubbish. Hopefully by doing this you will have also reduced the likelihood of it getting too smelly which the crew will be very grateful for, as it may have to be stowed in the anchor locker or lazarette for a few days before the opportunity arises to get rid of it. If you have guests on board it is not acceptable to walk past them with bags of rubbish, so either remove it before they get up in the morning or after they have retired for the night.

Cleaning

It is essential that the galley is kept spotless at all times; there is just no circumstance that would be an exception to this rule. It is entirely acceptable for the captain to routinely inspect the galley for cleanliness and that includes delving into the back of the fridge and checking under and down the sides of the oven and other appliances. It therefore makes sense to draw up daily, weekly and monthly cleaning schedules and stick to them. That way, things like cleaning the oven and defrosting the freezer do not get put off and no opportunity arises for food to be forgotten, to be found at a later date going mouldy at the back of the fridge.

Make sure that you are familiar with the correct cleaning products for each appliance and or surface. You will not be popular if you get oven cleaner spray all over beautifully varnished galley surfaces, or use abrasive cloths on pristine stainless steel appliances. Always cover surrounding surfaces up if you think there may be a problem with the product that you are using.

During the course of your working day, make a point of clearing up as you go along, and always bear in mind that if you are at sea, there is always the chance of sudden erratic movement; therefore never have more than you need out on the work surfaces.

ENVIRONMENTAL PRACTICES

GREEN SEAL®

It makes onboard sense to utilise environmentally friendly products whenever possible. An American organization, Green Seal works closely with a range of key stakeholders to make a measurable impact on the environment, safety and profitability. More and more companies are recognising that environmentally responsible design and production are an integral part of their mission and the value they want to deliver to their customers. Although not directly linked with the superyacht industry, many of the criteria for obtaining Green Seal Certification fit snugly into 'good practice' thinking for onboard product purchase and waste management.

The Green Seal sends out a clear message: "We care about improving the health and welfare of people and the planet" and as more and more businesses have begun to recognize that environmental priorities can be translated into differentiated products and market advantage, they've turned to Green Seal certification to give them a competitive business edge.

By identifying, certifying, and promoting environmentally responsible products and services, Green Seal:

- Improves the environment by reducing toxic pollution and waste, conserving resources and habitats, and minimizing global warming and ozone depletion;

- Increases health and wellbeing, particularly in populations most affected by product choice, such as schoolchildren, service staff, and the elderly; and

- Demonstrates to various business segments, that environmentally responsible products, can improve quality and boost profitability.

Since 1995, Green Seal has partnered with the lodging industry (American terminology for the hotel sector), the nation's second largest employer, to promote environmentally responsible products and practices within lodging properties. Green Seal's campaign to inform around 54,000 U.S. hotels and motels, focuses on how environmental efforts can both improve the bottom line and benefit the environment.

The average US hotel purchases more products in one week than one hundred families typically do in a year. Furthermore, both hotel guests and staff may be exposed to many environmental toxins from products ranging from cleaners to paint to floor coverings. These all represent opportunities to reduce impact and improve sustainability.

What does Green Seal do?
Green Seal works in a variety of ways with the lodging industry and its users, providing technical guidance, case studies, and certification of green hotels. To qualify for GS-33 certification a hotel (think superyacht) must demonstrate sustainable practices in the following areas:

- Waste minimization, reuse & recycling
- Energy efficiency, conservation & management
- Management of fresh water resources
- Waste water management
- Hazardous substances
- Environmentally sensitive purchasing

Many of the issues noted above are clearly transferable into the superyacht industry and will be of specific interest those of you who are environmentally aware.

THE GREEN BLUE
Crew need to be aware of the impact that 'their boat' can be having on the environment, hence The Green Blue, which is an exciting environmental awareness initiative by the British Marine Federation and the Royal Yachting Association. Their aim is to promote the sustainable use of coastal and inland waters by boating and water sports participants, and the sustainable operation and development of the recreational boating industry. It hopes to educate and inform the recreational boating community about environmental impacts, emphasising how you can avoid or minimise these impacts, by taking a few incremental steps.

The Green Blue is for everyone who enjoys getting out on the water, or whose livelihood depends on boats and water sports. By working towards an environmentally, self-regulating boating community, we can save money, avoid red tape and safeguard the waters and habitats we enjoy for the future.

The programme consists of academic research, information provision and practical projects, focusing on six impact areas:

- Oil and fuel
- Cleaning and maintenance
- Anti-fouling and marine paints
- Waste management
- Resource efficiency
- Effects on wildlife

The Green Blue objectives are:

- To provide more readily available information to industry and users about potential environmental impacts of recreational water sports and effective mitigation measures.

- To raise awareness of how users can purchase, maintain and use their craft and equipment in an environmentally responsible manner.

- To promote sustainable boating so that increases in participation figures and the size of the recreational marine industry, are achievable while minimising environmental degradation.

- To encourage the design and production of innovative, environmentally friendly products, facilities and processes within the recreational marine industry.

- To raise awareness of the interaction with the local environment amongst providers of marine services and amongst water sports participants.

- To work with partners, authorities and managers to raise awareness and appreciation of coastal and inland water environments.

RECIPES

It was the charismatic celebrity chef Keith Floyd who said *"Don't ever go into the restaurant business. It kills marriages, it kills relationships, and it kills life. It kills everything".* Marco Pierre White says of him, *"Keith Floyd was a gastronomic icon. He inspired a nation to fall in love with food, cooking and with Floyd himself."*

Jamie Oliver writes of Floyd *"Keith Floyd was just the most brilliant food presenter in history."*

MY GASTRONOMIC HEROES ARE:

For their outstanding contribution to culinary excellence:
- Keith Floyd
- Paul Bocuse
- Raymond Blanc
- Joël Robuchon
- Marco Pierre White

For sheer simplicity and great food:
- Rick Stein
- Jamie Oliver

Newish chefs on the block:
- Matt Follas
- Michael Caines
- Yotam Ottolenghl

For my interest in Pacific Rim & Fusion cooking:
- Neil Perry
- Bill Granger
- David Chang & Peter Meehan

For my love of Mediterranean cooking
- Claudia Roden
- Elizabeth David

COOKING ON YACHTS & SUPERYACHTS

Having been an hotelier, chef/restaurateur and corporate hospitality manager, my advice for entering the galley world of yachts or superyachts is that you must have some cooking experience and basic culinary theory behind you before you set foot onboard. If it's the galley you're heading for, then get yourself some experience in a land-based kitchen, working in a good (small) restaurant or gastro-pub before you apply for that first job, or alternatively head for one of the great cookery schools, which we have here in the south of England. Ashburton Cookery School in Devon is outstanding. For those who are not UK based, I am sure that you will find equally good schools of gastronomy in your own country, so maybe check out the blogs, such as Dockwalk.com for some firsthand feedback.

The recipes which we use on our marine cookery courses have evolved over the last few years. Recipes which have proved to be popular have been retained and we have spent our down-time researching new ones which are happening out there on the water today. Many recipes in this book are tried and tested, some are new and experimental, but all should stand the test of time and will please most, if not all your onboard guests.

We have always worked hard to make sure that we train our students in basic kitchen techniques, food safety, relevant methods of cookery and presentation styles for the types of dishes which are suitable to prepare, cook and present on a diverse range of boat sizes.

The one thing that we have always stressed is that when on the water, it is very likely that you will be preparing and cooking fresh fish or shellfish on a fairly regular basis. It is also highly likely that your guests or crew will be hauling fish up on lines over the side, or snorkelling to bring 'home' the very freshest fish, which you will be expected to scale, gut and prepare for lunch, dinner or BBQ.

I have included one or two classic retro dishes, which appear to be making a comeback and hopefully will become popular once again. I remember going out to dinner with my family on 21 July 1969, the day of the first moon landing and had a wonderful prawn cocktail for my 'starter', served in a wine glass, with a wedge of lemon and a nice shell on prawn draped over the edge. Although the dish had virtually disappeared from English menus since its hey-day in the 60s and 70s, it is now making a bit of a renaissance. It appears in a range of different guises, either in its original format or something with a new twist which has morphed from the original, to bring new, bright ideas to the plate. The ubiquitous prawn cocktail certainly was "One small step for man, one giant leap for mankind" in the culinary world.

I have tried, not always successfully, to keep the ingredient content of my recipes to a minimum. As I say, I have not always succeeded, however I have tried to include some recipes which are very flexible and can be used for a lunch, starter or main dish in the evening. I do tend to work much of the time without recipes, however, I also work to the rule that if I am trying a new recipe, I will prepare it first as it is written, after that, I will experiment and quite quickly come up with my own interpretation. The original recipe was, maybe outstanding, but it wasn't mine. So I will research and work hard to produce new dishes, which I hope will delight my friends and provide you with some sound basics to help take your yachting career in the right direction. As you become more experienced, you will find ways of taking a recipe, idea or suggestion from a fellow chef and put your own twist on it.

I would like to think that many of the recipes I have included in this book would be acceptable in the category of Gastro-Pub or Rosette rated restaurants. The one thing I most certainly am not about is high-end fine dining, Michelin Star food; this is the territory of le Maître Chef; the Michelin Star and Relais & Château restaurant chef, whose ability most of us can only envy from a distance. We must leave this to the truly outstanding maître chefs, like Raymond Blanc, Marco Pierre White (no longer cooking commercially) and the French piano players like Bocuse or Mathieu Fontaine at the Château de Bagnols. What you should realise is that these outstanding chefs work to the extremes of high standards day after day, supported by a brigade of talented, professional sous chefs, chefs de partie and commis chefs. These 'troops' graft, working often exhausting shifts for their masters, to produce some of the highest quality dishes on the planet, but without whose support, the masters would be totally lost; unable to produce the volume of outstanding dishes, selected by their discerning customers, on their own.

Working on a superyacht is of course a whole different ball game, as the job requires a range of skill sets that many outstanding chefs would struggle to cope with. The yacht owner, his/her guests, captain and crew will be totally reliant on you, the chef, often working alone, to source, stow, prepare, cook and present 5*+ quality food three (or more) times a day.

When you have guests onboard, your days will be long and even though you may have planned and agreed menus with the owners or charterers, you should anticipate alterations at very short notice. Your menu plan is a starting point, a reference; something that you know will work, if you are only given the opportunity to produce the dishes you had intended. You have to be ready to prepare and cook your recipes stood on a floor that, at times will just not keep still, as it can pitch and heave from one side to another, occasionally rising up a wave and dropping violently down the other side, leaving you wondering why the hell you ever thought of doing this as a career.

Ask 3* Michelin chef Gordon Ramsey what it's like chefing on a superyacht, because this was the industry in which he plied his trade for over two years, working on M/Y Idlewood, owned at that time by Mr Reg Grundy. Who? I hear you say loud and clear. Well my friend, you may well know Mr Grundy a little better, when I link him as being one of Australia's most famous media moguls, founder of the Grundy Organisation. Mr Grundy's company was responsible for TV shows like, Young Doctors, Sons and Daughters and, most famously of all – Neighbours. Grundy sold his TV production company for (allegedly) around $400m a few years back and now lives a reclusive life in the Bahamas, where (when he's not onboard), he charters out his massive $95m superyacht Boadicea for around $400,000 per week.

I really do not like 'name-dropping', although I guess I have done that already here and there. I have already mentioned the famous Mr Ramsey and do so again, most unashamedly; although I have to say that I think his 'niche language' gets in the way of his massive talent. He states in his book 'Humble Pie' that if he could have only one wine in his kitchen, it would be the French vermouth Noilly Prat. Having owned a house in France for a number of years and come to love the unique vermouth, I totally agree with him 100%. I also have a strong conviction that if you are using wine for cooking, never, ever use anything that you would not drink yourself. I would never recommend that you use cheap, poor quality wine or the de-alcoholised rubbish that can be purchased commercially in the UK. The brilliant Monsieur Raymond Blanc, like all chefs, has his own opinions on the quality of wine you should use when cooking – check out Raymond Blanc's book - Kitchen Secrets.

I will always remember my all-time cooking hero, the amazing and much missed food presenter Keith Floyd, once making a Boeuf Bourguignonne on TV, when he used two bottles of Gevrey Chambertin to cook his lovingly prepared pieces of beef. Gevrey is a very expensive, top quality red wine from the highly acclaimed Côtes de Nuits in the northern half of the Côte d'Or in the Burgundy region of France and is certainly not a wine I would use for cooking. I am not going to tell you how much this fabulous red wine would cost today, rather I will make this your homework for next time you are on on-line, so you can search the www and find out for yourself. However, I have to say with total respect for the dearly departed Mr Floyd, that this is one of the most amazing culinary gestures I have ever seen made to some small pieces of beef!

So, forgetting Floyd's extravagance, you can always source some nice supermarket wine for your cooking. Mind, not all well known or supermarket labels are what they are purported to be on the label. Take a read of Malcolm Gluck's *'The Great Wine Swindle'* to see what I mean – a fascinating read and a real eye opener for those out there, pretentious enough, who think they know everything there is to know about wines of the world. For the uninitiated, I have included a useful section on grapes, wines, champagne, fortified wines, brandy, plus food and wine combinations towards the end of the book, from Page 252.

OK, I know, I said I don't like name dropping, but I'm on a roll, so just indulge me one more time. Many of you yacht crew newbies may never have heard of the gastronomic icon that is Nico Ladenis, who wowed diners in the late 80s and 90s to attain 3 Michelin Stars, one of the first in the United Kingdom. Nico, like Marco Pierre White, 'handed back' the coveted 3* rating he had attained at Chez Nico, to enable him to bring down prices and simplify his menu, although this was not Marco's reason for handing back his stars. Others will have followed suit in the early 'naughties', as many gastro' followers find themselves no longer able to afford the credit card bruising prices charged at these temples of gastronomic excellence. Nico had very strong culinary convictions and his philosophy on food was driven by the marriages of tastes, which make the practice of gastro' dining such an enjoyable experience. I just love Nico's thinking on the basic 'food marriages made in heaven', many of which you will already be familiar with:

- Steak and chips
- Lamb with garlic
- Port with cheese
- Duck with orange
- Caviar with vodka
- Scallops with garlic
- Tomatoes with basil
- Chicken with morels
- Pears with chocolate

- Fish soup with rouille
- Fried eggs and bacon
- Chicken with tarragon
- White truffles with pasta
- Strawberries and cream
- Turbot with lobster sauce
- Foie Gras with Sauternes
- Cold lobster with mayonnaise

When you hit the 'main course' section of my book, you will quickly note that I have used only a limited number of cookery methods, mainly pan frying and roasting or a combination of both. I have done this because if you find yourself cooking on smaller sailing yachts, your cooking facilities and space is likely to be fairly limited. Your cooker might be a two burner hob over a 'gimbal' oven/grill, which usually don't have the accurate thermostatic controls of a domestic or commercial oven. Planning and preparation will be an essential part of your daily routine to achieve the maximum potential out of your limited resources.

I have deliberately avoided complex cookery methods, as I want you to start off by utilising what is here as a starting point to something better and more challenging as the synergy of your experience and repertoire start to produce food cooked in your style and not someone else's. Some of my grad students have been lucky enough to work on yachts, whose owners have paid for them to go and take a Thai cookery course, when their yacht is in that part of the world. A couple of my yachtie friends even paid for themselves to fly out there to do a one week cookery course to add that extra dimension to their skills base.

My international cookery influences are many, but truly focus on the western Mediterranean. My parents lived in Andalucia in the southern Spain for many years, so this had a big impact on my culinary thinking from the mid 1970's. Southern Spanish and Portuguese cooking is more-or-less totally influenced by their Moorish (Morroco) invaders and occupiers in the early 8th century AD. It is only recently that we have been able to access a couple of really good cookbooks for Morrocan or North African cooking, such as Arabesque and Moro.

My wife and I spent many years holidaying in central southern France and owned a house in that area of deep rural France for a number of years and this had a big impact on my appreciation of the delights 'local' produce, be it reared or grown. I also have a love for classical English cookery; however I have to admit that increasingly, littler-by-little, I find myself cooking less and less English style dishes and tend to concentrate far more on the Med and Fusion.

CONVERSION CHARTS
N.B. All conversions are approximate

WEIGHTS

Imperial	Metric		Imperial	Metric
½ oz	10g		6 oz	150g
¾ oz	20g		7 oz	175g
1 oz	25g		8 oz	200g
1 ½ oz	40g		9 oz	225g
2 oz	50g		10 oz	250g
2 ½ oz	60g		12 oz	300g
3 oz	75g		1 lb (16 oz)	400g
4 oz	100g		1 lb 8 oz	600g
5 oz	125g		2 lb	900g

Imperial	Metric		Gas	°F	°C
½ fl oz	15ml		1	275°F	140°C
1 fl oz	30ml		2	300°F	150°C
2 fl oz	60ml		3	325°F	170°C
4 fl oz	120ml		4	350°F	180°C
5 fl oz (¼ pint)	150ml		5	375°F	190°C
10 fl oz (½ pint)	300ml		6	400°F	200°C
20 fl oz (1 pint)	600ml		7	425°F	220°C
1 ¾ pints	1 litre		8	450°F	230°C
			9	475°F	240°C

NB: If using a fan oven, you will need to reduce the oven temperature in a recipe by approximately 20 degrees.

AMERICAN STANDARD CONVERSION

VOLUME (Liquid)

American Standard Cups & Quarts	American Standard Ounces	Metric Mill & Litres
2 tbsp	1 fl oz	30m
¼ cup	2 fl oz	60ml
½ cup	4 fl oz	125ml
1 cup	8 fl oz	250ml
1½ cups	12 fl oz	375ml
2 cups or 1pt	16 fl oz	500ml
4 cups or 1qt	32 fl oz	1000ml

DRY MEASURE EQUIVALENTS

Grammes rounded up or down			
3 tsp	1 tbsp	1/2 oz	14.5g
2 tbsp	1/8 cup	1 oz	28.5g
4 tbsp	¼ cup	2 oz	56.5g
8 tbsp	½ cup	4 oz	115g
12 tbsp	¾ cup	6 oz	.375 pound
32 tbsp	2 cups	16 oz	1 pound

Note: A pint isn't always a pint: in British, Australian and often Canadian recipes you'll see an imperial pint listed as 20 fluid ounces. American and some Canadian recipes use the American pint measurement, which is 16 fluid ounces as opposed to the 20 fluid ounces.

Finally, before I offer you some of my ideas for onboard galley recipes, I will share with you Nico Ladenis's thinking, which totally reflects my own, plus that, I think, of many celebrity chefs, specifically Jamie Oliver and Rick Stein: ***"Perfection is the result of simplicity"***.
"Don't you just love that?"

BREADMAKING

A lot of people avoid making bread onboard, because they think that it's "too difficult", or that they need special equipment. Can I just say, very loudly, *"It is not difficult!"*. I have also heard a lot of would be yacht chefs or existing ones for that matter, say those fatal words - *"I don't have time to bake bread"*. My reply to this is usually *"Nothing that a bit of advanced planning and organisation can't resolve"*.

Whilst I would never advise you to be a prisoner to your galley and encourage you to occasionally take short cuts when appropriate, you will find that bread making is a skill that is always worth mastering. Apart from being incredibly useful, there are few things more deeply satisfying to you than making a fresh, aromatic loaf of bread, or for your guests to get up in the morning and smell that distinctive smell of baking bread and freshly brewed Arabica coffee.

If after reading through the following section you still don't believe me, then try Emma's recipe for "Basic White Rustic Loaf" (Page 90) - it's simple, quick and quite delicious. You should have no problem knocking it out in even the smallest of galleys, whether you are hanging on by your finger tips at 45 degrees or languishing in a peaceful anchorage.

BREAD INGREDIENTS

- **Yeast** - is the raising agent necessary for bread making and is activated by heat and moisture; it is available in two forms - fresh or dried.

- **Fresh Yeast** - will keep in an airtight refrigerated container for approximately two weeks; it can be purchased from the bakery department of large supermarkets or from health food shops. Fresh yeast works by digesting the natural sugar content in the recipe ingredients, producing carbon dioxide causing the bread to rise. It is necessary to add sugar and warm water, or milk, to fresh yeast and allow time for it to froth up before using; on average you will need double the amount of fresh to dried yeast.

- **Dried Yeast** or fast action/easy blend - is the easiest to work with. Just add it to warm liquid and sugar and it starts to activate within five minutes. It is particularly suitable for yachts as it comes in sealed 7g sachets and is easy to stow, not needing any particular care.

- **Flour** - it is advisable to use a good, strong bread flour for your bread making. It has a much higher gluten content than ordinary plain flour, therefore producing a more elastic dough and lighter end product.

- **Whole wheat** - Wholegrain (Spelt flour) - flour should contain the whole wheat grain, ground so as to retain all its flavour and nutrients, with no additives or chemicals.

- **Granary** - flour contains crushed wheat and malt producing a texture with more bite, crunch and flavour.

- **Rye** - is rich in nitrogen and produces a darker close textured loaf than wheat flour.

- **Farmhouse flour -** contains 81% of the wheat, lighter in colour and less heavy in texture than whole wheat.

- **White cake flour** - is made from soft wheat and sifted to a fine texture, ideal for tea breads and fruit loafs.

BREAD MAKING PROCESSES

Making Basic Dough

If you are using fast action yeast, add it to some warm liquid and sugar, stir well and leave for five minutes to enable the yeast to 'start working'. Place the dry ingredients into a clean bowl, make a bay and add the wet ingredients. Gradually draw the dry ingredients into the liquid and as the mixture comes together, remove it from the bowl and place onto a lightly floured surface. Work the dough until it no longer sticks to your hand.

Kneading

By kneading, you are continuing the mixing process and helping to distribute the yeast evenly throughout the dough, whilst incorporating air into the mixture. As you continue to knead, you will notice that the dough will change texture from lumpy and coarse, to smooth, pliant and elastic.

Flour your hands and you are ready to start. Gather the outside edge of the dough and bring it into the centre, then use the heel of your hand to press it down. Continue this process. You will quickly get into the rhythm and could continue this for around ten minutes.

You will notice that the dough changes texture and becomes almost silky; you have now reached a stage where the dough can be left to rise in a draft free place. Simply clean out your mixing bowl with warm water, dry thoroughly and then lightly dust with flour and add your dough. Dust the top of the dough with flour and cover with cling film and place somewhere warm to rise/prove.

Rising

Letting your dough rise allows it to rest and double in size. When it comes to leaving your dough to rise you have a range options depending on your situation and available time.

Warm Rising

Most recipes recommend that you leave the dough in a warm place; this is the quickest method and is easily achievable on a yacht even if the outside air temperature is on the chilly side.

Cold Rising

Heat is not always necessary to make your dough rise – a lack of heat just means it will just take longer. Taking this one step further, you can put it in the fridge for its first rising, and this will slow down the whole process, but will produce a deeper richer flavour. It is also the easiest way to produce a loaf first thing in the morning, as you can start it the night before and then finish it off the next day. If you make a large batch it will keep (covered) in the fridge for up to three days, just break off what you need each morning and bring it up to room temperature before using.

Knocking Back

Once the dough has risen and doubled in size, most recipes will require you to "knock it back"; this literally means knocking the air/gas out of the dough, enabling you to let it prove for the second time and develop more flavour.

Simply hit the dough with your fist until flat then fold it up as you would a piece of paper. Try not to use too much flour. It should become quite firm, when you reach a stage when you cannot fold it any smaller and it is quite stiff, form it into a ball or whatever final shape you want to achieve. Alternatively, divide it between your loaf tins. If you are making rolls, shape the dough rolls at this stage, remembering that the dough will double in size, so size and shape them accordingly.

Proving
Now leave your bread to prove. This should take around 30 – 60 minutes - rolls approximately 20 - 30 minutes, this should allow the dough time to recover. Bear in mind that dough in a tin or container will take longer than "shaped" loaves or rolls that are to be cooked on baking sheets. It should have doubled in size and regained its smooth glossy appearance.

Finishing
Before baking your bread, you should consider whether you want to glaze the bread, therefore giving it a nice shiny finish, or whether you want a hard or soft crust - here are some suggestions.

Glazes
Brush with:

- olive oil for a shiny finish
- salty water for a crisp crust
- melted butter for a shiny finish
- beaten egg and grated cheese
- warmed honey for a sweet and shiny finish
- beaten egg yolk and cream for a rich finish

Toppings

- bran
- sea salt
- rolled oats
- dried herbs
- poppy seeds
- chopped nuts
- sesame seeds
- pumpkin seeds
- sunflower seeds
- snipped fresh herbs
- chopped sun dried tomatoes
- crushed brown sugar lumps
- chopped black or green olives

Slashing
Slashing the dough with a sharp knife, either diagonally, or in a cross, produces a more attractive loaf and also helps to control the expansion of the dough whilst baking.

Baking
Your oven temperature will vary according to the recipe, but as a general rule: the hotter the better. Always pre-heat your oven, so that it has reached the required temperature before your shaped dough is added, usually on a baking sheet. Typically, ideal temperatures would be Gas Mark 6-8 and Electric 220-230. A simple loaf should bake in 20-25 minutes. Take the loaves out of their tins and turn them upside down for the last ten minutes of baking; this helps to make the sides and bottom crisp.

Is it ready yet?
If you want to find out if the bread is cooked, remove it from the oven, turn it upside down and tap it on the bottom, it should sound hollow. Always place your cooked bread onto a wire rack to cool.

BASIC WHITE RUSTIC LOAF
This makes a delicious rustic loaf, with the advantage of only one rising, perfect served warm with preserves for breakfast, or superb prepared as rolls for mopping up a well dressed salad at lunch time.

Ingredients for two 1lb loafs or batches of rolls

- 500g strong white bread flour
- 1 tsp salt
- 1 tsp golden caster sugar
- 1 x 7g sachet dried yeast
- 325ml warm water
- vegetable or olive oil

Preparation

Accurately measure the warm water, add the sugar and dried yeast, mixing well for a few seconds with a fork. Leave for approximately five minutes to allow the sugar and yeast to start working and mix again.

Weigh the flour and place into a large plastic bowl and sprinkle in the salt and mix together. Draw the flour towards the sides of the bowl, making a bay (hole) in the middle of the flour ready for the liquid mixture.

Pour the yeast liquid into the bay and using your fork, work the mix in a circular motion, gradually bringing the flour from the edges of the bowl into the liquid. Keep doing this until the mixture starts to resemble sticky porridge and continue to work the mix until you can no longer mix it with your fork. You now need to work the dough with your clean hands, until all the flour has been absorbed and starts to come away cleanly from the sides of the bowl. You may need to dust the dough now and again with a little flour if it becomes sticky.

Dust your work surface with some flour, remove the dough from the bowl and start to knead the mixture on the surface by rolling and stretching with the heal of your hands. You should do this for around ten minutes, until you achieve a springy, soft, clear dough. If it remains sticky, continue to dust with flour and work the dough until it no longer sticks to the surface.

The dough now needs to rest for about fifteen minutes, so dust the worktop or bowl with a little flour, place the dough on top, dust with flour and cover with cling-film. You can also very lightly oil the inside of your bowl, as this will help prevent the dough from sticking. Once the dough has rested, you can cut it into as many pieces as you want

If making loaves, divide between two warm loaf tins, or simply shape into two rustic round loaves and place on a baking sheet. For rolls, divide the dough into 50g-75g (2-3 oz) balls and place on warmed baking sheets. Cover and leave to rise for about 30 minutes in a warm, draft free environment, until the dough has doubled in size. Glazing the top with a little egg wash, will help provide a nice golden colour to the end product.

Place in a pre-heated oven 230°C for 30 to 40 minutes or approx' 15 minutes for rolls. Bread is ready when golden brown and sounds hollow when tapped on the bottom. Remove from the oven, turn out and place on a wire cooling rack to cool.

This bread is best eaten on the day of baking but is perfectly good for toasting or rustic croutons for a couple of days.

MCB tip: The key to success with your bread making is to understand the qualities and characteristics of your basic ingredients.

Variations

Once mastered, you can try adding all sorts of goodies to this recipe. The following are particularly good:

- Fresh herbs
- Sun dried tomatoes
- Caramelised red onions
- Toasted seeds – pumpkin, sunflower, sesame or pine nuts
- Cheese: parmesan, blue, gruyere, strong cheddar or mozzarella

FLAT BREAD

Flatbreads are very similar to naan bread; very easy to make and an excellent accompaniment to curry, or great flavoured with garlic or chopped herbs and served with flavoured oils as a starter.

Ingredients for 8 flatbreads
- 500g strong white flour
- 2tsp salt
- 7g sachet dried yeast
- 3 tbsp olive oil
- 300m warm water

Preparation
Follow the same method as the previous recipe, placing your dough into a lightly oiled bowl and leave to double in size for approximately 1 hour.

Divide the dough into eight pieces and using a rolling pin or your hands flatten them into 15cm circles with a thickness of approximately 1cm. Leave them on a lightly floured surface to prove for five minutes.

Whilst they are proving get a good heavy based frying pan and heat to a medium temperature. Dry fry each flatbread on each side until golden brown, which should take about five minutes. Keep warm until the whole batch is done and then serve. Alternatively bake in your oven.

FRESH HERB FOCACCIA ROLLS

This recipe is based on the classic Italian Focaccia. These rolls can be served with many different types of food and are irresistible when they have just come out of the oven. There are many ways to finish off this dough, but using fresh herbs and cracked sea salt is my favourite. We often serve a basket of these rolls to our dinner guests, served with a couple of dipping oils.

Ingredients for four servings

For the bread
- 500g strong white plain flour
- 7g sachet dried yeast
- 350ml luke warm water
- 2 tbsp extra virgin olive oil
- 10g sea salt

For the topping
- extra virgin olive oil
- course sea salt & ground black pepper
- sprigs of fresh, young rosemary leaves

Alternatively, you can use any of the following herbs: basil, parsley, thyme, marjoram or chives.

Preparation

Pre-heat your oven to 220°C and lightly oil two baking sheets.

Sift the flour and salt into a large, clean bowl. Dissolve the yeast in the warm water, stirring well until completely dissolved. Make a well (bay) in the middle of the flour and pour in the yeast solution and oil and mix well with a fork, gradually drawing the flour into the liquid. Once it starts to reach a thick porridge state, you will need to use your hands to mix together until a dough is formed.

Remove the mix from your bowl, lightly dust your work surface and knead the dough for around five minutes, until the dough is smooth and elastic.

Lightly oil a bowl. Place the dough into the bowl and turn it through 360 degrees until it is coated all over. Cover the bowl with cling film and place to one side in a warm place for approx one hour, or until it has doubled in size.

 Knock the dough back to its original size and turn it out onto your lightly floured work surface. Divide the dough into eight equal sized balls. You can leave them round or roll them into thick (or thin) sausages. Place onto your baking sheets, making sure that you leave sufficient space between each one. Cover with a damp, clean tea towel and set aside to prove for thirty minutes.

Mix the rosemary and four dessert spoons of olive oil together. Dip your index finger into some flour and press several indentations into each roll and then spoon the rosemary mixture over each. Brush the oil round the sides of each roll and finish off with a sprinkling of Maldon salt.

Bake in the middle of your pre-heated over for between twenty and twenty five minutes, or until the rolls are well risen and golden brown. The base should sound hollow when tapped. Place onto cooling wires.

BREAKFAST DISHES

Breakfast on a yacht should be a leisurely experience; ideally eaten on the aft deck, or wherever your owner or guests decide. Different nationalities may require different approaches to breakfast, however a common solution is to provide some buffet style elements, cereals, fresh fruit platters, cheeses, cured meats, smoked salmon, breads: baguettes, croissants, brioche, bagels, muffins, German style rye bread (pumpernickel). In addition it is nice to offer a daily hot option e.g. choice of eggs, such as the ubiquitous onboard breakfast essential Eggs Benedict or scrambled eggs with smoked salmon. However it really is an opportunity to surprise your guests with a variety of fresh, seasonal or local ideas.

"Customer delight" is what you are all about – it is, after all, why you will be, or already are, working on the water. Your charter or private guests are your world when they are onboard and nothing will be too much trouble for you and the rest of the crew to tend to their every need. Something that your guests will love you for, is baking them some fresh bread, so the tried and tested recipe I have included is very flexible and also makes lovely rolls or mini-twists.

I have been greatly influenced by the inspirational book "Rose Bakery – Breakfast Lunch & Tea" by Rose Carrarini, who runs a contemporary "English Café" at 46, Rue des Martyrs, Paris. I have adapted one or two of Rosie's ideas, as they work so well and are really delicious.

It is important that you are aware that under-cooked eggs and soft cheese can be dangerous to pregnant women. If you are aware that you have a pregnant woman onboard who asks for a soft boiled egg, eggs Benedict or runny scrambled egg etc., ask the stewardess to advise the guest that eating undercooked eggs is not recommended and could have a negative effect on an unborn baby. Your yacht is likely to have protocols for managing such occurrences.

AMERICAN BREAKFAST PANCAKES

Ingredients make 8 x 4inch pancakes
- 255g plain flour
- 2 tbsp caster sugar
- 2 tsp baking powder
- 2 medium eggs – lightly beaten
- 250ml milk
- ½ tsp salt
- 50g unsalted butter – melted
- 1 tbsp vegetable oil

Preparation
In a bowl, beat together the eggs, milk and sugar. Add the melted butter and beat again.

Sift the flour, baking powder and salt together into a bowl. Make a bay in the centre of the dry ingredients and pour in the egg mixture. Using a wooden spoon, beat the mixture quickly to make a batter.

Heat a heavy based skillet or frying pan over medium low flame and melt a knob of butter. Pour in the batter to make discs approximately 8cm in diameter and cook until a few bubbles come to the surface of the mixture, this should take about a minute. Turn each pancake over with a palette knife and cook for a further minute or so until both sides are golden brown. Place to one side to keep warm.

Continue to cook until you have used up all the batter. Serve immediately with fresh fruit, maple syrup and pecan nuts.

APRICOT and VANILLA COMPÔTE

Compôtes are an altogether more gentle and comforting start to the day. A compote can be a breakfast or dessert dish, usually made of whole pieces of fruit, poached in a sugar syrup. Whole fruits are immersed in sugar flavoured water and spices and cooked over a gentle flame. Compôte can be served either warm or chilled and some recipes include dried fruits, soaked in a little water with alcohol added i.e. rum or kirsch (cherry). In France, a compôte can also be a fine purée of cooked fruit and is often used a base for other desserts, such as the famous Tarte aux Pommes – the classic French tart!

Ingredients for four
- 100g caster sugar
- 300ml water
- 1 vanilla pod – split, seeds scraped & retained
- 12 fresh apricots – halved and stoned
- 2 handfuls of blueberries (optional)

Preparation

Place a heavy based pan over a high flame and bring the water to the boil, add the sugar and turn down the heat, stirring until the sugar has dissolved. Add the vanilla pod and seeds. Add the apricots and poach gently until they deepen in colour and are just becoming soft - this will take around five minutes, depending on the size, ripeness and temperature of the fruit.

Lift the apricots out of the syrup and leave to cool. Put the syrup back over a high flame and reduce by about half, remove from the hob, poor into a bowl and then leave to cool. Pour the cold syrup over the apricots and add the blueberries (if using).

This compôte can be served warm or chilled from the fridge depending on preference. However, serving compôte cold is the accepted norm for breakfast service.

CRUNCHY GRANOLA
(Oat Cereal)

If you are looking for something less "wet" and with more crunch, this is easy and delicious. Do not be put off by the long list of ingredients; it really is worth getting them all out of the cupboard. You could make one large batch each week and keep it in an airtight container.

Ingredients for six
- 400g rolled oats
- 125g whole almonds
- 100g sunflower seeds
- 100g pumpkin seeds
- 50g sesame seeds
- 1 tbsp wheat germ
- 125ml sunflower oil
- 150ml honey
- 50g soft brown sugar
- several drops of good quality vanilla extract
- a pinch of ground cinnamon
- handful of sultanas

- handful of chopped dates
- milk or soya milk to serve
- 1 tsp salt

Preparation

Pre-heat your oven to 160°C.

Place the honey, sunflower oil, sugar, vanilla, salt and cinnamon in a heavy based saucepan, add 125ml of water. Bring to the boil, making sure that you stir the mixture constantly.

Mix together the oats, almonds, wheat germ and seeds in a bowl and pour the hot contents of the pan over, stirring well to combine. The mixture should be sticky but not wet and if it is, simply add a few more oats to the mixture.

Spread the mixture out evenly on a flat baking sheet and bake for approximately one hour. Keep checking it and giving the tray a shake to make sure that the cereal gets evenly baked.

Turn the oven down to its lowest setting and bake for a further hour to achieve a really crisp result. You can bake it less if you wish.

Remove from the oven, leave to cool, and then add the dried fruit and store in an airtight container.

If I want to sex this up a bit, I like to add sunflower seeds, dried cranberries, cherries and fresh blueberries – better than brilliant!

DREAMY CREAMY SCRAMBLED EGGS

It's so easy to destroy a pan of scrambled egg - so do not rush the cooking. If you want your eggs to turn out nice and creamy, then nice and easy does it!

Ingredients per person
- 2 eggs (free range)
- 25ml single cream
- 25g unsalted butter
- salt & freshly ground black pepper

Preparation

Break the eggs into a bowl and beat with a fork. Add a little seasoning and beat again.

Place a small heavy bottomed pan over a low flame and allow to heat through for a minute or so. Melt the butter and add the egg mixture and stir continuously with a wooden spoon until the egg is lightly cooked. Just before the egg is ready and starting to thicken, add a splash of cream and stir-in gently to heat through. The French culinary term for this consistency is "baveuse" – meaning just a bit runny, undercooked or moist.

Remove from the heat, check for seasoning and serve. Be careful because the heat from the pan will carry on cooking the eggs after you have removed them from the flame. So, have your plates, toast, muffins, smoked salmon etc ready for when the eggs are cooked.

MCB tip: If you cook your eggs too quickly, or over-cook them, you will finish up with rubbery, discoloured egg, which really does not look very appetizing and certainly won't impress your guests or crew.

EASY PEASY BANANA SMOOTHIE
I think the title says it all!

Ingredients for one
- 1 banana - skinned
- 1 tspn of honey
- 2 tbsp apple juice
- 125ml of natural yoghurt or soya milk

Preparation
Just place all ingredients in a blender, whizz together and serve immediately!

EGGS BENEDICT
Synonymous with the yachting industry, this is 'the' egg dish, the 'real deal', the 'doggies doo dahs' – this is the ultimate high end breakfast or brunch egg dish and there are differing accounts of its origin.

In an interview in the "Talk of the Town" column of 'The New Yorker' in 1942 (the year before his death), Lemuel Benedict, a retired Wall Street stock broker, claimed that he had wandered into the Waldorf Hotel (New York) in 1894 and hoping to find a cure for his morning hangover, ordered *"Buttered toast, poached eggs, crisp bacon and a 'hooker' (usually referring to a non-descript quantity of alcohol – a 'slug') of hollandaise"*. Oscar Tschirky, the famed 'maitre d'hotel' at the Waldorf, was so impressed with the dish, that he put it on the breakfast and luncheon menus, but substituted ham and an English muffin for the bacon and toast.

Ingredients for four
- 4 x English muffins
- 8 medium sized eggs – free range
- clear vinegar (white wine, cider, distilled or similar)
- 4 slices of good quality white ham or crispy pancetta
- hollandaise sauce (see below)

Preparation
Fill a shallow pan with about 7.5cm (3 inches) of water and bring to a gentle boil over a high heat and add 2 tablespoons of the clear vinegar, this helps the eggs maintain their shape when you break them into the pan. Reduce the heat to a medium-low flame until you obtain a steady simmer.

Break each egg carefully into a cup, remove any shell and then gently tip the eggs into the simmering water one-at-a-time and poach for between three and four minutes - this depends on the size and temperature of the raw egg. Remember, the more eggs you add to the liquid, the more the temperature will drop, so do not try to cook more than a couple at a time. Lightly toast the muffins under your grill. If you don't have a grill, you can heat them through in your oven, or bar-mark them in a ribbed griddle pan or just serve them warm.

Once the eggs are cooked, remove with a perforated spoon and drain them carefully on a paper towel. Place two halves of lightly toasted muffin onto each plate, top with muffin sized discs of ham and top each with an egg. Spoon a good amount of hollandaise sauce over each egg.

Cut the remaining pieces of ham into fine strips and neatly scatter over the top of each egg (remember to check for vegetarians). Serve nice and hot.

MCB tip #1: You can very easily turn this dish into an up-market bacon, egg and tomato breakfast. Simply slice a large beef tomato into four good round slices, brush with oil, lightly season and heat under your grill. Grill a couple of slices of smoked bacon or pancetta per serving. Place a slice of tomato onto each half muffin, add the poached egg and hollandaise to one half, then top the other half with a couple of rashers of crispy bacon and maybe some grilled mushrooms – breakfast heaven!

MCB tip #2: If you are likely to have a high demand for this dish, you can 'part-poach' your eggs well in advance of folk arriving for breakies! Poach the eggs as noted above and when about three quarters cooked, remove them from the pan with a slotted spoon and gently place them into a bowl of well iced water. This will instantly stop them from cooking. When needed, all you need to do is use them on demand, placing them back into a simmering pan of lightly salted, simmering water. Another minute or so will heat them through nicely.

For the Hollandaise Sauce

This sauce is known in the trade as an 'emulsion' of butter and lemon juice (or clear vinegar), using egg yolks as the emulsifying agent, usually seasoned with salt and little black or white pepper or cayenne pepper. Despite the name, it is a French sauce, which requires some skill and knowledge to prepare; care must be taken to 'hold' it properly after preparation. Correctly made, the sauce should be smooth and creamy; the flavour rich butter, with a mild tang. Overheating will cause the sauce to break or "split", so caution is required.

Ingredients
- 225g unsalted butter
- 1 tbsp white wine vinegar
- 1 tbsp lemon juice
- 3 egg yolks (free range) – lightly beaten
- pinch of salt

Preparation
Place the butter in a small pan and melt very slowly over a gentle heat.

Put the wine vinegar and lemon juice into a small shallow pan and bring to the boil. Pay attention, because this will happen quickly. Reduce by three quarters, remove from the heat and cool a little by adding a spoon or two of cold water. Gently whisk in the egg yolks.

When the butter has melted take off the heat and gradually whisk into the egg mixture, little-by-little, pouring slowly in a steady stream. Make sure that you do not add the milky deposits from the bottom of the pan. The sauce will thicken and is ready to serve.

If the sauce over-thickens, you can thin it a little with some hot water until you reach the desired consistency. Keep the sauce warm in a stainless bowl, placed over a pan of gently simmering hot water until ready to serve. Do not overheat or the sauce will split.

MCB tip: If the sauce splits, place an egg yolk into a clean bowl and gradually whisk in the split sauce.

FYI: I have included a couple of alternate methods of preparing Hollandaise in the Basics section on Pages 228 & 230.

FLAT OMELETTE

This is by far the easiest of my omelette recipes.

Ingredients for one

- 2 eggs per person – corn fed free range are best
- salt and white pepper
- spray vegetable oil or a little butter

Preparation

Break the eggs into a bowl, beat well with a fork or whisk thoroughly and lightly season just before cooking.

Ensure that your omelette pan is thoroughly clean, then heat over a medium-low flame. Spray lightly with vegetable oil or melt a small knob of butter until it melts.

Add the eggs and reduce the flame a little. Cook quite slowly, without stirring the egg mix. To help set the top of the mix, I find it helpful to cover with a lid, or a plate will do.

Once the mix is set, remove the pan from the heat and using a palette knife, ease the omelette away from the edge, tilt the pan away from you and fold the omelette in half. Tap the bottom of the pan on a folded tea towel, over a firm surface, to move the omelette up to the edge of the pan. Tilt the pan completely and turn the omelette out onto a plate.

Tidy up the shape and serve immediately.

FRIED EGGS

I love to serve uniform sized fried eggs on a lightly toasted half muffin, drizzled with a little grind of black pepper. Place some crispy pancetta over a warm, thick slice of beef tomato on the other half muffin.

Frying eggs should really be so simple to cook, but there are so many factors that can turn this relatively easy process into a near-disaster, there really are too many to tell you about. So let's keep it simple:

Eggs – size (medium), temperature (not too cold), freshness (very), battery v free range (always) What to cook them in – lard (pork product), vegetable oil (sunflower or corn oil), butter (use clarified), too hot (singed edges), too cold (eggs spread).

Preparation

Allow one to two eggs per portion. Place a non stick frying pan over a medium flame and add a little oil. Allow the oil to heat through and add the eggs. Cook gently, spooning a little hot oil over the yolks until they start to glaze and the eggs are lightly set. Use a fish slice to remove the eggs, drain of surplus fat and serve.

MCB tip #1:   To prepare an outstanding fried egg, it is essential that you use the very best quality, freshest, free range eggs.

MCB tip #2:   To get a uniform shape, you can buy round, stainless egg moulds for frying. These are v.useful, as they can double up for making tians, stacks or similar.

MANGO LASSI

Ingredients for two/four
- 100ml single cream
- 200ml skimmed milk
- 400ml natural yoghurt (unsweetened)
- 400ml mango purée (or fruit purée of your choice)
- 2 dsp golden caster sugar

Preparation
Blend the ingredients together first thing, pour into a jug, cover and refrigerate until required. Serve over ice.

If you have children onboard, they will love this; just add chunky straws.

MELON and GINGER SALAD
This makes an incredibly refreshing and cleansing start to the day.

Ingredients for four to five
- 100g caster sugar
- 4cm piece of fresh root ginger – very finely chopped or shredded
- 1½ lemons – juiced
- 1 orange fleshed melon - peeled and deseeded
- 1 green fleshed melon - peeled and deseeded
- 1 large wedge of watermelon

Preparation
Place 250ml of water in a saucepan over a high flame and bring to the boil. Add the sugar, turn down the heat a little and stir until the sugar has dissolved and the liquid has reduced by 50%. Add the ginger, turn the heat off and leave to infuse and cool.

Once cooled, strain the syrupy liquid into a large bowl and add the lemon juice. Carefully cut the melons into equal sized cubes, add to the syrup and refrigerate for half an hour before serving.

OMELETTES
An omelette is one of the quickest and easiest dishes you can make for breakfast, lunch or dinner and it can be "knocked up" in seconds – equally, it can also be made to look like the proverbial 'dog's breakfast' if you don't follow some simple rules. For the novice cook, the use of a non stick frying pan will help you a great deal, while a professional galley chef will have special omelette pans which are seldom used for anything else.

Claire and I like to show our students how to make three or four different types of omelette. What we would call a restaurant style omelette, a folded flat omelette, a soufflé omelette and a savoury Frittata or Spanish style omelette. Ideally omelettes should be cooked in a heavy bottomed 20cm (8") omelette or non-stick frying pan.

As a guideline, you will often find that the guys will go for three eggs and the girls usually prefer only two. Your breakfast stew will need to ask, don't just assume what your guests want.

POACHED EGGS
There is definitely a skill to producing the perfect poached egg. I do not expect you to become the best egg poacher overnight, however I hope this info' will provide you with a good starting point.

I have already mentioned the fresh egg thing and this applies equally for poaching, as they have a thicker white (albumen) and therefore are less likely to 'spread' in the simmering water. Poor quality eggs are difficult to manage, as the white is thin, it spreads in the simmering water and falls apart.

Your well prepared poached egg should have a firm, but tender white, surrounding the slightly thickened, unbroken yolk. I usually always use cider vinegar, white wine vinegar, or distilled which also make the white more tender and whiter.

Preparation
Fill a shallow pan with about 7.5cm (3 inches) of water and bring to a gentle boil over a high heat and add 2 tablespoons of the vinegar to the water, this helps the eggs maintain their shape when you break them into the pan. Reduce the heat to a medium-low flame until you obtain a steady simmer.

Break each egg carefully into a cup and remove any shell. Rotate the simmering water with a spoon to create a vortex and then gently tip the eggs into the simmering water and poach for between three and four minutes - this depends on the size and temperature of the raw egg. Remember, the more eggs you add to the liquid, the more the temperature will reduce, so do not try to cook more than a couple at a time. Once the eggs are cooked, carefully remove with a perforated spoon and place into a bowl of iced water (not necessary if you are serving immediately).

Trim the white off the egg if necessary to provide a uniform shape. Re-heat as your guests arrive à table. When required, place into a shallow pan of hot, lightly salted water for around one minute. Remove carefully with a perforated spoon, drain on a clean kitchen cloth and serve hot.

MCB tip #1:   Eggs from corn-fed chickens, which you find in many Mediterranean countries, have the most wonderful golden yellow yolks, which look fabulous when cut into.

MCB tip #2:   Never use dark malt vinegar, as this will discolour the eggs and may create a 'scum' on the top of the water. Alternatively a squeeze of lemon juice will help, but don't use too much.

RESTAURANT STYLE OMELETTE

Ingredients for one
- 2/3 eggs per person – corn fed free range are best
- salt & white pepper
- knob of unsalted butter

Preparation
Break the eggs into a bowl, beat well with a fork or whisk thoroughly and lightly season just before cooking.

Ensure that your omelette pan is thoroughly clean, then heat over a medium flame. Add around 12g butter and heat until it foams. As soon as the bubbles start to subside, add the eggs and cook quickly, moving the mixture continuously with the back of a fork until the eggs are nearly set and spread fairly flat in the bottom of your pan.

Remove the pan from the heat and tilt pan away from you and fold the omelette in half. Tap the bottom of the pan on a folded tea towel, over a firm surface, to move the omelette up to the edge of the pan. Tilt the pan completely and turn the omelette out onto a plate. Tidy up the shape and serve immediately.

This type of omelette can have a range of fillings, such as: tomato concassé, mushrooms, bacon, chorizo, chopped fresh herbs etc etc….

SMOOTHIES

A smoothie is a blended, chilled, sometimes sweetened 'beverage', usually made from fresh fruit or vegetables. In addition to fruit, many smoothies include crushed ice, frozen fruit, honey or frozen yoghurt – although some smoothies are made from 100% fruit.

They have a milkshake-like consistency, which is thicker than 'slush' drinks. Unlike a milkshake, smoothies should never contain ice-cream, but they can contain milk. Some recipes may include ingredients such as: soy milk, whey powder, green tea, herbal supplements or nutritional supplement mixes.

SOUFFLÉ OMELETTE

Out of my three omelette recipes, this can be the most time consuming and difficult to get right. Practice, practice, practice people! You will also get some ultra-thin guests who appear to be on a "no food" diet, who are likely to ask for a plain egg white omelette. The production method is very similar to this recipe, just leave out the yolks and serve with some dry fried mixed peppers with a little tomato concassé, chilli and chopped fresh herbs.

Don't panic folks – this isn't one of those mega-technical, stressful propa soufflés that you have to timed to perfection, just to find that your guests have decided to hit on another round of Mojitos! This recipe can take as little as five minutes if you have an electric whisk – if not it will take a little longer and leave your wrist aching just a tad!

Ingredients for one
- 2 large eggs – corn fed free range are best
- salt & freshly ground black pepper
- 10g (1/2 oz) unsalted butter
- salt and black pepper

Pre-heat your grill and have a warm plate ready for serving.

Separate the eggs; whites into one bowl, yolks into another. Separating the whites one at a time into a cup or mug is a good idea, then transfer them into a spotlessly clean bowl, so if one egg breaks, you don't ruin all the whites by getting any yolk into them. If this happens, the whites will not whisk up properly.

Whisk the egg yolks with a small balloon whisk until they are light and fluffy, season well with a little salt and pepper. Whisk your egg whites with either an electric hand whisk or a balloon whisk, until they form soft peaks. Place your omelette pan over a low flame to heat through. Using a large metal spoon, carefully fold the egg yolk mix into the whisked egg whites.

Increase the flame just a little and add the butter to your pan and once the bubbles start to subside, spoon in your egg mixture. Using the back of a fork, flatten out the top of the mix and cook for approximately one minute. Remove from the heat and using a palette knife, ease the omelette away from the edge of the pan.

Place your pan under the grill flame. Make sure that there is sufficient 'head room', as the omelette (as the name suggests) will rise under the heat. Let the omelette cook for another minute, depending on the heat of your grill. This is the time when you do not want to be distracted – a few seconds can mean the difference between the perfect golden omelette and a burnt offering!

Remove the pan from under the grill, fold in half with the aid of your palette knife or a fish slice, turn out onto the warmed plate and serve immediately.

TRADITIONAL MUESLI

This is so simple and so much nicer than opening a dusty old packet of supermarket muesli. This is a good basic recipe and you can always add fruits or seeds to taste.

Ingredients for four

- 150g rolled oats- soaked in 250ml apple juice for one hour
- 125ml natural or Greek yoghurt
- 1 crunchy apple – (peeled or unpeeled) – grated
- 2 heaped tbsp chopped almonds
- 1 tbsp wheat germ
- 1 tbsp honey - more for serving (best quality you can afford)
- 1 handful of sultanas
- 1 handful each of pumpkin and sunflower seeds

Preparation

Blend together and serve. Alternatively, set up individual bowls on the breakfast buffet of these ingredients. You can also offer guests bowls of summer or autumn fruits, so they can make up their own 'designer' muesli.

SOUPS

There is so much I could write about soups, be they hot or cold, consommé (clear), cream, velouté, purée, broth or bisque. The opportunities for serving hot soup may be fairly limited, so I am going to include a couple of classics, both hot and cold. Think seriously about the weather conditions when planning your menu. Maybe think about a little bowl of chilled Gazpacho, drizzled with some top quality olive oil as a 'muse bouche' – to stimulate your guests' palates. However, something like a lamb broth with chunky vegetables can equally be a god send in poor, cold weather and may go down well with crew doing a crossing or delivery.

CHILLED CUCUMBER SOUP with PRAWNS

I appreciate that for much of the time, most of you will be working in the hot climates of the Mediterranean, Caribbean, BVIs, Indian Ocean, Pacific etc..., so a chilled soup may be a great little starter or even a 'muse bouche', to tantalise the taste buds of your guests, before you hit them with the real deal.

I have played around with this recipe for a number of years, but now I think that I have finally cracked it. Early efforts were either too insipid, caused by adding too much ice and too little cucumber, or I added too much mint or too little ice, so I decided to look at a totally different way to produce a high quality soup.

One of the important bits of kit that you will find invaluable in the galley is an electric hand blender and you will need one to get the best result with this soup

Ingredients for four
- 25g unsalted butter
- 2 shallots – finely chopped
- 1 firm cucumber – peeled, de-seeded and diced
- 1 clove of garlic – crushed
- 300ml cold milk
- 300ml whipping cream
- 100g cooked, peeled prawns (shrimps)
- 4 large prawns – shell on
- 1 dsp each of finely chopped mint and chives
- 1 lemon
- salt & freshly ground black pepper

Optional garnish
- 4 large cooked peeled prawns – finely sliced across the body
- picked fresh dill and chopped chives

Preparation
Place four French soup bowls into your freezer, if you are lucky to have one large enough for the job!

Place a medium size pan over a low flame and gently melt the butter. Add the shallots and garlic and sweat (cover with a lid) without colour until soft and translucent. Add the cucumber of cook for a few minutes more until tender.

Add the milk and bring to the boil and immediately reduce the flame and simmer for a further five minutes. If you have a food processor onboard, then poor in the mix and blitz until smooth. Alternatively, use your hand blender, taking care not to decorate the galley with your milky broth.

Transfer the mixture into a separate container, season to taste and leave to cool. To speed up the cooling process, you can place the container over or into a bowl of ice. When cool, add the cream and chopped herbs and stir thoroughly. Check the seasoning, cover with cling-film and transfer to your refrigerator to chill for a couple of hours.

About 15 minutes before you serve the soup, spread the prawns out on a plate. Squeeze over with a little lemon juice and lightly season with salt and freshly ground black pepper. Just prior to serving, remove the broth from the freezer, drain the prawns, finely slice with a small sharp knife and mix together with the dill and chives.

To serve – remove the soup bowls from the freezer and using a suitable ladle, distribute the broth evenly, so all guests have the same size portion – don't overdo it. The outside of the soup bowls should lightly crystalize. Lightly scatter the prawn and herb mix over the broth and top with a whole prawn. Place the soup bowls onto an under-plate and serve.

CLAM CHOWDER

If you have problems finding fresh clams, then use frozen or canned clams to help create this classic recipe from New England in the United States. Reserve a few cooked clams in their shells for garnish. Classically, the soup is served with Saltine Crackers, which you may find in USA and possibly English delicatessens. Doriano crackers from Tesco are about as close as you might get in the UK or checkout www.costco.com

Ingredients for four
- 100g salt pork or un-smoked bacon – diced
- 1 large onion – chopped
- 2 medium sized potatoes – peeled & diced (1cm squares)
- 1 bay leaf
- 1 sprig of fresh thyme
- 300ml milk
- 400g cooked clams – cooking liquid reserved
- 150ml double or whipping cream
- salt, ground white pepper & cayenne pepper
- finely chopped parsley

Preparation

Place a saucepan over a medium-low flame, allow to heat through and add the salt pork or bacon and cook gently, stirring frequently, until the fat runs and the meat starts to brown. Add the chopped onion and cook over a low heat for about five minutes, until softened but not browned.

Add the cubed potatoes, bay leaf and thyme. Stir well to coat with the pork fat, then pour in the milk and the reserved clam liquid and bring to the boil. Turn the flame right down and simmer for about ten minutes, until the potatoes are tender, but still firm. Remove the bay leaf and thyme and discard.

Remove the clams from the shells, retaining some for garnishing. Add bulk of the clams to the pan and season the broth to taste with salt, pepper and cayenne. Simmer gently for a further five minutes, then stir in the cream. Heat until the soup is very hot, but do not let it boil. Pour the hot chowder into warmed soup bowls, making sure that the clams and diced potato are evenly distributed. Garnish with some of the clam shells and the chopped parsley and serve immediately.

GAZPACHO

Gazpacho is a chilled, Spanish, tomato based raw vegetable soup, originating in the southern Spanish region of Andalucia. This soup is widely consumed throughout Spain, Portugal (gaspacho) and parts of Latin America. The soup is mostly consumed during the extremely hot summer months, due to it's refreshing qualities. There are areas in Southern Spain, away from the coast, where summer temperatures can reach well over 40°C.

The ancient roots of Gazpacho include the theory of its origin as an Arab soup of bread, olive oil, water and garlic, which arrived in Spain with the Moors, or via the Romans with the addition of vinegar. The other is that it is a legacy of the New World, when Columbus returned from 'The Americas' with tomatoes and peppers. Whichever is true, once in Spain, it became part of Andalucian cuisine, particularly around the beautiful medieval city of Seville.

You can easily vary the flavours, thickness and textures of this Spanish classic, which is a great low fat summer lunch dish when it's too hot to cook. It is good with some nice pieces of crusty bread or toasted wheat bread. You can use green pepper instead of red, but I find that this tends to make the soup a little bitter and in my opinion, the red pepper gives it that little *je ne sais quoi*, or should I say, *No sé lo que*!

Ingredients for six
- 700g ripe tomatoes – peeled & chopped
- 2 red bell pepper – skinned, halved, de-seeded & chopped
- 1 small Spanish onion – coarsely chopped
- ½ cucumber – peeled, de-seeded and chopped
- 2 cloves of garlic – peeled and crushed
- 100g fresh breadcrumbs
- 4 tbsp olive oil
- 2 tbsp white wine vinegar
- 500g passata di pomodoro (tomato juice)
- 1 tbsp basil leaves – chopped
- flat leaf parsley – finely chopped
- ½ tsp of cumin
- ½ tsp sweet paprika
- salt & pepper to taste
- tomato purée (optional)

Preparation
Pre-heat your oven to 200°C.

Brush the red peppers with olive oil and roast in the hot oven for around thirty minutes or until soft. Remove from the oven and allow to cool a little. Remove the stalk and split in half lengthways, scrape out the seeds, remove the skin and roughly chop. Place the prepared peppers, tomatoes, cucumber, garlic, bread, olive oil and vinegar into a food processor and blend until smooth. Add the passata, basil, cumin and paprika and process briefly. If the soup is too thick, add a little cold water until you reach the desired consistency. I do like to add a dessert spoon of tomato purée, which really helps with that intense tomato hit.

Season to taste and refrigerate for about half an hour or more.

To serve, ladle the soup into bowls, lightly drizzle with a little olive oil or chilli oil and sprinkle with the chopped parsley and basil. Serve with chunks of local, rustic crusty bread.

MCB tip: My good friend, and professional superyacht chef Sarah Churcher, puts olive oil into an ice-cube tray to freeze and then places an 'olive oil ice cube' in the middle of the soup to serve. This looks great and keeps the soup cold as the 'ice' melts and the olive oil spreads over the surface.

PURÉE of ROASTED BUTTERNUT SQUASH & SWEET POTATO

This is a soup which my wife makes during the colder winter months. It is very straight forward to make and tastes delicious. Chickpeas are high in protein, so make a great meat or fish substitute contribution for a stable diet.

Ingredients for four

- I butternut squash – peeled & cut into 3cm dice
- 1 large sweet potato – peeled & cut into 3cm dice
- 2 medium carrots – peeled & cut into 3cm dice
- 1 x 400g tin chickpeas – liquid retained
- 1lt vegetable stock
- fresh rosemary – a stem
- crème fraîche
- olive oil
- coriander – chopped
- sea salt & black pepper

Preparation

Pre-heat 180°C

Place the prepared vegetables into a bowl and drizzle with olive oil, mixing well to make sure the vegetables are thoroughly coated. Spread the vegetables out onto a baking tray, drizzle with a little more olive oil and season with salt and freshly ground black pepper. Place into the middle of your pre-heated oven and roast for minimum of twenty minutes.

Once the vegetables are soft, remove from the oven and turn out into a heavy based saucepan, add the rosemary and cover with hot vegetable stock. Place the pan over a high flame and bring to the boil. Reduce the flame to medium-low and simmer the broth for around twenty minutes.

Remove the pan from the heat. Remove the rosemary stem and whizz up with your hand blender. If the soup is too thick, then just add a little more stock or hot water. Check for seasoning and adjust to taste. Return the pan to your hob over a medium-low flame and add two dessert spoons of crème fraîche and whisk gently to incorporate.

Ladle the purée into warmed soup bowls, garnish with a teaspoon of crème fraîche and some chopped coriander.

SOOTHING ASIAN BROTH

Although I have provided you with a list of ingredients, these are by no means prescriptive. What we have here is a starting point, as this is a soup that you can adapt to suit what you have in your fridge. You can add a range of different ingredients to suit the occasion, such as: headless de-shelled prawns, white crab meat or even tofu. I love to use Udon noodles, thick wheat flour noodles, popular in Japanese cuisine, although I have used rice vermicelli here. It is important that you put the chilli in at the last minute, otherwise the heat can become overpowering.

Ingredients for four
- 750ml good quality chicken or vegetable stock
- 500g pre-cooked headless tiger prawns (shelled)
- 1 pak choi – split lengthways & shredded
- 2 spring onions – trimmed & cut into 2cm lengths
- 25g rice vermicelli
- 50g bean sprouts
- 1 chilli – split, de-seeded & finely chopped
- 2.5cm piece of root ginger
- 1 stalk of lemon grass (outer layers removed – finely sliced)
- 1 tsp soft dark sugar
- 1 tbsp fish sauce (nam pla)
- 1 tbsp light soy sauce
- 1 star anise (optional)
- 2 limes – zested & juiced
- fresh coriander – select some nice leaves for garnish and chop the remainder

Preparation
Peel the ginger, slice thinly, and then cut into fine batons. Pour the stock into a heavy based saucepan and place over a medium flame, bring to the boil and reduce to a simmer. Add the half the ginger, sugar, half the lemon grass, fish sauce, soy sauce, lime zest and star anise (if using) and simmer for approximately ten minutes, so that the stock takes on all the wonderful flavours.

Place a small pan of water over a high flame and bring to the boil. Add a pinch of salt, turn off the heat and add the vermicelli, agitate with a fork and leave for three to four minutes.

Bring the stock up to a gentle simmer and add the prawns and cook for one minute, before adding the bean sprouts, pak choi and the remaining ginger, lemon grass and the chopped coriander. Simmer for another thirty seconds and remove from the heat.

Using some kitchen tongs, divide the vermicelli between four bowls, and then ladle the soup over them, making sure that the prawns are evenly distributed. Garnish with whole coriander leaves and serve.

STARTERS

AUBERGINE, TOMATO and GOAT'S CHEESE STACK
This dish is easy, quick, great tasting, fabulous food - you don't have to be a vegetarian to enjoy this recipe.

Ingredients for four
- 125ml olive oil
- 2 cloves of garlic – crushed
- 2 small aubergines
- 2 firm red tomatoes
- 150g goats cheese log
- 8 basil leaves
- rocket leaves to garnish
- 150g jar of sundried tomatoes – drained
- 1 clove of garlic – crushed
- 2 tbsp good quality mayonnaise

Preparation
Place the oil and two crushed cloves of garlic together in a bowl and mix together. Cut each aubergine into 1cm slices; you will need twelve slices altogether. Cut the tomatoes into 1cm slices; you will need eight slices in total. Dip a small, sharp knife into hot water and cut the goats cheese into eight 1cm thick slices.

Using half the oil mixture brush both sides of the aubergine slices and then heat a heavy based frying pan over a medium flame and fry in batches until golden on both sides. Take out of the pan and place onto kitchen paper to keep warm. Repeat the process with the tomato slices, until they are warmed through and slightly softened and keep warm with the aubergine.

To make the dressing, roughly chop the sun dried tomatoes and crushed garlic together, then whizz them up in your blender with a tablespoon of olive oil, until smooth. Transfer to a bowl and stir in the mayonnaise to reach your desired consistency.

To assemble, place an aubergine slice on each plate. Top with a slice of tomato, then a basil leaf and a slice of cheese. Repeat with the remaining ingredients to give two layers, finishing off with a slice off aubergine on the top. Finish with a generous spoonful of dressing and arrange the rocket around each stack. Serve immediately.

MCB tip: This tastes just as good made with some Mozzarella cheese.

BAKED WHOLE VACHERIN MONT d'OR
Mont d'Or is not too far away from where I used to live in France and I was introduced to this dish by a mate who used to go there for ski trips.

We always found that this dish was a wonderful way to intro' a meal and a great conversation piece when friends arrive for dinner, particularly as not many folk had seen cheese cooked this way before. At the time of writing, this has become quite en vogue at dinner parties in the UK and still has the ability to intrigue the uninitiated.

The soft cheese, Vacherin Mont d'Or is now certified and protected by a label of origin (AoC) and is the sixth French cheese to obtain this major distinction. This requires each stage of production, from milk to finishing, to take place within its region – the Valée de Joux in the Jura foothills in the

Canton of Vaud. It lays down strict requirements that producers must respect, under the control of independent certification body. The AOC protects Vacherin Mont d'Or from imitations, assuring customers that it is a fully authentic cheese they are buying.

The recipe below is for a shared hor's d'oeuvres; something that guests can dip into before sitting down for their main meal.

Ingredients for four
- 2 x 250g Vacherin or Camembert – medium to ripe
- Garlic clove – peeled, trimmed & cut into slivers
- dry white wine or Noilly Prat
- fresh rosemary or thyme
- extra virgin olive oil
- 500g new (Anya) potatoes – scrubbed
- 125g cornichons (small gherkins) – French are best

Preparation
Pre-heat your oven to 180°C.

Place the potatoes into a pan of cold, salted water. Bring to the boil and cook for 12 – 15 minutes until tender. Drain, return to the pan and cover to keep warm.

While the potatoes are cooking, remove the cheese from the box and remove the paper wrapping. Cut a thin slice off the top of the cheese. Return the cheese to the box and place the wooden lid under the base, so you have a double box below the cheese. Pierce the top of the cheese a few times with a fine skewer, spike with the garlic slivers and drizzle with a little white wine (or Noilly) and olive oil and top each with a sprig of fresh rosemary or thyme. Place onto a baking sheet and bake in the oven until the cheese is hot and has softened all the way through.

Put the cheese, in its box, into the centre of a large serving platter. Surround with the warm potatoes, cornichons and chunks of crusty bread for dipping and serve straight away.

CAESAR SALAD
Caesar Salad all but disappeared from hotel and restaurant menus some years back. This was specifically due a political scare about salmonella in chickens and eggs in the UK. At this time, it was not deemed to be good practice to use raw eggs in un-cooked sauces. However, in recent years this dish has started to make a bit of a renaissance – often supported by a proprietary sauce i.e. Caesar Cardini's, who is said to have invented the original dish. It is essential that you use crispy lettuce for this recipe.

Ingredients for four
- 1 cos lettuce – roughly chopped
- 2 little gem lettuce – roughly chopped
- 1 large handful of rocket leaves
- 1 small tin/jar of anchovies – drained and cut into fine strips

For the croutons
- 150g bread – cut into 1cm cubes
- 25ml corn oil
- 25g unsalted butter
- salt & freshly ground black pepper

For the dressing
- 2 egg yolks – free range
- 100g fresh parmesan cheese – finely grated
- 1 clove of garlic – crushed
- 150ml olive oil
- 1 lemon – juice only

First make the croutons. Place a heavy bottomed frying pan over a medium-high flame. When heated through, add the olive oil and butter. Once the butter has bubbled, add the cubes of bread and fry until golden. Remove the croutons from the pan and drain on some kitchen paper.

To make the dressing, place all of the ingredients, including 50g of the grated parmesan into a large bowl and whisk thoroughly. If you do not have a refrigerator on board, then this must be done at the very last minute.

Toss the lettuce in the dressing. The idea is to coat the leaves evenly with the dressing to give them a beautiful glazed effect. Arrange the leaves on individual bowls and arrange strips of anchovy over the top and add the croutons. Sprinkle the remaining parmesan over the salad to finish. Thin slivers of parmesan also work extremely well with this dish.

MCB tip: This dish can easily be enhanced by the addition of some thin slices of Parma or Serrano ham or some delicate strips of smoked chicken breast. I like to pan fry some Bavarian Smoked Ham and place a couple of crisp rashers over the top of the salad.

You can also vary the dressing, depending on what you have on board. Try using some Greek yoghurt, for a nice creamy texture and finish.

CLASSIC PRAWN COCKTAIL

Back in the 'swinging sixties' it was "certainement de rigueur" to have a prawn cocktail as your 'starter'. Sadly the dish went out of fashion; however it still makes a wonderful starter/appetizer, most of which can be prepared in advance, including the classic Marie Rose sauce. So here is my Retro Cuisine version of this wonderful dish, which can also be made quite sexy by garnishing with sliced lobster tails, langoustine or caviar.

Ingredients for six
- 1 crisp green lettuce – cos or romaine
- half cucumber – peeled, de-seeded and finely chopped
- 750g cooked peeled prawns (shrimp)
- 6 large whole cooked prawns trimmed, tail on
- 1 lemon – cut into 6 wedges
- salt, ground black pepper & cayenne pepper
- thinly sliced buttered brown bread – crusts removed

Marie-Rose Sauce
- 4 heaped tbsp mayonnaise
- 1 heaped tbsp ketchup
- splash of Worcestershire sauce
- 1 tbsp brandy (not cooking)
- juice of one lemon

Preparation

For the sauce, simply mix the ingredients together, until they are fully blended together. Add a little lemon juice, salt and black pepper to taste.

Drain the prawns and spread them out over a plate or baking sheet. Sprinkle with the remaining lemon juice, salt and black pepper and allow to marinate while you prepare the lettuce.

Wash the lettuce, drain well and finely shred (chiffonade). Fill six individual glass bowls one third full with the lettuce and top with the prepared cucumber.

Drain the prawns again and fold them into the Marie-Rose sauce and spoon the mixture over the cucumber in each bowl. Very lightly sprinkle over a little cayenne and a light twist of the pepper mill.

To finish off, drape a whole prawn over the rim of each bowl.

Place the bowls onto a doylied under-plate with a discreet wedge of lemon and a teaspoon.

MCB tip: I have always made it a golden rule never to use frozen prawns for this dish, although sometimes you will find that needs must.

FYI: It is always nice to serve this dish lightly chilled, so if you have the space, place the finished bowls into your refrigerator for half an hour before serving, or build at the last minute if you are stuck for fridge space.

CONCH FRITTERS
with dipping sauce

Conch (pronounced "konk") is a common seafood throughout the Caribbean and the Florida Keys. Good quality conch should be white, with pink and orange edges. Always avoid conch with a grayish colour. Like other seafood, it should not smell fishy. If there are any dark pieces of skin, trim them off.

Because of its firm texture, conch needs to be tenderised before being cooked. This can be accomplished by placing the meat between cling film and pounding it with a meat tenderiser, but don't beat it to a pulp, smooth and flatten it to the desired thickness. Treat it like squid, either barely cook it, or cook the hell out of it. After heating briefly, conch will begin to toughen until it is essentially inedible. However, after being cooked for a while i.e. simmered in a stew for an hour, the conch should become tender again.

I suggest that you finely grind the conch through a meat grinder or food processor for this recipe.

Ingredients
- 250g conch meat (ground)
- medium onion – finely diced
- ½ red pepper – de-seeded & finely diced
- ½ green pepper – de-seeded & finely diced
- 2 sticks celery – finely diced
- 2 cloves garlic - crushed
- 100g self-raising flour
- 1 egg
- 120ml milk

- cayenne pepper
- salt & black pepper
- 1lt vegetable oil (for frying)

For the dipping sauce
- 30ml ketchup
- 30ml fresh lime juice
- 15ml mayonnaise
- 15ml hot sauce (Trappey's or similar)
- salt & pepper to taste.

Preparation
Prepare the dipping sauce first by blending all the ingredients together thoroughly. Cover with cling film and set to one side in the refrigerator.

Place a sauteuse over a medium-low flame, add a slug of vegetable oil and allow to heat through. Add the diced onion, celery, red and green peppers and cook for a couple of minutes without colour, until they become soft. Add the prepared conch, stir to blend the ingredients and cook for another three minutes or so until the conch is just cooked. Remove from the heat and cool.

Take a bowl and mix the flour, cayenne, egg and milk and whisk to create a thick batter. Add a pinch of salt and a couple of grinds of black pepper, whisk again. Fold in the cooled conch and vegetable mixture and blend thoroughly.

Take a medium sized saucepan and add one litre of vegetable oil and place over a medium flame and heat to 185°C, do not leave the pan of oil unattended at any time. (See Deep Frying in the Glossary of Cookery Terminology – Page 241). While the oil is heating, get yourself set up and ready to do some deep frying. You will need some absorbent kitchen paper, a lasagne dish or similar, spider to remove fritters from the hot oil and a couple of tablespoons for shaping the fritters.

When the oil is up to temperature, gently place a heaped tablespoon of the conch batter, one at a time, into the hot oil. When the fritters pop back to the surface, roll them around in the oil to brown them evenly on both sides. Remove and drain on the kitchen paper. Season immediately with Creole Seasoning and serve hot on absorbent paper, with the dipping sauce on the side.

MCB tip: Superyacht chef Victoria Allman has a great recipe, called Frankie's Conch Salad in her fabulous book Sea Fare A Chef's Journey Across The Ocean. It is said to have great restorative capabilities following a heavy night out on the local rum!

FYI: Conch harvesting is currently illegal in Florida, so any you buy in that State will have been imported.

CRAB and RICOTTA TARTLETS
We are totally blessed living here on the Isle of Wight, to be able to buy Ventnor Brown Crabs, local fresh lobsters and 'catch of the day' fresh fish from Jeff and Cheryl Blake at The Ventnor Fish Haven on the south coast of the island. You need to use the white meat from a freshly cooked crab weighing in around 500g, if not, look for some frozen white crab meat and defrost thoroughly in your fridge before using.

Ricotta is a healthy cheese, as it is made from the whey, the liquid separated from the curds in cheese production. It is a fresh cheese, as it is not ripened as most other cheeses. Like many fresh cheeses, it is highly perishable.

Ingredients for four
- 300g short pastry – (see Basics – Page 233)
- butter for greasing
- 4 basil leaves
- 100g baby spinach leaves
- 4 cherry tomatoes – sliced
- nutmeg – freshly grated
- 100g ricotta cheese
- 75g white crab meat
- 1 tsp whole-grain mustard
- 2 egg yolks – free range
- 100ml double cream
- sea salt & freshly ground black pepper

Preparation
Preheat your oven to 200°C

Remove your prepared short pastry from the fridge and bring up to room temperature. Lightly dust your work surface and rolling pin. Roll out your pastry to approx' 3mm thick. Cut out rounds big enough to cover the base and sides of four 10cm tartlet tins. Line the pastry cases with baking parchment (greaseproof paper or tin foil will do) and fill with dried baking beans. Bake blind for ten minutes in the middle of your pre-heated oven. Remove the paper and beans. Reduce the oven heat down to 180°C and return the tartlets to the oven for a further ten minutes to dry out and start to turn a light golden brown. Remove the tartlets from your oven and place to one side.

Tweak the oven temperature back up to 200°C.

Heat a frying pan over a low flame until hot, then add a spoon of water and heat through. Add the spinach and cover with a lid and cook until the spinach has just wilted, this will only take a few seconds. Remove from the pan and drain well. Squeeze out any surplus liquid from the spinach and place onto a chopping board. Roughly chop and place and place to one side.

Place the egg yolks, cream and mustard into a bowl, season with salt and freshly ground black pepper and whisk together. Add the ricotta, crab meat, prepared spinach, shredded basil leaves and mix together thoroughly. Season to taste with a little salt and freshly ground black pepper and mix again. Spoon the ricotta mixture into the bottom of your tartlet cases, spread to cover the base and top with tomato slices.

Transfer the tartlets to the oven and bake for 20 – 30 minutes, or until golden brown and bubbling. Remove and cool slightly before serving.

These lovely tartlets are equally good served cold for lunch or cut into quarter wedges and, using one or two wedges per person, serve them as a starter for dinner.

ENSALADA de MOJAMA
The nice clean lines of this dish make it an attractive, light and interesting starter on a warm summer evening. Most folk will not have heard of Mojama, which is cured, air-dried tuna. It is predominately produced in the south of Spain along the La Costa de la Luz. It is thought that the name 'mojama' is typically derived from the Arabic/Moroccan word 'musama', which means to dry.

Mojama can be served as tapas or is becoming equally popular served as part of a plated hors d'oeuvres/salad. Its appearance is similar to Parma/Serrano ham and it also has similar lasting qualities and should keep, if well wrapped, in the fridge for eight to twelve weeks. Mojama starter salads can work really well with caperberries, anchovies or piquillo peppers, which will really stimulate the palate.

Ingredients for four
- 200g mojama – approx 6 slices per person
- 4 x medium free range eggs – soft boiled, refreshed, shelled & quartered
- 8 asparagus spears – prepared, poached & refreshed
- 12 black olives – pitted & cut in half lengthways
- 250g cherry plum tomatoes – halved lengthways
- salad leaves – peppery works well
- 4 tbsp lemon mayonnaise (juice from half lemon)
- 1 lemon (small) – quartered & trimmed

Preparation
The mayonnaise needs to be slightly runny. This is achieved by the addition of the lemon juice and maybe a little boiling water, added little-by-little until the desired consistency is achieved.

To build the dish, strategically place a few salad leaves onto large white plates, add the asparagus, cherry tomato halves, olive halves and egg quarters. Discreetly drizzle over sufficient lemon mayonnaise. Top with the slices of mojama and finish with a lemon wedge to serve.

FENNEL and FETA SALAD
with pomegranate seeds and sumac
I only discovered Sumac very recently, with its stunning burgundy colour and a delicious tangy, sour, slightly salty flavour. Sumac powder is the ground berries of the sumac bush; native to the Middle East, which is used liberally sprinkled over rice in Turkey and Iran, and also used as a dry seasoning on salads in the Middle East.

When used to flavour meat or fish, the sour flavour of sumac mellows slightly on cooking and is a great flavour enhancer. Some people say that Sumac is a useful replacement if you run out of lemons. You can also use sumac as a dry seasoning for vegetable, meat or fish kebabs on your barbeque.

Ingredients for four
- ½ pomegranate or 100g pk of pomegranate seeds
- 2 medium sized heads of fennel – trimmed, retaining the leaves
- 1½ tbsp extra virgin olive oil
- 1 dsp sumac
- juice of one lemon
- tarragon leaves
- 2 tbsp flat leaf parsley – roughly chopped
- 100g feta cheese – crumbled
- salt & black pepper

Preparation
First of all comes the tricky part of releasing the pomegranate seeds from the fruit. I have seen this done in loadsa different ways, but find the best is to cut the pomegranate across 'the equator', hold the flat side of the fruit against your hand and, over a large bowl, hit the back (rounded side) with a wooden spoon. If you hit it too hard, you'll bruise the seeds. Usually the seeds will just fall out; however you will need to pick out the creamy yellow skin which may fall out, as this is quite bitter and will spoil the appearance.

Remove the leaves from the fennel, keeping a few to one side for garnishing. Trim the root end, making sure that you leave enough in place to hold the slices together. Cut the fennel in half end-to-end and slice very thinly.

Take a medium sized bowl and mix the olive oil, lemon juice, sumac, herbs plus some salt and pepper. Add the slices of fennel, stir and coat with the marinade. Check for seasoning, but you must remember that the Feta cheese is quite salty, so easy does it.

Using a nice white serving plate or lipped soup bowl, layer the fennel slices, then the feta and pomegranate seeds. Garnish with shredded fennel leaves and lightly sprinkle over with sumac and serve immediately.

MCB tip: This dish makes a great individual, plated salad starter.

GINGER and CHILLI SPIKED PRAWNS

This is one of Emma's fabulous recipes, which she tells me has evolved over the last ten years, depending on what ingredients she has to hand. After a recent cooking and culture trip to Venice, she has come up with this definitive version.

Great big plump fresh prawns are what you are after from the local fish market. If you are serving this as a starter, then use three large prawns per person, for lunch - 5 would be plenty. Guests should be encouraged to slurp and suck the prawns as the flavour is fantastic. Finger bowls and copious napkins will be necessary, plus maybe a bowl to put the shells in. Not all guests like shell on prawns so if you want a slightly more sophisticated version remove the shells and de-vein before cooking.

Ingredients for four
- 20 x large prawns or tiger prawns – shell on
- fresh root ginger – thumb size
- 2 cloves of garlic
- 2 lemons – 1 zested, the other cut into wedges
- fresh parsley – small bunch
- 2 small red chillies (dried chilli flakes will do)
- olive oil
- rocket Leaves

Preparation
Take a good small sharp knife and carefully peel the ginger and garlic, then dice it as finely as you can and put to one side.

Prepare the fresh chillies by topping and tailing them, slitting them along their length – scrape out the seeds and discard, then slice very finely. Remove the stalks from the parsley and finely chop. Wash and dry a lemon and, using the finest side of a grater to remove the zest. Use a knife to scrape it all away from the grater and add to the garlic and chilli mix.

Take a heavy based frying pan and place over a low flame. Drizzle in enough olive oil to cover the base of the pan, add the garlic, ginger, lemon zest and chilli. – the idea being to let the flavours infuse into the oil as it gently warms up. Let the oil gently bubble for a couple of minutes, whilst just keeping things moving around the pan with a wooden spoon. Turn up the heat to medium and add the prawns to the pan; you can do this in a couple of batches, if necessary.

Give the pan a good shake and cook for about 3 minutes per side, until they have changed colour to pink. Arrange on a plate, pour over the pan juices and sprinkle with the chopped parsley. Serve with some dressed rocket leaves and freshly baked ciabatta.

To serve as a starter
Use large white plates if possible. Take a small pile of rocket leaves scrunch them slightly in your hand and place in the middle of the plate in a small mound, drizzle with a little olive oil. Pile the prawns on top, spoon over some pan juices and then drizzle the remainder, in a spiral, around the plate, finish with lemon wedges and parsley.

MCB tip: Always wash your hands well after preparing chillies and do not rub your eyes.

GREEK SALAD
There are so many different variations of this dish, but I have found that this one works well. You can always play around a little with the ingredients, but Feta cheese and black olives are a must. This is my variation on a theme, which I originally put together when I lived in France. It always went down well as a starter at dinner parties or as a lunchtime dish served with local 'boule' (flat, round country bread) and some chilled rosé. Although you have to bear in mind that in France, lunch usually lasted around three hours, so we drank quite a lot of rosé.

Ingredients for four
- 200g Feta cheese – cut into 2 cm dice
- 50g black olives – pitted
- 100g mixed peppery salad leaves – include some rocket & fresh coriander
- 3 firm red tomatoes – cut into 2 cm dice
- 1 cucumber – de-seeded & cut into 2 cm dice
- 1 red pepper – de-seeded & diced
- ½ red onion – finely sliced
- 6 tbsp extra virgin olive oil
- 2 tbsp raspberry vinegar
- 2 tsp Dijon mustard
- salt & freshly ground black pepper

To start off, prepare the salad dressing. Take a bowl and add the Dijon mustard, black pepper, pinch of salt and the raspberry vinegar. Mix these ingredients with a fork or small whisk, then gradually incorporate the olive oil and mix thoroughly.

Divide the salad leaves between four bowls or plates and mound up the leaves to a dome towards the centre of the dish. Mix all the remaining salad ingredients together in a bowl and distribute over the salad leaves and top off with the olives and Feta.

To finish off your master-piece, give the salad dressing a final whisk and drizzle over the four salads.

MCB tip: This dish is also lovely served with a couple of scrunched up slices of Parma or Serrano ham over the top for the non-vegies!

LANGOUSTINE RISOTTO

Ingredients for four
- 16 langoustine – uncooked
- 900ml fish stock (fonds or bouillon) – hot

- olive oil
- salt & freshly ground black pepper
- 2 shallots – finely chopped
- 2 cloves garlic – crushed
- 400g aborio or carnaroli rice
- 25ml Noilly Prat or dry vermouth
- 25ml dry white wine (nothing cheap)
- 75g unsalted butter
- 1 lemon – juiced
- 75g fresh parmesan – finely grated
- fresh basil – small bunch

Preparation

Place a large pan of water over a high flame, bring to the boil and add a good pinch of salt. Blanch the langoustines for 2-3 minutes. Drain and, when cool enough to handle, remove the heads, wash, drain, cover and refrigerate.

To make the risotto, place a shallow heavy-based pan (sauteuse) over a medium-low flame. Melt the butter and add the shallots and half the garlic, cover with a lid and sweat for a few minutes until softened, without taking on any colour. Add the rice and stir for a couple of minutes to coat the rice with the butter. Add the wine and cook until the liquid is absorbed.

Add the hot fish stock ladle-by-ladle, stirring continuously, allowing the liquid to be absorbed each time, before adding more stock, until it is almost completely absorbed. When the rice is just becoming tender and creamy, add the vermouth, the remaining butter and a small squeeze of lemon juice. Once the vermouth is absorbed, sprinkle in two thirds of the parmesan, stirring continuously. Taste and season with a little salt and black pepper, if required.

Heat a couple of slugs of olive oil in a heavy based frying pan, place over a medium flame and add the remaining garlic and the langoustines and fry for a couple of minutes without colour.

Spoon the creamy risotto into warmed bowls and arrange the langoustines neatly on top. Finish off by sprinkling with the remaining parmesan and some torn basil leaves.

RISOTTO

Risotto is a traditional Italian rice dish and is one of the most common ways of cooking rice in Italy. It's origins are in the north, specifically in the beautiful Piedmont, Lombardy and Veneto regions. It is one of the pillars of Milanese cuisine.

A round, high-starch, medium grain rice is used to make risotto. Such rice has the ability to absorb liquids and to release starch, so it is stickier than long grain varieties. The principal varieties used in Italy are Carnaroli and Vialone Nano and to a lesser degree Arborio.

Risotto is one of those dishes that folk tend to be wary of making, because someone told them it was difficult. For sure, it's not easy to perfect and you can finish up with a savoury, sticky rice pudding if you are not careful. But, like many such dishes, there really is not a great deal to it if you carefully follow the recipe and instructions on your packet of risotto rice.

MARINATED ROMANO PEPPERS
with buffalo mozzarella

My favourite peppers in the whole wide world are the sweet flavoured Pimiento Romano (Romano peppers). My darling wife introduced me to these peppers a few years back, when she stuffed them with roasted Mediterranean vegetables, her special couscous, topped with brie or mozzarella and then baked them in the oven. I have played around with her idea and created a fabulous summer lunch dish, served with some crispy salad leaves dressed with a citrus vinaigrette and of course, served with a nicely chilled Rosé from Provence.

Ingredients for four
- 4 romano peppers
- 2 tbsp coriander – finely chopped
- 2 tbsp flat leaf parsley – finely chopped
- 1 clove of garlic – crushed
- virgin olive oil
- 2 tbsp white wine vinegar
- 100g peppery leaves
- 250g buffalo mozzarella
- sea salt & ground black pepper

Preparation
Pre-heat your oven to 225°C.

Drizzle a little oil on a roasting tray and brush over the surface, so that it has a light covering. Add the peppers and drizzle with a couple of tablespoons of the olive oil, sprinkle with the sea salt and black pepper. Place into your oven and roast for around fifteen minutes or until the skin becomes coloured.

While the peppers are roasting, take a bowl and add the crushed garlic, vinegar, chopped coriander, parsley and approx' 75ml olive oil and mix thoroughly. If the seasoning is not quite right, add a little extra salt and ground pepper (I sometimes add a little lemon juice).

Place the warm peppers into a lasagne style dish, pour over the marinade and leave un-refrigerated for fifteen minutes or so to start the cooling process. Cover with cling-film, then place into your refrigerator to lightly chill.

To serve, dress your salad leaves with a slug or two of olive oil and mound them up in the middle of each plate and rest one pepper over each mound of leaves. Tear the mozzarella end-to-end into smallish chunks and add to the remaining marinade for only a few seconds. Dot the mozzarella over and around the peppers and drizzle over the remaining herb oil and finish with some chopped coriander and parsley.

MEDITERRANEAN SALAD
with basil

This is a great little lunch time salad, or ideal as a starter for one of those special dinners for guests, when you're at anchor watching the sun go down in a secluded bay in the Agean (or anywhere else in the world for that matter!).

Ingredients for four
- 225g fusilli
- 150g fine green beans
- 4 medium eggs – hard boiled, refreshed & shelled

- 4 medium, ripe vine tomatoes
- 200g tin good quality tuna in oil – drained & roughly flaked
- 25g anchovy fillets – drained & split head to tail
- 50g black olives – pitted
- 25g basil leaves
- 1 tbsp capers
- salt & ground black pepper

Dressing
- 6 tbsp extra virgin olive oil
- 2 tbsp white wine vinegar or lemon juice
- 1 clove garlic – crushed
- ½ tsp Dijon mustard
- 2 tbsp shredded basil
- salt & black pepper to taste

Preparation
Place all of the ingredients for the dressing into a small bowl and whisk thoroughly, season with salt and pepper to taste and put to one side to allow the flavours to develop.

Place a small saucepan of water over a high flame. Once the water starts to boil, add a little salt and the green beans and blanch them for about 3 minutes. Drain, retaining the water, and refresh the beans in some iced water.

Return the 'bean water' to the saucepan, top up a little if necessary, bring back to the boil and add a couple of slugs of olive oil. Add the pasta and cook until 'al dente', drain well, refresh, drain again, place into a bowl and add a little olive oil and stir well, this will help stop the pasta from sticking together. Cover and set to one side.

While the pasta is cooking, place the green beans onto a chopping board and top & tail them and then cut them in two.

Using four appropriate sized, wide-rimmed soup bowls. Cut the vine tomatoes into thin slices and arrange on the base of each bowl, grind over some black pepper and moisten with a little of the dressing and cover with some of the basil leaves. Sprinkle over some of the green beans and moisten with a little more of the dressing. Toss the pasta in some of the dressing and add to each bowl. Add some more of the basil leaves and the flaked tuna.

Cut the eggs into half lengthways and add two halves to the centre of each bowl. To finish off, add a few strips of anchovy, a few black olives, a few capers and the remaining basil. Drizzle each salad with a little of the remaining dressing and serve immediately.

MCB tip: If you want to add a little extra something to the salad, try adding some marinated olives from the local supermarket – alternatively, if you have time, you can always create your own bespoke flavoured olives.

MOULES GRATINÉES
There are many fabulous mussel dishes produced around the world and this is really one of the most easy to produce. Different people will tell you that this location or that produces the best mussels in the world. Some say that the treacherous northern coast of Spain produces the best, I love the wonderful large, fleshy mussels from the Dartmouth Estuary, or if you can get hold of them – New Zealand Green Lipped Mussels are absolutely gorgeous.

Ingredients for four
- 500g fresh large mussels
- 2.5cl dry white wine
- 25g unsalted butter – melted
- 1 tbsp olive oil
- 3 tbsp parmesan cheese – finely grated
- 2 cloves of garlic – finely chopped
- 2 tbsp flat leaf parsley – finely chopped
- 25g toasted pistachios – finely chopped
- 2 tbsp bread crumbs
- ground black pepper
- peppery salad leaves

Preparation

Soak the mussels in cold water for about an hour. Scrub them thoroughly and scrape off any barnacles with the back of a knife, remove the gritty beards and discard. Some of the mussels will have opened, so tap them with the back of a knife; throw away any that fail the close or any with broken shells.

Take a large heavy based pan and place over a high flame. Add the white wine and bring to the boil. Immediately add the prepared mussels. Cover with a lid and place over a medium-high flame and steam for about 5 minutes, or until the mussels have opened.

While the mussels are cooking, take a small bowl and add the melted butter, olive oil, parsley, chopped garlic and black pepper – mix well. In a separate container, mix the parmesan, pistachios and breadcrumbs together.

Drain the mussels and throw away any that have not opened and allow to cool a little. Remove the top shell from each mussel, discard, and loosen the flesh attached to the bottom part of the shell.

Arrange the flesh filled shells into a flameproof dish, trying to arrange them so that stay as level as possible. Pre-heat your grill to high. If you don't have an effective grill on board, then a high setting on your oven should do.

Take a teaspoon and add a small amount of the garlic mixture to each mussel, pressing down lightly on each. Sprinkle each with a little of the breadcrumb mixture. Place under the grill (broiler) for a minute or so, or until they are sizzling and the tops turn golden brown.

Serve the mussels in their shells, resting on some salad leaves.

MCB tip: You can replace the garlic mixture with pesto, thinned with a little dry white wine.

OPEN GOAT'S CHEESE PASTY

This recipe is a bit of a variation on a theme. I love the oozy, creamy texture of the Vacherin Mont d'Or and the grilled goat's cheese in my Salad Corrèzienne. I have prepared a similar dish before, as an open puff-pastry tart with spinach, which works really well, so when one of our students suggested a cheese pasty, we thought – why not? It took a bit of while for us to get it right, as the goat's cheese has to be of a certain texture, so you will need to get hold of some that is not too soft. Goat's cheese cylinders, with a nice rind on them work really well and I always use ready-made puff pastry, which you can pick-up pre-rolled, although for this recipe, you are better off buying a slab and rolling it yourself.

Ingredients for four
- 250g ready-made puff pastry
- 2 cylinders of soft goat's cheese
- 1 egg – beaten for egg wash
- fresh herbs – young rosemary shoots or thyme
- peppery leaves
- olive oil

Preparation
Pre-heat your over to 220°C.

Lightly dust a clean work surface and roll out your puff pastry to approximately a quarter of a centimetre thick and cut into 4 x fourteen centimetre squares. The size will depend on the diameter of the cheese and the length you cut the cylinders. I usually cut each cylinder into two pieces of around five centimetres each, which is ample per portion.

Place the half cylinders into the centre of each square of pastry. Using a pastry brush, paint the edges of the pastry with the egg wash. Crimp the corners of the pastry together, pressing firmly to make a tight parcel around the cheese. The pastry should come up to the top of the cheese, leaving the top open. Very lightly drizzle the top of the cheese with a little olive oil and place a couple of baby sprigs of rosemary or thyme over the top of each one.

Place the pastries onto a prepared baking sheet and bake in your pre-heated oven for approximately fifteen minutes until the pastry turns golden brown and the cheese has gone soft.

Serve hot with a few dressed peppery leaves.

OYSTERS ROCKEFELLER

Oysters Rockefeller is 'the' classic cooked oyster dish. John Davison Rockefeller Senior (1839 – 1937), was an American industrialist and philanthropist, who revolutionized the petroleum industry. He had always believed, since he was a child, that his one purpose in life was to make as much money as possible. He became the world's richest man and the first U.S. dollar billionaire.

Preparing oysters
Oysters should be kept in a cold storage area or refrigerator to keep them moist and alive. The shells should be tightly shut; this indicates their freshness.

Many people have pre-conceived ideas that there is some sort of mysticism to opening an oyster. Admittedly, when you first try it you may not find it too easy. However, after a bit of practice and using the 'right' piece of kit, you should develop your own technique in no time.

Scrub off any grit or sand from the shells. Oysters should be carefully opened, using a special oyster knife to ensure that the inside of the shell is not scratched. Wrap one hand in a thick tea towel and hold the deep, rounded part of the shell in your hand with the flatter shell on top.

Take an oyster knife in your other hand and push the point of the knife into the hinged end of the oyster, located at the narrowest point. Work the knife backwards and forwards between the two halves of the shell to break the hinge. Twist the knife to lever the top shell upwards and remove, trying not to let any fragments fall onto the oyster and keeping the bottom shell level, so as not to lose any of the juice. Pick out any little pieces of shell that might have broken off into the oyster. Slide the point of the knife under the oyster to sever the ligament that joins the oyster to the bottom shell.

Oysters are usually served by the half dozen on a bed of crushed ice, accompanied by quarters of brown bread and butter, wedges of lemon, ground black pepper and maybe a little chilli vinegar.

MCB tip #1:   Do not attempt to open oysters with such things as kitchen or steak knives. A friend of mine who did this recently, finished up having stitches on both sides of his hand after the blade had been removed – he assures me it was a very painful experience. I offered to buy him a proper oyster knife, but he told me he has gone off opening oysters for a while!

MCB tip #2:   Oysters are usually sold as 1s, 2s and 3s, according to their relative size.

Ingredients for six
- 400g course sea salt (+ extra to serve)
- 24 medium sized oysters (2's) – opened, drained & loosened
- 50g unsalted butter
- 2 shallots – finely chopped
- 400g baby spinach leaves – wilted, drained & finely chopped
- 4 tbsp celery leaves – finely chopped
- 6 tbsp white breadcrumbs
- 4 tbsp flat leaf parsley - chopped
- chilli sauce (Tobasco or similar)
- 3 tsp Pernod
- salt & ground black pepper
- 2 medium sized lemons – cut into wedges

Preparation
Pre-heat your oven to 220°C.

Take a large baking sheet and prepare a bed of course salt. Set the flesh filled, rounded half-oyster shells on the bed of salt, which will keep them steady.

Take a small saucepan and place over a medium flame. Melt the butter and add the chopped shallots, reduce the flame to low and cook them for 2 – 3 minutes until they are softened. Add the spinach, chopped parsley and celery leaves and cook gently for another two or three minutes. Season with a little salt, black pepper and chilli sauce.

Very lightly drizzle a little Pernod over each oyster. Spoon the stuffing over the oysters, spread to a thin topping. Sprinkle the breadcrumbs over the top and bake in the oven for approx' five minutes, until bubbling and golden brown.

Serve on a heated platter on a bed of coarse salt with some lemon wedges.

MCB tip: It is said, by some, that there is only one wine to drink with oysters and that is Champagne, although I would go for a good Montrachet. However, with this particular dish, it is a difficult one to select the right wine, because the flavour of the Pernod will predominate. Personally, I love this dish without the Pernod, but I had to go authentic.

PIRI-PIRI PRAWNS
Prawns (shrimps) are usually very popular with most guests and are wonderfully versatile. This is a very simple dish to make, however the golden rule when cooking shellfish applies – do not overcook, or the prawns will turn chewy. I usually peel the prawns, so that they draw down more flavour from the liquid. This is a very spicy (hot) dish and can be easily adjusted by adding less chilli.

Ingredients for four
- 1 tbsp sunflower oil
- 2 cloves of garlic – peeled & finely chopped
- 3 ripe tomatoes – skinned, de-seeded & chopped (concassé)
- 1 fresh red chilli or tsp chilli flakes
- 1 fresh green chilli – split, de-seeded & chopped
- 16 cooked king prawns (jumbo shrimp) - peeled & de-veined
- 4 fresh king prawns – shell on
- 1 dsp tomato purée
- 2.5cl dry white wine
- 1 tsp lemon juice
- 2 spring onions – trimmed and chopped
- fresh coriander - chopped
- coarse salt & ground black pepper
- fresh coriander

Preparation
Place a medium sized heavy based frying pan over a medium/low fame, add the oil and when heated through, add the garlic, cover with a lid and cook for one minute, without colour.

Add the tomatoes, red and green chilli, lemon juice, wine, tomato purée, a pinch of salt and a turn of black pepper. Cook, stirring occasionally, for five minutes. Check for seasoning and adjust to taste. Add the prawns and heat through.

Ladle the mixture into heated serving dishes or bowls and garnish with one king prawn per bowl and top with the chopped spring onion and some fresh coriander.

PRAWN, MANGO & AVOCADO SALAD
with Thai coconut dressing

Fresh, pretty and full of flavour, this is easy and looks stunning on the plate, perfect for hot lazy days onboard. As with many of the recipes that we use on our courses, this can be served as a starter or a lunch dish.

Ingredients for four (lunch)
- 2 ready to eat avocados
- 2 ready to eat mangos
- 16 cooked shell on tiger prawns (king prawns or langoustines are fine)
- handful of rocket leaves or similar
- fresh coriander – finely chopped

For the Dressing:
- 250ml thick coconut milk
- 1 small red chilli – de-seeded & finely chopped
- 1 tbsp fresh coriander
- 2 tbsp lime juice
- 1 tbsp fish sauce

Preparation

Combine dressing ingredients in a screw top jar and shake well to combine or place in a bowl and whisk together, cover and refrigerate.

Prepare the avocados by slicing in half end-to-end. Carefully remove stone from the avocado and discard. Place each half cut side down on chopping board and cut lengthways down through the green skin until the knife meets the flesh. Carefully ease off the skin endeavouring to keep the avocado as intact and neat as possible. Cut each half lengthways into slices, sprinkle with lime juice to prevent the flesh from discolouring, cover and refrigerate.

Prepare the mango by slicing in half lengthways as close as possible to the large elliptical central stone. Place each half, skin-side down on to a chopping board and using a sharp flexible knife (a fish knife is remarkably good for this), slice the flesh away from the skin, again keeping the flesh as intact and as neat as possible. Cut lengthways into slices, trying to keep the width of each slice consistent and equal to those that you have just done with the avocado.

Finally prepare cooked shell on prawns; carefully peel the shell away from the tail, leaving the head and feelers intact.

I usually serve this dish on white rectangular plates 25 x 12.5cm. Making a fan of the sliced mango in opposite corners, overlap half-way down the mango with strips of avocado. I scrunch up the rocket into a mound in the centre and top with a mini-salsa from the remaining mango and avocado, which I then top with the prawns.

Whisk or shake the dressing briefly to amalgamate ingredients and carefully dribble attractively over the prawns and fruit. Scatter over a little rocket and the coriander – chopped or leaves.

ROASTED PORTOBELLO MUSHROOMS
with Taleggio and fresh herbs

Portobello (portobella or portabella) mushrooms are a 'brand name', dreamt up by marketeers to raise the image, profile and sales of large, open field mushrooms. Taleggio is an Italian cheese with a strong aroma, but its flavour is comparatively milky with an unusual fruity tang; this cheese melts and spreads beautifully over the top of the mushrooms.

Ingredients for four
- 4 Portobello mushrooms
- 1 x 200g Taleggio cheese
- 75g button mushrooms – finely chopped
- 1 tbsp thyme, basil & parsley – roughly chopped
- ½ lemon
- 1 shallot – finely chopped
- 1 clove garlic – crushed
- 200g baby spinach leaves – wash & shake
- peppery salad leaves
- good quality olive oil
- salt & freshly ground black pepper

Preparation
Pre-heat your oven to 200°C.

Place a large pan over a low flame and add two or three table spoons of water. Add the spinach leaves, cover with a lid and allow to take on some heat until they start to wilt. Remove from the heat, drain well and then squeeze out any surplus liquid. Allow to cool a little, place onto a chopping board, shred with a sharp knife and place into a bowl.

Trim around the top of the open edge of the portobello mushrooms and remove the stalks. Cut a thin sliver off the bottom of the mushrooms, so they will sit flat on a plate. Place a large, heavy based frying pan over a medium flame, heat through and add a couple of slugs of olive oil. Add the mushrooms and cook the underside for a couple of minutes until the bottom of the mushrooms start to take on some colour. Remove from the pan and place them into lightly oiled oven-proof dish. Drizzle a little olive oil over each mushroom and season with a little sea salt and freshly ground black pepper.

Take a clean heavy based frying pan and place over a medium-low flame. Add a little olive oil and the chopped shallot and crushed garlic, cook for two minutes without colour. Add the chopped mushrooms, cover with a lid and cook for two or three minutes, remove the lid and add the spinach, chopped herbs, a mini-squeeze of lemon juice. Season with salt and black pepper.

Spoon the spinach mixture into the four mushrooms and allow to cool a little.

Trim the outer skin from the Tallegio and cut into 1/2 cm slices. Place one slice of each mushroom and pop your baking sheet into the pre-heated oven. Allow around fifteen minutes for the mushrooms to cook through, depending on their size. The Tallegio will melt evenly over the top of the spinach and mushroom mix.

Remove from the oven and serve immediately, garnished with some dressed peppery salad leaves.

MCB tip: These stuffed mushrooms are great as a main course garnish.

SALAD NIÇOISE

This is my last 'classic' salad in this section and to get the very best results from this dish, the Niçoise salad should be prepared using thinly cut, fresh tuna steaks.

This dish makes an excellent lunch time meal and if you want, you can always buy larger tuna steaks for the crew with a real appetite. The fish can be cooked in the galley on a ridged griddle pan, to enhance your guests' visual plate experience.

Ingredients for four
- 4 x 120g fresh tuna steaks (cut thin)
- 400g new potatoes – cooked & quartered
- 150g French beans – blanched, refreshed & drained
- 1 bag of mixed lettuce leaves
- 4 firm, ripe plum tomatoes – quartered
- 2 x little gem lettuce hearts – quartered lengthways
- 1 x small red onion – finely sliced
- 4 x eggs – hard boiled, refreshed, shelled & cut in quarters lengthways
- 75g black olives – pitted

Salad dressing
- 8 tablespoons olive oil
- 2 tablespoons white wine vinegar
- ½ lemon – juiced
- 2 tablespoons flat leaf parsley – finely chopped
- 1 clove of garlic – crushed
- salt & freshly ground black pepper

Preparation

Take a lasagne dish or similar and add the olive oil, white wine vinegar, lemon juice, chopped parsley, garlic, salt and pepper and mix together thoroughly.

Place your tuna steaks into the marinade and immediately turn them over, so that both sides are coated. Cover with cling film or tin foil and refrigerate for an hour or so, turning the steaks every now and again, so that the acid in the marinade starts to 'cook' them on both sides.

Arrange the salad leaves onto four plates or bowls. Position the quartered eggs and black olives over the salad, then the remaining salad ingredients and cooked beans.

Heat your griddle pan over a medium to high flame so that it takes on a good deal of heat. Remove the tuna from the marinade and drain away excess oil. Cook the steaks for 1 -2 minutes on either side, this depends on the thickness and how your guests like their fish cooked. However, tuna cooked so that the middle is still 'pink' is often the norm. Over-cooked tuna steak has all the eating characteristics of a Wellington Boot.

Neatly place a cooked tuna steak on the top of each salad and finish the dish by drizzling a little olive oil over the tuna.

SALT COD FISH CAKES
with aoli

Since the very first EMC course, we have always included a demonstration and practical session on 'Luxury Fish Cakes'. From a training perspective, this covers a broad range of skills, processes and techniques i.e. fish quality points, filleting, skinning, pin-boning and poaching suprèmes of salmon. This is followed by the process of the blending and balance of different composites in the filling, the shaping and size of the product, then the panéing (bread crumbing) of the fish cakes, before finally shallow frying them and presenting them for service. Some of this will become clear from the recipe below.

I decided to include this salt cod recipe because you will usually be able to find dried salt cod in many areas throughout the Caribbean and Mediterranean - it is very popular in Spain, where it is called Bacalao. This dish is great for lunch, sundowners or used as a 'different' starter.

Salt cod can be kept for months under the right conditions. It has become an integral part of the cuisine of many nations, thanks to its common historic use as a staple on board ships and in the colonies. The flavour is radically different from fresh fish, as is the texture. You will often see it in such dishes as soups, stews, tapenades and the popular dip known as Brandade of Salt Cod.

Ingredients for six

- 450g salt cod – cut into four pieces
- 300ml fresh milk
- 450g floury potatoes – peeled
- 4 spring onions – trimmed & finely chopped
- 2 tbsp extra virgin olive oil
- 4 tbsp chopped fresh parsley
- juice of ½ lemon
- 4 eggs (free range) – beaten
- plain flour – for pané
- 100g breadcrumbs – made from stale bread
- sunflower oil
- salt & ground black pepper

- lemon wedges
- salad leaves to serve
- 1 mixture of Aioli (see Basics – Page 221)

Preparation

Soak the salt cod in cold water for at least twenty four hours. You will need to change the water two or three times during this period. The dried fish should swell up as it rehydrates. Drain well and dry out on kitchen paper.

Cut the potatoes into roast potato sized pieces and boil in lightly salted water, until you can pierce them easily with a small sharp knife. Drain and return to the pan, cover with a lid and place over a high flame for a few seconds, shaking the pan vigorously until the potatoes go 'fluffy'. Remove from the heat and mash thoroughly with a fork or potato masher.

Pour the milk into a shallow pan, place over a medium flame and bring to a gentle simmer. Add the cod and poach gently for approximately fifteen minutes, or until the fish flakes easily. Remove the cod and drain thoroughly. Remove any skin and bones which may be present.

Flake the cod into a bowl, add a few tablespoons of the mashed potato and beat them together with a wooden spoon. Add the olive oil and lemon juice and mix in thoroughly, before gradually adding the remainder of the mashed potato, stirring thoroughly to blend the ingredients. Check for seasoning – you may need to add a little salt and pepper, however the fish should provide sufficient 'saltiness' on its own. Sprinkle in the spring onions and two tablespoons of chopped parsley. Add the yolk of one egg to the mixture and stir thoroughly one final time. Cover with cling film and place in your fridge until the mix firms up.

Remove the potato mixture from the fridge and shape into about sixteen balls. Using the heal of your hand, gently flatten each ball into a disc shape.

Now you are ready to pané your fish cakes, so you will need to have everything ready before you start. Place approximately 125g of flour into a bowl and lightly season. Place the beaten eggs into another bowl, add a little milk and whisk together. Place the prepared bread crumbs into a bowl or dish and add the remaining chopped parsley and mix together thoroughly.

Coat each fish cake in seasoned flour and shake off any surplus. Dip them in the beaten egg and milk mix, shake off any surplus, and then dip in the breadcrumbs. Place the prepared fish cakes onto some silicone paper, on a tray and refrigerate until ready to pan fry in half vegetable oil, half butter until golden brown on both sides.

To serve, place a few dressed salad leaves on a plate with a couple of wedges of lemon (labels removed) and a ramekin of your home made Aioli (see Basics)

MCB tip: Try to buy salt dried cod that is white and preferably cut from the middle of the fillet. However, the ones I usually see in the Med are whole sides of salted, dried cod. Avoid any vendor who may try to palm you off with fillets that are thin or yellowish in colour, as they are likely to be too dry and salty.

SEAFOOD PROVENÇALE

This safe-bet dish can be prepared anywhere in the world, but works particularly well in the Med, so give your guests a treat at the start of the season, for the Cannes Film Festival or the Monaco Grand Prix. The idea of the dish is so simple, that I use it as an interesting base for a number of different seafood and pasta dishes.

Ingredients for four

- 2 shallots – finely chopped
- 1 clove of garlic – crushed
- 24 good sized tiger prawns – cooked & shelled
- 500g mussels – prepared (see Moules Gratinées)
- 500g clams – cleaned & ready to cook
- 2 tomatoes – ripe & firm – de-seeded and chopped
- 15cl vegetable stock
- 15cl dry white wine
- 4 tbsp finely chopped flat leaf parsley
- 25g unsalted butter
- 1 lemon
- sea salt & freshly ground black pepper

Preparation

Place a medium sized, heavy based pan over a medium-low flame. Melt the butter, add the shallots, cover and sweat without colour for five minutes, reducing the heat if you need to. Remove the lid, tweek up the flame to high, immediately add the wine and bring to the boil, add the mussels, cover and cook for two to three minutes until the mussels open. Place a fine sieve over another pan (or bowl) and drain the mussels, retaining the cooking liquor. When the mussels have cooled a little, remove the meat from the opened shells and discard the unopened ones, cover and set to one side.

Place a deep sided frying pan or sauté pan over a medium-high flame, add the wine liquor, bring to the boil and reduce by half. Add the vegetable stock, boil again and reduce the flame to medium, so the liquid simmers gently. Add the clams, tomatoes, garlic and parsley and cook for a couple of minutes until the clams open. Add the prepared mussels, prawns, crushed garlic, half the chopped parsley and a squeeze of lemon juice. Season to taste and serve immediately in a wide-rimmed, white soup bowl and garnish with the remaining parsley.

MCB tip: If you want to serve this as a more wholesome main course dish, cook approximately 250g potato gnocchi, drain and place a small mound in the middle of each bowl and garnish with parsley.

SEARED SCALLOPS NIÇOISE
with sauce vierge

The scallop, or should I say its shell has, for hundreds of years, been the symbol of Santiago de Compostella, in Galicia, North West Spain. Christian pilgrims flock there to worship at the tomb of St James and, on arrival buy and eat a scallop, attaching the shell to his/her hat or cloak, to prove that s/he had made the journey to this holy place. In 1985 the city's Old Town was designated a UNESCO World Heritage Site.

I advise that you always use the freshest scallops on the shell. Frozen ones are often soaked in water to plump them up and you find that when they have defrosted, that you have scallops which are half the size they were when you bought them, with the texture of a sponge. Unless baking or grilling fresh scallops in their shell, the orange coloured roe should be separated from the white meat.

Scallops should be washed in plenty of cold water. Place the scallop on a chopping board, with the flat shell facing upwards; carefully slide the blade of a short filleting knife between the two shells. Try to make sure you keep the blade of the knife close to the top shell and probe for the ligament which joins the meat of the scallop to the shell and cut right through it. Remove the top shell and pull out everything in the shell except for the bright orange coral and the white muscle meat. Remember my warning about sharp knives and shellfish when I spoke about oysters (Page 122), so take care.

You would normally be expected to serve a minimum of two scallops per person, I just happen to think that serving three looks a lot better on the plate.

Ingredients for four

- 12 fresh large scallops – shelled with coral removed
- 4 quails eggs – lightly boiled, refreshed & shelled
- 250g fine green beans – blanched, refreshed & trimmed to even lengths
- 4 small black olives – pitted & halved lengthways
- 8 fresh, marinated anchovy fillets (not the salty ones)
- 16 sundried cherry tomatoes – drained
- 24 baby capers in Sherry vinegar – drained
- salt & freshly ground white pepper
- sauce vierge (see Basics)
- olive oil

Preparation

Firstly you will need to prepare one quantity of sauce vierge – Page 233.

Using large white serving plates, round, square or rectangular, you will need to dress them with the other ingredients before you start to cook the scallops. You can of course create your own design; alternatively I suggest two mini-bundles of the cooked beans placed onto the middle of the plate in parallel, but off-set from each other, about 4cm apart. Top each bundle with half an olive. Cut the quail's eggs in half and trim a sliver off the rounded side and place a half on opposite sides of the plate, yolk facing upwards. Place an anchovy fillet to the outside of each bundle of beans. Strategically place four sundried cherry tomatoes on each plate and dot the six baby capers around the plates like a clock-face. Drizzle some sauce vierge around each plate, making sure that the tomato concassé is evenly distributed.

Fresh scallops are very delicate and require hardly any cooking at all. Like most shellfish, an overcooked scallop will lose its flavour and become very chewy. Rinse the scallops and pat dry and place onto a dish, lightly brush with a light olive oil and very lightly season.

Place a heavy bottomed frying pan over a medium flame and allow to heat through and spray with a fine mist of vegetable oil. Gently place the scallops into the pan flat side down and cook for one to two minutes, depending on how well cooked you wish them to be. Do not disturb the scallops until you are ready to turn them over to cook the other side. You want to obtain a beautiful golden colour on either end of the scallop. Remove the scallops from the pan onto kitchen paper to take up any surplus oil. Place three scallops in the space between the bundles of beans and very lightly drizzle with a little of the sauce vierge and serve immediately.

MCB tip: You can serve some freshly made, warm bread with this dish.

SUSHI

Sushi is a skill which I have not truly mastered, so, I am going to provide you with a brief overview of the basics. If you are really interested in 'doing' sushi, I suggest you consider buying one of the many good books currently on the market, or take the opportunity to try a couple of speciality short courses.

Maki Rolls and Sushi

The secret of sushi-making is to always keep your hands wet, otherwise the fish will dry out and the rice will stick to your fingers. Knives also are best used wet and should be cleaned frequently; either wipe the blade with a damp cloth or wet the knife in a solution of 2 tablespoons of rice wine vinegar and 500ml water.

Only use the best cuts and most tender slices from the freshest fish for sushi or sashimi. I love to use tuna loin or salmon.

Sushi Rice

This is the basic technique for producing the glutinous, vinegar-flavoured rice that forms the basis for all types of sushi. A fairly consistent recipe is to use equal amounts of rice and water. Some recipes go for the water being one inch above the rice, but I would go with the one-to-one ratio.

Preparation

Wash the rice thoroughly, three or four times, until the water runs clear. Drain for 30 minutes (if time allows) as this will allow the grains to absorb moisture and start to swell, although this is not necessary.

Put the rice and water in a pan with a tight fitting lid. Place over a high flame and bring to the boil. Reduce the flame to medium-low and simmer for about 10 minutes. Do resist the temptation to lift the lid while the rice is cooking as you will lose the steam. Turn off the heat, keep the lid in place and set to one side and leave for ten minutes.

Spoon the hot rice into a bowl and pour sushi vinegar evenly over the surface of the rice, mixing it into the rice with quick cutting strokes. You should use one tablespoon of vinegar per cup of rice. At this stage, I usually spoon the rice onto a flat tray and spread it out evenly and place into my fridge to cool.

Basic terminology

Sushi – ovals of rice you see topped with ingredients such as fish or shellfish.

Maki – rolls made with sheets of nori seaweed and rice with fish and/or vegetable in the centre.

Futomaki – is a very fat maki roll, like a Japanese burrito. Always made with the same ingredients: Japanese omelette, radish, sweet, bright pink fish powder and other vegetables.

Tekkamaki – which has raw tuna at the centre as its main ingredient. This version derives from the Japanese word for gambling parlors – Tekka, and was invented rather like our sandwich to be eaten at the gaming tables.

The above are usually spiced with Japanese wasabi and served with pickled ginger and soy.

THAI MOULLES

My darling daughter worked in a Bistro style restaurant on the south coast when she was between jobs. I took her there for lunch one day and she said I just had to try the Thai Mussels. I did, and they were amazing. Afterwards, as you do, I asked for the recipe, but this was a total no go area and no form of incentivisation would encourage the chef to part with his prized recipe. So, I thought, how could I recreate this tasty dish and replicate it with my own version. This is brill' and a great way to serve mussels.

Ingredients for four
- 2kg mussels
- 2 sticks of lemon grass – outer skin removed & finely sliced
- 3 cloves of garlic – crushed
- sunflower oil
- fresh coriander bunch – chopped
- ½ tsp green Thai curry paste
- 1 tin of coconut milk
- 2 limes – zested & juiced

Preparation

Fill your sink or a large bowl with cold water, add the mussels and give a good swill around and preferably soak for around an hour. Use a small sharp knife to remove all the barnacles and pull the hairy beards away and discard. Any mussels that are damaged, or remain open at this stage and don't shut when tapped with the back of a kitchen knife, should be discarded.

Take a large heavy based pan that will hold all the mussels and place over a medium-low flame. Add a couple of slugs of oil, heat through and add the garlic and the lemon grass. Stir and cook without colour until the garlic softens and the lemon grass starts to release its unique aroma.

Pour in the coconut milk, lime zest, lime juice, Thai curry paste and half the chopped coriander and bring to the boil. Drain the mussels and add them to the pan and shake well, cover with a lid. Allow the mussels cook for about 3 minutes until they are all open. As they open, their lovely juices mix with the coconut milk and create a really fragrant broth

Have some warm large rimmed soup bowls heated and ready. Using a slotted spoon, transfer the mussels to the soup bowls, taking care to discard any unopened ones. Spoon the fabulous juices over the mussels and sprinkle with the remaining chopped coriander.

MCB TIP: Serve with some fresh granary bread or similar.

TIAN of CRAB & AVOCADO
with crème fraîche

A tian is really just a stack, sometimes made up of different layers, although modern thinking certainly empowers chefs and gastronaughts alike to put their own spin on dishes.

This is an amazing recipe, which is really quite easy to put together, it just takes a little time, but the effort's so worth it. This is a real fusion starter, seamlessly blending Mexican and Thai cuisines. The great thing with this recipe is that it is so flexible and I sometimes replace the crab with cooked tiger prawns which have been marinated for a while in peanut oil, lime juice, grated ginger and chopped coriander.

Ingredients for six
- 2 ready to eat avocados – halved, stoned & roughly chopped
- 2 firm ripe tomatoes – skinned, de-seeded & chopped
- clove of garlic – crushed
- fresh chilli – de-seeded & finely chopped
- 1 lime – zested
- 1 lemon – zested
- 200g crème fraîche
- 200g white crab meat
- 6 large prawns – shell removed

- extra virgin olive oil
- flat leaf parsley – finely chopped
- fresh coriander – chopped
- salt and black pepper

Preparation

Take a bowl and add the chopped avocado, garlic, chilli and crush with the back of a table fork. Add half the crème fraîche and lime zest and mix well, then gently fold in the chopped tomatoes and chopped parsley. Add a touch of salt and a couple of grounds of black pepper to taste. If you think it needs it – add a little lime juice, but do not make the mixture too loose.

Place the crab meat into a bowl and add the chopped coriander, half the lemon zest, juice from half the lemon, a drizzle of olive oil, very lightly season and blend together. Taste and add a little more seasoning if necessary. Place the crab mixture into the fridge for half an hour or more.

Using six stainless steel rings, very lightly oil the inside of each and place onto a baking sheet. Remove the crab mixture from the fridge and drain thoroughly, squeezing gently with the back of a spoon to remove the surplus liquid. Spoon the guacamole mixture into the rings and fill about half way – press and smooth with the back of a spoon.

Spoon the crab mixture into the rings, but do not fill completely. Loosen the remaining crème fraîche by stirring vigorously with a spoon or fork. Spoon the crème fraîche over the crab and smooth with the back of a spoon. Sprinkle with a little dried chilli flakes and finely chopped herbs and neatly place one prawn on the top of each.

Slide a fish slice or palette knife under each tian and place onto serving plates. Gently remove the rings. Dress some rocket or chard leaves and scatter around the outside of each plate.

MCB tip #1:   This dish can be made in the morning and served later for lunch. Just build the rings, tightly cling film and refrigerate. Be aware that the avocado will discolour if prepared too far in advance.

MCB tip #2:   If you don't have any rings, use 7 - 8cm ramekins, very lightly oiled and build the dish upside down, before carefully turning out onto serving plates.

TUNA SALAD
with an oriental dressing

This recipe was inspired by Bill Granger's brilliant book Sydney Food. We have gradually been introducing more Pacific Rim style dishes to our cookery courses and this one works so well. It needs to be prepared with the freshest tuna, so I suggest buying straight off the dock or check out the local fish market. The end product has close visual similarities to fillet of beef carpacio.

Ingredients for four
- 500g tuna loin
- 2 tbsp ground black pepper corns
- 1 dsp sea salt
- 50g chopped coriander (cilantro) – finely chopped
- 50g chopped parsley
- 75g oriental radish - shredded
- 75g cucumber – peeled, split lengthways, de-seeded & cut to 1cm slices
- 75g mangetout or snow-peas – shredded on the diagonal
- 75g pak choi – split lengthways and shredded 1/2cm thick

- coriander leaves for garnish
- mint leaves for garnish
- light olive oil
- sea salt and freshly ground black pepper
- chive oil (see Basics – Page 223)

For the dressing
- 50ml soy
- 50ml mirin
- 3 tbsp rice wine vinegar

Preparation
Place the dressing ingredients into a bowl and blend with a fork. Cover and refrigerate until required.

Place the salt, pepper corns, chopped coriander, parsley and olive oil in a bowl and stir to combine. Cut the tuna loin into approx' 5cm square batons and place onto a plate and pour over the herb mixture, pressing into the fish on all sides.

Place a large non-stick frying pan over a high flame and heat through. Add the pieces of tuna and cook for twenty seconds on each side. Remove from the pan and place onto some kitchen paper and refrigerate for one hour.

Mix the radish, cucumber, mangetout and pak choi together in a bowl, dress with a little olive oil and very lightly season with sea salt and a little ground black pepper.

When rested, slice the tuna into 1/2cm slices and arrange on individual plates and top with the mixed oriental salad. Drizzle some of the soy-mirin dressing over the salad and some chive oil towards the edge of the plate.

WARM MUSSEL & POTATO SALAD
with pistou
There are so many variations of this fabulous dish, however I am going to give you a base recipe and then you can play around with your own version another time.

Ingredients for four
- 400g new potatoes – nutty Anya potatoes are best
- 750g medium/large mussels – prepared & ready to cook
- 100g peppery salad leaves (rocket, watercress etc)
- 1 large vine ripened tomato – skinned, de-seeded & chopped
- 50g frisée (curly endive)
- 1 lemon – juiced
- 150ml olive oil
- 2 handfuls of fresh basil leaves
- 2 cloves of garlic – chopped
- 100ml extra virgin olive oil
- 75g parmesan – finely grated
- sea salt & freshly ground white pepper

For the pistou

Place a small pan over a medium-low flame. Add a couple of tablespoons of cold water and the fresh basil; cover with a lid for a few seconds until the basil wilts. Drain and refresh immediately in iced water. Drain again and squeeze out any remaining liquid.

Place the basil, garlic, tomato and parmesan into a mini-food processor and blend to a fine purée, then gradually add the oil little-by-little until you reach a mayo-like consistency. Season with sea salt and freshly ground white pepper. Place into a clean container, cover with cling film and place into your fridge until needed.

Gently clean the potatoes. If you have some which are much larger than others, cut those on a diagonal, so that the potatoes are the same size and they cook at the same rate. Place the potatoes into a pan and barely cover with cold salted water and bring to the boil over a high flame. Cook for ten minutes or so, or until just cooked and still slightly firm. Drain, but do not refresh. Return to the pan and cover to keep warm.

To cook the mussels, place a pan over a medium-high flame and heat thoroughly. Add around 2.5cl of water and the mussels; cover with a lid and cook for two or three minutes until the mussel shells open, discarding any that do not open.

Place a colander over a suitable sized saucepan and drain the cooked mussels and retain cooking liquor. Allow the mussels to cool a little, and then remove the meat from the shells, retaining both; cover and keep warm.

Place the pan of cooking liquor over a medium-high flame, bring to the boil and reduce a little. Place four tablespoons of the pistou into a small bowl and add a couple of spoons of the reduced mussel liquor to thin out the pistou a little.

To serve, very lightly dress the salad leaves and place a mound of leaves onto four serving plates. Slice the warm potatoes approx' 1cm thick and arrange them neatly over the leaves. Add two or three mussel shells facing upwards and then distribute the mussel meat between the four plates.

To finish, drizzle your beautiful pistou over the salad and a light squeeze of lemon juice. I like to serve this while both the potatoes and mussels are still nicely warm.

MCB tip: We used to serve this dish in France with Persillade and drizzle a little truffle oil over before serving.

PASTA & PIZZA

Pasta, the Italian word for "dough" which originates from the same word in Latin meaning: "dough, pastry cake or paste". It is a generic term for the Italian variant of noodles – food made from a dough of flour, water and/or eggs. We know the word these days to mean a dish which contains pasta, in one shape or another, as the primary ingredient, which is served with a sauce or seasonings. There are said to be approximately 3,500 different pasta shapes.

There are two basic styles of pasta that you can buy: dried and fresh. Dried pasta, made without eggs can be stored for up to two years in ideal conditions; unfortunately the humid atmosphere on your yacht is not, in the long term, necessarily one of them. Fresh pasta will keep for a couple of days or more in your refrigerator.

Making pasta is no big deal - it's not complicated. Honestly, I'm not kidding you - pasta really is easy to make. There is no mystique, all you need to remember is 1 egg = 100g flour. However, and equally important to remember – eggs and flour are always slightly different. I always recommend that you use fresh free-range eggs and if you can get hold of eggs from corn-fed chickens, even better, because you will finish up with the most beautiful golden coloured pasta imaginable.

The type of flour you use is also critical in making a successful pasta, so always use strong pasta flour (Tipo '00'). Once you have made your pasta, if you think that the end product is a bit too wet or sticky, add a little more flour and if it's too dry, add a little more egg.

You can also buy some quite outstanding "fresh" pasta from the supermarkets these days. Many products cook in no time flat, so as well as delighting your guests, such products can also be very useful for crew cooking. Using a 300g pack of shop brought tortelloni, for instance, you can literally prepare, cook and serve a couple of really tasty bowls of pasta in ten minutes flat.

BASIC PASTA

Ingredients for six hungry people

- 600g Type 00 flour or strong bread flour
- 6 medium free range eggs (the freshest you can buy)
  or
- 12 free range egg yolks (produces a rich pasta)

Preparation

Place the flour in a large clean bowl or if you are feeling adventurous, onto a chopping board or your worktop, (very clean obviously), make a well in the centre of the flour and crack your eggs into it. If you have any suspicions about their quality crack them individually into a mug, then add them one at a time, that way if one is not at its best it won't ruin the whole thing.

Take a fork and lightly whip the eggs and then gradually start incorporating the flour until it all comes together. Flour your hands well and start kneading the dough. As with bread making, you are aiming for smooth elastic dough, which does not take long to achieve. You can use the dough straight away but if your galley is hot, you might want to wrap it in cling film and put it into the fridge for 30 - 40 minutes, to rest and firm up.

Although a pasta machine is very useful, there is not a lot you can't do with a rolling pin and a knife. The easiest thing to do with your pasta dough is to roll it out flat on a well floured surface. You can then cut it into rectangles for lasagne, cut it into thin ribbons for tagliatelle, squares for ravioli etc etc.....

Cook your pasta in a pan of boiling salted water or stock and cook until "al dente", so it still has a little "bite" to it and drain off the liquid. Make a simple sauce and *"presto pronto"* – fast fabulous food.

HOME MADE PIZZA DOUGH

Pizza has got to be one of the most famous dishes in the world and should be really simple to put together. Don't be tempted to go for too many toppings; this does not always work. So, roll out the base thinly and keep the toppings down to a minimum.

This is a great recipe and sooooo easy to make and I have to say, makes the best pizza I have ever had. It does help if you have got a good sized oven; a gimble oven rather limits your ability to produce a meal, however with a little common sense and ingenuity you will manage fine. My youngest, Ash, uses this dough to make a thin, crisp garlic bread, which is simple but sensational – the type you might be served, cut into wedges as a mixed 'bread' starter in an Italian restaurant.

I have included this recipe because Pizza is a favorite with both adults and kids alike and getting a home-made pizza onboard will be a bit of a treat. If you have kids onboard, getting them involved in making Pizzas can be a welcome distraction for mums and dads. Students on our cookery courses love the session on pizzas and make their own designer pizzas for lunch.

I usually roll my bases out really thin, around 2.5 - 5mm thick. This recipe will provide you with up to eight medium sized pizzas – roll them out more thickly if you wish; they don't have to be rolled out round and look great if they are quite 'random'. If we are entertaining at home, we make three different varieties, cut them into wedges with a pizza wheel and serve them on big platters in the middle of the table for people to help themselves.

Ingredients for 4 or 8 pizzas (depending on thickness & size)

- 500g strong white bread flour
- ½ tsp table salt
- 1 x 7g sachet of dried yeast
- 1 dsp golden caster sugar
- 325ml warm water
- 1 quantity Really Simple Tomato Sauce or Topping (see Page 140)

Preparation

Weigh the flour accurately and sieve into a large plastic bowl and sprinkle in the salt. Draw the flour towards the sides of the bowl, making a bay (well) in the middle, ready for the liquid mixture. Accurately measure the warm water and add the sugar and dried yeast, mixing well for a few seconds with a fork, then leave for approximately five minutes to allow the sugar and yeast to start working and mix again.

Pour the yeast liquid into the bay and using your fork, work the mixture in a circular motion bringing the flour from the edges of the bowl into the liquid. Keep doing this until the mixture starts to resemble sticky porridge and continue to work the mix until you can no longer mix it with your fork. You now need to work the dough with your clean hands, until all the flour has been absorbed and starts to come away cleanly from the sides of the bowl. Dust with a little more flour if the dough is too sticky.

Dust your work top and your hands with some flour, remove the dough from the bowl and start to knead the mixture by rolling and stretching with the heal of your hands. You should do this for around ten minutes, until you have a springy, soft, clear dough.

The dough now needs to rest for about fifteen minutes, so dust a bowl with a little flour, add the dough, dust the top with flour and cover with cling-film and set to one side.

Once the dough has rested, you can cut it into as many pieces as you want. I usually cut it into four or eight pieces, wrapping each in cling-film, dusted with flour and placed into the fridge until I need it. Depending on what yeast you use, your dough should remain beautifully light and springy, even while refrigerated.

I tend to roll out my bases around fifteen minutes or so before I am ready to cook them. Remove a ball of dough from the fridge. Dust your worktop, rolling pin and dough with flour and roll out into a shape that will fit your baking sheet. Take your oven tin, brush lightly with olive oil and dust with flour, then place your rolled out pizza base on top. Make up as many pizza bases as you need.

See below for building your pizza.

MCB tip: You can roll out your pizza bases, dust each with flour, stack on top of each other, wrap in cling-film and refrigerate for use later. This is fine if you have a large refrigerator, but not recommended for a locker type of fridge. It's really useful doing this for mini-pizzas for the kids, who will just love creating their own 'designer' pizzas.

BUILDING YOUR PIZZA
OK, you have made some wonderful pizza dough and a great little tomato sauce, so you are now ready to build your own pizza, so here goes. I will give you the basics and you can alter it any which way you like.

Pre-heat your oven to 250°C, or 20° or so less, if you are going to roll the base out quite thick. Take a table spoon and smear each base with your tomato sauce, leaving about 1cm free around the edges. Now you can add your toppings, such as: slices of mozzarella, Parma ham, chorizo, fresh anchovies, capers etc etc..... Sprinkle with a little grated cheese, oregano or both and finish with some torn fresh basil leaves. Brush a little olive oil around the edge of the dough and cook in the middle of the oven for approximately ten minutes.

It is useful to have a pizza board and a pizza wheel. Serve whole or cut into wedges.

MCB tip: If you are stuck for time, you can buy some really good readymade sauces, but if you do have the time and want to be totally authentic, my recipe is so easy and quick to knock up.

LINGUINE PUTTANESCA
This is derived from the classic Italian dish: Spaghetti alla Puttanesca (tart's or whore's spaghetti), which is a spicy, tangy and somewhat salty dish, which some culinary experts regard as modern, therefore reflecting regional market ingredients, rather than those from the garden. The ingredients are usually easy to find and are typically Mediterranean. Italians refer to the sauce as *Sugo alla Puttanesca*.

This is not a gentle or mild dish, on the contrary it is full of gutsy flavour hence its name "puttanesca" (lady of the night). Ideally accompanied with a large glass of red Chianti, you could serve this as a lunch dish with a rocket based green salad served separately, depending on your guests' nationality and preference.

Ingredients for four
- 400g fresh linguine
- 500g fresh tomatoes – skinned, de-seeded & chopped
- 100g olive oil
- 100g black olives – pitted & halved
- 30g anchovies – drained
- 30g large capers – drained
- 2 tbsp tomato purée
- 2 cloves of garlic - crushed
- 1 red chilli – deseeded & chopped
- flat leaf parsley - chopped
- parmesan cheese – grated

Preparation
Put a heavy based pan and plenty of water over a high flame, adding a little olive oil (no salt) and bring to the boil.

Place a smaller heavy based shallow pan over a low flame; add the olive oil, chilli and garlic and cook until soft, being very careful not to let the garlic take on too much colour. Add the anchovies and mash them into the oil, then add the chopped tomatoes, black olives, capers and tomato purée. Stir well, cover with a lid and simmer very gently for twenty minutes.

While the sauce is cooking and once the water has boiled, add the linguine and cook 'till "al dente". When the pasta is cooked, drain, return to the pan, add the sauce and stir to combine well. Timing is critical.

This dish looks lovely served in one large dish or can be served individually on large white plates or pasta bowls. Serve topped with freshly grated parmesan cheese and garnished with chopped flat leaf parsley or basil.

MCB tip: Be careful not to season with salt when you are already using salty ingredients like anchovies or capers.

PASTA SCIALATIELLI
with clams
This has to be one of my very favorite Italian pasta dishes. This type of pasta is popular around the coast of Amalfi in Southern Italy. Scialatielli are like short, slightly widened strips of tagliatelle, and are sometimes 'pinched' in the middle. This recipe, made with fresh clams, is an ideal lunch time dish, served with a crisp, citrusy, dry white wine.

Ingredients for four

For the pasta
- 400g plain flour
- 100g milk
- 4 basil leaves – finely chopped
- salt and black pepper
- 2 tablespoons extra virgin olive oil
- 25g pecorino cheese – finely grated

For the sauce
- 1 kg fresh clams – washed thoroughly

- 1 large or 2 small cloves of garlic
- extra virgin olive oil
- flat leaf parsley – chopped
- sea salt & black pepper

Take a good sized bowl, add the flour and make a well in the middle. Pour in the milk and add the remaining pasta ingredients. Using a fork, draw in the flour and when the mix reaches a porridge-like consistency, use your hands to continue mixing together until the dough is smooth. Allow to rest for around thirty minutes, and then roll out the dough, using a rolling pin or pasta machine. Cut into long strips, which should be a little thicker than spaghetti, but slightly shorter in length. I find my pasta machine gets the thickness just right.

Place a large pan of water over a high flame and bring to the boil. Add a good pinch of salt and a little vegetable oil. Fresh pasta takes no time to cook, so make sure that your clams are almost ready before cooking.

Place a large, heavy based frying pan over a medium-low flame. Add a couple of slugs of olive oil and add the crushed garlic. Cook without colour for a minute or so. Add the washed and drained clams, cover with a lid and steam until opened. Do not cook for too long, as they will shrink and become chewy. Do not drain any liquid from the pan, as this will give your sauce a great flavour.

Cook the pasta in the boiling salted water until al dente. Drain, then add to the clams and toss together in the pan so that all the juices coat the pasta.

Serve garnished with freshly chopped parsley.

MCB tip: I also like to finish the sauce with a little crème fraîche. If you want to give the dish a vibrant colour, it also is nice to add some shredded blush sun dried tomatoes.

REALLY SIMPLE TOMATO SAUCE TOPPING

Ingredients: sufficient for the pizza dough recipe above
- 1 shallot – sliced
- 1 clove of garlic – peeled & finely sliced
- 1 hand full of fresh basil
- 1 x 400g tin chopped tomatoes
- 1 dsp tomato purée
- salt & ground black pepper
- extra virgin olive oil

Preparation
Heat a small saucepan over a low flame, add a small slug of olive oil, the prepared shallot and garlic and cook gently for a few minutes, stirring now and again until they start to turn a light golden brown. Add the chopped tomatoes, basil and a small pinch of salt and a good grind of black pepper. Bring up to the boil, reduce to a steady simmer and cook for around twenty minutes, stirring now and again. You can mash the tomatoes or blitz them with a hand-blender. Your source is now ready to use.

SPAGHETTI with GENOESE PESTO
(Pesto alla Genovese)
Once you have tasted homemade pesto, bursting with massive flavours, you will realise that the shop bought jars do not even start to compare. This is an authentic Italian recipe.

Ingredients for four
- 450g dried spaghetti
- bunch of fresh basil
- 25g pecorino (Sardinian ewes milk cheese) – finely grated
- 1 handful of pine nuts – lightly toasted
- 3 cloves of garlic – roughly chopped
- 1 glass of extra virgin olive oil
- 25g of grated or processed parmesan cheese
- extra virgin olive oil
- 1 tsp coarse sea salt

Put the basil leaves, garlic and the coarse salt into a marble mortar and crush to a smooth paste with a pestle; you could also do this in a food processor or even use a bowl and the end of a rolling pin. Gradually add the two types of cheese until you have a homogenous mixture. Transfer the mix to a clean bowl and add the olive oil.

Add a little olive oil to a pan of boiling, salted water and cook the spaghetti until "al dente". Drain and reserve a tablespoon of the cooking water; add this to the pesto before combining with the pasta and serve in warmed bowls.

MCB tip: This dish also looks particularly attractive served on one large, warmed shallow serving dish with torn fresh basil scattered over the top.

SPAGHETTI with PRAWNS, GARLIC & CHILLI
If you are lucky enough to be shopping somewhere that sells really fresh prawns then always choose those and only use frozen prawns as a last resort. This dish looks very pretty on the plate and lends itself well to being served at lunch time.

Ingredients for four
- 400g dried spaghetti
- extra virgin olive oil
- 2 cloves of garlic – crushed
- 1-2 dried red chillies – crumbled
- 400g peeled raw prawns (as large & fresh as possible)
- 50ml dry white wine
- 6 sun-blushed tomatoes – shredded
- 1 lemon – zested & juiced
- 2 handfuls of rocket – roughly chopped
- sea salt & freshly ground black pepper

Preparation
Place a large pan of water over a high flame and bring to the boil. Add a good pinch of salt and a couple of slugs of olive oil and cook the spaghetti.

Place a large frying pan over a medium-low flame, add a couple of slugs of extra virgin olive oil, heat through, add the garlic and chilli and cook until the garlic starts to take on a little colour. Tweak up the heat, add the prawns and sauté them for a minute or so on both sides. Add the white wine and sun-dried tomatoes, stir well to and simmer for a couple of minutes.

When the pasta is cooked, drain well, reserving a little of the cooking liquor. Toss the spaghetti with the sauce, squeeze in the lemon juice, add half the chopped rocket adding a little of the reserved cooking liquid to loosen the sauce slightly. Check for seasoning and add a little salt and pepper if needed.

Divide the pasta between four large bowls and finish off by sprinkling with the grated lemon zest and the remaining rocket leaves.

FISH & SHELLFISH MAINS

It will come as no surprise to you that fish and shellfish rate very highly on the food popularity list for owners, charterers and crew. As well as being incredibly versatile, an important advantage of using seafood is that it is low in fat and high in proteins, minerals and vitamins. Fish oil can improve health by helping lower cholesterol levels. Is it any surprise that the Japanese, who eat copious amounts of raw fish, have the lowest recorded incidence of heart disease in the world.

Omega 3 is the collective name given to fatty acids, which have a lowering effect on blood fats, thus decreasing the chances of blood vessels closing up with cholesterol. They can also help maintain the blood flow more easily, reducing the likelihood of a heart attack. Omega 3, found almost exclusively in oily fish, also reduces inflammation from rheumatoid arthritis and psoriasis.

Cooking fish can be the simplest process, however this has to be complimented by the selection of a reputable supplier, purchasing the freshest produce possible, taking great care with handling, storage, immaculate preparation and perfectly timed cooking.

One of my great pleasures when we lived in deep rural France, was that, even though we lived approximately four hours drive from the coast, the bi-weekly Thursday market brought me and mine the delight of a massive blue trailer, displaying a dazzling array of brightly coloured fresh fish and shellfish, presented on top of mountains of crushed ice.

Seafood is extremely versatile and very rewarding to cook. One of your great pleasures of going ashore in strange foreign lands will be visiting the local food markets, where you will often find the fish market is located separately to the meat, poultry, fruit and vegetable market. The fish markets in particular will open your eyes to fish of shapes, sizes and colours that you have never seen before.

A good place to start in deciding what to buy, is what you need to support your menu plan and how this can be achieved. Do you need to buy flat or round fish? Round fish will always have more meat on it, so if it's 'round' and you can't find what you are looking for; ask yourself what can you buy that is similar and will fit seamlessly into your menu plan. Can you prepare and cook it the same way as the fish you had hoped to buy – quite often the answer to this would be yes. The tip is, that unless you have been asked for a specific type of fish, then visit the fish market (daily when possible) with an open mind. This will give you the opportunity to select the freshest fish available and sometimes offer you the chance to impress your guests with a surprise fish that they have maybe never tried, or even heard of before!

FISH purchasing and quality points

If you are in an unknown environment, you may need to find a supplier quickly and there are some obvious options available to you. Check to see if other boats know of good local suppliers or reputable fishing boats to buy from direct. Alternatively, check with the harbour master or marina office to see if they can direct you – if not, head for the local market, you will usually be pleasantly surprised.

There are a number of recognised quality points that you should observe when buying fresh fish and they should be:

Purchase:	Daily if possible
Eyes:	Clear and bright – not cloudy.
Skin:	Covered with fresh sea slime, or be smooth, moist and shiny.
Flesh:	Firm to the touch. When pressed the impression should quickly disappear.
Gills:	Gills are suffused with oxygenated blood and should be bright red to rosy pink. They undergo colour changes as the blood decomposes, from: red – dark red – brown – purple – green, when they smell of stale cabbage
Scales:	Flat against the fish, moist and plentiful.
Smell:	Pleasant with no hint of ammonia or other 'off' smells.
Storage:	Well iced, so that it arrives onboard in good condition.
Size:	Medium sized fish are often better than large. Small fish tend to lack depth of flavour.

Deliveries

If you place advanced orders with a supplier to have your fish delivered at the dockside, there are a few things to consider, so make sure that you:

- inspect the condition of the delivery immediately on arrival
- reject if the condition of the fish is not up to standard
- take a 'core temperature' sample, using a temperature probe.
- reject frozen food if it is delivered at an external temperature above -10°C (NB commercial freezers should operate at -18°C)
- never re-freeze fish once defrosted
- reject refrigerated fish if it has a core temperature above 6°C
- place food into appropriate storage as soon as possible
- keep cooked and raw food separate

This advice is considered good practice, however time constraints with guest arrivals, schedules and itineraries can make all of these difficult to perform, so my advice is – be very comfortable with your supplier or go and buy yourself, where you can be assured of the quality by using the sensory checks noted above.

Cooking methods

Although there are numerous methods of cooking, I have included the ones which you are most likely to use onboard.

Fish will cook very quickly, when compared to other types of fresh high protein food; therefore it is very easy to overcook, so take a great deal of care and attention, especially when you are using small, boneless pieces of fish. Timing is everything.

Initially, you may wish to use a temperature probe to check the internal temperature exactly. You can also take a small, sharp, pointed knife and part the fish at the thickest point – if it is cooked through, the fish will have changed colour from translucent to solid white or pink depending on what fish you are using. However, once you become more experienced, you will be able to tell by sight and touch whether or not your piece of fish is cooked.

I have included a guide at the end of the book, which provides you with the translation of fish and shellfish names into French, Spanish and Italian. See page 296.

BAHAMIAN GRILLED LOBSTER

Since the very early days of the EMC course, we have always demonstrated the classic shellfish dish: Lobster Thermador and for whatever reason, this has always been one of my jobs. The great thing about our recipe, is that it covers a number of different methods of cookery and techniques, such as boiling, simmering, flambé, grilling, making a basic white sauce (velouté – see Basics) and turning it into something really quite sexy. I wanted to include some Caribbean recipes in my book, so once you have mastered this dish, you will find Lobster Thermador just as easy to prepare.

Ingredients for four
- 4 medium sized lobsters – boiled & cooled
- 1 small onion – finely chopped
- 1 clove of garlic – crushed
- 2 tbsp flat leaf parsley – finely chopped
- 25g unsalted butter
- 25ml brandy
- 1lt fish velouté (Page 236)
- 200g button mushrooms – sliced
- 100ml crème fraîche (double cream will do)
- 100g breadcrumbs
- 2 tsp Worcestershire sauce
- few drops of chilli sauce – Trappey's or similar
- salt & freshly ground black pepper

Preparation
Halve the lobsters and carefully remove the meat, wash in cold water, pat dry, cut into 2cm pieces. Discard remaining debris from the shells, thoroughly wash, pat dry and put to one side.

Place a sauteuse over a medium-low flame, add the butter and melt until it bubbles subside, add the chopped onion and gently cook, until they turn a light, golden brown. Increase to a medium flame, add the lobster meat and garlic and heat through for a few seconds. Pour over the brandy and tilt the pan forwards so the juices gather at one side near the flame and the brandy will ignite. Do not panic, the flames will subside in a few seconds. Add the mushrooms and simmer for a minute or so.

Stir in the chilli and Worcestershire sauce and cook over a low heat for a minute. Increase the flame to medium; add the hot velouté little-by-little until the pieces of lobster are nicely coated in the velvety sauce. Add the crème fraîche, chopped parsley and fold the ingredients together. Check for seasoning and adjust as required.

Place the shells onto some scrunched up tin foil on a baking tray and fill each with the lobster mixture and coat evenly with any residual sauce, sprinkle liberally with the breadcrumbs and place under a pre-heated grill for a minute or so to glaze. Serve the lobster over some dressed peppery salad leaves.

BAHAMIAN PIGEON PEAS and RICE
Pigeon peas, popular throughout the West Indies, are small, oval beans with a nutty flavour. Look for them in Caribbean markets, or substitute with kidney beans or black-eyed peas. I've used canned pigeon peas, because they're more readily available than dried. This dish is also noted by some as being Puerto Rico's national dish.

If you are going to use dried kidney beans, you must soak them thoroughly overnight. If not thoroughly soaked, they can cause severe stomach cramps.

Ingredients for eight

- 1 x 400g can pigeon peas – drained
- 200g long grain rice
- 2 bay leaves
- 1 tsp dried thyme
- 1 tsp dried oregano
- 1 medium onion – chopped
- 2 cloves garlic – crushed
- 1 green pepper – de-seeded & chopped 1cm dice
- 3 slices bacon or salt pork – cut into 1cm lardons
- 300g large shrimp (large prawns) – shelled & de-veined
- 300g conche – chopped and marinated in lemon juice
- 400ml chicken stock
- canola or corn oil
- salt & freshly ground black pepper

Preparation

Place a medium sized pan over a medium-low flame, add a mini-slug of oil and allow to heat through. Add the bacon to the pan and fry until lightly golden. Add the onion, stir, reduce to a low flame and cover with a lid to sweat until soft and translucent. Remove the lid and add the green peppers and garlic and cook until soft.

Add the rice and stir well to coat the rice with the bacon fat and it just begins to cook. Add the herbs, peas, a little salt and pepper and sufficient stock to just cover the rice. Increase the flame and bring to the boil, reduce the flame to a simmer, cover with a lid and cook for approximately fifteen minutes. Add the prepared conch and stir well. Cover and continue to cook for a further ten minutes. Add the prawns (shrimp) and continue to cook until all of the stock is absorbed (add a little more stock if necessary). Check for seasoning and serve as a main dish.

MCB tip: Do not add too much stock, or you will finish up with a savoury rice pudding.

CANOLA OIL

Canola oil is pressed from tiny canola seeds produced by beautiful yellow flowering plants of the Brassica family. Canola was bred naturally from its parent rapeseed in the early 1970s. Canola, however, is NOT rapeseed - their nutritional profiles are very different.

Consumers recognize canola oil for its nutritional attributes as it contains the lowest level of saturated fatty acids of any vegetable oil. It is high in monounsaturated fatty acids, which have been shown to reduce blood cholesterol levels and contains 11% plant-based Omega 3 fat. It is also a rich source of vitamin E. Like all vegetable oils, canola oil is cholesterol free.

BAKED RED MULLET
with glazed prosciutto and poached quails eggs

I discovered this dish on a recent visit to the Ashburton Cookery School in Devon, which is one of the best cookery schools in the UK. If you ever get the chance to do a course there; it's totally worth the experience and cost. This recipe incorporates some basic cooking principals, so as long as you get your planning sorted, you should find the preparation and cooking relatively straight forward. However successfully pulling it all together will be a true test of your ability. Get it right and your guests will love the combination of flavours and textures.

Red mullet is widely found in the Mediterranean and this much admired fish has great flavour and texture; the larger the fish, the less troublesome the bones. Some species are found all around the world, but few can match the texture and flavour of those found in European waters. It is fast becoming a popular fish for pan-frying or grilling in the galley, or if you are heading for the beach or dockside, it marinades well and is fabulous on the BBQ.

Ingredients for four
- 4 x scaled red mullet fillets (120-150g per fillet)
- 1 lemon – juiced
- olive oil
- sea salt & ground black pepper
- 4 thin slices of prosciutto (Parma or Serrano)
- runny honey - warmed
- 12 quails eggs
- white wine vinegar
- crisp peppery salad leaves

Preparation
Pre-heat your oven to 180°C.

Take four ramekins and carefully crack 3 quail's eggs into each. Add a splash of white wine vinegar and leave for 5-10 minutes. This will start to 'cook' the eggs and will help form a nice shape when you poach them.

Place a small pan of water over a medium-high flame and bring to the boil, reducing the flame so the water simmers gently. Add a splash of white wine vinegar to the simmering water. Prepare a bowl of cold water and ice, which you will need for your soft poached eggs, when they are cooked.

Take a spoon and stir the simmering water in one direction, creating a vortex. Gently pour the first three quails eggs into the water and poach gently for approximately one minute. It is important that the egg yolks remain runny, so timing is fairly critical. Take a slotted spoon and gently remove the eggs from the water and place into your bowl of iced water. This will immediately arrest the cooking process. Once they are cold, remove them from the cold water and place into a container covered with a sheet of damp kitchen roll. Cook the rest of the quail's eggs in the same way. Clean out the pan, replenish with fresh water and place back over a low flame.

To prepare the prosciutto, simply lay the strips of Parma or Serrano ham onto a baking sheet, lined with some silicone paper (or mat). Bake for approximately ten minutes, until the prosciutto goes crispy, remove the tray from the oven and place the ham onto a cooling wire. Once cooled, brush each one with a little of warmed honey.

To prepare the fish fillets for cooking. Leave the skin in place and remove all the pin bones with tweezers. Place the fillets, skin side up onto a baking sheet lined with silicone paper (or mat), drizzle with a little olive oil and lightly sprinkle with a little sea salt and cracked black pepper. Bake in your pre-heated oven for approximately four minutes or until the fish is just cooked.

While the fish is cooking, take sufficient salad leaves for four plates and using a bowl, lightly dress with a little olive oil and a minute splash of white wine vinegar. Place a pile of leaves onto each plate and carefully rest a baked fish fillet onto each one. Cut the lengths of prosciutto in half with some scissors and place one on either side of the fish.

Using your slotted spoon, quickly, but carefully lift the quail's eggs into your pan of hot water; re-heat for thirty seconds to one minute without overcooking the yolks. Remove from the water, drain, pat dry and arrange three eggs onto each plate. Sprinkle each egg with a little finely ground black pepper. Squeeze a little lemon juice over each fillet and serve immediately.

MCB tip: For something totally different, lightly sprinkle the eggs with sumac.

FYI: Sumac is a red berry spice from North Africa.

BAKED WHOLE FISH
with herb salsa
This works so well if you are able to barbeque the fish; alternatively, a grill or oven will produce a great result too. To really get yourself in the mood for preparing this dish, get up really early one morning and seek out the delights of your local fish market. You are looking for either one or two large fish, which should feed all your guests or small to medium size fish which would be perfect for individual servings. Just make sure that what you buy will fit in your oven or under your grill, otherwise you will be making last minute alterations to your menu plan.

Gilthead Sea Bream (Daurade), usually available at around 20 – 40cm, are a nice size for between two or more people. It is probably the best of the sea bream family and is highly rated on mainland Europe.

For a starter even the humble (but very tasty) sardine is worth consideration, allowing two to three per person is ideal, depending on size. The relish I use is very similar to my "Salsa Verde" recipe (see Basics) but a slightly simpler method.

Ingredients for four

For the herb salsa
- 1 tbsp capers – drained
- good handful flat leaf parsley
- good handful basil leaves
- small handful mint leaves
- 4 spring onions
- 100ml olive oil
- 2 lemons – 1 juiced & 1 cut into wedges
- sea salt & freshly ground black pepper

If you are lucky enough to have a blender on board then simply whiz all the ingredients together until a smooth sauce is formed. If not, then finely chop the herbs, capers, spring onion and then add all the remaining ingredients – this will produce a slightly more rustic salsa but just as delicious. Place to one side.

For the fish
- whole fish (amounts as above) de-scaled & cleaned (head & tail removed if guests prefer)
- 100ml olive oil
- 1 red chilli – de-seeded & chopped
- 2 cloves of garlic - crushed
- sea salt & freshly ground black pepper
- lemon wedges

Preparation
Put the olive oil, chilli, garlic, salt and pepper in a blender and process until smooth. Rub this mixture all over the fish and leave to marinate for an hour. Drain excess oil from fish and place them onto an oiled baking sheet and grill for 4-5 minutes each side, or until cooked through.

If barbequing: make sure that all flames have died down and the coals are white hot, place fish on the barbeque and grill for 3-4 minutes each side. I would recommend investing in hinged fish grills, as this makes it so much easier to turn the fish as it cooks and helps to stop the fish sticking to the barbecue grill.

To serve
Place the cooked fish onto a serving dish, garnish with some dressed summer leaves and finish with the lemon wedges and a few generous grinds of black pepper. Serve the salsa separately on the side.

CHAR-GRILLED SWORDFISH
with tomato chilli salsa
You can prepare and cook this dish very quickly and it is totally ideal for when you hit the beach and set up the barbi. You can just as easily use tuna steaks, small whole sea bass, or sea bream (Dorade). Simply serve with a chilli spiked salsa and some ice-cold beer, both fresh out of your chiller box. Swordfish and tuna can easily be cut into cubes and placed onto brochettes for easy eating.

Ingredients for four
- 4 x 150g swordfish steaks
- 1 small lemon – juiced
- 4 tbsp olive oil
- 2 cloves garlic – finely sliced
- 1 tbsp flat leaf parsley – chopped
- sea salt & freshly ground black pepper

For the salsa
- 2 ripe & firm tomatoes – de-seeded & chopped (5mm dice)
- 1 x red bell pepper – de-seeded & chopped (5mm dice)
- 3 spring onions – cut into ¼s lengthways & finely chopped
- half cucumber – peeled, de-seeded & chopped (5mm dice)
- 1 green chilli – split, de-seeded & finely chopped
- 2 tbsp fresh coriander – roughly chopped
- 2 tbsp flat leaf parsley – roughly chopped
- 1 large clove of garlic – finely chopped
- 1 lime – zested & juiced
- extra virgin olive oil
- salt & freshly ground black pepper

Preparation

For the salsa, take a bowl and add the prepared tomato, red pepper, lime zest, cucumber, coriander, parsley chilli and a drizzle of olive oil. Lightly season with salt and ground black pepper, mix well together, cover and place into your fridge.

Place the lemon juice, olive oil, garlic, chopped parsley, salt and pepper into lasagne dish and mix together. Add the swordfish steaks, turning once to make sure that both sides start to take on the flavour from the marinade. Cover, refrigerate and marinate for one hour, turning the fish after half an hour.

Light the barbecue, grill or place a ribbed griddle pan over a medium-high flame. Drain the swordfish of any surplus oil and cook for around three minutes on either side, depending on thickness. Serve with a good spoonful of salsa spread over the top or placed to one side.

MCB tip: I would recommend serving ice cold San Miguel, Sol or Corona beer to compliment this dish and beat the heat from the salsa.

ESCOVITCH LOBSTER

If you've been to Jamaica, you will have already heard of Escovitch, which is a traditional way of cooking or serving fish in the Caribbean. If your guests love lobster and spicy food, then this is maybe the recipe for them. I originally found this recipe on the www.jamaicans.com website and as many Europeans would never think of serving lobster in such a 'fiery' way, I have given the recipe a little bit of a Euro twist and lightened up on the spices a bit.

The original recipe required that the lobster tails be fried whole in semi-deep oil, so for onboard safety's sake, I am going to take the pragmatic viewpoint and cook them in a more conventional way.

INGREDIENTS for six
- 6 lobster tails
- 250ml vegetable oil
- 175g plain flour
- 1tsp salt
- 1tsp ground black pepper
- 1tsp onion salt
- 1 tsp dried thyme
- 1tsp paprika
- 1 tsp cornflour (cornstarch)
- 175ml milk
- 3 egg – beaten

For the 'sauce'
- 125ml white vinegar
- 2 tbsp vegetable oil
- 2 tbsp sugar
- 1 tbsp ground black pepper
- 3 onions – thinly sliced
- 2 sweet red peppers – de-seeded & thinly sliced
- 1 scotch bonnet pepper
- 20 pimento seeds (whole allspice)

Preparation
For the 'sauce'
Slice the onions, red pepper and the scotch bonnet pepper, removing any seeds. Place a heavy based frying pan over a medium flame and add a couple of slugs of oil. Add the sliced onion, red peppers and scotch bonnet and cook for a few minutes until they start to soften a little.

Combine the vinegar, the sugar and oil in a small saucepan. Place over a medium flame and bring to the boil and add the onion mix and cook for a further five minutes. Remove from the flame and allow to cool. Strain off the liquid, retaining sufficient to barely cover the vegetables in the bottom of a small saucepan. This can either be served hot or cold.

For the lobster
While the sauce is cooling, take a bowl and combine the flour, thyme, sugar, salt, black pepper, onion salt, paprika and cornflour together. In a separate bowl, combine the egg and milk and beat well.

Take a large pan and half fill with cold water. Place over a high flame and bring to the boil and add a dessert spoon of salt. Add the lobster tails and cook for ten minutes. Remove from the pan and place to one side to cool a little.

Split the shell lengthways, remove the cooked lobster meat and, wash thoroughly and pat dry. Cut into bite sized pieces. Dip the pieces of lobster into the egg, then the flour mixture.

Place a high sided frying pan over a medium-high flame and heat the oil to around 200°C. Place the pieces of lobster (a few at a time) into the hot oil and fry until crisp and golden brown. Turn the pieces over and cook until golden. Adjust the flame as necessary. Place the pieces of cooked lobster into a warmed oven proof dish and pop into a low oven to keep warm.

Re-heat the onion mixture and spoon equal amount onto serving plates. Top with the pieces of lobster and garnish with some peppery salad leaves. Serve with plentiful amounts of ice cold beer, preferably Red Stripe.

FYI: The original recipe included four scotch bonnet chillies, which I felt was just too intrusive on the sweet flavour of lobster tails.

FRESH TUNA NIÇOISE
This recipe is a timeless classic and a very popular lunch dish, starter or evening main course. You decide when you are putting your menu plan together.

Ingredients for four
- 4 fresh 150g tuna steaks
- 225g fine beans – cooked al dente & trimmed
- baby spinach leaves
- bag of peppery leaves
- 250g new potatoes – cooked & quartered
- 4 ripe plum tomatoes - quartered
- 4 medium eggs – hard boiled & chopped
- 8 anchovy fillets – drained & split lengthways
- 1 tbsp fine capers in vinegar – drained
- 75g black olives – pitted
- fresh basil leaves
- virgin olive oil
- sea salt & black pepper

For the dressing
- 1 tbsp Dijon mustard
- 30ml white wine vinegar
- 120ml virgin olive oil
- I lemon – juiced
- salt & freshly ground black pepper

Preparation
For the dressing; place all of the dressing ingredients into a bowl and whisk together, cover and set to one side. I usually use a squeezy, extra wide neck, plastic sauce bottle, which can be stored in your fridge and will keep for days.

For the salad, put the dressing into a heavy based frying pan over a low flame and allow to heat. Add the prepared beans, potatoes and tomatoes and toss them together in the warm dressing, remove from the flame.

For the fish; place a ribbed griddle pan over a medium high flame to heat through. Brush the tuna steaks with olive oil and lightly season with the salt and pepper on both sides. Cook the tuna steaks for a couple of minutes on either side and keep warm while you cook off the other steaks.

To serve, place the salad leaves into a bowl and dress with a little olive oil. Build the leaves in a mound on serving plates or bowls and distribute the warm vegetables, capers and anchovies, then spoon over the warm salad dressing. Place a cooked tuna steak on top of the salad. Add a little chopped egg and sprinkle over with shredded basil.

GILT-HEAD BREAM (Daurade)
with a cherry tomato salsa and pecorino romano
This wonderful dish is great served as a light lunch or a very tasty starter for dinner. Make the cherry tomato salsa first, as the fish only takes a very short time to cook. You will find this fish right across the Med, but expect to buy them whole, so you will need to practice your filleting skills. This extremely attractive fish has juicy white flesh and large, easily handled bones. For a light lunch or starter, you might want to serve one fillet between two, depending on the size you buy, so one good sized fish could feed up to four for lunch. Although I might go for four fillets off two smaller sized fish.

Cherry tomato salsa
- 24 x red cherry tomatoes – cut in halves
- 10 x spring onions – trimmed, cut on an angle into 1cm pieces
- 1 large clove of garlic – finely chopped
- smoked sweet paprika
- 1 x Thai chilli (optional) – de-seeded & finely sliced
- 20 x medium basil leaves
- 1 tsp sherry vinegar (balsamic would work)
- pecorino romano
- virgin olive oil
- caster sugar
- sea salt & black pepper

Preparation
Place a non-stick frying pan over a low flame, add a little olive oil and heat through. Sweat the spring onions until they start to soften, add the garlic, chilli and a pinch of the smoked paprika. Continue cooking over a low flame for another minute.

Add the cherry tomatoes and a splash of sherry vinegar and turn up the heat a little. Once the tomatoes start to soften, tear up the basil leaves and add them along with a drizzle of olive oil, a little sea salt, a grind or two of black pepper and a good pinch of caster sugar. The basil leaves will wilt in the salsa. Taste and add more seasoning, vinegar or olive if necessary to balance the sweet/sour flavours. Remove from the flame while you cook the fish, cover and keep warm.

Ingredients for four (as a main course)
- 4 x fillets (approx 120g each) – pin-boned
- 1 x lemon – juiced
- corn oil
- 50g unsalted butter
- sea salt & black pepper

Preparation
Cut the fillets into two or three pieces on a severe angle. Place onto some kitchen paper, skin side up, pat dry and lightly season with sea salt.

Place a non stick frying pan over a medium flame and drizzle in a little corn oil and a knob of butter. The butter will melt and when it starts to foam (bubble), place the fillets into the pan skin side down, reduce the flame and cook gently for around four minutes or until the skin has started to turn golden in colour. Meanwhile, return the salsa to a medium-low flame to heat through again.

Using a palette knife, turn the fish over carefully and cook for another minute until it is perfectly cooked in the middle. Remove the fillets from the pan and drain onto kitchen paper.

Spoon a line of salsa across the serving plates and neatly arrange the fish pieces over the top. Return the fish pan over a high flame, add the butter and when it has melted, bubbled and the bubbles start to recede, add the lemon juice and shake the pan vigorously to blend the juices. Remove from the flame and spoon the golden nectar over the fish.

Finish off with some finely shaved Pecorino Romano over the fish and serve immediately.

GRILLED TERIYAKI MAHI-MAHI
with mango salsa
Mahi-Mahi (in Hawaiian) is also known as dolphin fish (not Dolphin as we know it), dorado, rakingo, calitos, maverikos or lampuki (Maltese delicacy). This fish, which is usually found in warm waters, tastes similar to flounder, tilapia and many other white fish. It is found widely in the Caribbean, North and South Americas, Costa Rica, Gulf of Mexico, Southeast Asia and many other areas. When removed from the water, the fish often changes colour through several hues (this being the reason for the Spanish name, Dorado Maverikos), finally fading to a muted yellow-grey.

After reading superyacht chef, Victoria Allman's recipe for Mahi-Mahi with a Mango Salsa, in a recent edition of Dockwalk, I decided that I just had to give it a go and include a recipe of my own for this fabulous fish. I have taken some of Victoria's ideas and thrown them up in the air with some of my own. I hope your guests enjoy the outcome.

Ingredients for four
- 4 mahi-mahi fillets – approx 150g each
- 2 tbsp runny honey
- 2 tbsp soy sauce
- 2 tbsp sweet Sake or Mirin (sweet rice wine)
- 1 tbsp vegetable oil
- 1 tbsp light brown sugar
- 1 tsp grated fresh ginger
- 1 clove garlic – crushed
- vegetable oil

Salsa
- 1 ripe mango – de-stoned, peeled & diced
- 2 firm, red tomatoes – skinned, de-seeded & chopped
- ½ cucumber – peeled, quartered, de-seeded & finely chopped
- 2 spring onions (scallions) – trimmed & chopped
- 1 lime – zested & juiced
- 1 red chilli – split, de-seeded & finely chopped
- fresh coriander (cilantro) – chopped
- salt & freshly ground black pepper

Preparation
To make the salsa; place the prepared ingredients into a bowl and stir to combine. Cover the bowl with cling film and place into your refrigerator until you are nearly ready to serve.

To prepare the marinade, take a small bowl and add the honey, soy sauce, sweet sake/mirin, vegetable oil, sugar, ginger and minced garlic and whisk together and set to one side.

Place the prepared mahi-mahi fillets into a large zip-lock bag and pour over the marinade, squeeze out the air and seal tightly. Shake the bag gently to coat the fillets with the marinade and refrigerate for around twenty to thirty minutes. If you don't have any zip lock bags, then place the fish into a lasagne dish, pour over the marinade and cover with cling film, then refrigerate.

Take the fillets out of the bag and dispose of the marinade. Brush or spray both sides of the fish fillets with vegetable oil and place onto a lightly oiled baking sheet.

Heat your grill to high and cook the fish through, this should take around four to five minutes each side. Serve the fish hot with the salsa.

ITALIAN STYLE FISH STEW
Fish soups and fish stews, mostly tomato based, are to be found on restaurant menus throughout the Med and about every French port where I have ever eaten.

My Italian variation is a straightforward recipe, guaranteed success every time. It is a feast of fish and shellfish in a tasty tomato broth. It can be served at lunch or dinner and can only be improved by using fresh tomatoes and adding a nice spoon of Rouille (see Basics – Page 232).

Ingredients for four

For the broth
- 2 tbsp olive oil
- I medium onion – roughly chopped
- 2 sticks celery – roughly chopped
- 2 carrots – roughly chopped
- 1 tsp dried thyme
- 2 dsp tomato purée
- a few threads of saffron
- 2 cloves of garlic – crushed
- 2 x 400g tins of chopped tomatoes
- 175ml dry white wine
- 2 dsp sweet paprika
- pinch of cayenne
- 2lts fish stock

For the seafood
- 4 x 100g pieces of white fish fillet – skin on, pin-boned
- 400g monkfish – membrane removed, cut into pieces
- 400g fresh mussels – scrubbed & de-bearded
- 220g small squid – cleaned & cut into rings
- 8 x large langoustine
- 2 tbsp chopped fresh basil or parsley
- salt & ground black pepper
- thick slices of rustic country bread to serve

Preparation
Pre-heat your oven to 200°C.

To make the broth, heat the oil in a heavy based pan over a medium flame. Add the onion, celery, carrots, thyme, cayenne and salt. Reduce to a medium-low flame and cook, stirring occasionally, for about eight to ten minutes until the vegetables start to take on a little colour. Add the tomato purée and garlic and cook for another minute. Increase the heat and stir in the tomatoes, white wine, saffron and hot fish stock. Bring to the boil, reduce the flame to low, cover with a lid and simmer gently for around thirty minutes. Strain the broth through a fine sieve into a clean pan and discard the vegetables. Cover with a lid and place the pan over a low flame to keep hot.

Ladle sufficient broth to cover the base of a shallow lasagne style dish. Add the fish and shellfish in four portions and pour over sufficient broth to cover. Wrap the dish with some tin-foil and place into your pre-heated oven for approximately twenty minutes until the mussels have opened. Discard any that remain closed.

Using warmed, large, wide rimmed soup bowls, add equal amounts of seafood to each and ladle over the broth. Top each dish with two langoustines and sprinkle with shredded basil or chopped parsley.

Serve with great big chunks of rustic country bread.

JAMBALAYA

Jambalaya is a Louisiana Creole dish with Spanish and French influences and is a close relation to the saffron coloured Spanish Paella. There are two primary methods of making this dish, with the most common being the *Creole Jambalaya*, also known as 'Red Jambalaya'. Firstly meat is added to the 'trinity' of celery, peppers and onions; the meat is usually chicken and sausage, such as andouille or smoked sausage. Next, vegetables and tomatoes are added to cook, followed by seafood. Rice and stock are added in equal proportions to finish.

The second style, more characteristic of south western and south-central Louisiana, is *Cajun Jambalaya*, which contains no tomatoes, the idea being that the closer you get to New Orleans, the more common tomatoes are in dishes. Meat is browned in a cast iron pot, so that it sticks a little to the pan and caramelises, which gives the Cajun Jambalaya its brown colour and flavour. The 'trinity' of 50% onions, 25% celery and 25% green bell pepper is added and fried in the meat fat until soft. Stock and seasonings are added and brought to the boil. The rice is added after around an hour.

Ingredients for four
- 1 red chilli – chopped
- 3 tbsp vegetable oil
- 2 cloves garlic – chopped
- 2 bay leaves
- 1 tsp cayenne pepper
- 1 tsp sweet paprika
- 1 green bell pepper
- 2 medium onions – chopped
- 3 sticks of celery – trimmed & chopped
- 150g smoked sausage – andouille or chorizo cut into 1/2cm thick slices
- 4 chicken breasts – cut into bite sized pieces
- 1 x 400g can chopped tomatoes
- 2 tbsp tomato purée
- 100g long grain rice
- 16 tiger prawns – shelled
- 250-500ml chicken stock
- small bunch parsley – chopped
- salt

Preparation
Heat the oil in a large heavy based pan over a medium flame. Add the chopped onions, bell peppers, celery, cayenne and chilli with a good pinch of salt. Stir regularly, while browning the vegetables for about ten minutes or until they are caramelised and taking on a good brown colour. Scrape the bottom and sides of the pan to loosen any browned particles.

Add the sausage and sweet paprika and cook, stirring for five minutes or so, scraping the bottom and sides of the pot to loosen any browned particles. Season the chicken pieces with salt and a little cayenne, add to the pan with the bay leaf and cook until it starts to brown. Add the garlic, tomatoes, tomato purée and 250ml of chicken stock and stir well to combine. Bring to the boil and reduce the flame to a simmer.

Add the rice and stir well. Cover and cook for around twenty minutes, without stirring or until the rice is nearly cooked. Remove the lid and add the prepared tiger prawns and a good handful of chopped parsley. Cook for another five minutes or so until the liquid has been absorbed. You may need to add a little more stock.

Remove the bay leaves and serve in large white, wide-rimmed soup bowls. Sprinkle with chopped parsley and serve.

LUXURY FISH CAKES

This dish is very adaptable and can be used for a light lunch or as an evening starter. All you need to do is adjust the size or shape. You can also prepare 'mini' luxury fish cakes and serve them with cocktails and dips once you've dropped anchor.

Ingredients for eight or more
- 400g waxy potatoes
- 300g salmon fillet - skinned
- 300g smoked haddock fillet
- 100g smoked salmon – shredded
- 100g cooked prawns
- 25g unsalted butter
- 1 lemon – zested & juiced
- sea salt and black pepper
- fresh thyme - few sprigs
- 1 lemon sliced
- 10 black peppercorns
- handful flat leaf parsley – finely chopped
- handful fresh coriander – finely chopped
- 6 tbsp plain flour
- 3 medium eggs – lightly beaten
- 75g fresh breadcrumbs
- milk
- sunflower oil

Preparation

Prepare a pan of salted water. Peel the potatoes and cut into even-sized pieces and add to the water. Place the pan over a high flame and bring to the boil. Reduce the flame to a rolling simmer until the potatoes are tender when pierced with a small sharp knife. Drain thoroughly into a colander and place the potatoes back into the pan. Place over a medium-high flame, cover with a lid and shake the pan vigorously for a few seconds, until the potatoes appear 'fluffy'. Remove from the flame. This process helps to remove any excess moisture from the potatoes. While still hot, thoroughly mash the potatoes and add the butter, lemon zest ,a table spoon of lemon juice and season with salt and freshly ground black pepper. Place the potato mixture into a clean bowl and allow to cool.

To cook the salmon, take a shallow pan and add the peppercorns, thyme, lemon slices and sufficient cold water to cover the salmon. Place the pan over a medium high flame and bring to the boil; reduce to a simmer, add a little salt and the salmon and poach for five minutes or until cooked through. Remove the salmon and place to one side to cool.

When the fish is cool enough to handle, break it into flakes, discarding any pin-bones. Add the fish, smoked salmon, prawns, chopped herbs (reserve a spoonful of herbs) and a little seasoning to the mashed potato and mix together; check for flavour and adjust if needed.

Dust your work surface with a little flour, divide the mixture into the required size and shape into neat patties or spheres. Put the flour into a bowl and season with a little salt and pepper. Place the eggs and a little milk into another bowl and whisk thoroughly. Place the breadcrumbs into a third bowl with the remaining chopped herbs and blend together.

First coat the fish cakes in the seasoned flour, dip into the egg and finally into the breadcrumbs, turning to coat evenly all over. Reshape them as necessary and place on a tray covered with greaseproof paper. Place into your fridge and chill for an hour or so.

To cook, place a non-stick frying pan over a medium low flame. Add the olive oil, heat through and reduce the flame. Fry the fish cakes for a couple of minutes on either side until they turn golden brown. If you need to keep the fishcakes warm, place into a pre-heated oven at 160°C, or serve immediately with some dressed peppery salad leaves and some lime mayonnaise.

MAHI-MAHI – FRUITY BAKE
with a lime and coriander couscous
This recipe was given to me by one of our grad students - Emma McIntyre, who is travelling the world with her husband Terry on their yacht. Emma recently posted some great photos on Facebook of a Mahi-Mahi that Terry had caught en route from Portugal to the Canaries. Emma did the business and prepared the whole fish and cut the fillets into suprèmes, which she cooked in various ways.

One of her ideas appealed to me as a great way of using up any fruit that you have spare, to create a really unusual fish meal. Emma says that this dish is really lovely and a bit different; making use of all the bits of fruit she had onboard for the passage.

Ingredients for four
- 4 x 150g mahi-mahi suprèmes
- 1 small sweet white onion – finely sliced
- 1 clove of garlic – crushed
- 1 mango – de-stoned, skinned & diced
- ½ small pineapple – skinned & diced
- 1 firm banana – peeled & diced
- 1 papaya – peeled, de-seeded & diced
- 1 lime or lemon cut into wedges
- ½ green pepper – de-seeded & sliced
- ½ red pepper – de-seeded & sliced
- handful of coriander – chopped
- 4cl tropical fruit juice
- 1 tsp mixed herbs
- 1 tsp paprika

Preparation
Pre-heat your oven to 180°C.
Prepare the lime and coriander couscous in advance and allow to cool.

Place all of the prepared fruit and onion into a bowl, drizzle with some light vegetable oil and mix together well. Take a lasagna dish and very lightly brush with olive oil. Add the Mahi-Mahi, lightly season on both sides and cover with the mixed fruit and vegetables. Pour over the fruit juice and sprinkle over the paprika and mixed herbs.

Cover the dish with tin foil and bake in your pre-heated oven for twenty to thirty minutes, until the fish is cooked through.

Using a fish slice, lift a fruit and vegetable topped suprème onto each plate and spoon some of the juice over the top. Sprinkle with chopped coriander. Turn out a ramekin of couscous onto each plate and serve.

PAELLA

Paella (pronounced pie-ay-ya) is a rice dish that originated in its modern form in the 19th century near Albufera, close to the eastern coast of Spain's Valencian region.

Many non-Spaniards view paella as Spain's national dish, however, most Spaniards consider it to be a regional Valencian dish and most Valencians regard it as one of their identity symbols. The dish has gained considerable popularity throughout most of the Spanish speaking world and among Hispanics in the USA.

There are three widely known types of paella: Valencian (Paella Valenciana – beans, green vegetables, rabbit), seafood paella (Paella de Marisco – shellfish and calamares) and mixed paella (Paella Mixta – free style), there are many variations.

Paella can be the easiest of dishes to cook, if you follow a few simple rules, you will find the end result makes for a hearty informal lunch or dinner. If you have BBQ time on your hands, it is also great cooked over glowing barbecue coals in the summer evening sun. You should be able to access most of the ingredients anywhere in the Med'.

Ingredients for six people
- olive oil – extra virgin is best
- 4 chicken breasts
- 500g diced loin of pork (optional)
- 6 langoustines
- 500g large prawns, shell on
- 1k mussels – de-beard & discard any open shells
- 250g calamares – prepared & cut into rings
- 100g clams (optional)
- 2 medium sized onions – roughly chopped
- 3 cloves of garlic
- 2 sweet red peppers – halved, de-seeded & chopped
- 150g French beans – top and tail & cut in half
- 250 g paella rice (long grain will do)
- chicken or vegetable stock (2½ x volume of rice)
- 1 sachet of Paellero paella seasoning
- 2 large fresh lemons
- flat leaf parsley – chopped
- salt & black pepper

Preparation
Cut each chicken breast into three or four pieces and the pork into bite sized chunks. Coarsely chop the onion, peppers and garlic and lightly fry in the olive oil over a medium flame until they start to soften. Remove the ingredients and place into a bowl. Add a little more oil to the pan and fry the chicken and pork until they turn golden brown. Return the vegetables to the pan and mix the cooked ingredients together before adding the rice and paella seasoning, followed by ¾ of the hot stock.

Cover the paella pan with some tin foil and cook over a low heat (or in the oven) until nearly all the stock has been absorbed by the rice. After about 20-30 minutes, check to see if the rice is cooked. If necessary, top up with a little more stock.

Mix in the mussels, calamares, clams, beans and the prawns. Decorate the top of the paella with the langoustines, by placing them on top of the other ingredients like the numbers on a clock face, replace the foil and finish cooking for a further five to ten minutes.

Cut the lemons into large wedges. Remove the pan from the heat and decorate with the lemon wedges and sprinkle liberally with the chopped parsley. Place the pan in the middle of the table with a ladle or very large spoon and just let everyone help themselves.

MCB tip: It is great to use a paella pan, however this is not always possible as your hob size may be extremely limited. This is an excellent dish to cook on the dockside or beach on a large barbi.

PAN FRIED FISH with a ZINGY GREEN SALAD

I decided to include a recipe which does not specify the type of fish to use. As I mentioned earlier, you should try to buy fish on a daily basis when you can. Visit a local fish market or buy direct from a fishing boat, tied up at the dockside. This gives you the opportunity to vary your menu plan, by replacing the fish you had planned to use, for another, which is wonderfully fresh. Use fillets of sea bream, sea bass or snapper for this recipe. There are over 250 different species of snapper and these include: Bordemar, Bourgeois, Therese, Red Snapper, Job Gris and Job Jaune; these all have good firm flesh with an excellent flavour.

Ingredients for four
- 4 white fish fillets – as noted above
- plain flour
- 25g unsalted butter
- sunflower oil
- salt and ground black pepper

For the salad
- 15g fresh cilantro leaves (coriander) – chopped
- 15g flat leaf parsley – chopped
- 15g fresh mint leaves - shredded
- 3 shallots – finely sliced
- 100g mangetout – shredded diagonally
- 2 fresh limes – zested & juiced
- large red chilli – split, de-seeded & sliced diagonally
- coarse sea salt

For the dressing
- 2 tbsp soft brown sugar
- 2 tbsp caster sugar
- 2 tbsp water
- 2 tbsp fish sauce (Nam Pla)
- fresh lime – zested & juiced

Preparation

Prepare the green salad first, by adding the prepared chilli, cilantro, mint, parsley, shallots, lime zest and mangetout to a bowl and mixing well together. Cover with cling film and put to one side and lightly refrigerate until you are ready to serve.

Add three to four tablespoons of flour to a shallow dish, add a good pinch of salt and a few twists of black pepper and mix thoroughly. Dip the fish fillets into the seasoned flour on both sides and shake off any surplus flour.

Place a large heavy based frying pan over a medium flame, add a couple of slugs of oil and allow to heat through. Add the butter and allow to bubble. Carefully place the fillets into the oil, cooking the presentation side first for a couple of minutes before gently turning and cooking for a further two minutes on the other side.

While the fish is cooking, create the fabulous dressing, by placing a small saucepan over a low flame; add both sugars and water and stir until the sugar dissolves. Continue to cook over a medium-low flame until the mixture starts to turn golden. Remove from the flame and stir in the fish sauce (Nam Pla) and two tablespoons of fresh lime juice and stir thoroughly to blend.

To serve, place one fillet onto each plate and top each fillet with the green salad. Drizzle the warm dressing over the salad and then around each plate.

MCB tip: When I first tested this recipe, I also added some peppery salad leaves as a side on the plate, drizzled with some extra virgin olive oil. This helped to create a third dimension and balance out the sweet and sour dressing.

PAN FRIED RED MULLET
with tahini sauce

Many of my Global Research Team have worked on yachts out of Greece, Turkey, Cyprus and Egypt and have experienced some amazing Lebanese influences in the 'local' food they have tried in that part of the Eastern Med. Having personally experienced the intense frenzy which occurs when you arrive by taxi at the fish restaurants down at the fishing ports of some North African countries, you have to understand that all the hassle is definitely worthwhile. The food produced in these havens of fish and shellfish cookery is to die for – simple, fresh and tasty.

Female crew would be advised to visit fishing ports accompanied by male crew, as the attention you will receive, although well-meaning, can be very intimidating to the uninitiated.

One of the most popular items on menus in many of these fish restaurants, along the Lebanese coast, is deep-fried red mullet, which is accompanied by a fabulous tahini (sesame paste) sauce. Because many of you will be working in galleys, which are not always ideal environments for deep frying, I am going to give you a recipe for pan frying the fillets, which is easier and safer to cook in the confines of the smaller galley.

Ingredients for four
- 8 x 100g red mullet fillets – skin on
- mixed salad leaves
- 2 tbsp extra virgin olive oil
- 50g unsalted butter
- 1 lemon
- sea salt & ground black pepper

For the tahini sauce
- 75ml tahini – stir well before using
- 75ml cold water
- 1 lemon – juiced
- 1 clove garlic – crushed
- sea salt

Preparation
To make the sauce, take a small bowl, add the tahini and lemon juice and beat with a fork; the tahini will thicken to a thickish paste. Add the water and beat briskly until you reach the consistency of pouring cream. Add a pinch of salt and the crushed garlic and pour into one or more ramekins ready to serve.

Place the red mullet fillets onto some kitchen paper, skin side up, pat dry and lightly season with sea salt and ground black pepper. Place a large, non-stick frying pan over a medium flame, add the olive oil and heat through, add half the butter and allow to bubble. Add the fish fillets, skin side down and cook for approx' two minutes, then using a fish slice or palette knife, turn the fillets over and cook the other side for a minute more. Remove the fish fillets from the frying pan and place onto some kitchen paper to remove some of the oil. Place a small mound of salad leaves onto each plate and strategically place the fish fillets over the leaves.

Return the frying pan to a medium-high flame, add the unsalted butter, melt and allow the butter to foam. Once the bubbles start to subside, add the lemon juice and shake the pan vigorously. Remove from the flame and pour a little of the 'amber nectar' over the fish fillets.

Serve immediately and let your guests add the tahini sauce, which you can serve separately.

PAN FRIED SWORDFISH
with lemon and capers
If we are talking simple, then things don't get much easier than this. Emma has cooked this dish, charter after charter and always found that it went down a storm. It is quick and simple and yet manages to hit the mark every time. Perfect food for a balmy Mediterranean summer evening. The mixture of lemon, capers and nut brown butter (beurre noisette), served with white fish, and is one of the classics - a marriage made in heaven.

Ingredients for six
- 6 swordfish steaks (not too thick)
- corn oil
- 1 lemon - halved
- 2 tbsp capers – drained
- 75g unsalted butter – chopped into dice
- flat leaf parsley – roughly chopped
- sea salt & black pepper

Preparation
Take your swordfish out of the fridge to let it come up to room temperature. Pat the fish dry and season well.

Take a large heavy based frying pan and place over a medium flame and pour in a good slug of corn oil and half the butter. Once the butter melts and the bubbles start to subside, cook the swordfish for approximately 2-3 minutes on each side depending on thickness, until golden. Keep warm while you are cooking the remaining swordfish.

Arrange the swordfish on serving plates. Working quickly, add a slug of corn oil and increase the flame. Add the remaining butter and once the bubbles start to subside, add the capers and lemon juice. Shake the pan vigorously. Remove from the flame and dress the fish with the caper and butter sauce.

Finally sprinkle with chopped parsley and serve.

To serve as a lunch dish
Keep it simple and let the flavours speak for themselves, I would serve it with a really good green salad, maybe just very lightly dressed with olive oil, a squeeze of lime and lightly sprinkled with some dried chilli flakes.

To serve as a main course
To make it more substantial I might serve it on a bed of braised fennel and some baby new potatoes.

To take it in another direction
Simply replace the lemon with lime and add chopped coriander instead of flat leaf parsley – simple!

PAN ROASTED COD
with a fresh herb and toasted pine nut crust

Ingredients for four
- 4 thick pieces of cod fillet (120-140g)
- 4 tbsp flat leaf parsley – finely chopped
- 4 tbsp basil – finely shredded
- light olive oil
- 2 cloves of garlic – finely chopped
- 1 lemon – zested and juiced
- 1 lemon – cut into eight neat wedges
- 2 tbsp pine nuts
- 75g breadcrumbs
- 50g unsalted butter – melted
- salt & ground black pepper

Preparation
Pre-heat your oven to 200°C.

Take a lasagna style dish and add half a dozen good slugs of olive oil, half the lemon juice, half the crushed garlic, one dessert spoon each of chopped parsley and chopped basil. Season with a little salt and three or four turns of your pepper mill. Coat the cod on both sides and place into your fridge for around thirty minutes to take on all the wonderful flavours.

Place a small frying pan over a low flame; add the pine nuts and dry fry. Turn regularly and cook until golden brown. Remove from the flame and put to one side. Take a bowl and mix together the breadcrumbs, lemon zest and the remaining parsley, basil and garlic. Lightly season with salt and a little black pepper, then add the melted butter and remaining lemon juice. Mix together thoroughly.

Remove the cod from the fridge and place into a clean, shallow, buttered, ovenproof dish and press the herb crust firmly onto the cod to form an even covering. Sprinkle the toasted pine nuts over the herb crust and gently press down.

Place the fish into your pre-heated oven for around twenty minutes until the crust is lightly browned and the fish is cooked through. Serve immediately.

PANCETTA WRAPPED COD LOIN
with asparagus and lime mayonnaise

Although I have used cod loin for this recipe, you can just as easily do a more up-market version and use Monkfish instead. This is a great dish to serve at lunch with a little salad or as a starter or main course for an evening meal. Obviously if you are using this for a starter, then you will need to downsize the portions just a tad. This method of roasting fish is something we have always shown our students and by just allowing the pancetta to take on a little colour before it goes in the oven, helps to produce a lovely moist and very tasty end product.

I often use ready-made mayo' for this recipe and thin it slightly with lime zest and juice, to give a more runny consistency. Classically mayonnaise is served with cold asparagus and hollandaise is served with hot asparagus. As I am serving the hot asparagus, I will bend the rules a little.

Ingredients for four
- 4 x 150g nice round cod loin fillets
- 12 thin slices of pancetta (or prosciutto)
- 1 lime – finely zested and juiced
- 24 fresh asparagus spears – trimmed & ready to cook
- freshly ground black pepper
- 4 fresh young shoots of rosemary – very finely chopped
- 4 tbsp mayonnaise
- 1 tbsp sunflower oil
- 25g unsalted butter

Preparation
Pre-heat your oven to 180°C

Firstly, season your pieces of fish with just a little black pepper, half the lime zest and finely chopped rosemary. To wrap each portion of fish, lay three pieces of pancetta onto a clean chopping board. Place a portion of fish in the centre and wrap the pancetta over and round neatly, so that your piece of fish is fairly well covered.

Place a medium sized, heavy based frying pan over a medium flame, heat through and add the oil and butter. Once the butter has melted and starts to bubble, add your pieces of fish, presentation side down and cook for about one minute, taking on a little colour. Carefully turn over and cook for a further minute, before transferring to a hot baking sheet and finish off cooking in your pre-heated oven. This should take around another ten minutes.

While the fish is cooking, place a pan of shallow water over a medium flame and bring to the boil. Reduce to a steady simmer and add a little salt. If the asparagus is not too thick, it should only take a couple of minutes and cook, retaining a little crispness. Drain and keep warm.

Place the prepared mayo' into a bowl and add the remaining lime zest and juice little-by-little until you reach the desired consistency.

Remove the fish from the oven and place to one side for a second. Using four shiny white plates, add six asparagus spears to each plate. Add the cooked fish, slightly overlaying the bottom of the asparagus, with the tips showing. Finish each plate with a good drizzle of mayo' and serve immediately.

MCB tip: I sometimes use a thin Hollandaise sauce to go with this recipe, so check out one of the recipes in the Breakfast or Basics section and add a little boiling water to thin the consistency a little.

RED THAI CURRIED PRAWNS
This recipe is equally good used with fish, pork or chicken.

Ingredients for one large curry
- 750g prepared tiger prawns – uncooked
- 1 shallot – chopped
- 1 lemon grass stalk – trimmed & finely sliced
- 2-4 dried red chillies – re-hydrated in warm water, drained & chopped
- 4 cloves garlic – sliced
- 1 thumb of root ginger – peeled & sliced
- 1 tbsp tomato purée
- ½ tsp ground cumin
- 1 tsp ground coriander
- ¼ tsp ground white pepper
- 3 tsp Nam Pla (fish sauce)
- 1 tsp shrimp paste
- 1 tsp caster sugar
- 1 dsp chilli powder
- 1 can thick coconut milk or cream of coconut
- 1 lime – zested & juiced
- handful fresh coriander or basil – chopped for garnish

Preparation
Either place all the ingredients, excluding the prawns and coriander, into your food processor and whizz-up with a little coconut milk, or for the more energetic and maybe more authentic version, take fifteen to twenty minutes grinding up the dry ingredients with a pestle and mortar into a sticky paste.

If you are using immediately, fry the paste in a little oil over a medium-low flame to release the fragrance before adding the prawns. Stir the prawns to cover with the paste. Add the remaining coconut milk to create the curry sauce. If more sauce is required, add a little chicken or vegetable stock.

Taste for seasoning and adjust if required, before serving with fragrant Thai rice, garnished with the chopped coriander or basil. If not sufficiently salty, add more fish sauce. If too salty, add another squeeze of lime juice. If too sour, add more sugar. If too spicy, add more coconut milk.

MCB tip: If you want to prepare your curry paste in advance and store it. Spoon it into an airtight jar or container and place in your refrigerator. It should keep for around one week. Alternatively, it freezes really well and a great idea is to have a dedicated ice cube tray and freeze it down into individual portions. Once frozen, you can turn out into a zip-lock bag, label, date and pop back in the freezer.

SEARED TUNA
with soy, avocado and cilantro

This recipe was 'given' to us by a great guy from Canada called Matt Speight, so a big thanks to you fella. Emma and I were blown away by the immense flavour of this dish.

Ingredients for four
- 4 fresh tuna steaks (or swordfish)
- 2 big handfuls of fresh cilantro (coriander) – finely chopped
- 1 ready to eat avocado – stoned, peeled & finely chopped
- 1 tbsp of fresh grated ginger
- 1 garlic clove – finely chopped
- juice of two limes
- two tbsp soy sauce
- salt & ground black pepper
- extra virgin oil
- corn oil

Preparation
Combine the cilantro, ginger, garlic, lime juice, soy sauce, salt, pepper and two tablespoons of olive oil. Stir until well combined, brush both sides of the tuna steaks with the dressing and set aside an hour or so. Refrigerate the remaining dressing.

Place a heavy based frying pan over a medium-high flame, add a little oil. Season the tuna and carefully place into the very hot frying pan. Sear for 1 minute on each side to form a thin crust. Spoon half of the remaining cilantro mixture over the fish in the pan and heat through. Transfer the steaks to serving plates and sprinkle the prepared avocado over the fish and spoon the remaining mixture over top. Voila!

SEA BASS with a MUSTARD CREAM SAUCE

This simple but tasty recipe was created by my young son Ash, who found that the blend of crème fraîche, Dijon mustard with a touch of lemon juice works really well. The mustard sauce will go with many different types of pan-fried or grilled fish fillets. If you have unexpected guests onboard for dinner and have the opportunity to nip down to the fish market, this can make a quick, easy and tasty dish for a dinner party dish, as a starter or main item.

Ingredients for six
- 3 medium sea-bass – filleted (or 6 x 150g fillets)
- peppery salad leaves
- 1 lemon – cut into fine wedges
- 2 tbsp Dijon mustard
- 350g crème fraîche
- ½ lemon - juiced
- ½ tsp caster sugar
- 25g butter – melted
- sunflower oil
- sea salt & freshly ground black pepper

Preparation
Pre-heat your grill.

To make the sauce, combine the mustard, crème fraîche, sugar and one teaspoon of lemon juice together in a small saucepan over a low flame – stir constantly with a wooden spoon. Simmer the sauce and stir constantly until the sauce thickens. Check for seasoning and consistency and add a little more lemon juice if necessary. This sauce can be made in minutes and needs little cooking time. Cover and set aside to keep warm.

Check the fillets for pin-bones and remove. Cut the fish fillets into two or three pieces on the diagonal (leave whole if you prefer), brush with a little melted butter on both sides and lightly season with salt and black pepper, and place onto baking sheet skin side up. Cook under your pre-heated grill (not too near the flame) for two minutes or so, until the fish is nearly cooked through. Carefully turn the fillets, brush with melted butter and finish cooking for another minute or so until cooked through.

Transfer the fish to serving plates and spoon some sauce to one side. Garnish with a few salad leaves and lemon wedges. This dish is great served simply with some new potatoes and French beans.

SKATE WING
with preserved lemon and garlic olives
This is an unusual fish, as the flesh is rather stringy in appearance as opposed to flaky as you expect with most fish. Some writers claim that a strong smell of ammonia is natural to skate, this is wrong and any smell of ammonia should disappear on washing and if it doesn't, then the fish is likely to be 'off'.

Skate does not need to be 'played with'. Keep the cooking process nice and simple, to compliment the delicious flavour and texture of this fish.

This recipe is my version of a dish we were lucky enough to try when we were on holiday in Morroco a couple of years back. We were served poached skate with Morrocan spices, which was so unusual, that I just had to create something that was typically Morrocan, but with my stamp on it. I felt that leaving out the spices would give the dish a 'cleaner' flavour.

Ingredients for four
- 4 very fresh skate wings (around 200g each) – trimmed
- extra virgin olive oil
- peel from one preserved lemon – chopped
- 2 x lemons – one juiced & one quartered to serve
- 16 x green garlic olives – pitted (make these yourself – see below)
- 1 x clove garlic – crushed
- 25g unsalted butter
- handful of flat leaf parsley – finely chopped
- sea salt & black pepper

Preparation
Half the olives and place into a bowl with the crushed garlic, half the parsley and a good slug of olive oil, lightly season, stir well, cover and put to one side.

Place a non-stick frying pan over a medium flame, add three to four tablespoons of olive oil, lightly season the skate wings with sea salt and place into the pan service side down. Reduce the heat a little and cook for around four minutes. Using a fish slice, gently turn over the skate wings, add the lemon juice and cook for a further four minutes or until the fish is cooked and starts to come away from the bones. As skate wings are quite big, you will need to cook them one at a time or start them off on the hob and place into your oven to finish cooking.

Remove the skate wings from your oven and place onto serving plates. Return the frying pan to a medium-high flame and add the chopped, preserved lemon peel, garlic olives, remaining parsley and the butter. When the butter foams, turn off the heat and shake the pan vigorously for a couple of seconds. Spoon the butter sauce over each skate wing and garnish with a wedge of lemon.

MCB tip: The classic way to serve pan fried skate is with black butter. This is very simple to cook, however the black butter requires care and attention. I also like to go for a beurre noisette, a nut-brown butter with lemon juice, which is beautiful. I also like to add a handful of capers which compliment skate wing perfectly.

SWORDFISH BROCHETTES
with pak choi coleslaw

I use a similar style marinade for this dish as I do for my Char grilled Swordfish recipe, but replace the lemon with lime, parsley with coriander and add a few dried chilli flakes to give the fish that extra blast. This type of marinade is very simple and effective, as the fish takes onboard all the wonderful flavours of citrus, herbs, garlic and olive oil. Brochettes are readily available in supermarkets and are usually made of wood. I usually buy 7" (18cm) Tiger Tiger, bamboo skewers from Akram's, our local Asian store. My recipe suggests that you soak the brochettes in cold water for a while before spiking the food, as this will help stop the brochettes from charring too much over an open flame.

Ingredients for four
- 2 swordfish steaks (2.5 cm thick)
- 2 cloves garlic – finely sliced
- pinch of dried chilli flakes
- 1 tbsp coriander – chopped
- 1 lime – juiced
- 2 limes – cut into eight wedges
- 4 tbsp olive oil
- 100g pak choi (bok choy) – split end-to-end & shredded
- 100g mangetout – finely sliced on the diagonal
- 1 stick of celery – trimmed & finely sliced on the diagonal
- 4 spring onions – trimmed & roughly sliced on the diagonal
- 1 tbsp sesame seeds – lightly toasted
- salt & freshly ground black pepper

For the dressing
- 1 tbsp light sesame oil
- 3 tbsp light soy sauce
- 1 tbsp sherry vinegar
- 1 tbsp golden caster sugar
- 1 lime – juiced
- 2 red chillies – split, de-seeded & finely chopped

Preparation
Soak your bamboo skewers in cold water for approximately one hour. Cut your swordfish steaks on the diagonal into 2.5cm squares.

Place the lime juice, olive oil, garlic, chopped coriander, chilli flakes, salt and pepper into a bowl or lasagne dish and mix together. Add the pieces of swordfish and turn to coat all sides with the marinade. Cover and refrigerate for an hour.

Light your barbecue or pre-heat your grill. Alternatively, get ready a ribbed griddle pan and place over a medium flame to heat through.

Place the prepared pak choi, mangetout, celery and springs into a bowl, very lightly season with a pinch of salt and a couple of grinds of black pepper, toss together, cover and refrigerate.

Build the skewers by alternating three pieces of swordfish with two wedges of lime per skewer. Try to make sure that you pass the skewer through the skin of the fish and lime wedge, as this will help to hold everything together.

Build the coleslaw into a mound on your serving plates and drizzle over some soy dressing and sprinkle with sesame seeds.

If you are using a barbi, make sure the coals have got a good grey/white ash over them and cook the swordfish   for around two minutes on either side. Carefully remove the skewers from the heat and rest over the coleslaw to serve.

SWORDFISH WAGAMAMA

Wagamama has become a well known global brand, comprising of a range of retail food products and a chain of restaurants, specialising in Pan-Asian food in the style of a modern noodle bar. My daughter Alanna, first visited Wagamama in Brighton a while back and was totally blown away with the mélange of flavours – I recall the description of her meal as "a time-bomb of Asian flavours" – which was maybe not the most sensitive of descriptions in the early twenty fist century, post 9/11 and 7/7 era!

The first Wagamama restaurant opened in 1992 off Gower Street in Bloomsbury, London, which I understand still exists today. The chain now includes branches all over the UK plus a couple in Ireland – not forgetting outlets in Denmark, Belgium, Holland, Switzerland, Cyprus, Greece, Turkey, Egypt, Dubai, Australia, New Zealand and USA.

The chain's website translates the word "Wagamama" as a "willful or naughty child"; however, a more accurate translation of the Japanese adjective is "selfish". Their trademark slogan is: *"Positive eating + positive living"*. Mmmmmmmm – not too sure about that one!!

I first discovered Wagamama sauce in early 2009 and thought about how I could create a simple, tasty fish dish to serve with some pasta or noodles, hence the recipe below.

Ingredients for four
- 4 x 175g fresh swordfish steaks (2cm thick)
- Wagamama fragrant coconut, ginger & lemongrass sauce
- 400g fusilli – or similar fresh egg pasta
- 250g crème fraîche (Greek yoghurt is OK)
- 4 peppadew – finely shredded (baby sweet piquant peppers)
- 1 lime – zested & juiced
- 100g unsalted butter
- small bunch coriander – finely chopped
- olive oil
- salt & black pepper

Preparation
Pre-heat your oven to 160°C.

Pour a small amount of Wagamama sauce into a ramekin or similar, then using a pastry brush, lightly coat both sides of each fish steak with the sauce. Cover and set the swordfish to one side to refrigerate for approximately one hour.

Cut the butter into small dice (1/2 cm) and place into a medium sized bowl. Grate the whole lime into a fine zest and add to the butter with a little of the juice, plus a good tablespoon of finely chopped coriander. Using your hands, squeeze and soften the butter and other ingredients together until thoroughly blended. Take a square of grease-proof paper (foil will do) and shape the butter mix into a cylinder, place onto the paper and roll into a sausage shape, twisting the ends to seal. Place into your fridge for thirty minutes or more.

Timing now becomes critical. Place a heavy based saucepan of water over a medium flame and bring to the boil, add a little salt and a couple of slugs of olive oil.

Place a griddle pan over a medium flame, lightly brush with sunflower oil and heat thoroughly. Remove the swordfish from the fridge and fry for three to four minutes on either side. Remove, place onto a baking sheet, brush again with Wagamama sauce and keep hot in your oven. Repeat this process until all the fish is cooked.

While the last piece of fish is cooking, pour the fusilli into the boiling water and cook until al dente – this should only take two or three minutes. Drain the pasta and put back into the pan and add the crème fraîche and shredded peppers. Sit well and return to a low heat and season to taste.

Arrange the pasta in four bowls or plates and top each with a tuna steak. Remove the butter from the fridge, cut into slices and top each steak with one or two discs of the savoury butter and serve.

TUNA CHARMOULA

Charmoula, chermoula or carmoula is a marinade used in Algerian, Moroccan and Tunisian cooking, usually to flavor fish or shellfish, but it can also be used on lightweight meats such as chicken, pork or lamb or vegetables.

Charmoula is often made of a mixture of herbs, oil, lemon juice, preserved lemons, garlic, cumin and salt. It may also include onion, fresh coriander, ground chilli peppers, black pepper and saffron. However, there are many different recipes that use different spices and the proportions vary widely. In most recipes, the first two prime ingredients are garlic and coriander.

Tuna Charmoula is an authentic Moroccan dish, suitable for any occasion. It is absolutely delicious and easy to prepare - don't let your guests miss out on a real treat!

Ingredients for four
- 4 tuna steaks – not too large
- 2 tsp toasted cumin seeds
- ½ tsp cayenne pepper
- 2 tsp sweet paprika
- 1 lemon – juiced
- 3 cloves garlic – roughly chopped
- handful each of fresh coriander & flat leaf parsley
- olive oil
- ½ tbsp salt

Preparation

Blend the coriander, parsley, cumin, cayenne, paprika, garlic, lemon juice, salt and two tablespoons of olive oil for a couple of minutes. When it comes out of the blender, the mixture needs to be chunky rather than smooth - that is Charmoula!

Rub the charmoula over the tuna steaks evenly on both sides. Put the steaks in a dish and cover with cling film and place into your 'fridge for a couple of hours, turning them every fifteen minutes or so.

Heat some olive oil in a pan until it's nice and hot. Carefully place the tuna steaks into the pan and fry for approximately four minutes on either side, depending on their thickness. You want the tuna to be slightly pink in the middle. Serve immediately.

ZARZUELA
Catalan fish stew

I used to drive down to the south of Spain every autumn and spend a month or so unwinding after a busy summer season in my restaurant. Driving back through the Basque area in the early 90's, I stopped at a hotel in the Pyrenees with my family and remember being treated to Zarzuela, one of the most fabulous fish stews I have ever tasted. The dish was a mixture of white fish and shellfish, such as king prawns, clams and mussels, with garlic, tomatoes, red peppers and chilli, served bubbling away in a sizzling hot terracotta dish. Since then, I have come to realise that this dish can be delicious or a disaster, depending on where you eat it and who cooks it.

My all time foodie hero, Keith Floyd, used to tell the 'uninitiated' that Zarzuela was a type of fish only caught in the Mediterranean waters off the South coast of Spain – what a character!

Ingredients for four

- 4 halibut steaks – skinned
- 250g prepared squid – cut into pieces
- 500g mussels – cleaned & de-bearded
- 250g tiger prawns – uncooked
- 4 Dublin Bay prawns – uncooked
- 16 clams - scrubbed
- 2 x medium Spanish onions – sliced
- 100g chorizo – cut into ½cm dice
- 4 cloves of garlic – chopped
- 4 almonds – toasted, skinned & roughly chopped
- 2 slices of thin white bread – crusts removed
- 400g tomatoes – skinned, de-seeded & chopped
- 50ml Spanish brandy (Magno works well)
- sea salt & ground black pepper
- 1 dsp tomato purée
- 1 tsp sweet paprika
- 150ml dry white wine
- 1 lemon – juiced
- flat leaf parsley – roughly chopped
- flour for dusting
- extra virgin olive oil

Preparation

Place a large heavy based casserole over a medium flame, add two tablespoons of olive oil, allow to heat through and sauté the onion for a couple of minutes until it turns golden brown. Add the tomato concassé, tomato purée, half the garlic and paprika, reduce the heat and cook until the oil separates and appears on the top of the tomato mixture, this is called a 'sofrito'. Put to one side.

While the sauce is cooking, heat a little oil in a frying pan and fry the bread on both sides. Cut into small squares and place into a mortar with the chopped almonds, the remaining chopped garlic and a little olive oil and pound to a fine paste; this is called a 'picada'. Put to one side.

Put three tablespoons or so of flour into a bowl and add a good pinch of salt and a twist of black pepper. Add the pieces of fish and dust with flour, shaking off any surplus. Heat five teaspoons of olive oil in a heavy based frying pan over a medium flame and fry the pieces of fish until they turn golden brown. Next pan fry the prawns, squid and Dublin Bay prawns. Place each item of fried seafood into at clean, high sided casserole dish and place over a low flame. Pour over the brandy and flame (flambé). Pour over the white wine and lemon juice and add the "sofrito", gently stir, bring to the boil and simmer for three to four minutes.

Now add the mussels and clams, cover with a lid and steam over a low flame for around five minutes, until the mussels and clams have opened, discarding any that remain closed.

Place the "picada" into a bowl and add a few tablespoons of the tomato broth, to thin the mixture a little. Mix thoroughly together and pour back into the casserole, stirring gently into the broth, taking care not to break-up the fish. The "picada" will thicken the sauce. Finally, add the chopped parsley and gently stir into the broth, season to taste and serve in large white, wide rimmed soup bowls.

MCB tip: It's a big "must", to serve freshly baked crusty bread or ciabatta with this dish.

FYI: Zarzuela, by the way, is also the name of the Spanish Royal Palace in Madrid. It is the official residence of King Juan Carolos and his wife Queen Sofia of Spain, who do not actually live there, rather choosing instead to live in the more modest Palacio de la Zarzuela on the outskirts of Madrid.

I am only telling you this because, King Juan Carlos and his family spend their summer vacations in Majorca and are often seen out and about in a very public arena. The connection of course, is that Palma is one of the global hot-spots for yachts and superyachts, so if by chance you bump into them one day, just mention my name!

MEAT MAINS

My mantra for cooking on yachts and superyachts has always been two fold – *"keep it simple"* and *"easy eating"*. I believe that the owner, charterer and crew, should be able to sit down for a meal and not have to pick their way through bones and other non edible food items, which some chefs seem to think look attractive on a plate. I also firmly believe that *"less is more"*, as I would always prefer to serve a beautifully presented plate of food to a guest that shows a good percentage of *'white space'*. If I can achieve this, as opposed to an over-crowded plate, which my guests would struggle to plough through, I know that there is a high percentage chance that plates will return to the galley 'clean'. This thinking is of course two fold. Firstly you are not setting your guests a challenge; rather you are providing them with an interesting plate of tasty, well balanced, attractive food. Secondly you need to consider the stowage of residual food waste. To put this into a simplistic context - the less decaying food debris you have to contend with, the better.

Marinating

This is the process of covering food with a seasoned, often acidic liquor before cooking. The origins of the word allude to the use of brine (aqua marina) in the pickling process, which led to the technique of adding flavour by immersion in liquid. The liquid in question, the 'marinade' can be acidic with ingredients such as vinegar (seldom malt), lemon, lime or orange juice, wine, fruit juice, or more savory with soy or supermarket purchased preparatory sauces. Other essential ingredients may include oils, chilli, garlic, lemon grass, tamarind, herbs (preferably fresh) and spices – the list is fairly endless; however I am sure you get the idea.

A marinade is commonly used to flavour foods, but also to tenderize tougher cuts of meat. The process may last for seconds or days. Different marinades are used in different international cuisines. For example, in Indian cuisine, the marinade is usually prepared with yoghurt and spices.

With meat, the acid causes the connective tissue to break down, allowing more moisture to be absorbed and giving a juicier end product. However, too much acid can have a detrimental effect on the end product. A good marinade will have a delicate balance of herbs, spice, acid and oil.

Always cover food tightly while marinating. The more completely the food is coated with a marinade, the quicker the flavouring process. If marinating in a dish, place some cling film directly on the food in order to expel any air. A useful onboard tip, is the use zip-lock bags for marinating, or even plastic roasting bags work well, coating food completely in a marinade, without it splashing all over the place in rough weather.

Always use non-reactive containers for marinating. Use plastic, stainless steel or ceramic. Never use glass, aluminium foil, cast-iron or copper.

Always make sure that you shake excess mixes off the food before cooking. Oil that drips onto BBQ coals for instance, will cause a flare-up and provide you with the opportunity to screw-up all your hard work, finishing up with unusable, singed food.

Finally, be very aware of cross-contamination. Do not place grilled food back into the same dish you used for marinating. Bacteria will still be in the raw juices left behind in the dish, so be sure to place cooked food onto a clean dish.

Do not confuse the word marination with maceration, which is a similar process, usually related to flavouring fresh fruits. This is mainly done by using spirit, liqueur (flavoured, sweetened spirit), fruit syrups, sugar syrup, honey, vanilla etc, etc…

Right, before I kick off with some more recipes, I must explain that I have tried to keep the number of core ingredients to a minimum and particularly ones which usually only require a minimum of cooking. My thinking is that once you have mastered the preparation, cooking and presentation of these ingredients, you will progress to experimenting with new ingredients,

BARBECUED FILLET OF LAMB
marinated in rosemary, shallots and honey

I love cooking with fillet of lamb, as it takes no time at all to cook and the meat is so tender, and juicy, especially when cooked pink. Other very tender cuts of lamb include saddle (boned), loin (fillet removed), rosettes and noisettes; these are very versatile, fabulous cuts of meat, which will delight your guests. If you want to use lamb for a barbie, then use any of these, cut to size and marinated for an hour or so. Thread onto sturdy rosemary stems, with a spray of leaves at the tip, or onto flat, stainless brochettes, with marinated Mediterranean vegetables of your choice.

I have included this simple recipe, because this is one I use a great deal on warm summer evenings at home cooking on my brilliant my Weber barbi and I just know it's always going to turn out great, so I hope your guests love it as much as my family does.

Ingredients for four

- 100ml light olive oil
- 2 tbsp acacia honey (try Agave syrup from Mexico)
- 2 shallots – finely chopped
- ½ lemon – juiced
- 440g of lamb fillets (4) or loin – trimmed
- 2 tbsp fresh young rosemary leaves – roughly chopped
- Mediterranean vegetables – such as:
  red onion, courgette, romano pepper – prepared for kebabs
- sea salt & freshly ground black pepper

Preparation

Place a small saucepan over a low flame, gently heat the olive oil until warm, add the shallot and cook for a minute or so without colour. Add the honey, lemon juice, rosemary and seasoning, stir well. Remove the pan from the heat and set to one side to infuse. Allow to cool.

When cooled, transfer the marinade to a lasagne style dish. Cut the lamb fillets into 2-3cm cubes and add to the marinade, turning once or twice to make sure all the pieces are evenly coated. Cover with cling-film and refrigerate for at least one hour. The flavour is immense if you refrigerate overnight. I usually add my prepared Mediterranean vegetables to the marinade as well, but the choice is yours.

Remove the lamb and veggies from the marinade and skewer alternate vegetables and lamb onto your brochettes or rosemary stalks. When cooked, this is great served in some wraps or pitta bread, with some crunchy leaves, drizzled with a little Tzatziki.

Before heading for the shore, dockside, or wherever else you are going to set up your barbie, wrap the brochettes in cling film, plastic roasting bags or zip-lock bags and pop them into your cool box.

MCB tip #1:   This dish is also great smothered with some freshly made Charmoula, Cucumber Yoghurt Raita or a Chilli Lime Mayo.

MCB tip #2:   Alternatively, you can pan fry the whole fillets over a medium-high flame for two or three minutes, until brown on all sides. Transfer to a pre-heated oven (180°C) and roast for five to seven minutes, or until the lamb is cooked, but pink in the middle. Remove from the oven, set to one side and allow to rest for five minutes. To serve, carve the lamb end-to-end into long, thin slices and thread each slice onto a prepared rosemary 'skewer', concertina style, season with freshly ground black pepper and serve with roasted Mediterranean vegetables.

AGAVE NECTAR

Produced in Mexico from a diverse range of Agave plant types (large cactus). Agave tequiliana (blue Agave) is used to make Tequila. Vegans commonly use agave nectar to replace honey in recipes. It can also be used as a sweetener for cold beverages, such as iced tea because of its ability to dissolve quickly.

Agave nectars are sold in light, amber, dark and raw varieties. Light agave nectar has a mild, almost neutral flavour and is therefore sometimes used in delicate tasting food and drinks. Amber has a medium intensity, almost caramel flavour and is therefore used in foods and drinks with stronger flavours. Dark has stronger caramel notes and imparts a distinctive flavour to dishes, such as some desserts, poultry, meat and seafood dishes. Both amber and dark agave nectar are sometimes used "straight out of the bottle" as a topping for pancakes and waffles.

BARBECUED PORK RIBS

This is a really simple recipe given to me by Nicola, one of my catering students, who now lives in the South of Spain. It makes really nice, tasty, sticky finger food.

Ingredients for four
- 750g prepared pork flat ribs
- 4 tbsp plum jam (like jelly)
- 2 tbsp runny honey
- 2 garlic cloves – crushed
- 1 tbsp fresh ginger – grated
- 4 tbsp soy sauce
- ½ tsp dried chilli flakes

Preparation
Place all the ingredients into a small pan over a low flame. Allow to heat through and stir thoroughly to combine. Remove from the heat and allow to cool.

Place your prepared pork ribs into a lasagne style dish and spoon the marinade over the top. Turn and coat the other side of the ribs. Cover and put to one side for around an hour, so the ribs take on the lovely flavours.

This dish is always great served with home-made burgers and spicy chicken wings, so strike up the barbie, crack open some Mexican beer for your guests and off you go!

CÔTELETTE DE PORC aux MOUTARDES
pork chops with a grain mustard cream sauce

This is one of my favorite ways to serve pork chops or cutlets. I use some Côtes de Provence Rosé in this recipe, which I know is quite unusual, but it really does work so incredibly well and doesn't intrude too much into the wonderful pork and mustard flavours.

Ingredients for four
- 4 regular pork chops (bone out for quicker cooking)
- Maille Moutarde fins Gourmets (course grain mustard)
- 125ml Côtes de Provence Rosé
- 200g champignons de Paris (button mushrooms)
- 150ml cream or 200g crème fraîche
- 35g unsalted butter
- corn oil
- sea salt & black pepper

Preparation
Pre-heat your oven to 175°C.

Place the chops onto your chopping board, flatten a little with the heal of your hand and lightly season with a salt and ground black pepper. Thinly 'butter' each chop on one side only with some coarse grain mustard.

Place a heavy bottomed frying pan over a medium flame and when hot, add a couple of slugs of corn oil and a knob of butter. Once the butter has melted and the bubbles start to subside, add the chops to the pan, 'mustard side' down and cook until well sealed and lightly browned, this should take two or three minutes. Turn the chops over and cook the other side for another two, or three minutes depending on the thickness of your pork chops. Adjust the flame as necessary.

While the chops are cooking, clean the grit from the stems and underneath of the Champignons de Paris, rinse in a colander, pat dry and trim the stems before slicing them.

Remove the chops from the frying pan and place onto a roasting tin or baking sheet and place into your pre-heated oven, while you make the sauce.

Increase the flame to medium-high and add the sliced mushrooms to your frying pan and fry until nearly cooked (the mushrooms should take up any surplus oil left in the pan). Add the rosé and allow to reduce down by around fifty percent. Turn the flame down to medium-low and add a dessert spoon of the coarse grain mustard, stir well then add the cream or crème fraîche and stir well to combine. Remove the chops from the oven and pour the juices into the sauce and stir well to incorporate all of the wonderful flavours. Taste and adjust the seasoning and consistency to your liking.

Place one pork chop onto each of four hot plates and pour the sauce over the top or around the edge of each.

FILLET STEAK with MADEIRA SAUCE

Here I am telling you how to make a traditional style Madeira Sauce. If you wanted to make a red wine sauce instead, then just replace the Madeira with double the amount of red wine.

Ingredients for two

For the steak
- 2 x 200g fillet steaks (Tournedos – middle cut)
- corn oil
- 1 tbsp unsalted butter
- sea salt & freshly ground black pepper
- 50ml Madeira

For the Madeira sauce
- 150ml Madeira
- 100ml red wine
- I carrot – finely chopped
- 2 shallots – finely chopped
- 1 stick celery – finely chopped
- 1 clove garlic – crushed
- 2 mushrooms – chopped
- 1 tomato – chopped
- 1 tbsp tomato purée
- 1 tbsp balsamic or sherry vinegar
- 1 tbsp dark brown moscovado sugar
- parsley stalks, fresh thyme & bay leaf
- olive oil
- 100ml beef stock
- salt & freshly ground black pepper

Preparation

For the sauce

Place a medium sized heavy based pan over a medium-low flame and add a slug of olive oil. Add the prepared carrot, shallot, celery and fry until the vegetables turn a light golden brown.

Add the mushroom, tomato and garlic and cook for another couple of minutes. Add the tomato purée, vinegar and brown sugar and stir well, before adding the beef stock, red wine and herbs – stir well and allow to simmer for 15 minutes.

Increase the flame a little and reduce the liquid by around half. Add the Madeira and cook for a further five minutes, then remove the pan from the flame. Using a clean pan and a sieve, pass the sauce into the clean pan. Season to taste and finish the sauce by whisking in a knob of butter.

For the steaks

Pre-heat your griddle pan or frying pan so it is nicely hot. Season your steaks at the last minute. If you are using a griddle pan, then lightly brush or spray with a light oil; if using a frying pan, then add a little corn oil and a knob of unsalted butter.

Allow the butter to bubble, then add your steak and pan fry for four minutes on either side, depending on how your guests want it cooked. Once you have put the steaks into your pan, leave them alone, there is no need to keep moving them around. Remove the steak from the pan, cover and allow it to rest for a couple of minutes.

While the steak is resting, start building your plate with vegetable and potato of your choice. Add the steak and a pool of Madeira sauce.

MCB tip: I like to serve this with crushed new potatoes and sweet potatoes, infused with a little fresh rosemary, and oven roasted like a potato cake, plus fine green beans and long fingers of 'just cooked' carrot.

LAMB KLEFTIKO

Kleftiko (in Greek) means 'stolen meat'. According to legend, this dish would be made with a lamb stolen from a flock as it grazed on the hillside. The thief would cook the meat for many hours in a hole in the ground, sealed with mud so that no smoke or steam could escape to give him away. In more modern times it can be made in a sealed earthenware dish, alternatively in a casserole dish, covered in aluminium foil, works just as well. It is also nice to present this dish by making individual parcels of meat wrapped in baking parchment or aluminium foil.

Ingredients for four
- 1 shoulder of lamb – boned & cut into fist sized pieces
- olive oil – drizzle
- 1 lemon – zested & juiced
- 1 tsp dried oregano
- 1 pinch powdered cinnamon
- 1 bay leaf
- 4 large potatoes – peeled & cut into four
- sea salt & freshly ground black pepper

Preparation
Pre-hat your oven to 150°C.

Take a large bowl and add the pieces of lamb. Add the remaining ingredients and mix them together thoroughly, making sure that the lamb pieces are well coated with the herbs and seasonings.

Cut a one metre length of aluminium foil and lay on your work surface. Place the ingredients in the centre and fold the foil, so that you form a sealed package. Place into a casserole or onto a roasting tray and transfer to the middle of your pre-heated oven and slow-roast for two to three hours, until the meat is very tender.

Remove the meat from your oven and place to one side to rest for around fifteen minutes in a warm place. Place the lamb and potatoes onto four serving plates and drizzle over the herby juices before serving.

MORROCAN LAMB TAGINE
with apricots and almonds

A "Tagine" is a type of terracotta cooking pot used in the North African cuisines of Morocco, Tunisia and Algeria. The dish is subsequently named after the special, heavy clay pot in which the food is cooked. A traditional tagine is formed entirely of heavy clay, which may be colourfully painted or naturally, as glazed terracotta. The tagine consists of two parts, the base, which holds the food, is flat and circular with low sides; the cover or lid is designed to encourage the movement of condensation, which should return from the lid to the bottom, keeping the dish moist. The cover is usually removed when the base is taken to the table for serving, after the food has been liberally sprinkled with freshly chopped herbs, usually coriander.

Moroccan tagine dishes are stewed or braised at low temperatures, usually resulting in tender meat, poultry and fish with aromatic vegetables and sauce. Often used for cooking less expensive cuts of meat; the ideal ones are neck, shoulder or shank of lamb, cooked with a mixture of spices, fruits and fresh herbs.

Ingredients for six
- 1 x shoulder of lamb – de-boned
- 3 tbsp Argan oil (or olive oil)
- 1 large white onion – roughly chopped
- 2 cloves garlic – finely sliced
- 2.5cm fresh ginger – peeled & chopped
- 1 good pinch of saffron threads
- salt & ground black pepper
- 1 cinnamon stick
- 1 dspn ground cumin
- 1 dspn ground coriander
- 250g dried apricots – ready to eat
- 1lt stock – lamb, chicken or vegetable
- 100g ground almonds

Garnish
- 2 tbsp fresh coriander – roughly chopped
- 2 tbsp sesame seeds – lightly toasted

Preparation
Using a large sharp knife, cut the lamb into 3cm sized pieces. Place a large heavy based pan over a medium flame, add the oil and allow to heat through before adding the prepared meat. Seal the pieces of lamb on all sides until golden brown, remove and place onto some kitchen paper. Now add the onion to the pan and cook for five minutes, until lightly browned. Return the lamb to the pan and add the garlic, ginger, saffron, cumin, coriander, cinnamon stick, salt and ground black pepper, stir well to coat the meat.

Barely cover with stock, bring to the boil and immediately reduce to a gentle simmer, cover with a lid and cook gently for approximately 1½ hours. Add a little more stock or water if necessary, although the lid should create sufficient steam, which will help to keep everything nice and moist. Stir well, add the ground almonds and stir again. Check for seasoning and adjust to taste. If the sauce is too thin, add a little more ground almond.

Place a small frying pan over a medium low flame and lightly dry fry the sesame seeds until they turn golden brown.

Serve the tagine in warm bowls and garnish with the toasted sesame seeds and the roughly chopped coriander.

Serve with Tasty Morrocan Couscous (see Basics).

MCB tip: This recipe takes approximately twenty minutes to cook - in a pressure cooker.

PORK TENDERLOIN
with a fricassee of clams and summer vegetables
This excellent dish was inspired by a recent research weekend at the Ashburton Cookery School in Devon, delivered by the inspirational team of James Knight-Pacheco and Luke Garnsworthy.

The recipe offers a slightly unusual combination of melt in the mouth pork tenderloin and shellfish with cider, which works really well. Pork tenderloin, which can weigh in at around 500g, is often sold as pork fillet, which is very tender and only takes a short amount of cooking time.

Ingredients for four
- 4 x 150g pieces of thick pork tenderloin
- 4 sprigs fresh thyme
- 1 lemon – zested
- corn oil
- knob of butter
- sea salt & cracked pepper

For the fricassee
- 500g fresh clams
- 8 x small artichoke hearts – prepared, cooked & sliced (tinned hearts in oil can work well)
- 150g fresh peas (or defrosted)
- 80g unsalted butter
- 3 x shallots - sliced
- 2 x eating apples (Cox's or Braeburn)
- 200ml sweet cider
- 1 tbsp chopped fresh tarragon
- sea salt & cracked black pepper

Preparation
Pre-heat your oven to 200°C

Using a small, sharp paring knife, neatly trim the pork tenderloin, removing any excess fat and sinew, finishing up with nice 'clean' pieces of pork from the centre of the fillet.

Take a sharp knife and butterfly the tenderloin by cutting along the full length of the fillet (end-to-end). Cut approximately three quarters of the way through and open up the fillet, gently flattening out with the heal of your hand. Season well with the salt and pepper and add the zested lemon and thyme leaves. Roll the pork back into a barrel shape and usng some butcher's string, tie the meat firmly ready to cook.

Place an oven-proof frying pan over a medium-high flame, add a drizzle of oil and the knob of butter. Allow the butter to melt and bubble; as the bubbles subside, carefully place the tenderloin into the pan and seal well on all sides for two or three minutes until they turn golden brown.

Place the frying pan into your hot oven for eight to ten minutes.

While the pork tenderloin is roasting in your oven, prepare the fricassee, so that you are ready to assemble the dish when the pork is cooked.

Wash to clams well. Place a heavy bottomed pan over a high flame; heat through and add the cider and bring to the boil, immediately add the clams and cook for a couple of minutes or so until they open. Remove the pan from the heat; drain the clams, retaining the cider cooking liquor. Pick out the clam meat and retain with the shells.

Peel the apples, cut into quarters and remove the core. Cut the quarters into half lengthways to create neat wedges.

Place a medium sized heavy based pan, over a medium-low flame. Add half the butter and sweat the shallots gently, without colour, then add the prepared artichokes, peas and apple wedges. Add the retained cooking liquor and simmer until it has reduced a little. Reduce the heat, add the remaining butter and shake well, so the fricassee starts to emulsify, add the tarragon and clams, taste and season if required, cover with a lid and simmer very gently.

Take the pork tenderloin from the oven, remove from the frying pan, cover and allow to rest for a couple of minutes. Remove the string and carve on a severe angle into 4-5 pieces.

Select good sized plates and spoon the fricassee onto each one. Neatly arrange slices of the pork over the fricassee, drizzle over the juices and serve.

ROAST FILLET OF BEEF
with Correziènne stuffed tomatoes

The very first time I cooked roast fillet of beef, was for a senior member of the British Royal family at a private party. My cooking and this dish have moved on a million miles since that time in my life.

It seems such an innocent little menu item, but there are a few rules which you must consider when buying your tomatoes. The size of the tomato is important; as it must be of a reasonable size – definitely not too small – Marmande or beef tomatoes are good. Also the texture and colour – don't use tomatoes which are over-ripe or too green; the colour has to be that 'ripe tomato red', something that is going to look special on the plate.

Ingredients for 4 people

For the beef
- 1 x 2k beef fillet – trimmed, tail & chain removed
- olive oil
- sea salt and freshly ground black pepper

For the tomatoes
- 2 medium to large tomatoes
- 150g Champignons de Paris (button mushrooms) – finely chopped
- 2 shallots – finely chopped
- 2 cloves of garlic – crushed
- 3 tbsp flat leaf parsley – finely chopped
- 4 sprigs of fresh young thyme – leaves only
- handful of dried breadcrumbs
- dried herbs de provence
- extra virgin olive oil
- unsalted butter
- salt & freshly ground black pepper

Preparation

Wash the tomatoes in cold water and pat dry. Cut the tomatoes in half (not through the stalk) and using a teaspoon, scoop out the seeds and discard. Cut a fine sliver off the bottom of each tomato half, so that they will stand upright when served. Place the tomatoes, base-side-down onto a plate; season the insides with a little salt, freshly ground black pepper and a small knob of butter.

Place a small pan over a medium-low flame and add a splash of olive oil and a small knob of butter. Add the prepared shallots, mushrooms and garlic, stir well and cover with a lid. Reduce to a low flame and sweat the vegetables for five minutes without colour.

Remove the pan from the heat and add the breadcrumbs, parsley and thyme and stir thoroughly and allow to cool. Stuff the tomato halves and lightly sprinkle the top of each with a mixture of the remaining breadcrumbs and herbs de Provence and drizzle with a little olive oil.

For the fillet

Pre-heat your oven to 200°C.

Place a lightly oiled roasting tray into your pre-heated oven. Place a large heavy based frying pan over a medium-high flame and add two dessert spoons of oil. Brush, or rub the whole fillet with olive oil and season well with sea salt and freshly ground black pepper. When the oil in your frying pan starts to smoke, gently add the fillet and sear for a minute or so on all sides, until evenly coloured.

Transfer the seared fillet to your roasting tray and add the prepared tomatoes and return to the hot oven and roast for a further fifteen to twenty minutes. Remove the fillet from the oven, wrap in tin-foil and allow to rest for a few minutes. Leave the tomatoes in the oven to crisp off the top – being careful not to overcook, or they will fall to pieces when you transfer them to the serving plates.

To serve, remove the fillet from the foil onto a chopping board. Using a very sharp knife, carve into thick slices and divide between four serving plates. Add a stuffed tomato to each, drain off any fat from the roasting tray and drizzle the cooking juices over the beef.

This dish is great served with some crunchy ratatouille infused with fresh rosemary and some pan fried, diced potatoes.

MCB tip #1:   The idea of this dish is to serve the beef 'nicely pink'. If you have guests who prefer to eat their beef more well done, then you can simply carve their beef and sear off their 'steaks', to their desired level of cooking.

MCB tip #2:   Make sure that your butcher removes the 'chain' from the fillet – this is the inedible strip that runs down one side of the whole fillet. If left on, you must remove this yourself as there is nothing you can do with it, except 'bin it'. It is equally essential that the inedible sinew is removed from the thick end of the fillet.

ROAST FILLET OF LAMB
with summer vegetables

This is a wonderful, light, summery dish, which always proves to be popular with guests.

Ingredients for four

For the lamb
- 4 x 150g lamb fillets - fully trimmed
- 8 small shoots fresh young rosemary

- 6 garlic cloves – skin on
- 2 tbsp extra virgin olive oil
- sea salt & freshly ground black pepper

For the vegetables
- 3 firm, red plum tomatoes – sliced 5mm
- 2 medium sized courgettes – sliced 5mm on an angle
- 1 small aubergine – sliced 5mm
- 3 – 4 tbsp olive oil
- sea salt & freshly ground black pepper

For the sauce vierge
- see Basics, using lime juice & rosemary shoots
- rocket leaves to serve

Preparation
Preheat your oven to 210°C

Place the aubergine slices into a dish, lined with kitchen paper and sprinkle with sea salt, which will draw out surplus liquid.

Place your trimmed lamb fillets onto your chopping board and using a sharp knife, cut a pocket into the side of each fillet and insert two small young shoots of rosemary into each. Season the lamb with salt and freshly ground black pepper

Place an oven-proof frying pan over a medium flame and add the olive oil, garlic and the lamb fillets. Fry the fillets on all sides until they turn golden brown all over, then transfer to your pre-heated oven to roast for 4 – 6 minutes, or until nearly cooked through. Remove the frying pan from the oven, carefully remove the lamb and place onto kitchen paper, cover and allow to rest for 3 – 4 minutes. Reduce the heat of the oven to low.

Place a cast iron griddle pan over a medium-high flame and very lightly brush with oil. Pat the aubergines dry and place into the griddle pan a few at a time. Do not move them for a couple of minutes, allowing the slices to take on the bar marks from the pan; turn and colour the other side. Place the cooked aubergines into a roasting tin, lined with kitchen paper and keep warm in your oven.

Place a non-stick frying pan over a medium-high flame, add the olive oil until hot and add the sliced tomatoes and courgettes. Season with a little sea salt and ground black pepper and fry for two minutes on either side, until just tender and turning golden. Add the vegetables to the roasting tin to keep warm with the aubergine.

To make the sauce vierge, wipe out your frying pan, return to a low flame and add the olive oil and warm through. Add the lime juice, rosemary, season and finish off by adding the chopped parsley and tomatoes.

To serve, place thee slices of each vegetable (tomato, courgette and aubergine), just overlapping, into the centre of your serving plates. Carve the lamb into thick slices at an angle and place on top of the vegetables. Spoon the sauce vierge over the lamb and around each plate. Add a small handful of dressed rocket leaves to finish.

ROASTED LOIN of LAMB
with braised cabbage and a red wine jus

Ingredients for two
- 1 X 400g loin of lamb – boned, fat on & tied
- 2 garlic cloves
- 2 tbsp corn oil
- 2 tbsp fresh rosemary shoots – finely chopped
- 2 tbsp fresh young thyme – finely chopped
- 2 tbsp fresh mint – finely chopped
- sea salt & freshly ground black pepper

For the braised cabbage
- 1 small leek – trimmed & finely shredded (white only)
- ¼ small savoy cabbage or similar – finely shredded
- 150ml vegetable stock
- 25g unsalted butter
- sea salt and freshly ground black pepper

For the red wine sauce
- 1 shallot – finely chopped
- 1 garlic clove – crushed
- 175ml red wine (something reasonable please)
- 50g unsalted butter
- sea salt & freshly ground black pepper

Preparation
Pre-heat your oven to 180°C.

To cook the cabbage, place a small saucepan over a medium-low flame. Add the butter, shredded leek and cabbage, cover with a lid, reduce the flame and sweat without colour for five minutes. Add the vegetable stock, bring up to the boil, reduce the flame to low, cover with a lid and braise for around 10 minutes until nearly cooked, but still a little crunchy.

Your loin of lamb will be quite long, so maybe cut in half width-ways, sprinkle with salt and pepper and roll in the chopped herbs. Heat the corn oil in an ovenproof pan until very hot. Add the lamb and brown on all sides and the using kitchen tongs, seal the ends as well. This should take around five minutes in total.

Transfer the pan to your pre-heated oven and roast for around eight minutes, which should cook the lamb to a medium stage, leaving it slightly pink in the middle. Leave it in the oven for longer if you want it cooked through. Remove from the oven and transfer the lamb to a warm plate, cover and allow to rest for a further five minutes.

To make the sauce, return your pan to the hob over a medium-low flame, add half the butter, melt and add the chopped shallot, and cook without colour for a minute or so. Add the red wine and turn the heat right up and reduce the liquid by around half. Strain the reduced liquid into a small saucepan, re-heat and whisk in the remaining butter to help thicken your sauce and give it a really nice sheen. Season to taste.

To serve, using a slotted spoon, portion the cabbage onto the centre of each plate. Carve the lamb fillets and place neatly overlapping around the outside of the cabbage. To finish, drizzle some of the red wine gravy over or around the slices of lamb, but don't over-do it.

ROASTED PORK SCALLOPS
with a cilantro salsa

The salsa is similar in some ways to my Charmoula recipe, which I used in the previous section. However, this recipe has some unusual twists and the inclusion of honey and spices, would point in the direction of North Africa, if this wasn't a pork dish.

Ingredients for four

- 4 x pork loin scallops (boneless steaks – approx' 2 cm thick)
- 1 large handful of cilantro (fresh coriander)
- 2 large cloves of garlic – crushed
- 1 tsp dried cumin (freshly ground seeds are fine)
- 1 tsp dried coriander (as above)
- 1 tbsp runny honey
- 1 lemon – zested (retain juice)
- 2 tbsp olive oil
- ½ tsp dried white pepper
- salt & freshly ground black pepper

Preparation

Pre-heat your oven to 200°C.

Take the pork scallops and trim away any surplus fat, leaving approximately half a centimeter of fat surrounding the meat. Take a sharp knife and score the fat on the diagonal. Place into a roasting tin, cover and put to one side.

Take the remaining ingredients and pop them into your food processor and blitz for a minute or so, until the consistency resembles a rough paste. Taste for seasoning. You may want to add a little more salt and pepper and maybe a touch of lemon juice. If you don't have a food processor, then use powdered spices and combine the ingredients by hand.

Place a heavy based frying pan over a medium flame. Add a little olive oil and fry both sides of the scallops to seal. Remove and place into a roasting tin. Spoon the salsa over each steak.

Place the roasting tray into the middle of the oven and cook for twenty minutes or so until the meat is cooked through.

Alternatively this dish tastes wonderful when cooked slowly over a charcoal barbecue.

MCB tip #1:   This dish is great served with mango salsa, which you will find in the previous chapter under my recipe for Grilled Teriyaki Mahi-Mahi.

POULTRY MAINS

In my mind chicken is one of the most flexible ingredients that you have at your disposal. I say this because chicken is an incredibly versatile product, which is high in protein, low in fat (low fat, or no fat if the skin is removed). It can be cooked in a myriad of different ways, served hot or cold, used for lunch, sundowners, starter, intermediate or main course, I could go on-and-on, but I think you've got the idea.

I guess that I have never given it much thought before, but when 'Jo Public' (UK) refer to poultry, the majority tend to talk about chicken and turkey. Even the early editions of the catering students' bible (UK), 'Practical Cookery' (Ceserani, Kinton and Fosket – Hodder & Stoughton), paid scant regard to duck or goose recipes, which just seems plain odd to me.

If you find yourself shopping for chicken in the South of France, the birds to go for are Label Rouge, free-range, corn fed chicken, reared in the grassy open air or open space buildings with low quantity flock sizes and access to an open air environment. This type of bird will cost two or three times more than you would expect to pay in the UK. Back in 2004/5, we used to pay up to €15 for a spit-roasted chicken at our twice monthly town market. You didn't have to ask if it was free-range bird; because if you did, everyone in the queue would laugh at you! You just knew that you were buying the very best chicken that was available in that part of France. There are some things I miss in life, and my bi-weekly visit to our local market 'en Corrèze' is definitely one of them!

So folks, always buy the very best quality and freshest chicken that you can. You will find varying quality all over the world; however, if you can get your hands on some Poulet de Bresse, these are acclaimed by the top chefs as the best chickens you will buy anywhere in the world and don't let anyone try to persuade you otherwise.

COCONUT RED STRIPE CHICKEN

This is fairly typical of the style of recipe you will find in Caribbean cuisine. It is fairly simplistic and tastes great.

Ingredients for four
- 1k chicken legs/thighs – trimmed
- 1 can coconut milk
- 1 cup Red Stripe beer
- 1 large onion – chopped
- 2 cloves garlic – crushed
- 1 large green bell pepper – de-seeded & sliced
- 3 tbsp vegetable oil
- salt & pepper

Preparation
Place a heavy based frying pan over medium flame, add the vegetable oil and allow to heat through. Carefully add the chicken pieces and cook through on both sides until golden brown. Remove and place to one side on absorbent kitchen paper.

Pour off any residual oil, leaving around two tablespoons in the frying pan. Add the onion, bell pepper and garlic and cook until the onion becomes soft and translucent.

Return the chicken to the pan and add the coconut milk and Red Stripe beer. Increase the flame and bring the liquid up to the boil, reduce the flame and allow to simmer gently for approx' thirty minutes.

Season to taste and simmer for a further fifteen to twenty minutes, to allow the liquid to reduce and thicken. If the liquid evaporates before the chicken is done, moisten with a little more Red Stripe and/or coconut milk.

PAN FRIED CHICKEN
with emmental and parma ham

This is a recipe which my son Ashley loves cooking. He sometimes cooks this when we have guests round for dinner and serves it either as a main course or cut into strips and served over crisp dressed salad leaves, as a starter.

Ingredients for four

- 75g emmental – grated
- 2 tbsp chopped basil
- 2 tbsp chopped flat leaf parsley
- 2 tbsp chopped coriander
- 4 skinless chicken breasts
- 8 slices of parma ham (Serrano is also good)
- salt & freshly ground black pepper
- 12 baby asparagus
- 25g butter
- 1 lemon - zested
- olive oil

Preparation

Pre-heat your oven to 180°C.

Place the chicken breasts onto a chopping board, round side up, and one at a time, pummel them with the heal of your hand to start the flattening process.

Mix the chopped herbs and lemon zest together. Liberally sprinkle each chicken breast with the cheese, followed by the herb mix. Lay two slices of cured ham over each, slightly overlapping. Cover each breast with cling film and flatten them to around 1cm thick with a rolling pin, meat tenderiser or the base of a frying pan. Remove the cling film and discard.

Place a heavy based frying pan over a medium flame and add a little olive oil and heat through. Gently add the chicken breasts, cured ham side down into the pan and cook for approximately three minutes on each side.

Place the chicken breasts onto a baking sheet and into your pre-heated oven to keep warm. Trim the base of the asparagus and add a knob of butter to your frying pan and place over a medium flame. Add the asparagus and cook for a couple of minutes only, turning occasionally.

Place the chicken onto serving plates and garnish with the asparagus and a wedge of lemon. This is lovely served with some crispy salad and new potatoes.

MCB tip: If you want to serve this as a starter, allow half a chicken breast per person and cook them earlier in the day. Cut them into strips and lay over a small mound of dressed salad leaves, serve with cold asparagus and some lemon mayonnaise.

PAN ROASTED DUCK BREAST
with a cassis gravy

It may seem a bit odd, but I suggest that you prepare the cassis gravy before you start cooking the duck breast. You could even do this in the morning, cool, cover and refrigerate for use later.

Ingredients for two

For the cassis gravy
- 1 shallot – finely chopped
- 150ml red wine
- 300ml brown beef stock
- 1 tbsp cassis
- 20g unsalted butter
- 16 large blueberries

Preparation

Place a small saucepan over a low flame and add half of the butter. Once melted, add the chopped shallot and cook gently without colour until softened.

Add the red wine and reduce quickly until the liquor turns thick and syrupy. Add the stock and reduce again until you have around 100m of liquid remaining. Strain the liquid into a bowl, cover and set to one side or refrigerate.

To finish the sauce (while the duck is in the oven), place a small saucepan over a low flame, add the sauce and the remaining butter and whisk thoroughly into the sauce. Add the blueberries and a final splash of Cassis, taste and correct the seasoning and you are ready to serve.

For the duck breast

- 2 medium sized duck breasts (200g)
- five spice
- sea salt

Preparation

Pre-heat your oven to 200°C.

Trim the duck breasts, removing any surplus fat from the edges and sinew from the flesh side. Score the skin with a very sharp knife on the diagonal, to create a diamond pattern.

Place the duck breasts into a cold frying pan, skin side down and place over a medium flame and cook for three or four minutes or until the skin turns golden brown. You do not need any extra oil.

Pour off the surplus fat from your pan, turn the duck breasts over and cook the other side for one minute. Return to the skin side down and season with a little more salt and five spice and place into the oven for approximately ten minutes, until the duck breast is cooked medium-rare.

Remove the pan from the oven, place the duck breasts to one side, cover and allow to rest for a few minutes before carving.

MCB tip: I love to serve this dish with lightly glazed baton carrots, crunchy sugar snap peas and a mixed vegetable rösti (potato, courgette, apple and spring onion).

PROSCIUTTO WRAPPED CHICKEN BREAST
stuffed with goat's cheese & spinach

This recipe is from my book Dix Neuf – Cuisine du Terroir Correziennne, although this version has a new twist of Italian Tomato Sauce and Parsely Purée.

I used to cook a similar dish quite often when we were entertaining friends and guests at our French Chambres d'hôte. It really is simplicity personified and the beauty of this dish is that you can prepare it all in advance, wrap the chicken breasts in cling film and refrigerate, ready for cooking later in the day. This has now become a very popular way of preparing and cooking chicken (I take no credit), primarily because you can stuff your chicken with so many different fillings.

Ingredients for four
- 4 chicken breasts (butterflied)
- 12 slices of parma ham (or similar)
- 1 small bag of baby spinach leaves
- 2 crottin de chèvre (goats cheese)
- Italian tomato sauce (see Basics – p 228)
- good handful of fresh parsley
- freshly grated nutmeg
- olive oil

Preparation
Pre-heat your oven to 180°C.

Prepare one quantity of Italian Tomato Sauce.

To prepare the stuffing, place a pan over a low flame and add a couple of tablespoons of cold water. Add the spinach leaves, cover with a lid, heat through and wilt for a minute or so. Drain the spinach, cool and squeeze dry. Place onto your chopping board and chop through, as you would with chopped parsley. Chop the goats cheese into ½ centimetre dice and add to a medium sized bowl. Add the chopped spinach, lightly season and add a small pinch of grated nutmeg. Drizzle with a little olive oil and stir well. Place to one side while you prepare the chicken breasts.

To butterfly the chicken breasts, use a clean dry chopping board and a small, sharp knife. Lay a chicken breast on the board flat side down, insert the point of your knife into the thickest fleshy end of the breast and slice towards the narrow end. Being careful not to cut all the way through, make sure that you have enough space to add your 'stuffing'. Season the inside of each breast with a little salt and black pepper and using a dessert spoon, add some stuffing to each breast, but don't overfill. Fold the flap back over the stuffing.

On a clean chopping board, lay three prosciutto slices side-by-side, slightly overlapping and place a stuffed chicken breast on top, round side down. Wrap the prosciutto around, rolling up tightly.

Heat a large frying pan over a medium-low flame, add a good slug of olive oil, heat through and cook the chicken breasts for 2-3 minutes on each side, or until they start to turn a light golden brown. Transfer the chicken to your pre-heated oven and finish off cooking until they are completely cooked through. Remove from the heat and allow to rest.

For the parsley purée, wash the parsley and squeeze dry, place into a mini food processor with a little olive oil and blend until smooth.

To serve, slice the chicken breast on the diagonal. Spoon some of the tomato sauce in the centre of a serving plate and place the slices of chicken breast on top, then drizzle over the parsley purée and serve.

MCB tip: This dish works really well served with a small portion of buttered tagliatelle.

SCALOPPINE DI POLLO CON ERBE
Chicken scaloppini with herbs

I bumped into the well known Italian restaurateur Antonio Carluccio at Hotelympia a few years back and to cut a long story short, I finished up getting a copy of his book, Antonio Carluccio's Italian Feast, which he signed for my darling wife. I have included my own version of Antonio's recipe, which is packed with flavour and the presentation is so unique that few people I know have ever seen chicken served this way. The dish makes a great light lunch dish, served with crisp summer leaves or a salad of mixed beans, cooked al dente and mixed with fresh mint, crushed garlic, olive oil, a little lemon juice and seasoned to taste

Ingredients for four
- 4 chicken breasts – bone in, skin removed
- 2 tbsp plain flour
- 75g unsalted butter
- 1 tbsp extra virgin olive oil
- 1 tbsp each of finely chopped: flat leaf parsley, basil, mint, chervil, dill & rosemary
- 1 clove garlic – finely chopped
- ¼ fresh red chilli – finely chopped
- 1 x lime – zested and juiced
- 4 tbsp chicken stock
- 4 tbsp dry white wine
- 2 dsp crème fraîche
- sea salt & freshly ground black pepper

Preparation
Pre-heat your oven to 160°C.

Place the chicken breasts onto your chopping board and using a sharp knife, cut each breast in strips from where the meat joins the bone, making four cuts down the length of the breast, so that you finish up with five fingers or tentacles, a bit like an octopus. Cutting the meat enables more flavour to be absorbed and the cooking time is reduced.

Place the flour into a bowl, season with salt and pepper and dust each chicken breast, shaking off any surplus flour.

Place a large, heavy based frying pan over a medium flame, add the oil and half the butter and when butter foams, add the chicken breasts presentation side down, fry for a couple of minutes on either side until golden brown. Transfer the chicken to a baking sheet and place into your oven to keep warm.

Reduce the flame to medium and return the pan to the flame. Add the remaining butter; add the herbs, garlic, chilli, lime juice, zest, stock and white wine and stir well together. Return the chicken to the pan and poach for about another five minutes until cooked.

Transfer the chicken to serving plates, spoon some of the herb sauce over each and serve.

SPICY CHICKEN SALAD
with lime and sesame

This is a zingy, spicy, tasty sensation on a plate. A bit of Pacific Rim influence, utilising a Chinese, shredded chicken recipe, brought up to date with an Australian twist. Great for lunch on a blisteringly hot day, perfect as a light starter too.

Ingredients for four

- 4 chicken breasts – skin on (bones removed)
- 1 cucumber
- 100g mangetout – shredded lengthways
- 2 spring onions – trimmed & thinly sliced on the diagonal
- 1 good handful fresh coriander – including stalks
- 1 good handful mint leaves
- 1 tbsp fish sauce
- 3 tbsp lime juice
- olive oil
- sea salt & freshly ground black pepper

To Serve

- ½ small iceberg lettuce – shredded
- lime wedges
- 10g toasted sesame seeds
- light sesame oil

Preparation

Pre-heat your oven to 200°C.

Place a heavy based frying pan over a high flame. Add a little olive oil and add the chicken breasts, skin side down. Sear for two minutes on both sides, but no longer, and then transfer to a baking tray and place in your pre-heated oven for approximately 15 minutes, or until the juices run clear when the meat is pierced with a skewer. Remove from the oven and leave to cool and rest for 20 minutes. Remove the skin and shred the chicken into thin strips on the diagonal.

Top and tail the cucumber and cut in quarters lengthways, remove the seeds with a sharp knife and cut into one centimeter slices on the diagonal.

Finally place the prepared chicken, cucumber, mangetout, spring onions, coriander and mint into a large bowl, sprinkle with fish sauce, sesame oil, lime juice and toss together until well combined.

Divide the iceberg lettuce between four large white plates. Pile the chicken mixture on top, add a light drizzle of sesame oil around the plate and scatter toasted sesame seeds over to finish. A totally cosmic lunch crunch!

MCB tip: The reason I use iceberg lettuce, is because it will stay nice and crisp on the plate and not wilt in the heat.

SWEET & SOUR CHICKEN THIGHS

When I started writing this book, I promised myself that I would not include a chicken thigh recipe. I have already told you how I feel about debris coming back into my galley on guests' plates. However, this is one of those recipes which I use loads at home and chuck onto my Weber on a balmy summer evening, while slurping down the odd cocktail or a glass of chilled Sancerre, so I really just had to share!

Ingredients
- 6 large chicken thighs – bone in (trimmed)
- 1 tbsp black peppercorns – roughly crushed
- 2 lemons – juice only
- acacia honey – three tablespoons
- 1 tbsp course grain mustard
- 4 garlic cloves – crushed
- light olive oil
- sea salt
- 2 preserved lemons (in brine)
- 16 pitted green olives – roughly sliced
- flat leaf parsley – roughly chopped

Preparation
Preheat the oven at 200°C.

Take a large bowl and add the crushed black pepper, lemon juice, honey, mustard and half the garlic and mix well together.

Using a small sharp knife, slash the chicken thighs two or three times across the thickest part of the flesh. Take a roasting tin and very lightly brush with olive oil. Add the chicken thighs and spoon some of the lemon and honey mixture over each one, allowing it to take on the flavour of the marinade for around thirty minutes.

Sprinkle the thighs with sea salt, and then cook in your hot oven for around 45 minutes, turning a couple of times and basting with any residual marinade. The thighs will become lovely and sticky.

While the chicken is cooking, drain the preserved lemons. Open them up and remove the soft inner flesh and discard, leaving you with the skin only. Using a sharp knife and a chopping board, cut the skin into fine strips, place in a bowl and add the sliced olives, crushed garlic, chopped parsley and a couple of slugs of olive oil. Stir to blend.

When the chicken is cooked, present the thighs onto plates and spoon over the lemon and olive mixture.

MCB tip: This recipe works equally well on chicken wings. Using the honey and mustard marinade above, add half a preserved lemon, finely chopped, a dessert spoon of tomato purée and a good sprinkle of dried chilli flakes. Marinade the wings for half an hour, then slap them on the barbi or griddle for finger food heaven!

YUCATAN RECADO CHICKEN
with citrus mango & avocado salsa

This is an authentic grilled Mexican dish, which uses some of my favorite spices, such as: cumin, coriander, cinnamon and black pepper. It works particularly well on the barbi.

One of the keys to the brilliant flavours of the Mexican grill, is the family of seasoning mixtures used on meats, fish, poultry and vegetables before they are grilled. These little known seasoning gems, for the most part, from Yucatan cooking are called *recados*, meaning "complements". Part marinade, part spice mix; *recados* do indeed complement the flavours of the foods they season.

Ingredients for four
- 4 chicken breasts – skin on & bones removed
- citrus mango & avocado salsa (see Basics – page 223)
- 2 cloves garlic – crushed
- ½ tsp ground cumin
- ½ tsp ground coriander
- ½ tsp ground cinnamon
- ½ tsp ground black pepper
- ½ tsp Mexican oregano
- ½ tsp lemon thyme
- 1 tsp ancho chilli powder
- 1 tbsp dark brown moscovado sugar
- 2 tbsp corn oil
- 1 lime – zested & juiced
- 1 small orange – juiced
- sea salt

Preparation
Pre-heat your grill.

Combine the garlic, chilli, oregano, thyme, cumin, coriander, pepper, cinnamon, sugar, oil, lime zest and juice and four tablespoons of orange juice and a couple of grinds of black pepper and mix together well. Add the chicken breasts and turn to ensure that they are evenly coated. Place into a zip-lock bag and refrigerate for an hour or so.

Place the marinated chicken breast onto a baking sheet and place under your hot grill, skin-side-up. Cook for a few minutes until the skin goes crisp. This should take around five to seven minutes. Turn the chicken breasts over and continue to cook for another five minutes or so, until cooked through, with no trace of pink.

Place the chicken breasts onto serving plates, top each with a spoon of salsa and serve with some crispy salad leaves. Serve with a spoonful of salsa on the side of each plate.

MCB tip: I love to play with this recipe and sometimes cool the grilled chicken, shred and serve with the salsa and some shredded lettuce as a filling for Mexican Chicken Wraps, finished off with a little chilli and lime mayo' and hot chilli sauce. Plus of course, the ubiquitous chilled Mexican beer.

HAPPY EVER AFTERS

There is so much information I could give you about desserts, sweets, puddings, 'afters' or whatever you like to call them. However, I have decided to include more recipes for cold desserts than hot ones, for the fairly obvious reason that you will mostly be working in hot or very hot, humid climates, therefore a hot, heavy pudding may not really go down too well with your charter guests. However, this does not mean that you should not serve hot desserts to your onboard guests. I have included some cooked recipes, which you can prepare and cook in the morning and serve cold for lunch or dinner with sorbet, ice cream, crème fraîche, natural yoghurt, fromage frais, or cream.

Just remember to try to balance your menu plans; a rich dessert is fine after a light main course and vice-versa. For every guest who claims they are watching their weight, there will always be another who cannot wait for dessert each night, so it's a good idea to have a repertoire of low calorie options available to balance out the status quo.

It is important for you to check with your guests to ascertain if they want to eat their dessert before their cheese or vice-versa. The French follow their main course with cheese, which is traditionally followed by dessert; this knowledge will also help you to make decisions about which wines to serve. If your guests have been drinking red wine with their main course, then it is appropriate to finish off the wine with cheese (savoury), rather than drinking it with a sweet food (dessert), which would destroy the flavour on their palate. You can then serve a nicely chilled sweet white, such as Sauternes from Bordeaux, or somewhat less expensive wines from across the River Garonne from Loupiac, Ste-Croix-du-Mont or St Macaire. For a budget buy, but quite acceptable quality, try a Blanc Moelleux de Bordeaux. The wine does not have to be from Bordeaux, as sweet whites are produced in many different ways all over the world.

If you are working on a very high end yacht, you may spot the odd bottle of Chateau d'Yquem (Bordeaux), which is the world's most famous and expensive sweet white wine, which can cost hundreds or thousands of pounds (Sterling) per bottle.

Fortified wine from the South of France called Banyuls or Muscat Beaumes de Venise (a sweet fortified or vin doux naturel wine), Muscat de Rivesaltes, Muscat de Frontignan, or Tokay Aszu from Hungary can also go quite nicely with some desserts. There is also a less know generic term to be aware of – Eiswein (pronounced 'ice vine') from Germany.

FYI: Always serve dessert wines nicely chilled.

Wine and chocolate: Chocolate is not the easiest food to match wine with. A nicely chilled Asti Spumante goes well with a light fluffy chocolate mousse. Powerful flavours tend to work well with other chocolate dishes. Try Tokay Azsú from Hungary. I love Banyules from SW France or a nice tawny port. Alternatively why not experiment with a rich red, such as a new world Shiraz.

BAILEY'S CRÈME BRULÉE

This is a fabulous alternate to the excellent Crème Brûlée recipe on page 195. It is very rich, so be careful that you don't plan this into a menu following an equally rich main course.

Ingredients for six
- 8 egg yolks
- 50g caster sugar
- 450ml double or whipping cream
- 150ml Bailey's
- 2 tbsp demerara or golden caster sugar

Preparation
Pre-heat your oven to 150°C.

Mix the egg yolks and sugar together in a bowl. Pour the cream and Bailey's into a small saucepan and place over a medium flame and heat to pre-boiling point. Remove the pan from the flame and whisk the cream mixture into the egg yolks and sugar. Strain into a jug.

Place six ramekins into a deep-sided roasting tray and pour in the brulée mix just short of the top. Fill a jug with boiling water. Place the roasting tray onto the middle or lower shelf and carefully pour the boiling water into the roasting tray, to reach half way up the sides of the ramekins. Cook for around forty five minutes until just set. There should be a slight wobble in the centre of the set custard. Remove from the oven, take out the ramekins and set aside to cool. Refrigerate to chill.

Pre-heat your grill to very hot. Sprinkle the top of the custard with the sugar and place under the grill. Keep a careful eye on this until the sugar caramelises to a rich golden brown.

MCB TIP: See my Crème Brûlée recipe below for advice on the use of a chef's blow-torch.

BRIOCHE BREAD & BUTTER PUDDING
with whisky and marmalade
Born in frugal times, when nothing in the kitchen was thrown away, this original version of this dish, bread and butter pudding, was an ideal way of using up stale bread. Not that I am suggesting that you serve revived stale bread to your guests; I am suggesting that this is a great use-'em-up if you have brioche or croissant left over from breakfast; either ingredient will turn this into a great dessert, which will be loved in equal measure by guests and crew alike.

Ingredients for four
- 50g unsalted butter
- 3 eggs
- 400ml whole milk
- 100ml single cream
- 6 brioche breakfast rolls – split lengthways
- Old English marmalade
- whisky
- 100g ready to eat dried apricots – shredded
- 3 tbsp golden caster sugar
- fresh nutmeg

Preparation
Pre-heat your oven to 180°C

Butter the cut sides of the brioche rolls, spread with marmalade and cut each slice in half (side-to-side). Take a baking dish and lightly butter, arrange a layer of brioche over the base. Sprinkle with the shredded apricots and then cover with another layer of brioche, then the remainder of the apricots. Drizzle some whisky over the brioche.

Take a measuring jug; add the eggs, half the sugar, cream and whisk together thoroughly. Add the milk and top up to 1pt or 600ml.

Pour the cold liquid over the brioche, press down with the back of a fork. Sprinkle over some freshly grated nutmeg, and bake in the oven for approximately thirty minutes, until all the liquid has been absorbed. Serve warm with some delicious Italian vanilla ice cream.

MCB tip: If you want to big-up the presentation for your guests, you can cook this in the morning and set aside to cool. Later in the day, you can cut out individual portions of pudding, using a metal ring or pastry cutter and gently warm the individual portions in your oven, then plate up and serve with ice cream, crème fraîche or crème anglaise and summer fruits and a sprig of mint.

CLASSIC CRÈME BRULÉE

Ingredients for four
- 500ml double cream
- 2 vanilla pods – split, seeds scraped & retained
- 75g caster sugar
- 5 egg yolks – free range
- demerara sugar

Preparation
Pre-heat your oven to 150°C.

Place a heavy based pan over a medium flame, add the cream, vanilla pods and seeds and bring to a simmer. Immediately remove from the flame and put to one side.

While the cream is warming up, take a large bowl and add the caster sugar and all of the egg yolks and whisk together until the mix turns pale and fluffy.

Remove the vanilla pods from the cream and pour the liquid over the egg and sugar mixture, whisking continuously until the sugar has dissolved. Strain the liquid into a measuring jug, as this makes the next step easier.

Place four ramekins into a deep-sided roasting tray and pour in the crème brulée mix just short of the top of the ramekins. Fill a jug with boiling water. Open your oven and place the roasting tray onto the middle or lower shelf and carefully pour the boiling water into the roasting tray, to reach half way up the sides of the ramekins; being careful not to get any water into the ramekins. This 'water bath', is called a 'bain-marie'. Cook in the oven for approximately 45 minutes, or until the custard has set firm, but still has a slight wobble.

Carefully remove the bain marie from the oven and place safely onto a work surface. Remove the crème brulées from the bain marie and set aside to cool slightly. Safely dispose of the hot water. Once sufficiently cool, cover the brulées with cling film and place into your refrigerator to chill until required.

When the crème brulées are needed for service, sprinkle the surface of each with some demerara sugar and using a chef's blow torch, heat the sugar until it melts and caramelises. I sometimes like to give the tops a second coating of sugar, if I am after a nice crunchy end product.

MCB tip #1: You can buy a good quality Mini Chefs Blow Torch from a good cook shop for around €20. You can use different types of sugar to produce a different finish to the brûlée – icing sugar, caster sugar, golden caster sugar etc etc..... Use a sugar sifter/dredger or a very small chinoise (sieve) to dust your Crème Brûlées when using icing sugar.

MCB tip #2: If you have a lot of mini air-bubbles on top of your brulée mix in the ramekins, just give the top a wee blast with your gas gun before you cook them – presto, no bubbles!

Di's INCREDIBLE CHEESECAKE

Di is my darling wife and I'm really not too sure where she found this recipe, maybe she just created it one day, however it works - and how! This is one of those never fails, everyone loves, cheesecakes that can be knocked up in no time flat. This is Di's banker, the dessert she often pulls together when we are having a dinner party.

Di and I prepared and cooked a four course meal for 14 on a 70' Challenge yacht not so long ago and she made two of her cheesecakes. Needless to say, there were only a few sweet biscuit crumbs left on the mess table as evidence that a cheesecake had ever existed on that yacht. I guess that the only problem with the recipe is that it's a concentrated cholesterol time-bomb.

Ingredients for eight
Base
- ½ packet digestive biscuits
- 75g unsalted butter

Topping
- 1 x 300g tub philadelphia (medium fat soft cheese)
- 600ml double cream
- 75g caster sugar
- 1 lemon – juiced
- vanilla essence – few drops

Preparation
Pop the biscuits into a zip-lock bag and crush with a rolling pin, or whatever comes to hand. Place a small pan over a low flame to melt the butter, add the biscuit crumbs and mix together thoroughly. Spoon into the bottom of a spring form (spring release) cake tin and press down to form a firm base. Di uses a potato masher for this and it really works so well.

Place the cream cheese and half of the cream into a mixing bowl and whisk together slowly with a hand-held electric mixer. Add lemon juice, vanilla and sugar and whisk together into a thick mixture. You may need to add a little more cream.

Spoon the cream mixture over the biscuit base and smooth out the top. Pop into your fridge and chill for three hours, or preferably overnight.

Serve on its own or with your choice of summer or tropical fruit topping and as you have some cream left – why not?

ETON MESS

This is another big time "get-out-of-jail-free-card". I find that this is about as universally popular as Crème Brûlée and needs no cooking at all, except for the meringues, which you can make yourself or purchase ready-made.

This classic English dessert consists of a mixture of strawberries, strawberry purée, pieces of meringue and whipped cream. It was traditionally served on at Eton College's annual cricket match, when pupils played against students from Winchester College. It is now served on the playing fields following the annual school prize giving ceremony.

An Eton Mess can be made with many other types of summer fruit, but strawberries are regarded as more traditional. The dish is said to date back to the 1930s, when it was served in the school's "sock shop" (tuck shop), and was originally made with either strawberries or bananas mixed with ice-cream or cream. Meringue was a later addition.

Due to the temperamental nature of the ovens on many smaller yachts, I suggest that you use shop bought meringues. Certainly in France, you should have no problem finding a pâtisserie that produces the lightest caramel coloured meringues. The last thing you want to do is go and buy the horrible white ones, which you sometimes find in British supermarkets.

Ingredients for six

- 250g fresh strawberries – hulled
- 570ml double cream
- 2 tbsp caster sugar
- 3 large meringues (6 small)
- 2 tbsp icing sugar

Preparation

Chop one quarter of the strawberries and whizz them up into a purée in your blender with the icing sugar. Pass through a sieve into a clean bowl.

Chop the remaining strawberries and place into a bowl and add the caster sugar and stir to coat. Whip-up the double cream to a peak, taking care not to over mix.

When you are ready to serve, break up the meringues into rough 2.5 cm pieces and place them into a large mixing bowl. Add the chopped strawberries and the resulting sugar syrup, and then fold the cream in and around them. The sugar syrup will give a lightly marbled effect, similar to Fraise Romanoff.

Finally spoon into serving dishes or glasses and drizzle the strawberry purée over the top and serve immediately.

FRAISES ROMANOFF

Celebrity chefs such as Marco Pierre White and Gordon Ramsay might be forgiven for thinking that they have little in common with the great chef Antonin Carême, born in 1783.

Certain aspects of Antonin's life, however, would strike a chord. He also rose from being a humble apprentice to become famed throughout the land. He too was a tireless self-promoter and, towards the end of his life, he wrote with great sympathy and experience of the appalling conditions, stress and ill-health suffered by kitchen workers.

Carême was a refining influence on post-Revolution French gastronomy, rigorously documenting the methods, techniques and recipes of French cuisine of his day, thereby providing a classic foundation for "la grande cuisine".

In 1816 he was engaged by the Prince Regent and installed at Brighton. After this, he went to work in Russia for Tsar Alexander, for whom he created Fraises Romanoff, in which strawberries are macerated in orange juice and Cointreau and served with chilled Crème Chantilly.

Ingredients for four

- 600g ripe, firm strawberries
- 30ml freshly squeezed orange juice
- 30ml Orange Curaçao, Cointreau or Grand Marnier
- 300ml double cream
- 2 tbsp sifted icing sugar
- 1 tsp fresh lemon juice
- ½ tsp vanilla extract

Preparation

Remove hulls, wash the strawberries and pat them dry. Cut into quarters top to bottom and place in a deep bowl, add the orange juice and liqueur, cover with cling film and refrigerate for an hour or two, turning gently once or twice.

Just before serving, gently whip the double cream, icing sugar, vanilla and the lemon juice, until it just starts to thicken. Carefully spoon some strawberries and a little juice into the bottom of wine glasses, glass tumblers or glass bowls. Drain the remaining strawberries and retain the liquid. Gently fold the remaining strawberries into the whipped cream (crème chantilly), until it streaks like rose marble.

Spoon the cream mixture into the glasses, decorate the top with a strawberry fan and serve with Caprice wafers.

MCB tip: This dish is totally amazing if you use passion fruit in place of strawberries.

FYI: For a more health conscious option, use mascarpone or thick Low-Fat Greek yoghurt instead of cream. The surplus alcoholic liquid is fantastic when used in cocktails, especially mixed with chilled Champagne or Cava.

FROZEN WHITE CHOCOLATE & COINTREAU PARFAIT

This dish was inspired by James Knight-Pacheco and Luke Garnsworthy on my visit to the Ashburton Cookery School in Devon. You can of course use whatever flavour of liqueur you like to create this dish, but this will depend on what you are serving with the parfait, so be careful that your flavours don't clash. I always think that orange is a fairly safe bet, although Amaretto and chocolate together are truly amazing.

You can either use a terrine lined with cling film, or individual stainless steel rings. I prefer the latter as they are far easier to 'plate-up' quickly and efficiently.

Ingredients for approximately 8 x 7cm rings
- 8 x egg yolks – free range, medium
- 100g caster sugar
- 8 tbsp Cointreau
- 200g good quality white chocolate
- 600ml double cream

Preparation

Place a pan of hot water over a medium flame and bring up to a gentle simmer; reduce the flame to low. Place a stainless steel bowl over the pan, making sure the base is not touching the hot water. Gently melt the chocolate, stirring only occasionally. Stirring too much will make your chocolate go grainy, at which point you will have to start over again.

Using the same method of a bowl over hot water, whisk the egg yolks and caster sugar to achieve a sabayon, where the mixture doubles in volume and becomes light, fluffy and leaves a ribbon trail in the liquid. Do not allow the mix to get too hot, or you will finish up with scrambled egg. Remove the sabayon from the heat, discard the hot water and continue to whisk until the mixture cools a little.

Whisk the cream in a separate bowl until it is semi-whipped and starts to form soft peaks.

Add the melted chocolate to the sabayon and mix in with a stainless spoon. Add the cream to the mixture and work well until you achieve soft peaks. Add the Cointreau and fold into the mixture.

If you are using stainless rings, wrap one end tightly with cling film and place onto a baking sheet, roasting tray or similar. Spoon your mixture into the ring or mould and place into your freezer for a minimum of six hours, or over-night is good.

To serve
Whatever you are serving the parfait with, it should be plated up first, so you need to think where on the plate the parfait will go and make sure all the plates look identical.

Now remove the cling film from the moulds. Using a chef's gas gun, and one at a time, give the outside of each mould a very light blast of flame. Slide a palette knife under the mould, transfer to the serving plate, remove the palette knife and simply lift the mould off the parfait, VOILA - PARFAIT!

LAVENDER CRÈME BRULÉE
with caramelised nectarines
My home is on the Isle of Wight, where we produce some beautiful, fragrant lavender, which I buy (dried) from Isle of Wight Lavender at Staplehurst Grange, near the market town of Newport. This is not, I have to say, produced in quite the quantities as the picturesque rolling fields of the French Departments of: Alpes-de-Haute-Provence, Vaucluse, Drome and Hautes Alpes in the South of France, where you are constantly aware of the fragrance of lavender in the air in the summer months.

You will note, quite quickly, that this recipe is different to the Classic Crème Brulée recipe which I gave you earlier. The subtle flavour in this brulée is created by infusing dried lavender in warmed cream, to create one of those 'talking point' dishes.

Ingredients for four ramekins

For the brulée
- 400ml double cream
- 5 medium egg yolks – freshest free range
- 40g caster sugar
- 1 dsp dried lavender

For the nectarines
- 2 x nectarines (ripe but firm)
- 10g unsalted butter
- brandy
- golden caster sugar – pinch
- mixed spice – pinch

Preparation
Pre-heat your oven to 130°C.

Take a medium sized, heavy based saucepan, add the cream and lavender and place over a low flame. Gently warm to a light simmer (do not allow to boil). Remove from the flame, cover with some cling-film and place to one side to infuse for one hour.

Cut each nectarine into eight wedges (north to south), remove from the stone. Place a non-stick frying pan over a medium-low flame, add the butter, heat and melt until it starts to foam. Once the foam starts to subside, add the prepared wedges and pan fry for a minute or so on either side until they start to soften. Add a splash of brandy, flambé with care and burn off the alcohol. Add the sugar and mixed spice and cook until the juices start to caramelise. Remove the fruit and liquid from the pan and place into a suitable container and set aside to cool.

Remove the cling-film from the infusion and gently re-heat the cream (not too hot). While this is happening, whisk the egg yolks and sugar together in a bowl, until the mixture turns pale in colour. Pour the warmed cream infusion over the egg mixture, gently whisking all the time. If you whisk too hard, you will create a lot of froth, which will form on the top of your brulées as bubbles.

Pass the cream mixture through a sieve (chinoise) into a pouring jug to remove the lavender. Place your ramekins into a roasting tin and three quarters fill each with some of the cream mixture. Place the roasting tin into your oven, and fill with water so it reaches three quarters the way up the sides of the ramekins. Cook for approximately ninety minutes until just set, but check regularly for progress.

Once cooked, remove the roasting tin from the oven. Remove the ramekins and refrigerate for around three hours. When you are ready to serve, sprinkle a thin layer of demerara sugar over the top of the set creams and caramelise with a blowtorch. Gently re-heat the nectarines and serve with the brulée, garnished with some fresh mint.

MCB tip: You can serve the nectarines hot or cold.

LEMON & PISTACHIO SHERBERT
This is one of those amazing recipes, which I would never have thought about making myself, until superyacht chef Claire Everard demonstrated this to a group of our students recently. This recipe presses every single button from top to bottom and if you don't try making this, you will miss out big time. *You will require a 1 litre milk or fruit juice carton – thoroughly rinsed with boiling water.*

Ingredients for eight
- 275g caster sugar
- 2 tbsp liquid glucose (or sugar syrup)
- 3 lemons - finely zested
- 500g Greek-style yoghurt
- 250ml double cream – thickened
- 100g pistachios – roasted
- 8 sponge finger biscuits - cut into 1cm pieces
- 2 tablespoons lemon juice
- 500g strawberries – hulled & quartered

Preparation
Place sugar, glucose, zest and 125ml water in a small saucepan, place over a medium flame and bring to the boil, reduce the heat and simmer for 5 minutes. Remove from heat and leave to cool.

When cool, whisk all but 80ml of the syrup into the yoghurt. Using an electric mixer, whisk the cream until firm peaks form, then fold into the yoghurt mixture with pistachios and biscuits.

Spoon the mixture into the rinsed milk carton, fold the top tightly closed and wrap firmly in layers of cling film. Place into your freezer overnight and refrigerate the reserved syrup.

To serve, combine reserved syrup, lemon juice and strawberries in a bowl.

To remove sherbet from carton, cut the top with scissors, and then tear away sides. Serve sherbet slices with strawberries and syrup.

LIMONCELLO and BLUEBERRY AMARETTI SYLLABUB

Ingredients for four
- 300g blueberries
- 4 tbsp limoncello
- 3 tbsp caster sugar
- 300ml double cream
- 6 tbsp sweet dessert wine
- 12 amaretti biscuits– crushed

Preparation
Put the blueberries, one tablespoon limoncello and 1 tablespoon of sugar into a pan and poach over a low flame for about one minute until the mixture has a more intense colour but the berries are not bursting. Transfer to a bowl and allow to cool.

Pour the cream into a bowl and add the remaining limoncello and dessert wine. Whisk until floppy and just holding a soft shape. Put some of the blueberries in the bottom of four sundae glasses, scatter over some crushed amaretti biscuits and spoon over some of the syllabub. Repeat this layering twice more, ending with a layer of syllabub, and top with a few blueberries and some crushed amaretti biscuits. Chill for 30-60 minutes before serving.

MANGO & CARDAMOM CREAM
This recipe was given to me by one of my grad students who has done a couple of seasons out in the BVIs. She tells me that her guests absolutely love this dish and regularly ask for it a second time during their charter, therefore destroying her carefully planned charter menus. Nothing, of course, that she couldn't handle!

Ingredients for eight
- 4 ready to eat mangoes – peeled & stones removed
- 10 green cardamom pods – seeds only
- 275ml whipping cream (heavy cream)
- 2 limes – zested & juiced
- 100ml golden Jamaican rum
- 2 passion fruit – scooped out
- 1 small bunch of fresh mint

Preparation
Finely chop two prepared mangoes, cover and refrigerate.

Roughly chop the remaining mango flesh, place into a food processor, blend until smooth and place in a bowl. Add half of the finely chopped mango and fold in. Return the remaining half of finely chopped mango to your fridge.

Using a pestle and mortar, grind the cardamom seeds to a fine powder. This aromatic spice gives off the most unique perfume. Place the crushed seeds into a bowl with the lime zest, juice, icing sugar and rum. Stir well to combine and add the cream and whisk until soft peaks form when the whisk is removed.

Spoon the mango purée mixture into serving dishes. Add the cream mixture and a spoon of passion fruit, topped with the remaining finely chopped mango and garnish with sprigs of mint.

NECTARINE and PLUM TART

One of my favourite pastry recipes is Marco Pierre White's version of sweet pastry (Marco Pierre White, Wild Food from Land and Sea). Although Marco's is the very best sweet paste recipe I have ever used, I have not included it here. For the uninitiated cook/chef, Marco's recipe can be difficult to handle, as it reacts to temperature changes and takes a certain level of technical knowhow to perfect. So, I have come up with an alternate sweet shortcrust pastry (see Basics – page 234), which you should find fairly straightforward to get right.

For this recipe, make sure you use firm, ripe fruit. Try to buy the largest, firm, ripe plums you can find on the market. **Use one quantity of Sweet Short Crust Pastry.**

Ingredients for eight
- 2-3 nectarines – stoned
- 6 large plums – stoned
- 3 eggs – free range
- 100g golden caster sugar
- 2 tbsp plain flour
- 90g unsalted butter – melted

Preparation
Pre-heat your oven to 180°C.

Remove your prepared pastry from the chiller and allow it to come up to room temperature. Lightly flour your work surface and roll out the pastry in a round until it is approximately 3mm thick.

Roll the pastry onto your rolling pin and gently un-roll it over a prepared 23cm tart tin and gently press the pastry into the base and up the sides, trimming off any surplus. Prick over the base with a table fork and set aside in your fridge to rest for thirty minutes.

Remove the tart tin from the chiller and line with a disk of baking parchment (grease-proof paper or tin foil will do fine). This must cover the base and up over the sides. Pour sufficient baking beans (most any dried pulse will do) over the parchment to weigh the pastry down and stop it from rising in the oven. Bake in the middle of your oven for ten minutes. Remove from the oven and gently remove the paper and lentils and put to one side. Return the tart to the oven for another ten minutes, to allow the base to dry out. Remove from the oven and leave to cool.

Cut the nectarines and plums into halves. Remove the stones and cut each half into two or three pieces depending on the fruit size. Arrange skin side down in the pastry case.

Break the eggs into a bowl and add the sugar and whisk until it thickens and turns a pale colour. Sift the flour and add, with the butter, to the egg mix and gently combine.

Pour the filling over the fruit. Bake for 30-40 minutes, or until golden and set in the centre.

MCB tip: When I test cooked this recipe, I used nice firm nectarines. The contrast in flavours between the slightly tart fruit and the sweetness of the 'sabayon' was absolutely fantastic.

PAIN PERDU
with cinnamon sugar & caramelised apples
Known in the UK as French Toast or Eggy Bread, this dish is often served at breakfast in Europe, Bermuda, Brazil, USA and Canada.

My recipe is a little different form the norm and provides you with a great 'use-em-up' opportunity for any brioche, which you may have left over from breakfast. The end result is excellent and goes down a storm with any children you may have onboard – including some of the grown up ones!

Having lived in France, I always say that this is their version of the English bread and butter pudding, but a lot more sexy. You can, of course, use slices of bread instead if you wish, but brioche has that wonderful sweet, buttery flavour which only benefits the end product.

Ingredients for four
- 8 slices of brioche
- 75g unsalted butter
- 450ml milk
- 40g caster sugar
- 3 large eggs – beaten
- 1 vanilla pod (essence or vanilla sugar would be fine)
- ground cinnamon

For the apples
- 75g unsalted butter
- 4 dessert apples – peeled, cored & thickly sliced
- 110g caster sugar
- 110ml double cream
- 2 tbsp calvados (apple brandy)

Preparation
For the apples
You will need to clarify both lots of butter first. This is done by putting the butter into a small pan and gently heat over a low flame, until the butter melts and the milky solids have dropped to the bottom of the pan. Divide the clear butter liquid between two bowls, discarding the solids.

Place a frying pan over a medium low flame and add a little of the clarified butter from the first bowl. Add the apple slices and fry for around two minutes, before turning them over to cook the other side until they are just soft (this will depend on the thickness of the slices and how firm your apples are). Lift out the apples and place onto some kitchen paper.

Turn the flame down to low and add the remaining clarified butter to the pan with the sugar, stirring with a spoon. As the sugar heats and dissolves, it will become a little grainy. Continue stirring until the sugar completely dissolves and turns a light toffee-colour. Remove the pan from the heat and add the cream and Calvados. Return the pan to a low flame and continue to cook, stirring all the time until any hard pieces of sugar in your pan melt into the sauce. Return the apples to the pan to keep warm and take on the lovely caramel flavours.

For the bread
Place a small pan over a low flame and add the milk, two thirds of the sugar and vanilla. Allow to heat slowly until almost boiling. Remove from the flame and allow to cool. Remove the vanilla pod and pour the milk infusion into a lasagne dish. Pour the beaten eggs into another shallow dish.

Slice the brioche 1cm thick. And then cut each slice diagonally, depending on size. Mix the remaining sugar and a half teaspoon of ground cinnamon together and keep to one side.

Place a heavy based non-stick frying pan over a medium flame and add a little of the clarified butter. Dip a couple or triangles of brioche in the milk, leave for around fifteen seconds, turn over and soak the other side for the same time. Your brioche should be moist, but not soggy. Now dip in the beaten egg on both sides and gently place into your frying pan and fry for around one minute on each side, until golden brown. Remove from the pan with a slice or tongues and place onto a tray and place into a low oven to keep warm, while you cook the remaining triangles of brioche.

Turn up the flame under the apples just a little to boost the heat. Arrange two triangles of Pain Perdu on each serving plate, dust with the cinnamon sugar. Divide the caramelised apples between the plates and spoon the rich apple juices over. Serve immediately.

PANNA COTTA
with poached strawberries
I believe that panna cotta is one of the classic European chilled deserts, made by the simple process of simmering together cream, sugar and vanilla and mixing this with soaked gelatine and letting it cool until set. Panna cotta literally means "cooked cream" and the dish is said to originate from the picturesque Northern Italian region of Piemonte.

The dish is eaten all over Italy, where it may be served with wild berries, caramel, chocolate sauce or a fresh fruit coulis, to which a good slug of fruit spirit can be added. Similar versions of this dish are also to be found in Greece and France.

Be aware of any vegetarians onboard, as they will not touch food containing gelatine. You can however, buy a vegetarian alternative, Agar-Agar (derived from seaweed), which will work equally as well and has no detrimental effect on the flavor of the end product. This is often available from health food shops, sold as flakes.

Ingredients for four people
- 3 sheets leaf gelatine
- 500ml double cream
- 225g golden caster sugar
- 2 vanilla pods
- ½ punnet of strawberries – hulled & halved
- ¼ bottle of champagne

Preparation
Place the gelatine leaves into a bowl of cold water for 10-15 minutes until soft.

Take a small heavy bottomed saucepan and place over a medium/low flame. Pour the cream and 75g of the caster sugar into a bowl and whisk gently and immediately transfer the mixture into the saucepan. Split the vanilla pods and scrape the inside and add both pods and seeds to the cream mixture.

Bring the cream infusion up to a light simmer (do not boil) and remove from the heat. Discard the vanilla pods. Remove the soaked gelatine from the water and squeeze out any excess liquid with your hands and add to the cream mixture; whisk or stir until completely dissolved.

When cooled a little, strain the liquid into a jug and poor into some ramekins or espresso cups, cover and refrigerate to set. This should take around two hours, although I prefer to leave them an hour or two more.

Pour the Champagne into a saucepan and add the remaining sugar. Bring to the boil, and then pour over the strawberries in a bowl with a little sugar. Leave to cool.

To un-mould the panna cotta, dip the ramekins individually into a container of very hot water to loosen from the sides. Cover with a side plate and holding the plate and ramekin firmly, turn them through 180° and give a quick shake – this should release the panna cotta onto the plate.

Transfer the panna cotta onto serving plates and decorate with the strawberries and pour over a little of the juice and finish with a small sprig of mint.

You can keep Panna Cotta refrigerated for a few days. Wrap completely in cling-film and place into a 'safe' area of your refrigerator, ready for a mid-night treat!

MCB tip #1:   Another great way to serve this dish is use half a bag of frozen summer berries. When your guests are eating their main course, turn out the Panna Cotta onto individual plates and scatter some small frozen berries around the plate; they should be half de-frosted when you are ready to serve. The sharpness of the berries contrasts wonderfully with this silky sweet vanilla-cream dessert.

MCB tip #2:   You will only use about half of the frozen berries, so in advance you can use the other half and boil them up with a little water and icing sugar, simmering for around 15 minutes or so. Remove from the heat, allow to cool a little, liquidise or pass through a sieve and presto – Summer Berry Coulis to enhance your dish.

PASSION FRUIT MOUSSE

Ingredients for six
- 12 passion fruit
- 1 large orange – zested & juiced (keep separate)
- 5 eggs
- 125g caster sugar
- 3 tsp powdered gelatine
- 315ml whipping cream

Preparation
Using a small sharp knife, cut the passion fruit in half across the equator, scoop out the flesh and place into a saucepan with the orange juice. Over a low flame, heat gently for 2- 3 minutes, pour into a bowl or jug, allow to cool, cover and refrigerate.

Take a large bowl and whisk the eggs, sugar and orange zest until thick and mousse-like. Sprinkle the gelatine over three tablespoons of water in a small bowl and leave to dissolve for 2 -3 minutes. To help the gelatine to dissolve more quickly, stand the bowl over a pan of hot water and stir gently until completely dissolved. When you have a clear 'gelatine liquid', fold into the egg mixture.

Sieve the chilled passion fruit mixture and stir half into the egg mousse, return the remainder to the fridge. In a separate bowl lightly whisk the double cream and fold into the mousse mixture. Spoon the mixture into a soufflé dish or individual serving glasses and chill until set.

If you are serving this dish straight onto individual plates, then make them look beautiful and surround each mound of mousse with a pool of passion fruit seeds and juice.

PEACHES in SAUTERNES
When my buddy Paul Rogers and I used to teach courses for the Wine & Spirit Education Trust, we always used the old trick of 'Taste the sweet wine' (some would like it, some wouldn't). OK so far? "Now eat a wedge of fresh, sweet peach, then taste the wine again" – presto! As if by magic,

the flavour of the wine is changed; balanced by the flavour of the food it is being served with. This is the essence of why we need to match the correct wine and food type/flavour.

When we lived in France, we could go down to our local market in Argentat (Corrèze) on a Thursday morning and buy trays of fresh apricots and peaches. We used to make beautiful apricot jam, which was loved by guests staying at our Chambres d'Hôte. Although we used to love eating the peaches, if we had guests book for dinner, we would think of different ways of preparing and serving lightly chilled fruit, to finish off an evening meal as the terrace lights came on and the candles were lit. This is the sort of dish we used to prepare.

Ingredients for four
- 4 firm ripe peaches
- 40cl Sauternes (or alternative – page 261)
- 500ml water
- 500g caster sugar
- 2 vanilla pods – fully split & de-seeded (seeds retained)
- 4 tbsp Crème de Pêche

Preparation
Remove any stalks and gently wash the peaches under cold running water. Take a medium sized saucepan, add the water and sugar and place over a high flame, bring to the boil, stir well and reduce the flame to a simmer. Using a perforated or slotted spoon gently lower the peaches into the liquid. Immediately turn off the flame and carefully remove the peaches and place into a bowl of well iced water, to cool. Retain the pan of liquid for later.

Once the peaches have cooled sufficiently, remove from the water and pat dry on some kitchen paper. Using a sharp knife, peel the fruit and cut round each peach, pole-to-pole. Gently twist the two halves in opposite directions to separate, remove and discard the stones. Place the de-stoned halves into a non-metalic bowl and pour over the sweet wine.

Place the pan of sugary liquid back onto your hob over a high flame. Add the vanilla pods and seeds, bring to the boil and then simmer for five minutes before pouring the liquid and vanilla pods over the peach halves. Place to one side to allow to cool a little before adding half of the crème de pêche. Cling film and place into your fridge.

To serve, remove the peaches from the fridge. For presentation purposes, trim a sliver of flesh off the base of the rounded half of four peach halves. Place one trimmed half and one 'normal' half onto a large, wide rimmed soup bowl and top with a split vanilla pod. Drizzle with some of the liquid and the remaining crème de pêche. Serve with a quenelle of crème fraîche, fromage frais or vanilla ice cream.

MCB tip #1:   Prepare this dish after breakfast, so that the flavours have all day to infuse into the peaches. The dish will be nicely chilled ready to serve with dinner.

MCB tip #2:   Check out the section at the end of the book on Dessert Wines. Sauternes is usually fairly expensive and your budget may not run to this extravagance. If you want to prepare this dish, but without the expense, I have offered you a range of less expensive alternatives, which will do a very similar job and work very well with the fruit.

PECAN PIE

This great dish is very American, very traditional, easy to slice and present; your guests will just love this recipe. It is not as heavy as you might think and is easy to make.

Ingredients for six

- 350g of short pastry (see Basics – page 233)
- 3 eggs – free range – beaten
- 225g soft brown sugar
- 110g golden syrup
- 110g melted butter
- 285g pecan nuts – halved
- 1 tsp vanilla extract
- icing sugar to serve

Preparation

Preheat your oven to180°C

Roll out the pastry to approximately 3mm thick and line a 25cm flan tin and bake 'blind'. This simply means that you lightly pre-bake the pastry before adding the filling, which helps to seal the pastry and should result in a light crisp finish. Cut a circle of baking parchment (grease-proof paper will do) and line the base of the pastry and up the sides and weigh down with baking beans or any dried pulse that you have to hand. Bake in your pre-heated oven for approximately 10 minutes. Take the flan out of the oven, remove the lining paper and baking beans and pop the flan back in the oven for another ten minutes for the base to dry out.

Place a heavy based saucepan over a low heat. Add the butter, golden syrup and sugar. When the butter has melted, remove the pan from the heat and allow to cool for around ten minutes. Add the beaten eggs to the mixture and stir well.

Arrange the pecan halves neatly in your part baked pastry case, retaining a good handful. Carefully pour the syrup mixture over the pecans.

Place the flan into your pre-heated oven and bake for around forty five minutes, until the pie is golden brown. The filling should still be slightly soft to the touch.

Remove the pie from your oven and transfer to a cooling wire. Once cooled sufficiently, decorate the top with the reserved pecan halves and dust with the icing sugar.

MCB tip: Try swapping the pecans with walnuts - it works just as well.

POACHED PEARS

in Moscatel, honey and thyme
with lime and yoghurt crème fraîche

We introduced this new recipe to our course in 2010 and it was an instant success. Many poached pear recipes utilize the 'mulled red wine' approach, leaving the pears a deep red colour, which looks great on the plate. However, I wanted to do something totally different from the norm and found the contrast of flavours in this recipe amazing. OK – so who ever thought of matching up pears and thyme? I like to serve this recipe with home-made vanilla ice cream.

Ingredients for four
For the pears
- 4 ripe William or Conference pears – halved & pips removed
  (The skin can be left on, removed or half & half)
- 1 bottle sweet white wine (Moscatel or Muscat)
- 125g clear honey (Acacia is best)
- 6 springs of fresh young thyme
- 2 lemons – finely zested

For the crème fraîche
- 100ml double cream – whipped to soft peak
- 100ml Greek-style yoghurt
- 2 limes – zested & juiced
- 1 tbsp icing sugar

Preparation
For the lime and yoghurt crème fraîche, place all of the crème fraîche ingredients, with half the lime zest into a bowl and mix together until combined. Cover and place into your refrigerator, while you poach the pears.

Pour the wine into a saucepan large enough to hold eight halves of prepared pears. Place over a high flame, add the honey, thyme and the lemon zest and bring to the boil. Reduce the flame and simmer gently for around three minutes to enable the flavour of the thyme to infuse in the liquor. Reduce the flame to low and add the pears, cover with a lid and cook for about five minutes or so until they are start to soften – test with a small sharp knife. The cooking time depends on the size, temperature and ripeness of the pears. Once the pears are nearly cooked, remove them with a slotted spoon and place to one side to cool.

Turn the flame back up to medium-high and bring the cooking liquor to the boil. Reduce the flame. As the liquid reduces it will become syrupy, so keep an eye on the pan. If you leave it too long, it will start to caramelise and burn quite quickly if unattended. Allow the liquid to reach a sugar syrup consistency.

Arrange the pears lovingly on four serving plates, spoon some syrup over the pears and add a large quenelle of your home made crème fraîche, sprinkled with a little of the remaining lime zest and a scoop of vanilla ice cream.

MCB tip #1:   If you are going to serve this dish cold, then preparing it in the morning is your best option. Place the cooked pears and liquid into a larger container, cover with cling film (prick a few holes in the top if still warm to release steam) and refrigerate. You can also prepare the crème fraîche and refrigerate, so everything is ready for service later that day.

EMC tip #2:   If you want to give this dish a real kick, splash a little Poire William liqueur over the pears directly before you serve to your guests.

POMEGRANATE
with honey and cinnamon cream
This is a great little dish which I threw together in an emergency a couple of years back. It has proved very popular with my students ever since. I sometimes replace the pomegranate with passion fruit seeds.

The pomegranate is native to Iran and has been cultivated and naturalized over the whole Mediterranean region since ancient times. It was introduced to Latin America and California by Spanish settlers around 1769 and pomegranates are now cultivated in many parts of California and Arizona for juice production.

For the health conscious, pomegranate juice has beneficial properties, which help our bodies in a number of ways. Studies have shown that pomegranate juice helps to inhibit hardening of the arteries, by preventing the build-up of material and reducing the chances of heart attack and stroke. By switching to pomegranate juice, we are protecting ourselves from heart disease, cholesterol and even stress! Pomegranate juice is also great served over ice in a hiball glass, with a dash of cointreau, a good shot of vodka and freshly squeezed lime juice, stirred – also preventing stress!

This dish is very simple to produce and requires only the bare minimum of time and ingredients.

Ingredients for four
- 2 medium pomegranates – de-seeded
- 1 x 500ml natural Greek yoghurt
- ground cinnamon
- runny honey
- 4 caprice wafers
- 50g amoretti biscuits – roughly crushed

Preparation
You will need two bowls – one for the pomegranate seeds and the other for the outer skin and debris. You will need to put on an apron to prepare the pomegranates, so do take extra care, as pomegranate will stain your 'whites'.

Cut the fruit in halves and with your hands, peel away the outer skin and discard. Now gently remove the seeds, which should be rosy pink to a bright, purple/red. Discard the creamy/white layers which grow inside the fruit. You should be left with a bowl of 'clean' pomegranate seeds.

Empty the yoghurt into a clean bowl and very gently, fold in 80% of the pomegranate seeds, retaining the remainder for your garnish. You do not want to finish up with a pink cream, rather a mélange of white and red, which is pleasing to look at.

Take four wine glasses or glass tumblers and divide the crushed amoretti biscuits amongst them. Using a table spoon, gently spoon the first layer of yoghurt mixture over the biscuits, trying to make sure that you keep the edges of the glasses clean. Sprinkle over a little ground cinnamon and a swirl of honey. Add another layer of yoghurt and so on, until you have used up all the mixture.

Top the cream with a final dusting of ground cinnamon, a swirl of honey and the remaining pomegranate seeds. Garnish by adding a Caprice wafer at a jaunty angle à la '99' ice-cream!

Place the glasses onto a doylied under plates and serve with a teaspoon.

ROAST FIGS
with honey and marsala
Figs are members of the Genus Ficus, belonging to the mulberry family and are one of the earliest fruits cultivated by man. The fig tree was mentioned very early on in The Bible and some scholars believe that the 'forbidden fruit' picked by Eve, was a fig rather than an apple. This would actually make more sense, as it was supposed to be a fig leaf which Adam chose to 'protect his modesty'.

Ingredients for four
- 8 large fresh, ripe figs
- 2-3 tbsp runny honey
- 8 tbsp Marsala wine (Port or Banyules are also good)
- vanilla ice cream

Preparation
Pre-heat your oven to 200°C.

Cut a deep cross down into each fig, from the top nearly down to the bottom, and then squeeze the sides of each fig to expose the juicy flesh. Place the figs into a lightly buttered baking dish.

Drizzle over the honey and Marsala wine, ensuring some runs down inside the figs. Cover with tin foil and bake in the oven for about 20 minutes.

Serve the figs immediately with ice cream and the boozy syrup from the baking dish. Alternatively, serve with cream, crème fraîche, mascarpone, or for the health conscious – on their own!

RICOTTA CHEESECAKE
I had hoped to include the fabulous Ricotta Cheesecake recipe by Rose Carrarini, who runs Rose Bakery, Rue des Martyrs, in Paris with her husband Jean-Charles. Unfortunately my request to her publishers was met with no response. If you get the chance to buy her book, Rose Bakery, it is well worth the investment.

My own version is smooth and creamy, but maybe not as rich as the American cheesecakes. It is best eaten on the day it is prepared, but will keep well for a few days in the fridge. Be warned – you will need to watch out for the phantom, night, fridge raiders!

Ingredients for eight

For the base
- 150g digestive biscuits – crushed
- 60g unsalted butter – melted
- pinch of ground cinnamon or ground ginger

For the filling
- 570g whole milk ricotta – drained
- 225g cream cheese – room temperature
- 200g caster sugar
- 15g corn flour
- 4 large eggs – beaten
- 1 lemon – zested
- 1½ tsp vanilla extract

Preparation
Preheat your oven to 180°C.

For the base
Wrap the base and sides of a 23cm spring form tin with a double layer of tin foil. Butter the base.

To make the base for the cheesecake, mix the crushed biscuits with the butter and ground cinnamon or ginger and press the mixture over the base of the tin.

For the filling
Place the cream cheese into a good sized bowl and beat until smooth and free of lumps. Add the ricotta and sugar and beat until smooth, scraping down the bowl when required. Beat in the corn flour.

Add the eggs little-by-little, beating to incorporate before adding more. Scrape down the sides of the bowl and add the lemon zest, vanilla extract and a pinch of salt, beating until fully incorporated.

Remove the base from your refrigerator, spoon in the filling and flatten with the back of a table spoon. Place the tin into a large roasting tray and pop it into your oven. Pour enough hot water into the roasting tray, to come about half way up the sides of the spring form tin.

Bake for around sixty to seventy five minutes, or until the top of the cheesecake has browned nicely. The middle of the cheesecake should move slightly when the pan is gently shaken.

Remove the pan from the water bath and place onto a cooling wire. When it has cooled down, cover and refrigerate.

Cut into wedges to serve.

MCB tip: This dish works well with soft summer fruits such as strawberries, raspberries or blueberries. You could also drizzle some Summer Berry Coulis over the cheese cake – see Panna Cotta MCB tip #2 – page 205.

TARTE TATIN
This is the famous upside down apple tart in which the apples are caramelised in butter and sugar, before the tart is placed into the oven to be baked. The story behind this dish is a tad on the lengthy, but worth telling – I think!

Folklore indicates that the Tarte Tatin was originally created by accident at the Hotel Tatin in Lamotte-Beuvron in France in 1898. The hotel was then run by two sisters, Stéphanie and Caroline Tatin. There are conflicting stories concerning the tart's origin, but the predominant one is that Stéphanie, who did most of the cooking, was overworked one day; she started to make a traditional apple pie, but left the apples cooking in butter and sugar for far too long. Smelling the burning sugar, she tried to rescue the dish by putting the pastry base on top of the apples, quickly finishing the cooking by putting the whole pan in the oven. After turning out the upside down tart, she was surprised to find how much the hotel guests appreciated the dessert.

The Tarte became a signature dish at the Hotel Tatin and the recipe spread through the Sologne region of France. Its lasting fame is probably due to the restaurateur Louis Vaudable, who tasted the tart on a visit to Sologne and made the dessert a permanent fixture on the menu at his famous, internationally renowned restaurant – Maxim's of Paris.

We included this dish in our cookery course since the early days and my good buddy Bucko, who is the 'Tatin Meister', always produces the most amazing dish. I am pleased to report that my research indicates that the genius Mr Heston Blumenthal creates his version of this dish in more or less exactly the same style as Bucko.

Ingredients for four

- 125g unsalted butter – cut into cubes
- 125g caster sugar
- 6 firm eating apples – Braeburn, Cox, Granny Smith – peeled & cored
- 250g pack frozen or chilled puff pastry (or ready rolled)
- calvados

Preparation

Pre-heat your oven to 200°C.

Allow the butter to soften a little and press it evenly over the base and up the sides of a heavy based frying pan with a steel handle, then sprinkle the sugar over the butter.

Cut the prepared apples in half and lay them, cut side up, in the pan. Fill the whole base of the pan with apple halves, packing them together tightly, as they will shrink a little during cooking. Try not to leave any gaps between the apples.

Place the pan over a medium-low flame. The butter and sugar will begin to bubble, gradually turning to a light golden colour as it starts to caramelise. As the sugar caramelises to a darker colour, sprinkle with a little calvados, cook for a few seconds more and remove the pan from the flame and put safely to one side.

Lightly dust your work surface with a little flour and roll out your puff-pastry into a disc, to between 5mm thick and about 2.5cm larger than the diameter of the frying pan.

Allow the apples to cool a little. Lightly dust your rolling pin and roll the pastry around the pin and unroll is over the apples, tucking the overlap inside the edge of the pan. Make a few strategically placed incisions in the pastry with a small, sharp knife.

Place the pan into your pre-heated oven for around 20 minutes to finish cooking. When the pastry turns a light golden brown in colour, it is ready to take out of the oven. Remove and allow to cool a little. However, you must turn the tart out while it is still warm, or else it is likely to stick. It is always a good idea, just to ease the pastry away from the edge of the pan with a palette knife before you attempt to turn out the tart.

Place a large serving dish or plate over the top of the pan and carefully, flip the two over, so that the pastry finishes up on the plate, with the caramelised apples, beautifully presented on the top.

MCB tip #1: Portion the tart onto individual plates and when you are ready to serve, add a scoop of vanilla or caramel ice cream or crème fraîche.

MCB tip #2: If you have space, this dish is great served as the centre piece at the table. Pre-sliced, so your guests can help themselves. I like to do this and add a little flaming calvados, before dimming the lights to serve. The effect is impressive.

FYI: If you are using a small gimbal oven, you may have to be creative in how or more specifically, what you cook this dish in.

CAKES & PASTRIES

If you are working on smaller yachts, or I guess big ones for that matter, and doing your thing in the galley, then you may find yourself needing to knock up some cakes, pastries or biscuits for afternoon tea. Other crew members will absolutely love you for your unchallenged ability to produce such wonderful tasty treats, because this type of 'any time of the day' finger food is always a total winner.

ANZAC BISCUITS

There are a number of theories surrounding the true origin of Anzac biscuits, which have long been associated with the Australian and New Zealand Army Corps (ANZAC) serving in Gallipoli (Turkey). What is certain is that they came about during World War 1 around 1914 – 15. The most widely believed theory is that they were created by Australian and New Zealand women, endeavouring to create a treat for their loved ones that would survive the long journey to the front-line. It has also been suggested that the biscuit is a variation of the Scottish Oat Cake.

Ingredients for 20 biscuits
- 85g porridge oats
- 85g desiccated coconut
- 100g soft flour – plain
- 100g caster sugar
- 100g butter – melted
- 1 tbsp golden syrup
- 1 tsp bicarbonate of soda

Preparation
Preheat your oven to 180°C.

Place the oats, coconut, flour and sugar in a bowl. Place a small pan over a low flame, add the butter, melt and stir in the golden syrup. Add the bicarbonate of soda to 2 tablespoons of boiling water and stir into the golden syrup and butter mixture.

Make a well in the middle of the dry ingredients and pour in the butter and golden syrup mixture. Stir gently to incorporate the dry ingredients.

Take a baking sheet and cover with a veneer of butter. Using a dessert spoon, add spoonfuls of the mixture, leaving approx 2.5cm between each to allow for spreading. Bake in batches for 8-10 minutes until golden. Transfer to a wire rack to cool.

BANANA CAKE

This is one of those recipes which is fairly well known by many chefs. Great when you have got some bananas which need using up. Really easy to make and enjoyed by those who have tried it.

Ingredients to serve eight
- 2 ripe bananas – overripe are best
- 175g golden caster sugar
- 175g flour
- 175g self-raising flour
- 175g soft margarine
- 3 medium/large eggs
- ½ tsp vanilla essence

Preparation
Pre-heat your oven to 180°C

Using your food processor, add all the ingredients and blend until thoroughly mixed.

Pour the mixture into a lined loaf tin and place into the middle of your pre-heated oven for approximately one hour.

Remove from the oven and place to one side on a cooling wire.

How's that for simple?

LARNIE'S CARROT CAKE
I am blessed to have three wonderful children who are, in their own different ways, very good cooks. My daughter, Alanna (Larnz) is the chief baker in the family and although we all love her home made cupcakes - in particular, I adore her carrot cake recipe.

Ingredients serve eight or more
For the cake
- 4 medium carrots (firm & sweet) – finely grated
- 250ml sunflower oil
- 225g golden caster sugar
- 3 large eggs
- 300g self-raising flour – sifted
- 1 tsp ground cinnamon
- unsalted butter – for greasing
- ½ tsp salt
- 100g walnuts – finely chopped (optional)

For the frosting
- 250g mascarpone cheese
- 25g golden icing cane sugar – sieved

Preparation
Pre-heat your oven to 180°C.

Grease and line a 20cm spring form cake tin with baking parchment.

Whisk the oil and sugar together, then whisk in the eggs one at a time. Gently fold in the flour, cinnamon, grated carrots and finally the chopped walnuts. Mix gently until thoroughly combined, then scrape out into your prepared baking tin, distributing evenly over the base.

Place into the middle of your pre-heated oven and bake for approximately forty minutes until golden brown and a cocktail stick, when inserted into the middle, comes out clean.

Remove from the oven and place to one side to cool for ten minutes. Turn out and place onto a cooling wire rack.

Mix together the mascarpone cheese and the golden icing sugar. Spread over the top and sides of the cake with a palette knife.

You can finish the top with either walnut halves or pecans. Both are equally good.

CHOCOLATE FUDGE CAKE

This is really one of the sexiest chocolate fudge cake recipes I have ever tasted. This recipe, inspired by Yotam Ottolenghi is fairly simple to prepare and has the odd twist of being baked in two stages. My son Ashley is the UK's #1 chocoholic and he thinks this recipe will be a big hit with your onboard guests and crew.

Ingredients for 8 people
- 240g unsalted butter
- 260g dark chocolate – 52% cocoa solids
- 95g dark chocolate – 70% cocoa solids
- 290g light moscovado sugar
- 4 tbsp water
- 5 large free range eggs (room temperature)
- cocoa powder
- salt

Preparation
Pre-heat your oven to 170°C.

Grease the inside of a 20cm springform cake tin and line the base and sides with baking parchment. Cut both lots of chocolate and the butter into small pieces and place into a large stainless steel bowl.

Take a small saucepan and place over a medium flame. Add the water and sugar, stir well and bring to the boil. Pour the syrupy mixture over the chocolate and butter and stir well until the ingredients have all melted, forming a runny chocolate sauce. Separate the egg white and yolks, making sure that you do not get any yolk in with the whites. Add the yolks, one at a time, stirring into the chocolate mixture. Allow to cool down to room temperature.

Place the egg whites into a large, clean, grease free bowl with a pinch of salt and whisk them until they form firm peaks. Using a large metal spoon or rubber spatula, very gently fold the meringue into the chocolate mixture a third at a time. Fully incorporate the meringue, but do not beat or you will knock the air out of the mixture.

Spoon around two thirds of the mix into the prepared cake tin and level out gently with the back of a large spoon. Cover the remaining cake mix with some cling film and place to one side.

Place the cake tin into the middle of your pre-heated oven and bake for approximately forty minutes, or until a skewer or flat brochette, inserted in the middle of the cake, come out almost clean. At this point, remove from the oven and leave to cool.

The centre of the cake will most likely have risen a little, so flatten the top down with the back of a large spoon or a palette knife. It doesn't matter if the top breaks a little. Now spoon the remaining mixture over the top of the cake and level again with the back of a large spoon. Pop the cake tin back into your oven and cook for a further twenty to twenty five minutes. After this time, check again with a skewer or flat brochette, which should still show slightly moist crumbs when removed.

Place the tin onto a cooling wire, but don't turn it out just yet. Allow to cool completely before you remove the springform sides. Dust the top with cocoa powder.

This is cake is great served on its own, with crème fraîche, lightly caramelised orange slices or summer fruit coulis.

MCB tip: If you just want to cook a one consistency cake, and then bake the whole thing in one hit – it still tastes great.

HAZELNUT SHORTBREAD BISCUITS

This seriously is one of the easiest baking recipes you will ever make and the fabulous light, short biscuits are a favourite either with mid-morning coffee or to accompany a summer dessert. For the former, make eight from the mixture and the latter, sixteen. The major problem that you will find is that these are 'magical disappearing biscuits'; because once the crew have tasted them and that distinctive baking smell becomes familiar, you will find yourself needing to bake twice as much as you actually need for your guests!

I have been known to pop some shelled hazelnuts into my mini-blender, whizz them up, not too fine, and presto – this adds an extra crunchy dimension to your biscuits.

Ingredients for 8 or 16 biscuits
- 75g plain flour
- 20g ground hazelnuts.
- 30g cornflour
- 90g unsalted butter – cut into dice
- 30g icing sugar

Preparation
Using a good sized bowl, sieve in the icing sugar, add the butter and cream together well. Sieve in the plain flour and corn flour, add the ground hazelnuts and mix until you have achieved a dough.

Here comes the sexy bit. Take two good sized rectangles of cling film and place onto your work surface. Add the dough and, using your hands, shape into a sausage shape. Roll up in the cling film and by holding tight onto the ends of the film; roll the cylinder into the desired thickness. Twist the ends of the cling film and pop into your fridge to rest for at least an hour.

To cook
Pre-heat your oven to 180°C

Remove your dough from the fridge; remove from the cling film and cut slices (discs) of the shortbread dough and place onto a silicone lined baking sheet, allowing a fair bit of space between each. When I make sixteen, I use two baking sheets. Bake in your pre-heated oven for fifteen to twenty minutes, until golden.

Remove from the oven and gently lift onto cooling wires with a palette knife. The biscuits may appear and feel undercooked, however the secret is to take a peek at the underside – light golden brown is perfect. You will find, as they cool, the soft texture will change and you will finish up in biscuit heaven!

MCB tip: You can make this dough days in advance if you wish and keep it in your fridge. Alternatively, make a large batch; break it down into cylinder shapes, wrap, label and freeze. All you need to do is to take a cylinder out of the freezer and pop it into your fridge the day before you are going to use it. Simple!

MALTESERS CUPCAKES

The fun thing about this recipe is trying to find someone in the crew who doesn't like Maltesers. Cupcakes and Maltesers have been around for as long as I can remember, yet it is only recently that cupcakes have made a massive resurgence in popularity. I have a good friend here on the Isle of Wight called Zoe, who makes the most amazing cupcakes you have ever seen. I wish I had her ability, patience and artistic talent.

Ingredients

For the sponge
- 100g maltesers
- 200g butter – softened
- 150g caster sugar
- 50g golden caster sugar
- 1 tsp vanilla extract
- 4 medium eggs – free range
- 200g plain flour
- 10g baking powder
- salt – pinch

For the butter cream
- 250g butter
- 500g icing sugar – sieved
- 1 tsp vanilla extract
- 60g maltesers – roughly crushed

Preparation
For the sponge
Pre-heat your oven to 180°C
Line a cupcake tin with 12 cupcake cases.

Take a bowl and add the butter and both sugars and cream together until the mix is light and fluffy. This can be done by hand or with a hand held whisk.

Add the eggs one-by-one, and all of the vanilla, whisking well after each addition. If the mixture looks like it is like it has curdled, add a couple of tablespoons of flour and beat well, until the mixture looks smooth.

Using a metal spoon, fold in the sieved flour, baking powder and salt together and then stir in the maltesers.

Using a dessert spoon, divide the mixture equally between the cupcake cases and bake in the middle of your pre-heated oven for around twenty five minutes or until a skewer or small sharp knife comes out clean. When cooked, remove from the oven and leave in the tin to cool.

For the buttercream
Take a bowl and using a hand held whisk, whisk together the butter, icing sugar and vanilla until it becomes pale and fluffy.

To decorate
Once the cupcakes have completely cooled, you can put a spoonful of the buttercream on top of each cupcake and spread it around with a small palette knife. To give the cupcakes the five star

treatment, use a piping bag and a 1cm star tube and pipe the buttercream on top. Sprinkle the crushed maltesers over the top to finish.

Original recipe from www.maltesers.com

SHORTBREAD

I always try to use unrefined caster sugar and salted or slightly salted butter, which I think tends to give the best flavour.

Ingredients for eight
- 150g soft flour (plain)
- 100g slightly salted butter – cut into pieces & softened
- 50g golden caster sugar
- caster sugar for sprinkling

Preparation
Preheat the oven to 160°C.

Place the flour into a mixing bowl, add the butter and rub between your fingers to make fine crumbs. Stir in the sugar and work the mixture together until it forms a ball.

Turn out onto a lightly floured work surface and knead briefly until smooth. Roll out and pat out on a very lightly floured surface to an 18cm disc. Smooth the surface of the pastry with your hands. Carefully slide the dough onto an ungreased baking sheet and flute the edges. Mark the circle into eight triangles with a knife, not cutting all the way through. Prick the surface all over with a fork.

Place the baking sheet into your pre-heated oven and bake for approximately 30 minutes or until cooked. Cooked shortbread should be very pale.

While still warm, cut through the markings and lightly sprinkle with castor sugar. Allow to cool before serving.

STICKY CHOCOLATE BROWNIES

There was only ever going to be one recipe that I can share with you for this famous finger food. My darling wife is the Chocolate Fudge Meister at chez nous, so for me to use my own recipe would have been far too high risk. So thank you my darling for letting me use your recipe in my little book.

Ingredients for 16 brownies
- 150g unsalted butter
- 260g caster sugar
- 110g dark muscovado sugar
- 185g good quality dark chocolate
- 1½ tbsp golden syrup
- 2 eggs
- 1½ tsp vanilla flavouring
- 150g plain flour
- 3 tbsp cocoa powder
- 1 tsp baking powder

Preparation
Pre-heat your oven to 180°C.

Lightly oil and flour a 23cm square cake tin or Pyrex dish.

Place a heavy based saucepan over a low flame and add the butter, sugars, dark chocolate and golden syrup and heat gently, stirring until the mixture is well blended and smooth. Remove from the flame and place away from the heat and allow to cool.

Take a plastic bowl and lightly whisk together the eggs and vanilla essence with a fork. Fold in the cooled chocolate mixture and then gently whisk again.

Sieve together the flour, cocoa powder and baking powder. Add the sieved cocoa mixture to the egg and chocolate mixture a little at a time, folding in carefully using a metal spoon or spatula.

Spoon the mixture into the prepared tin or Pyrex dish and bake in your pre-heated oven for 25-30 minutes until the top is crisp and the edge is starting to shrink away from the sides of the container. The middle will still be quite soft to the touch.

It is a good idea to mark the top and cut into squares and allow to cool in the container.

Similar to the hazelnut shortbread biscuits, this recipe will be very popular with the crew, especially for those on watch – so be warned!

MCB tip: When you have added the flour, the consistency needs to be at a good ribbon stage, so you may need to add an extra tablespoon of flour, it depends how 'gloopie' the mixture is (my wife's technical terminology!).

TOFFEE BROWNIES
This recipe was given to me by my mate Clair Etchell-Johnson and tastes ab-fab. Clair was one of my Btec National Diploma students some years back and has just returned to become a chef lecturer at The Isle of Wight College. Clare says that you have to use unrefined dark muscovado sugar, as this gives the brownies a sticky toffee flavour.

Ingredients to make 16 brownies
- 350g dark chocolate – broken into pieces
  (preferably around 60% cocoa solids)
- 250g unsalted butter, cut into pieces
- 3 large eggs
- 250g dark muscovado sugar
- 85g plain flour
- 1 tsp baking powder

Preparation
Preheat the oven to 160°C.

Butter and line the base of a shallow 23cm square cake tin. Melt the chocolate and butter together, then stir well and cool.

Whisk the eggs until pale, then whisk in the sugar until thick and glossy and well combined. Gently fold in the melted chocolate mixture, then sift in the flour and baking powder and gently stir until smooth.

Pour into your prepared cake tin and bake for 30-35 minutes, or until firm to the touch. Test by inserting a wooden cocktail stick into the middle; when removed there should be a few moist crumbs sticking to it. The mixture will still be soft in the centre, but will firm up on cooling.

Cool in the tin on a wire rack for at least 1 hour then cut into 16 squares and finish cooling on the rack.

BASICS

My basics section is essential to the culinary success of this book and improving your understanding of some 'cookery essentials'. It primarily covers two very important skills in the culinary world: pastry and sauces, both hot and cold. I need to give you a brief intro' to both, which you should make the effort to read before you prepare any of the recipes I have included.

PASTRY

I think that it is important to stress that you can buy some very good quality chilled, frozen or dried pastry products from supermarkets in many countries throughout the world. The merits or de-merits of these options are open to debate and should be put into context.

Buying pre-prepared pastry has the distinct advantage that you know, barring a total disaster of biblical proportions that it should work, giving you 'happy guests'. Making your own pastry provides you with the opportunity for what is commonly known as a 'cock-up', potentially giving you 'unhappy guests'. Pastry products and baking in particular are a science and as such require consistent ingredients, accurate measuring, temperature control, accurate cooking time and a certain amount of skill, which will come with experience.

I know this sounds like I am encouraging you to go for the soft option, however there are of course, going to be times when you can't shop and don't have the required pastry in your fridge or freezer, so I decided to provide you with a few simple recipes, which should see you through between provisioning trips when you may have run out of the factory made stuff.

Having owned a home in France, I swear by Pâte à Foncé, literally meaning lining pastry or pie pastry, which you will find in most major French supermarkets. The beauty of using this is that it is pre-rolled and chilled, so all you need to do is take it out of the packet, lightly dust your work surface or board with flour and off you go. Alternatively, you can use it straight out of the packet without further rolling. It also freezes well.

SAUCES
hot & cold

Sauces, prepared correctly, will enhance and complement a dish. You should, however, always avoid masking the flavour of the food you are serving, especially if the sauce has quite a distinctive flavour. The sauce and main ingredient should always flatter each other, as any conflict of flavours will be detrimental to the quality of the end product.

Simple sauces are ones which use the natural flavours from the ingredients to enhance the dish. Moules Marinière and dishes cooked en papillote are good examples of very simple 'thin' sauces which are full of flavour. The stock used, say, for poaching fish, gives you an excellent base for a sauce. If you want to enhance the flavour, add a little dry white wine or vermouth, simmer the stock rapidly to reduce, whisk in a knob or two of butter and some crème fraîche or natural yoghurt and you will have a wonderful sauce to serve over poached fish.

The great Antonin Carême designated four 'mother sauces' in the 19th century, these were: Béchemal, Hollandaise, Velouté and Espagnole. The famous French chef Auguste Escoffier would later classify tomato as a 'mother sauce' as well.

Simple sauces can be created when pan frying fish. Remove the cooked fish and keep warm, drain off any surplus oil from the pan and deglaze with some dry white wine, vermouth and cream. A dash of Pernod in some fish sauces is a marriage made in heaven. To finish off a sauce with a real blast of flavour, add some finely chopped fresh herbs just before you are ready to serve.

Another way of thickening a thin sauce is by adding what is called a beurre manié – equal quantities of butter and flour, kneaded together to form a paste. Whisk small nuggets of this mixture into your source, a little at a time and it will thicken beautifully and produce the most luxurious glaze on your sauce. Another is to use egg yolks to create a 'liaison', which will enrich, thicken and glaze your sauce. This is a specialised technique, but very simple to achieve if a little care is taken.

Finally, what might appear the most simple, is to whisk knobs of unsalted butter into your simmering sauce (Monté au Beurre), which will lightly thicken a sauce, while giving it the most beautiful silky sheen, looking heavenly on a plate.

AIOLI

Aioli is a sauce made of garlic, olive oil and egg yolks, which is very similar in texture to mayonnaise. There are many variations, such as the addition of mustard. In France and Spain, aioli is traditionally served with seafood, whereas in Australia it is served, like mayo' – with fries.

The recipe is traditionally prepared in a pestle and mortar, although this can be laborious. I have used a different method below, which you will find easier.

Ingredients

- 2 large garlic cloves
- 2 egg yolks – free range
- 300ml olive oil
- juice of ½ lemon – to taste
- salt

Preparation

Peel, top and tail the garlic; finely chop and sprinkle with salt. With the flat blade of a chef's knife, work the garlic until the oils are released – keep working it until you have crushed garlic. Transfer to a bowl and using a whisk; gradually work in the egg yolks.

Add half the olive oil little-by-little, whisking to incorporate. When the sauce is as thick as soft butter, whisk in 1 – 2 teaspoons of lemon juice. Continue to add the olive oil until the sauce is thick. Season to taste, adding more lemon juice if you wish.

MCB tip: With any emulsion type of sauce, the more oil you add, the thicker the sauce will become. If you want to 'thin it out' a little, just whisk in a spoon or more of hot water, whisking gently until you reach the desired consistency.

BASIC BÉCHEMEL SAUCE

I will always be very proud of the training I received as a teenager at Highbury College, where I was taught almost exclusively by master-chefs from France, Italy and Switzerland. One of my favourite stories is that even those fantastic chefs couldn't agree on one unified recipe for producing a Béchemal Sauce, one of the most basic, must have recipes for making white sauce.

Ingredients for four
- 50g unsalted butter
- 50g plain flour
- 500ml milk – heated
- 1 small onion – studded with a couple of cloves for savoury sauces

Preparation

Melt the butter in a small, heavy bottomed saucepan over a low flame. Add the flour and mix thoroughly with a wooden spoon and cook for a minute or so without colour. Remove from the heat. The butter and flour mixture is called a Roux.

Gradually add the heated milk, little-by-little at first and stir or whisk until smooth. Add the studded onion and place over a very low flame to simmer for approximately thirty minutes. Remove the onion and pass the sauce through a fine strainer into a bowl or clean saucepan. Adjust the seasoning and consistency.

If you want to use the sauce later, then cut some mini-knobs of butter and dot them over the surface of the sauce and cover with a cartouche (greaseproof paper disc), to prevent a skin from forming. Cool and refrigerate.

MCB tip: This basic white sauce recipe and method can be utilised to produce a vast range of roux based sauces i.e. parsley, mornay (cheese), anchovy, cream, mustard etc.... If using for a sweet sauce, then do not use the studded onion.

BÉARNAISE SAUCE

To create this sauce, you can simply add a couple of tablespoons of chopped fresh tarragon to the vinegar reduction and continue as per the recipe below for Hollandaise Sauce.

Cheat's Béarnaise

Follow the recipe for Hollandaise Sauce (below) and add a little tarragon vinegar instead of the lemon juice and a good handful of freshly chopped tarragon and parsley, mix well and serve with your favourite grilled steak or oily fish (tuna etc).

BEURRE BLANC

For some reason, many people are frightened of making this sauce, when in fact there is nothing complicated about it. If it separates, it is far easier to rectify than something like an egg based sauce such as Hollandaise.

- 3 shallots – very finely chopped
- 2 tbsp white wine vinegar
- 4 tbsp dry white wine
- 6 tbsp water or fish stock (court bouillon)
- 2 tbsp double cream
- 175g unsalted butter – cut into small dice
- lemon juice (optional)

Preparation

Place a small shallow pan (sauteuse) over a medium flame. Add the shallots, vinegar, wine and water, bring to the boil, reduce the flame and simmer until nearly all the liquid has evaporated. Add the cream and reduce a little more. Remove the pan from the heat and allow to cool a tad.

Little-by-little whisk in the butter until it is all amalgamated, to make a pale creamy sauce. Make sure that each piece of butter is fully incorporated before adding the next. Taste the sauce, then season with salt and white pepper and add a little lemon juice to taste, if you like.

MCB tip #1:　　If you are not serving the sauce immediately, place it in a metal bowl over a pan of gently simmering water. Do not allow the bottom of the bowl to come into contact with the hot water or the sauce will overheat and 'split'. If the sauce separates (splits), all you have to do is add a little more hot water and boil it vigorously to emulsify the butter and water. Use beurre blanc with poached or grilled fish.

CHARMOULA

Charmoula or chermoula is a marinade used in Algerian, Moroccan and Tunisian cooking. It is usually used to flavour fish or seafood, but can be used on white meat or vegetables.

Ingredients for four

- 1 handful flat-leaf parsley
- 1 handful fresh coriander
- 2 cloves garlic – crushed
- 1 tsp paprika
- 1 tsp ground cumin
- ½ tsp ground coriander
- ¼ tsp cayenne pepper
- 2 tbsp lemon juice
- 2 tbsp olive oil

Preparation

Place the garlic, herbs, spices, lemon juice an olive oil into a food processor or blender and pulse to a paste. Use to marinate lamb up to one day in advance of grilling, chicken breasts up to six hours in advance, prawns up to two hours in advance and fish up to thirty minutes.

MCB tip:　　You can make charmoula up to three days in advance, cover and refrigerate.

CHIVE OIL

Take half a bunch of chives and roughly chop. Place into your food blender, turn onto slow speed and drizzle in some light olive oil until you reach the desired consistency. Refrigerate.

CITRUS MANGO & AVOCADO SALSA

Ingredients for four

- 1 ready to eat mango – finely diced
- 1 ready to avocado – finely diced (prepare last)
- 1 small red onion – finely chopped
- 2 spring onions (scallions) – trimmed & chopped
- 1 red chilli – split, seeded and finely chopped
- 2 tbsp coriander – roughly chopped
- 2 tbsp mint – roughly chopped
- 2 small limes – zested & juiced
- 2 tbsp extra virgin olive oil
- chilli sauce (Trappey's or similar)
- salt

Preparation

Combine all of the prepared ingredients in a bowl. Blend together and add a little salt and chilli sauce to taste. Cover and place into your fridge for at least thirty minutes. Serve lightly chilled.

This salsa goes really well, served with grilled fish or chilli con carne with corn chips.

CLARIFIED BUTTER

Is butter that has been very gently melted, so all the milk solids and water content settle on the bottom of the pan and separate from the butterfat (liquid oil). Some solids may float to the surface and can be skimmed off. The liquid butter fat is slowly poured off into a separate container ready for use. Clarified butter has a higher smoke point than regular butter and is therefore preferred in some cooking applications which require a high heat.

Since the clarification process removes impurities, clarified butter keeps well – several weeks in your refrigerator and longer in the freezer. It is great served warm as a dip for lobster tails, crab or globe artichokes.

COURT BOUILLON

I have included two recipes for classic cooking liquors, which you can use for poaching fish and shellfish. This one is particularly good for cooking crabs; the other, Jus de Nage is outstanding for preparing fish sauces.

Ingredients to make approximately 1.75lts
- 3 leeks – split, cleaned & roughly chopped
- 1 carrot – peeled and roughly chopped
- 1 stick of celery – trimmed & roughly chopped
- 2 onions – roughly chopped
- 3 shallots – roughly chopped
- 1 leaf of bulb fennel
- 1 sprig each of thyme & tarragon
- handful parsley stalks
- 1 head of garlic – sliced across the equator
- 1.75lts cold water
- 250ml dry white wine
- 8 white peppercorns
- 1 tbsp salt
- 1 lemon – zested
- 1 star anise

Preparation

Take a large pan and add all of the prepared vegetables and the garlic. Add sufficient cold water to cover, place over a high flame and bring to the boil. Add the white wine, lemon zest, peppercorns, salt and star anise, re-boil and reduce the flame to a gentle simmer for around 35 minutes.

Pass the liquid through a fine sieve and discard the remaining ingredients. The court bouillon is now ready for use.

MCB tip: You can cool and refrigerate for use within a day. Alternatively this can be frozen, however this can mean taking up valuable and unnecessary freezer space on many smaller yachts.

COUSCOUS

Cereal grains provide more food energy worldwide than any other type of crop; they are therefore considered as 'staples' and an extremely valuable global harvest product.

Like many cereals and grains such as; rice, polenta, bulgur wheat and cracked wheat, all can be relatively flavourless when just cooked plain. Couscous itself is made from crushed and steamed durum wheat, coated in wheat flour. North Africans use couscous in the same way that many cultures use rice and it is extremely popular in Morocco, Algeria, Tunisia and Libya.

Couscous is traditionally steamed over a pot of simmering, spiced stew or broth made from chicken, lamb or mutton and various vegetables; the cereal then takes on the flavours of the dish below. Couscous and bulgur are also common ingredients in Turkish, Middle Eastern and Mediterranean dishes. You will find bulgur widely available in France, where it is generally sold as "Tabbouleh".

The great thing with cereals is that you can manipulate the flavour of the dish, and make it taste of whatever you want – within reason. So, you can follow my recipe below, or once you have 'cooked' the couscous (or Tabbouleh), you can manipulate the dish yourself and try out a different version every time you make it – making it your own bespoke recipe.

Ingredients for eight
- 500g couscous
- 400ml boiling water

Preparation
Poor the couscous grains into a bowl, pour over the boiling water and stir for a few seconds. Cover and place the bowl to one side untouched, to cool, while you prepare the additional ingredients.

Additional ingredients
I have included the kitchen sink version below, which produces a really lovely, tasty couscous. You can, of course, use far less ingredients and get an equally outstanding result.

- 2 medium red onions – finely chopped
- 1 small cucumber – peeled, de-seeded & finely chopped
- 1 red pepper – halved, de-seeded & finely chopped
- 100g ready to eat dried apricots – quartered
- 2 large cloves of garlic – crushed or finely chopped
- thumb sized piece of ginger – peeled & finely chopped
- 2 red chillies – split, de-seeded & finely chopped
- 1 large handful fresh coriander – finely chopped
- 12 fresh mint leaves – finely chopped
- 4 sun blushed tomatoes – roughly chopped
- 75g sultanas (or plump raisins)
- 2 limes (or lemon) – zested & juiced
- extra virgin olive oil
- 1 tbsp cumin seeds – roughly ground
- 1 tbsp coriander seeds – roughly ground
- salt & freshly ground black pepper

Preparation:

Take your cooled bowl of couscous and using the back of a table fork, gradually work the grains until they separate. This will take a little while, but just think of it as good therapy! Once you have a bowl of loose couscous grains, simply add all of the additional ingredients down to the sultanas, stirring well to incorporate all their flavours and textures. Sprinkle over the crushed spices and lime zest and stir again. Pour in a few slugs of the olive oil and stir well to lightly coat the ingredients. Check for flavour, add salt, black pepper and lime juice to taste.

MCB tip #1: Serve couscous or tabbouleh with tagines; alternatively serve as a side with summer salads.

MCB tip #2: My couscous recipe is about as extravagant as you might want to get, so if you prefer, you can leave out what you want, or even add a bit more of this or that.

CREOLE SAUCE

This sauce is quite outstanding served with fried or char-grilled chicken, seafood, or definitely over your favourite pasta. Creole sauce incorporates the classic Cajun trilogy of onions, celery and green bell peppers.

Ingredients for eight

- 2 medium sized onions – chopped
- 3 sticks of celery – chopped
- 1 green bell pepper – de-seeded & chopped
- 3 cloves of garlic – finely chopped
- 2 tablespoons olive oil
- 125 ml chicken stock
- 1 x 400g can of chopped tomatoes
- 1 x jar roughly chopped Passata
- 2 bay leaves
- 1 teaspoon oregano
- 1 teaspoon thyme
- 1 teaspoon basil
- 1 dessert spoon dark brown sugar
- 2 tsp Cayenne pepper sauce (Trappey's or similar)

Preparation

Heat a medium sized saucepan over a medium flame and add the olive oil. Add the onions, celery, green pepper and garlic and cook for five minutes until they take on just a little colour and are soft in texture. Reduce the flame a little and add the remaining ingredients and slowly bring to the boil and stir well. Reduce to a low flame and simmer for about another 20 minutes. Check for seasoning before serving.

CRUMBLE MIX

Katie C's Kiwi crumble mix

This recipe was given to me by a wonderful young lady from New Zealand called Katie. Those who were lucky enough to try it were very impressed with her Southern Hemisphere version of a crumble mix. It produces the most amazing flavours and textures for an outstanding crumble topping for both summer and autumn fruits.

You will see that Katie has not provided quantities, leaving the balance of the mix down to your own personal taste and creativity – give this a whizz and impress your guests, they'll love it!

Ingredients
- Oats
- Sultanas
- Brown sugar
- Caster sugar
- Runny honey
- Cinnamon
- Butter

Preparation
Mix together between fingers and layer over prepared fruit.

GAZPACHO COULIS
This is a really useful dressing to have in your repertoire. You will need a food processor and juicer for this recipe, although you can get away with using a hand blender, but the result is more rustic and maybe not quite as good.

Ingredients
- 1 tomato – peeled, de-seeded & chopped
- 1 tspn tomato purée
- 1 small cucumber – peeled, de-seeded & chopped
- 1 red bell pepper – de-seeded
- 1 clove garlic
- 1 stick of celery – trimmed (remove the stringy outside with your veg' peeler).
- extra virgin olive oil
- salt & ground black pepper

Preparation
Using your food processor, blitz the tomato, cucumber and tomato purée. Juice the red pepper, garlic and celery. With the food processor running, add the juice mixture and olive oil to the puréed tomato and cucumber. Season to taste and refrigerate ready for use.

GREEN GODDESS SAUCE
This is one of my favorites for knocking up in the warm summer months and using as a dip with crackers or corn chips. It is also great served with luxury fish cakes or grilled fish. There are so many variations of this recipe, which may include one of more of the following: tarragon, spring onions (scallions), parsley, mayo', yoghurt, crème fraîche, chives, capers, anchovies, zest or no zest – I think you get the picture! At the end of the day folks, I decided that my original version was pretty damn good, so I have stuck with what I know.

Ingredients
- 2 avocados – halved, stoned, peeled & roughly chopped
- 200ml olive oil
- 1 shallot – chopped
- 1 clove of garlic – roughly chopped
- 1 lime – juiced
- 1 lemon – juiced
- fresh basil – handful
- fresh coriander (cilantro) – handful
- ½ tsp sea salt
- ¼ tsp ground black pepper

Preparation

Place the herbs, shallot, garlic, salt and black pepper into a blender. Add two tablespoons each of both lime and lemon juice to the herb mixture and purée until the herbs and shallots are finely chopped. Add the chopped avocado to the herb mixture and whizz up in your blender until smooth. Little-by-little, drizzle the olive oil into the mixture with your blender set on the slowest speed – this will emulsify your sauce. Taste and add more seasoning if required.

HOLLANDAISE SAUCE

Ingredients for four
- 1 shallot – finely chopped
- 6 black peppercorns – crushed
- 50ml white wine vinegar
- 250g unsalted butter
- 2 egg yolks
- 2 tablespoons cold water
- ½ teaspoon salt

Preparation

Place the shallot, peppercorns, wine vinegar into a small pan, place over a high flame and reduce until you have one tablespoon of concentrated liquid. Add one tablespoon of cold water, allow to cool. Strain the reduction and discard the solids.

Melt the butter very gently in a separate pan until the solids sink to the bottom. Pour the clear clarified butter into a pouring jug and keep to one side. Discard the butter solids (buttermilk) at the bottom and allow the clarified butter to cool slightly – this will help prevent the sauce from splitting.

Put the egg yolks into a stainless steel bowl with the strained vinegar reduction and place over a saucepan of gently simmering water. Make sure that the bottom of the bowl does not touch the water and whisk the mixture until it becomes thickened and lighter in colour, this is called a sabayon.

Remove the bowl from the heat and very gently, little-by-little, whisk in the warm clarified butter, whisking until your sauce becomes thick and until the butter is thoroughly combined. To keep the sauce warm, rest the bowl over a pan of hot water.

If your sauce is too thick, add a little hot water until you reach the desired consistency.

MCB tip: For a really swift recipe, if you have a blender onboard, see Quick Hollandaise.

ITALIAN TOMATO SAUCE

I couldn't exist without a great, rustic, tasty tomato sauce in my galley repertoire. This sauce is so versatile and goes really well with pasta or pizza and is a perfect marriage with Gnocchi Piemontaise (potato gnocchi).

Ingredients for four
- 2 tbsp tomato purée
- 1 x 400g can of chopped tomatoes
  or equivalent roughly chopped Passata
- I medium sized onion – finely chopped
- handful of fresh basil – shredded
- 1 tsp dried oregano

- 1 clove of garlic – crushed
- 2 tbsp virgin olive oil
- salt & freshly ground black pepper

Preparation

Heat a medium to small saucepan over a medium flame and add the olive oil. Add the onion and garlic and cook for five minutes until they take on a little colour. Reduce the flame, add the tomato purée and cook for another couple of minutes, this will enhance the tomato flavour, and then add the chopped tomatoes or passata. Finish off the sauce by adding the herbs, and season to taste. Simmer until the sauce reaches the desired consistency.

MCB tip #1:   Replace the dried herbs with some shredded fresh basil and chopped flat leaf parsley, added at the last minute - for an outstanding result.

MCB tip #2:   I love the depth of flavour which can be derived from using tomato paste. So make sure you purchase yours in tubes for onboard use. This is space saving and is an excellent way to keep unused paste in top qualify condition.

JUS de NAGE

This exceptional recipe is ideal for poaching fish and shellfish, or to use in delicate fish sauces. It is ideal if you need to thin a fish velouté (see Basics – page 236).

Ingredients to make approximately 2lts

- 2 onions – roughly chopped
- 1 leek – split, cleaned & roughly chopped
- 2 sticks of celery – trimmed & roughly chopped
- 4 carrots – roughly chopped
- 1 head of garlic – sliced across the equator
- 6 lemon slices
- 8 white peppercorns
- 20 pink peppercorns
- 1 bay leaf
- 2 star anise
- 1.75lts of cold water
- 200ml dry white wine
- sprig each of parsley, coriander, tarragon, thyme & chervil

Preparation

Take a large pan and add all of the prepared vegetables, garlic, lemon, peppercorns, bay leaf and star anise. Add sufficient cold water to cover, place over a high flame and bring to the boil. Reduce the flame and simmer for a further ten minutes. Add the herbs and cook for a further two minutes.

Remove the pan from the flame and add the white wine. Pour into a large bowl or container, cover and leave to infuse for twenty four hours in the fridge.

Strain the stock through a very fine sieve and discard the remaining ingredients.

MCB tip: You can cool and refrigerate this stock, which will hold in the fridge for a few days. Alternatively this can be frozen, but this will often take up valuable and unnecessary freezer space on many smaller yachts.

MAYONNAISE

Although I do not recommend making fresh mayonnaise with eggs from an untrustworthy source, this is a handy recipe to have in the locker for emergencies. If you add the oil too quickly the mixture will split.

- 2 egg yolks – free range
- 1 tbsp Dijon mustard
- 2 tbsp white wine vinegar
- 500ml light oil – corn or sunflower
- ½ tsp salt & ground white pepper

Preparation

Place the egg yolks, mustard, vinegar and seasoning into a bowl and whisk together thoroughly. Gradually add the oil little-by-little at first, whisking continuously. When you have added around half of the oil, you can then start to add larger quantities until it has all been incorporated and the sauce is thick and creamy.

MCB tip #1: Your mayo' can split for a number of reasons, so be aware of: adding the oil too quickly; using oil that is too cold; not whisking sufficiently between additions of oil or using eggs which are not fresh.

MCB tip #2: If the sauce should become too thick, then add a little more vinegar or hot water to thin to the required consistency.

QUICK HOLLANDAISE

This is my quick method of making a hollandaise sauce, without all the fuss of making a vinegar reduction. Your sauce can 'split' (curdle), if you add the melted butter too quickly, or because of excess heat. It is not a good idea to re-heat or re-use this sauce at a later date.

Ingredients for eight

- 500g unsalted butter
- 4 egg yolks
- juice of 1 lemon
- 4 tablespoons of water
- small pinch of cayenne
- ¼ teaspoon of salt

Melt the butter very gently in a pan until the solids sink to the bottom. Pour the clear butter liquid into a pouring jug and keep to one side. Discard the butter solids (buttermilk) and allow the butter oil to cool slightly, which will help prevent the sauce from splitting.

Half fill a clean saucepan with water and place over a high flame and bring to the boil. Reduce the flame, so that the water simmers gently. Place a clean stainless steel bowl over the pan and pour in the water and eggs and whisk the mixture until it becomes thickened and lighter in colour.

Remove the bowl from the heat and, little-by-little, whisk in the cooled clarified butter, creating an emulsion, whisking until your sauce becomes thick. Whisk in the lemon juice to taste, plus the cayenne and a little salt.

For best results, use your hollandaise immediately. You can keep it for up to two hours, but it needs to be kept slightly warm over a pan of warm water, with a lid on.

ROMESCO SAUCE
(Catalan pepper sauce)

This sauce is said to originate from Tarragona, Catalonia in Spain. It is typically made from almonds (or hazelnuts), roasted garlic, olive oil and nyores (small, dried red chilli peppers). Other common ingredients are roasted tomatoes, red wine vinegar and onion. It is perhaps most often served with seafood, but can also be used with a wide variety of other foods, including poultry.

Ingredients

- 6 cloves of garlic – unpeeled
- 3 tomatoes – ripe & firm
- 2 tbsp olive oil
- 50g toasted almonds
- 2 tbsp sherry vinegar
- 1 tsp smoked paprika
- 1 tsp sea salt
- 2 dried ancho chillies
- 2 piquillo peppers
- 1 lemon – juiced
- 180ml olive oil

Preparation

Pre-heat your oven to 200°C

Toss the garlic and whole tomatoes in some olive oil, place into a roasting tin and roast for approximately forty five minutes. Allow to cool a little, peel the garlic and retain the flesh. This can be done by trimming off one end and squeezing from the other – the flesh inside should slide out. Toast the nuts in the oven for five minutes or so, until they give off a characteristic nutty aroma – allow to cool. Soak the ancho chillies in warm water for thirty minutes to re-hydrate, and drain.

Using a food processor, blend the nuts and chillies together. Add the garlic, tomatoes, piquillo peppers, sherry vinegar, paprika, sea salt and lemon. Blend together for twenty seconds or so. Little-by-little, drizzle the olive oil into the mixture with your blender set on the slowest speed – this will emulsify your sauce. Taste and add more seasoning if required.

MCB tip: This is not meant to be a smooth sauce, so don't worry if you still have a few lumps and bumps in the end product.

ROUGH PUFF PASTRY

This recipe makes a nice rich, buttery pastry. Ideally make this the day before you need it, to allow it to thoroughly rest and chill.

Ingredients

- 250g strong plain flour
- 1 tsp salt
- 250g unsalted butter – chilled
- 150ml water – ice cold

Preparation

Cut the chilled butter into small dice. Sieve the salt and flour into a bowl and add the butter. Mix the butter around the bowl with a large metal spoon to coat with flour. Using your finger tips, gently work the cubes of butter into the flour mix, until you finish with a mixture that resembles large breadcrumbs.

Make a well in the middle and add around two thirds of the cold water to the flour mixture and gradually draw in the flour mixture until the dough comes together to form a ball of pastry. You may need to add a little more water to reach this stage. Wrap in cling film and refrigerate for thirty minutes.

Turn your pastry out onto a lightly floured work surface and knead gently to form a rectangle. Lightly dust your rolling pan and roll the pastry in one direction only, until it is three times longer than it's width; around 20 x 50cm. Try to keep the edges straight and even. Don't overwork; you should have a buttery, marbled effect.

Fold the top third down to the centre, then the bottom third up over that. Give the dough a quarter turn (left or right) and roll out again to three times the length. Dust with flour if required. Fold as before, cover with cling film and refrigerate for at least thirty minutes before using.

MCB tip: Don't throw away any left-over pastry trimmings. Layer them on top of each other, lightly dust with flour and roll a little, then just fold into a neat little briquette, wrap in film and refrigerate or freeze. You can use trimmings for cheese twists or similar when you are serving Sundowners. Allow the paste to come back to room temperature before re-rolling.

ROUILLE

Rouille is the French word for 'rust'. This sauce varies greatly wherever you eat in France, so I hope my version is up to standard. It is served as an accompaniment with fish soups and stews, most famously Bouillabaisse, the classic fish stew from Provençe, most notably Marseilles.

Ingredients
- 1 medium potato – cooked in its jacket
- 2 cloves of garlic – crushed
- 2 red chillies – de-seeded & finely chopped
- 1 egg – free range
- pinch of saffron
- olive oil

Preparation
Split the potato in half and scoop the flesh out into a bowl. Add the crushed garlic, saffron, chillies and crush together with the back of a fork.

Transfer the mix to your food processor and with the motor running, drizzle in the olive oil little-by-little to make a smooth, shiny sauce that resembles a mayonnaise like consistency. Season with salt and add a pinch of cayenne if you need a fiery taste.

Spoon out into a container, cover and refrigerate.

SALSA VERDÉ

This sauce creates a whole mass of flavours and is one which I use a lot on char-grilled 'meaty' fish, such as tuna or shark steaks.

This sauce can be made in advance of your voyage and refrigerated, although it is always best prepared on board the same day.

Ingredients for eight
- 6 tbsp flat-leaf parsley – finely chopped
- 2 tbsp fresh mint leaves – finely chopped

- 10 anchovy fillets in oil – drained
- 3 tbsp capers – drained
- 2 tbsp Dijon mustard
- 2 cloves garlic
- 1 lemon – juice only
- 160ml extra virgin olive oil
- salt & freshly ground black pepper

Preparation

Place the finely chopped herbs into a bowl. Chop the capers, anchovies and garlic and add to the herbs. Add the mustard and lemon juice and around three-quarters of the olive oil. Check for seasoning and consistency. Add a couple of twists from your pepper mill, but remember the anchovies are salty, so you may not need to add salt. If the sauce is too thin, then drizzle in more of the olive oil and whisk until you reach the desired consistency. If it's too thick, then add a little more lemon juice or dry white wine.

SAUCE VIERGE

The name of this French sauce literally means "virgin sauce", which is made from olive oil, lemon juice, chopped tomatoes and basil. There are many variations, which may include other herbs such as chervil, chives, parsley etc. The sauce is usually served with shellfish, delicately flavoured white fleshed fish, such as cod and sometimes with pasta. It can be served either warm or cold. It is now a modern classic.

The sauce was made popular in the 80s by the famous French chef Michel Guérard (Le Grand Chef Relaise et Châteaux) at Les Prés de Eugénie, Eugénie-les-Bains in the foothills of the Pyrenees.

Ingredients for four

- 125ml extra virgin olive oil
- 1 lime or small lemon – juiced
- 2 firm ripe tomatoes – peeled, de-seeded & finely chopped
- 1 tbsp flat leaf parsley – finely chopped
- sea salt & freshly ground black pepper

Preparation

Place a small shallow pan over a low flame, allow to warm through and gently heat the olive oil. Add the citrus juice and shake the pan to combine. Remove from the heat and add the chopped parsley to infuse in the warm oil for a few minutes. Add the diced tomato and serve immediately.

I vary this dressing from time-to-time by adding some finely chopped, fresh, young rosemary shoots or some shredded fresh basil. Depending on what I am serving the sauce with, I sometimes gently soften a finely chopped shallot in the olive oil before adding the citrus juice.

SHORT PASTRY

Use short pastry for savoury pastry dishes. Traditional short pastry in the UK was always made with flour mixed with half butter and half lard. Unfortunately, lard is rendered pork fat, so I would advise that you use my recipe, to avoid situations with customers whose religion prohibits them from eating pork products.

Ingredients

- 200g soft flour – sieved into a bowl
- pinch salt

- 100g unsalted butter - chilled
- 2-3 tbsp water – chilled

Preparation

Cut the butter into small dice, add to the flour and using your finger tips, gently work the butter into the flour, until you finish with a fine crumbly mixture.

Make a well (bay) in the centre, add sufficient water and draw in the crumb to make a fairly firm paste.

Handle as little and lightly as you can. Wrap in cling film and chill for at least thirty minutes before use.

MCB tip: Remove the pastry from the fridge and bring back to room temperature before use. You will have to use your skill to judge this in very hot countries.

SWEET SHORTCRUST PASTRY

As long as you stick to the measurements below and follow the recipe exactly, you should be onto a winner. The cooler you can keep your hands the better. Use sweet short crust pastry for sweet, dessert pastry dishes.

This recipe works really well my Nectarine and Plum Tart (Page 202) and will make enough pastry for a 23cm flan tin.

Ingredients make 1kg of dough
- 500g plain flour – sifted (extra for dusting)
- 100g icing sugar – sifted
- 250g unsalted butter – chilled
- 2 large eggs (free range)
- milk - chilled

Preparation

Cut the butter into small dice. Break the eggs into a bowl with a splash of milk and beat together with a fork. In a large bowl, mix the sifted flour and sugar together. Add the cubes of butter and, using your finger tips, gently work into the flour mix, until you finish with a fine crumbly mixture.

Gradually add the egg and milk mixture and gently work everything together until you get a ball of dough. You may not need to use all of the liquid.

Sprinkle a little flour over the ball and also onto your work surface and set the ball on top. You do not need to work the pastry too much at this stage, or it will become elastic and chewy, not crumbly. Pat the ball until you have a flat round. Sprinkle it with a little bit more flour, then wrap it in cling film and refrigerate for thirty minutes, to rest the gluten in the flour before using.

TEMPURA BATTER

The aim of making tempura batter is to achieve a lacy, light crust on deep fried foods. I like to use this to cook small pieces of vegetables, such as: broccoli, courgette, mushrooms, peppers or seafood, such as squid, prawns, oysters, and fish.

You can use 'special' tempura flour or you can use plain flour mixed with cornflour (see below). Which-ever one you use, a minimal amount of stirring is best as it leaves the batter lumpy, with bits of dry flour around the edge of the bowl and floating on top, which is correct for tempura. It is critical to use ice cold sparkling water, as this helps to achieve the light batter.

Tempura should be cooked in 'clean' hot oil at a temperature of between 170 and 190°C, depending on the ingredient. It is important to scoop out any bits of batter floating on the surface of the oil between batches; if left, they will burn and leave a bad flavour in the oil.

The secret of a good end product is to make the tempura at the last minute, keep the oil at the right temperature and serve the food as quickly as possible after cooking, so that the coating remains crisp.

Ingredients
- 100g plain flour
- 100g cornflour
- pinch of salt
- ice-cold sparkling mineral water (new bottle)
- 4 tsp sesame seeds (optional)

Preparation
Sift the plain flour, corn flour and salt into a bowl (add the sesame seeds if using), then stir in the ice-cold water. The batter should be lumpy but thin, so add a little more water if necessary.

You will then need fresh oil for deep-fat frying. Heat the oil to 190°C, or if you don't have a thermometer drop a cube of bread in and watch to see if is 'fizzes' and turns golden in a few seconds. If doing your frying this way, you need to watch it like a hawk and turn the heat down immediately if the oil starts to smoke.

Dip the ingredients into the batter mix then into the oil and fry for about 1 minute until crisp. Lift out and drain briefly on kitchen paper and keep warm while frying the rest of your ingredients, then serve. Serving straight from your 'friture' is always best, but not always practicable.

MCB tip #1: You will need to be very focused on the cooking process. **Never, ever leave a pan of oil over a flame, to go and do something else** – it can be highly dangerous, as once your oil has reached smoking point; the next stage is that it will ignite.

IMPORTANT Check out Deep Frying in the Glossary of Cookery Terminology (page 241)

TRAIL MIX
This is something that we put together before we head off on a long trip. There is no fixed recipe, so I am going to give you a few thoughts, and then you can prepare your own 'designer trail mix'. This makes great crew grazing food.

Basic Trail Mix
Combine equal quantities of the following ingredients:
Unsalted peanuts, sunflower seeds, dried cranberries, dried cherries, dried apricots, raisins, chocolate chips, pretzels, Cheerios, Chex (Shreddies) and granola. Feel free to leave out any ingredients that don't sound too good. Mix together in a big bowl and store in an airtight container.

Ultimate Trail Mix
If you think that the more ingredients the better, when it comes to Trail Mix, then this recipe is for you. Combine the following ingredients in equal quantities:

Dried cranberries, dried blueberries, dried apple, dried pineapple, peanuts, cashews, almonds, chocolate chips, white chocolate chips, peanut butter chips, butterscotch chips and mini marshmallows. Mix thoroughly and eat before those sweets start to melt. Alternatively refrigerate until you drop anchor.

TZATZIKI

This well known Greek and Turkish 'meze' is traditionally served as an appetizer or pre-meal dip with freshly prepared vegetable sticks, pita triangles, kettle chips or taco shells, or it can be put on the table as an accompaniment with the meal. The key to great Tzatziki is the thick creamy texture that allows it to be eaten alone, as a dip, spread, or as a condiment.

Ingredients:

- 500g thick Greek yogurt
- 4 cloves of garlic – crushed
- 100g cucumber – peeled, de-seeded & finely diced
- 1 tbsp of olive oil
- 1 lemon – juiced
- fresh mint leaves – finely shredded

Preparation

Prepare all ingredients in advance. Combine the oil and lemon juice in a medium sized mixing bowl. Fold the yogurt in slowly, making sure you mix it completely with the oil. Add the garlic, according to taste, and the cucumber. Stir until evenly distributed. Serve well chilled.

VELOUTÉ

Velouté is one of the great French "mother sauces"; the term literally means 'velvety'. The principal is exactly the same as a Béchemal, except for the fact that you use a light chicken, veal or fish stock instead of milk and the sauce produced is commonly referred to by the type of stock used i.e. chicken stock = chicken velouté.

I have included this recipe because a velouté is widely used with poultry and seafood dishes, both popular en bateau.

Ingredients

- 50g unsalted butter
- 50g plain flour
- 500ml stock – chicken, fish, veal (as required)

Preparation

Melt the butter in a small, heavy bottomed saucepan over a low flame. Add the flour and mix thoroughly with a wooden spoon to a sandy texture (roux) and cook for a minute or so without colour. Remove from the heat.

Gradually add the hot stock, little-by-little at first and stir, or whisk, until smooth. Allow to simmer over a very low heat for approximately fifteen minutes, and then pass the sauce through a fine strainer into a bowl or clean saucepan.

If you want to use the sauce later, then cut some mini-knobs of butter and dot them over the surface of the sauce and cover with a 'cartouche' (greaseproof paper disc), to prevent a skin from forming. Cool and refrigerate.

MCB tip: For fish velouté, substitute 50% of the fish stock with half dry white wine and half Noilly Prat.

VINAIGRETTE #1

As salad dressings are an integral part of onboard cuisine, this is a great base recipe, which can be stored in a suitable container and used at will. This recipe requires the very 'clean' flavour of peanut oil. By making the quantity below, you can quickly change the end product by adding chopped fresh herbs or Dijon mustard to make an alternative dressing for your discerning customers.

Ingredients
- 75ml white wine vinegar
- 120ml peanut or sunflower oil
- 200ml olive oil
- salt & freshly ground white pepper

Preparation

Place the vinegar into a bowl and add a pinch of salt and pepper and stir to dissolve. Add the two oils and whisk to an emulsion. Taste and adjust the seasoning to your liking. Store in a plastic squeeze bottle and refrigerate.

MCB tip: This dressing should keep well, refrigerated for up to one week.

VINAIGRETTE #2

Ingredients
- 50ml red wine
- 50ml sherry vinegar
- 250ml peanut or sunflower oil
- 50ml olive oil
- salt and freshly ground white pepper

Preparation

Prepare, mix and store as in the previous recipe.

FYI: Sherry vinegar is usually available in most Western Med supermarkets.

WASABI LIME DRESSING

If you already know about wasabi (Japanese horseraddish), then it will come as no surprise that this unusual green dressing packs a big punch. I like to use this on salads and other foods which have fairly plain flavours. It is excellent, lightly drizzled over some char-grilled chicken fillets, but keep a bottle of nicely chilled beer nearby for when the heat kicks in.

Ingredients
- 1 lime – zested and juiced
- 4 tbsp sun flour oil
- 1 tsp Japanese wasabi paste
- pinch sea salt
- pinch table salt
- freshly ground black pepper – twist

Preparation

Take a clean bowl and add all of the ingredients including approximately half the lime zest and whisk thoroughly until completely combined. Check for seasoning. You may try adding a pinch of caster sugar to create a little bit more balance to the dressing.

GLOSSARY of COOKERY TERMINOLOGY

Aïoli – Aïoli (garlic mayonnaise) is a delicious accompaniment for cold or hot grilled vegetables, steamed or boiled artichokes, boiled potatoes, grilled or baked fish and shellfish. It also makes a great dip.

À la Nage – Cooking à la nage means poaching food, usually seafood, in a fragrant bouillon, which can also be used as an addition to fish velouté.

Al dente – An Italian expression applied in many western kitchens, generally to pasta and vegetables, cooked just until enough resistance is left in it to be felt 'by the tooth.'

Arborio – The name given to some of the best short-grained rice grown in the Po Valley in Italy, widely used as the rice of choice when preparing risotto.

Aromatics – Plant ingredients, such as herbs and spices, used to enhance the flavour and fragrance of food.

Arrowroot – A fine starch used to thicken liquids. The end result leaves a clear sauce, rather than the cloudy effect you get when using cornflour.

Bain-marie – A bain-marie is a pan or container of water that is used to help mixtures such as custards cook evenly and to protect them from the direct heat of the oven or, in some cases, the hob.

Barbecue – A cooking method involving grilling food over a wood or charcoal fire. Food is often flavoured with a dry-rub, wet marinade, sauce or glaze, which is applied to the item before, during and at the end of cooking.

Basmati – The name of the most deliciously flavoured long-grain rice from India. This rice needs thoroughly rinsing before cooking, or you will end up with very sticky rice.

Baste – To moisten food during cooking (usually roasting) with pan drippings, sauce, or other liquid. Basting helps to prevent foods from drying out during the cooking process.

Béarnaise – A warm, emulsified egg and butter sauce similar to hollandaise, but with the addition of white wine, shallots, and tarragon.

Beat – To agitate a mixture with the aim of making it smooth and introducing as much air as possible into it.

Béchamel – A classic white sauce made with whole milk, thickened with a white roux, and flavoured with aromatics.

Beurre Blanc – A rich butter sauce made by whisking small knobs of butter into a reduction of white wine, white wine vinegar, and shallots, and sometimes finished with fresh herbs or other seasonings.

Bisque – A soup, classically based on a strained broth of crustaceans. It is typically thickened with rice and usually finished with cream.

Blanch – A method of part-cooking, in which foods are plunged into boiling water for a few seconds, removed, and refreshed under cold or iced water, which stops the cooking process immediately. Blanching is used to retain colour and flavour, also to loosen skins on tomatoes. Blanching also helps to retain nutrients, particularly in green vegetables.

Boil – To cook in water or other liquid, heated until bubbling vigorously. Few techniques cause as much confusion as boiling, simmering, and poaching. Boiling is, in fact, often a technique to be avoided. Most foods—meat and seafood, for example—are simmered or poached instead, because boiling will have a detrimental effect of the quality of the end product. Some foods, however, are best cooked at a rolling boil i.e. rice and pasta cook more quickly and evenly in boiling water.

Bouillabaisse – One of the classic French fish soups, often found on restaurant menus along the Mediterranean coast.

Bouillon – French word for broth. Refers to the liquid resulting from simmering meats, vegetables, and aromatics in water. The term is often used to refer to proprietary brands of stock.

Bouquet Garni – A bundle of parsley stems, thyme, and bay leaf (aromatics), wrapped in a leek or celery and tied together and left to float freely in broth, stock, or sauce.

Braise – To cook food in a small amount of liquid. Sometimes referred to as stewing or pot roasting, but technically different. Different from poaching, in which the food is completely submerged in simmering liquid. Usually, the purpose of braising is to render more tough meat tender by slow cooking and to concentrate the food's flavours in the surrounding liquid.

Brioche – A highly enriched French breakfast bread. The high egg and butter content give it what is seen as a rich and tender crumb.

Broil – In America, when the heat comes from above, this is called broiling. Although the general term for broiling elsewhere can mean either overhead heat or over an open flame i.e. barbecue.

Broth – Broth is usually a soup or stew and means a flavoured liquid made by gently cooking meat, seafood, vegetables and pulses, often with herbs in liquid, usually stock.

Brown stock – An amber liquid produced by simmering browned bones and meat in water with vegetables and aromatics.

Buttermilk – A dairy liquid with a slightly sour taste similar to yogurt.

Calvados – Apple brandy, which is named after a town in the Normandy region of France.

Caramelise – The flavour of many foods, including vegetables, meats, and seafood, is often enhanced by gentle browning, which will caramelise natural sugars and other compounds and intensifies their flavour.

Cassoulet – A classic rich, slow cooked bean stew, originating in the South of France, containing white haricot beans and meat, typically pork (sometimes lamb), duck confit and Toulouse sausages. The dish is named after the 'cassole', a distinctive deep, round earthenware pot, with slanting sides in which a cassoulet is ideally cooked. Numerous regional variations exist, however, the best known are from Castelnaudary, the self-proclaimed 'Capital of Cassoulet', Toulouse and Carcassonne.

Chèvre – The French word for goat and by extension the cheese made from goat's milk.

Chiffonade – The fine ribbons obtained when leafy vegetables or herbs are tightly rolled into a cigar shape and finely shredded.

Chinoise – A fine-meshed strainer used for straining or passing liquids, sauces and coulis.

Chorizo sausage – A spicy Spanish pork sausage containing a mixture of pork, paprika, pepper, and chillies.

Chowder – A thick soup that usually contains potatoes, bacon, seafood and milk or cream.

Clarified butter – Because butter contains milk solids which burn at relatively low temperatures, it can't be used to sauté at the high temperatures required for browning most meats and seafood and some vegetables. Clarifying removes the water and milk solids in butter. You can purchase clarified butter called ghee (used for Asian cooking) at some larger supermarkets.

Colander – A perforated bowl made of metal or plastic that is used to strain the cooking liquid from foods.

Compote – A dish of fruit cooked in syrup flavoured with spices or liqueur.

Compound butter – Whole butter combined with herbs or other seasonings and served on grilled meat or fish.

Consommé – Broth or stock that has been clarified by simmering it with beaten egg whites, which attract and trap the impurities clouding the broth, leaving a clear liquid.

Cornichon – Small, crunchy pickled gherkins mixed with onions and other aromatics and preserved in seasoned pure wine or cider vinegar.

Coulis – A mixture, usually a fruit purée, which has usually been cooked and strained of tiny seeds or pieces of peel so it is perfectly smooth.

Court Bouillon – A vegetable stock, used for poaching fish. Made by simmering onions, leeks, carrots, celery, and sometimes other vegetables such as fennel, with a bouquet garni in water and often, white wine or vinegar.

Crème anglaise – A home-made egg custard or vanilla sauce.

Crème brûlée – A rich custard topped with sugar that is caramelized under a grill or with a chef's blow-torch before serving.

Crème frâiche – Heavy cream, cultured to give it a thick consistency and a slightly tangy flavor. Substitute with sour cream, if necessary.

Crème pâtissière – A thick sweet custard made with eggs, flour, milk, sugar, and flavourings, used to fill pastries or as the base for puddings, tarts, soufflés, and creams.

Crèpe– A thin pancake made with egg batter.

Crudités – French for a mixture of sliced raw vegetables, often served with savoury dips.

Cure – Food preservation and flavouring, especially of meat and fish; usually with salt, sugar, nitrates or nitrites. Many curing processes involve smoking.

Deep-frying – A method of cookery, which is not used a great deal on smaller yachts, because of the inherent danger of fire. I strongly recommend that you only use this cooking process if you have a thermostatically controlled deep fat fryer, professionally installed in your galley. However there are safety issues you still need to adhere to:

- Never overload your fryer
- Always use a frying basket
- Never place wet food into hot fat
- Have a 'spider' to hand to remove or turn food
- Only ever fill a fryer (friture) with oil to 2/3 capacity (max)
- Add food carefully to the hot fat – always away from you
- Wear rolled down sleeves at all times when using a fryer
- Do not attempt to move a pan of hot fat – this is extremely dangerous
- If the oil starts to rise towards the top of the friture, raise the frying basket or remove content immediately and safely
- Make sure that you have the correct firefighting equipment to hand and that you are familiar with its use
- If hot oil ignites – **never use a water based fire extinguisher**. Only use a foam extinguisher and/or a fire blanket

Deglaze – To add liquid to a pan in which foods have been sautéed or roasted in order to dissolve the caramelized juices stuck to the bottom of the pan. The purpose of deglazing is to make a quick sauce or gravy for a roast, steak, chop or piece of fish.

Degrease – To remove the fat that forms on the top of simmering broths, sauces, jus, and braising liquids.

Demi-glace – A mixture of equal parts of brown stock and brown sauce that has been reduced by half. This is the basis of many different brown sauces.

Dice – To cut into cubes (unlike chopping, which cuts foods into irregular pieces).

Duxelles – Finely chopped mushrooms, cooked slowly in butter with chopped shallots, usually flavoured with herbs.

Egg wash – Beaten egg yolks, whole eggs or eggs mixed with a little milk. Usually brushed over pastry and bread products before baking.

Emulsion – An emulsion is a smooth mixture of two liquids, such as oil and water that normally do not mix. Mayonnaise, beurre blanc, hollandaise, cream sauces and vinaigrettes are examples of emulsions.

En-croute – Food, usually fish, poultry or meat, wrapped in a pastry crust and baked in a hot oven.

Espagnole – The classic brown sauce made with brown stock, caramelized mirepoix with tomato puree, and seasonings.

Fettuccine – 1/2cm-wide ribbon noodles.

Fines Herbes – A mixture of finely chopped chervil, chives, parsley, and tarragon. There are many variations on content.

Fish sauce – Nam Pla. A clear, amber-tinted liquid, which is drained from salted, fermented fish. This is a very important flavouring in Thai cuisine.

Flambé – A cooking procedure in which spirit alcohol is added to food in a hot pan to create a burst of flame. It is typically done to create an impression at a dramatic point of preparing a dish. This is a practice that is not encouraged on most yachts, as it can create a fire hazard.

Foie Gras – The liver of goose or duck that has been force-fed a mixture of corn, lard, and salted water.

Frittata – A flat Italian, half-fried, half-baked omelette. À la Spanish omelette.

Garnish – To add an interesting, usually edible item to a plate or cocktail to make it look more attractive.

Gnocchi – Gnocchi are starchy dumplings that are made in various shapes. There are two basic types of gnocchi: those based on potatoes and those based on flour or cornmeal.

Gratin – is a widely used culinary technique in food preparation, in which an ingredient is topped with a golden crust, often using breadcrumbs, grated cheese and melted butter. Gratin originated in French cuisine and is usually prepared in a shallow dish, then baked in a hot oven or finished under a grill to form a golden crust on top.

Haloumi – Firm white cheese made from sheep's milk. It has a stringy texture and is usually sold in brine.

Haricot – French for bean.

Harissa – A hot spicy paste of red chilies, garlic and olive oil. This is used extensively in North African cooking, particularly Moroccan cuisine.

Hoisin sauce – A thick, sweet-tasting Chinese sauce made from fermented soy beans, sugar, salt, and red rice. Used as a dipping sauce or glaze.

Hollandaise – One of the "mother" sauces. It is made with a vinegar reduction, egg yolks, and clarified butter flavoured with lemon juice.

Jambalaya – A Cajun and Creole composition of rice, smoked sausage (andouille), chicken, cubed ham and aromatics. Based on the Cajun trilogy of onions, celery and green bell peppers.

Julienne – To cut into long thin matchstick size strips. Usually vegetables.

Jus – The natural juices released by roasting meats and poultry, thinned with an appropriate stock. A non-thickened 'gravy'. The term is now used liberally as a menu descriptor.

Jus-lie – As above, but thickened with cornflour (corn starch) or fécule (potato starch).

Kaffir lime – A variety of small lime with a bumpy outer skin. The fragrant leaves are crushed or shredded and used in cooking, and the limes are used for their juice, mainly in Thai cuisine.

Kosher – From the Hebrew 'kasher'. When talking about food, to prepare it at every stage in strict observance of the Jewish dietary laws. When talking about salt, kosher salt is a coarse salt that does not contain magnesium carbonate.

Lemongrass – A tall, lemon-scented grass, used extensively in Thai cooking.

Liqueur – A sweetened spirit, flavoured with fruit, spices, nuts and herbs.

Lox – Yiddish word, derived from the German word "lachs" for salmon and the name of salt-cured belly of salmon.

Mandoline – A kitchen gadget used for thinly slicing vegetables.

Marinade – A mixture of ingredients used to flavour and moisten foods. A marinade can be liquid or dry.

Mirepoix – Chopped carrot, celery and onion, sweated or pan-fried until golden brown. Used when preparing sauces, soups, stews, braised and roasted dishes.

Mirin – A heavily sweetened rice wine or sake.

Miso – A thick paste made from fermented and processed soy beans.

Mother Sauces – Mother sauces or Grandes Sauces, form the base of most all classic French sauces. The classification was updated in the early 20th century by August Escoffier; they are: Allemande, Béchemal, Espagnole, Hollandaise, Tomato and Velouté.

Mozzarella – A semi-soft Italian cheese, usually preserved in brine in vacuum sealed packages. Used mostly for topping pizzas and in salads. The best is Mozzarella di Bufala, produced using milk from domesticated water buffalo.

Nori – Sheets of dried seaweed, pressed into thin, square sheets (usually black), used for sushi, soups and Japanese cuisine.

Pan fry – Most chefs use the term "pan fry" and sauté, but technically they are different. Both refer to cooking food in a small amount of hot oil, clarified butter, ghee or other fat. Sautéing literally means to toss food items over a high flame, while pan frying describes cooking foods in a hot pan and turning once or twice i.e. a steak would be pan fried. A sauté pan is deeper than a frying pan and has rounded sides.

Papillote – Usually "en papillote", means food cooked in a parchment or tin foil bag, which is placed into a hot oven, where it will steam the food in its own moisture. Fish and chicken are great cooked this way.

Par boil – to partly cook in boiling water.

Parmigiano Reggiano – The king, queen and whole royal family of hard-grating Italian cheese, made from cow's milk. A processed, finely grated version is available in most European supermarkets.

Pâte brisée – Short pastry for making savory tarts. Usually available, pre-rolled, from French supermarkets.

Pecorino – This is referred to as Parmigiano's little brother. A hard, grating cheese, produced from ewe's milk, mostly made around Lazio and the island of Sardinia.

Persillade – Widely used in French cooking, this is a mixture of finely or coarsely chopped garlic and parsley (usually flat-leaf).

Pesto – Traditionally made of crushed basil leaves, pounded in a mortar with garlic, Pecorino (see above), pine nuts and olive oil. The word comes from the Italian "pestare" – to pound or crush.

Poach – To cook foods (usually fish or fruit) submerged in barely simmering liquid such as court-bouillon or sugar syrup.

Porcini mushrooms – A rich, heady, meaty mushroom; Porcini are one of God's great gifts to humanity. A true passion in Italian cuisine, they are found growing wild in the woods of Italy and are highly prized by gourmet chefs worldwide. They can be purchased dried, so they can be reconstituted in liquid, making them ideal for use on yachts.

Prosciutto – The term is almost always used for an aged, dry-cured, Italian ham. Usually thinly sliced and served uncooked (prosciutto crudo). The most famous coming from an area around the city of Parma.

Purée – To work or strain foods until they are completely smooth. This is usually done with a food processor, hand blender, or by passing food through a sieve or Moulis.

Quenelle – Is often a paste made of minced fish, poultry, or veal meat mixed with eggs and cream. Shaped between two spoons, poached in stock, and served with a sauce as a garnish.

Ragout – The tem (Fench ragoût) can refer to either a main dish stew, or to a sauce for noodles i.e. Bolognese sauce is a typical Italian ragout sauce.

Ragú – A global brand, owned by Unilever, is a marketed version of an Italian style sauce. It is said to be the best selling pasta sauce brand in the USA.

Ramekin – A small, round ovenproof dish, usually ceramic.

Reduce or Reduction – The technique of cooking liquids down so that some of the liquid they contain evaporates. Reduction is used to concentrate the flavour of wine, stock or sauce and, at times, to help thicken a sauce or syrup.

Refresh – To rinse, just-boiled vegetables, under very cold water to stop their cooking. Alternatively, plunge vegetables into a bowl of heavily iced water. This process helps to retain colour, texture and nutrient value.

Ricotta – A fresh cheese (as opposed to ripened or aged), grainy and creamy white in appearance, slightly sweet in taste and containing around 5% fat. Similar in texture to cottage cheese variants, though considerably lighter. Like many fresh cheese, it is highly perishable. Because ricotta is made from whey, rather than milk, it is a 'whey cheese' and therefore not technically a cheese.

Risotto – Is a creamy rice dish, made with short-grain rice. The rice is gently cooked in butter, olive oil and stock, often finished with parmesan cheese. The high starch content of the rice gives it a characteristic creamy consistency. Arborio, Carnaroli or Vialone Nano are all good.

Roux – Equal amounts of flour and butter, used to thicken sauces, soups, and gravies. Usually the butter is cooked with the flour in a heavy-bottomed pan over low heat, before adding hot milk or stock.

Sabayon – A light, frothy mixture made by beating egg yolks with water or other liquid over gentle heat.

Sashimi tuna – Finest quality tuna, cut in an Asian or Japanese style. It is very tender and used raw in Japanese cuisine.

Sauté – To cook over high heat in a small amount of oil or clarified butter in a sauté pan (sauteuse).

Scallions – Known as Spring Onions in the UK.

Sear – To brown the surface of pieces of meats and or fish by submitting them to intense, direct initial heat.

Sea salt – Salt produced by evaporating sea water. It is available refined, or unrefined, crystallized, or ground.

Shallot – A member of the onion family. Shallots, more delicate than onion, are used to provide a more mild flavor to dishes.

Shred – To cut into fine strips. Shredding is similar to cutting into chiffonade but less precise.

Shitake – A meaty, Oriental variety of mushroom with an almost steak-like flavour, used in soups, sauces and salads to provide a unique flavour.

Simmer – To gently cook liquids, by maintaining a constant temperature below boiling point.

Sorbet – A frozen dessert made with fruit juice or another flavouring, a sweetener (usually sugar), and beaten egg whites, which prevent the formation of large ice crystals.

Soufflé – A preparation made with a sauce base, whipped egg whites, and flavourings. The egg whites cause the soufflé to puff-up during cooking. Timing of cooking and serving is usually critical.

Steam – To cook in steam by suspending foods over (not in) boiling water or stock, in a covered pot or steamer. Steaming food under pressure in commercial hi-pressure steamers, reduces cooking time considerably.

Stew – A cooking method nearly identical to braising but generally involving smaller pieces of meat. Usually, the purpose of stewing is to render more tough meat tender, by slow, covered 'top cooking' (not oven) and to concentrate the food's flavours in the surrounding liquid.

Stir-fry – Chinese technique of cooking thin slivers of meat, shellfish, and vegetables in hot oil.

Sun-dried tomatoes – Plum tomatoes that have been dried slowly to produce a chewy, intensely flavorful ingredient. They are available for sale in oil or dry-packed. Blush Sun-dried tomatoes are now available and have a less intense flavour.

Sweat – An important cooking technique, to start cooking food without colour in a little butter or oil. Food is cooked over a gentle heat, usually covered or partly covered, until it releases its moisture. Vegetables and seafood are often sweated when making soups, stews, and sauces so that the foods release their juices into the pan and surrounding liquid.

Tamarind paste – A product from the ripe bean pods of the tamarind tree. It can be purchased as pulp or in the more convenient form of tamarind concentrate ready to use. Used extensively in Asian and Caribbean cooking, it has a distinctive sweet/tart flavour.

Tempura – A Japanese method of cooking vegetables and shellfish. They are coated with a light, cornstarch batter and deep-fried. Many yacht chefs will use sparkling mineral water as the liquid base in their recipe.

Tournedo – A steak cut from middle section the fillet (tenderloin).

Velouté – One of the "mother" sauces. A sauce of white stock thickened with a white roux. Also, a cream soup made with a velouté sauce base and flavorings, which can be finished with a mixture (liaison) of egg yolks and cream to enrich the end product.

Vinaigrette – The classic French salad dressing, made of one part vinegar and three parts oil. There are extensive global variations.

Wasabi – A spice that comes from a knobby green root of the Japanese plant wasbia japonica. A traditional condiment served with sushi and sashimi. Known as Japanese Horseradish, it has an extremely strong flavour similar to hot mustard.

Zabaglione – A whipped 'custard' made with egg yolks and sugar gradually diluted over heat with Marsala or other wine, fruit juice, or liqueur.

Zest – The thin, brightly colored outer part of the rind from citrus fruits. The oils make it ideal for use as a flavoring. Remove the zest with a grater, citrus zester, or vegetable peeler. Be careful to remove only the colored layer, not the bitter-white pith beneath it.

COCKTAILS

Although the preparation of cocktails on large yachts is something which would usually fall under the watchful eye of the Chief Stew; if you are working on a 'regular' small yacht charter, then that may mean cocktail preparation is down to you.

So, following some long discussions over which ones I should include and some even longer tasting sessions, I have identified a few popular cocktail recipes which might be useful to you at some time in the future. So without going too over the top, I have included ones which I hope your guests will enjoy. I have tried to create a balance of some nice, long cold drinks and a few less subtle, 'hit you between the eyes' ones as well.

If you are uncertain of the ingredients for a *"never heard of that before"* cocktail requested by a guest, then a good tip is to ask the guest what is their preferred recipe or the method for making the cocktail of their choice i.e. *"How would like your XX cocktail prepared this evening sir/madam?"*

All my recipes are for one serving and classify one shot as being 2.5cl or 25ml and all Units of Alcohol and ABV are approximate.

BLOODY MARY

Type:	Spicy
Glass:	Highball
Difficulty:	Medium
Units of Alc:	3
ABV:	13%

Recipe

- 2 dashes Angostura Bitters
- 2 shots standard Russian vodka
- 4 shots tomato juice
- 6 drops Tobasco sauce
- 0.5 shot Worcestershire sauce
- 0.5 shot lemon juice
- 1 pinch celery salt

Method

Pour liquid ingredients over ice, stir well. Add celery salt and stir again. Garnish with a little celery stick. Serve.

BLUE LAGOON

Type:	Fruity
Glass:	Highball
Difficulty:	Easy
Units of Alc:	2
ABV:	13%

Recipe

- 1.5 shots standard Russian vodka
- 1.5 shots Blue Curaçao
- top up with lemonade

Method
Build the vodka and Blue Curaçao into a highball glass, half filled with ice. Top with lemonade, stir and garnish with a slice of lime, lemon or orange. Serve.

CRANBERRY CHILLER
Type: Fruity
Glass: Highball
Difficulty: Medium
Units of Alc: 3
ABV: 13.5%

Recipe
- 1 shot standard Russian vodka
- 1 shot Triple Sec
- 1 shot Disaranno Amaretto
- 3 shots cranberry juice
- 2 shots of orange juice

Method
Fill a highball glass with ice cubes and build the ingredients: Triple Sec, Amaretto, Vodka, then add the cranberry and orange juices. Stir gently and squeeze in a little fresh lime juice. Serve.

DAIQUIRI
Type: Sour
Glass: Martini
Difficulty: Medium
Units of Alc: 2
ABV: 29%

Recipe
- 2 shots white rum
- 0.5 shot fresh lime juice
- 0.25 shot sugar syrup (Gomme)

Method
Pour ingredients into a shaker over crushed ice and shake vigorously and strain through a fine strainer into the glass to remove fragments of lime and ice.
(For something different, check out fresh mango daiquiri)

LONG ISLAND ICED TEA
Type: Dry
Glass: Highball
Difficulty: Medium
Units of Alc: 3
ABV: 30%

Recipe
- 0.5 shot London dry gin
- 0.5 shot Triple Sec
- 0.5 standard Russian vodka
- 0.5 shot white rum
- 0.5 shot tequila

- 1 dash of coke
- 1 teaspoon caster sugar
- 0.5 shot lemon juice

Method
Shake all of the ingredients, except the coke, with ice and strain into a highball glass filled with cubed ice. Pour the coke over the top and garnish with a wedge of lemon. Serve.

MAI TAI
Type: Fruity
Glass: Tumbler
Difficulty: Medium
Units of Alc: 4
ABV: 35%

Recipe
- 1 shot Woods dark rum
- 1 large dash Angostura Bitters
- 0.5 shot apricot brandy
- 0.5 shot De Kuyper Dry Orange
- 0.5 shot pineapple juice
- 0.5 shot lime juice

Method
Pour ingredients over ice into a shaker. Shake well and pour into a glass filled with crushed ice. Garnish with lemon wedge and a sprig of mint. Serve.

MOJITO
Type: Spicy
Glass: Tumbler
Difficulty: Medium
Units of Alc: 3
ABV: 14%

Recipe
- 3 dashes of angostura bitters
- 2 shots white rum
- 1 shot lime juice (fresh)
- 1 tsp sugar syrup (Gomme)
- soda water

Method
Muddle the mint leaves in a glass with the sugar syrup and lime juice to extract the mint oils. Fill the glass with crushed ice and add the rum and Angostura, then top up with soda water and stir. Garnish with a sprig of fresh mint. Serve.

PINA COLADA
Type: Fruity
Glass: Highball
Difficulty: Easy
Units of Alc: 2
ABV: 10%

Recipe
- 2 shots white rum
- 4 shots pineapple juice
- 1 shot cream
- 2 shots coconut cream

Method
Pour ingredients over ice into a shaker. Shake well and pour into a glass filled with crushed ice. Garnish with a pineapple wedge and a pineapple leaf. Serve.

MINT JULIP
Type:	Minty
Glass:	Tumbler
Difficulty:	Medium
Units of Alc:	2
ABV:	40%

Recipe
- 1.5 shots Bourbon
- 4 mint leaves
- 1 teaspoon caster sugar

Method
Lightly muddle together the mint leaves and sugar with a few drops of water in the bottom of the glass. Then almost fill the glass with crushed ice and pour the bourbon over it. Garnish with a sprig of mint. Serve.

SEX ON THE BEACH
Type:	Fruity
Glass:	Highball
Difficulty:	Easy
Units of Alc:	3
ABV:	11.5%

Recipe
- 1 shots standard Russian vodka
- 2 shot peach schnapps
- 3 shots cranberry juice
- 3 shots orange juice

Method
Build the ingredients over ice and stir. Garnish with a lime wedge. Serve.

SINGAPORE SLING
Type:	Sour
Glass:	Sling
Difficulty:	Easy
Units of Alc:	3
ABV:	16.5%

Recipe

- 1 dash of Angostura Bitters
- 2 shots London dry gin
- 0.5 shot Bénédictine D.O.M.
- 1 shot cherry brandy
- 0.5 shot lemon juice
- soda water

Method

Pour the bitters, gin, Bénédictine and cherry brandy into a shaker, over a little ice. Shake and pour over an ice filled sling glass, top with soda water, garnish with a slice of lemon. Serve.

FYI: Benedictine uses twenty seven ingredients of herbs and spices and the D.O.M. in its name, stands for Deo Optimo Maximo, which means – To God most good, most great.

WHITE/BLACK RUSSIAN

Type: Creamy
Glass: Tumbler
Difficulty: Medium
Units of Alc: 3
ABV: 20%

Recipe

- 1 shots standard Russian vodka
- 1 shot Kahlua
- 1 shot double cream
- 1 shots milk
- 1 dash coke

Method

Build over cubed ice.

Leave out the coke for a White Russian

FOOD & WINE

For many people, wine drinking has become an integral, if not an essential part of the meal experience and daily life. Consumption of wine in England continues to increase year on year and has in recent years become the drink of choice with 'trendy' young (and not so young) people, enjoying an after-work, relaxing drink in the company of colleagues and friends. Consequently our demand for knowledge of grapes, wine and what is actually in the bottle has increased greatly in the boom, before the bust culture of the late 'nineties' and early 'naughties'. People are now demanding higher and higher quality, plus dare I say, value for money – not an easy combination to reconcile when buying form commercially driven, 'you do it our way or not at all' supermarket chains.

To my mind, all interior crew should have at least a basic knowledge of wines of the world. I used to deliver advanced wine training courses for The Wine and Spirit Education Trust (WSET) and have no hesitation in recommending them (their courses) as the organisation of choice for global crew wine training. They are the recognised and acclaimed global leader in providing wine training courses. Get on their website (see below) and just click on 'where to study' and this will throw up a map of the world; click the country or continent of your choice and presto – the rest is down to you. WSET organises wine education courses, spirits courses and wine tastings for professionals and enthusiasts in 50 countries worldwide.

www.wset.co.uk
Tel: +44 (0)20 7089 3800

> **Négociant** is the French term for a wine merchant who assembles the produce of smaller growers and winemakers and sells the result under its own name.
>
> Négociants buy everything from grapes to grape must (freshly pressed grape juice that contains the seed, skin and stem) to wines in various states of completion. In the case of grapes or must, the négociant performs virtually all the winemaking. If he buys already fermented wine in barrels or 'en-vrac' - basically in bulk containers, he may age the wine further, blend in other wines or simply bottle and sell it as is. The result is sold under the name of the négociant, not the name of the original grape or wine producer.
>
> Some négociants have a recognizable house style. For example, Georges Duboeuf (Burgundy, Beaujolais & Rhône) was notorious for using yeast that produced a pronounced banana aroma.

You will quickly come to understand that wine has become an important part of an owner's or charterer's trips, therefore preference sheets have moved away from just asking charter guests if guests like red or white wine. You will increasingly find that preference sheets are now being completed by more knowledgeable guests, who will note an amazing amount of detail about which wines they want, vintages, regions, vineyards, vignerons, négociants etc etc .....

Supermarkets have, unsurprisingly, become the biggest 'off-licence' wine sellers in the Eurozone. We are, in my humble opinion, hit by far too wide a choice of mediocre and poor quality wines – often 'selected' for us via deals and handshakes made by wine buyers and négociants (see above), which can all too often provide us with shelf upon shelf of wines we have never heard of. However, when you are moored up at a marina in a foreign land, don't panic, because the information on the label should guide you to make a fairly accurate decision on what you are buying.

Everyone has their favourite wines and the decision to buy may be as simple as a choice of whether it's a red or white, although this is unlikely these days. Others may make far more complex decisions about a wine; from a highly respected grower (vineyard), using a single grape variety grown in a delimited area of production, from a specific year, bottled after a defined period in an oak barrel and then bottle aged for 'x' number of weeks, months or years – see how easy it is?

If you are relatively new to selecting (or even drinking) wines to compliment your weekly or fortnightly menu plan for the next charter, or for your discerning owner, you will want to stick to a few simple rules. However, no matter where you are in the world, the well known grape varietals will generally be found, so let these be your initial guide.

As a general rule of thumb, drink white wines and rosé fairly young, usually no more than two or three years old. As mentioned previously, you can be guided by much of the information provided on the label on the bottle. Large wine producing countries in Europe i.e. France, Italy, Spain, Portugal and Germany all have legally binding quality control systems in place, which guarantee that what's in the bottle is reflected by the description on the label.

Many reds may require to be left to mature and age in oak barrels and the bottle. A guide to this might be that the wine is a vintage – a quality wine from an especially 'good year' from a particular vineyard, indicated by a date on the label. Other reds, such as Beaujolais, should always be drunk young, and even slightly chilled. If you are sailing in a very warm climate and your guests want a lightweight red, then certainly do not be afraid to offer to chill the wine for an hour or so before serving. This is common practice in many rural areas of Central and Southern France, where the summer heat can be very intense, reaching unforgiving temperatures that would send the most ardent sun worshipper heading for some shade!

Whether your guests drink huge quantities of wine (there are some nationalities famous for it in the industry), or they can afford the very high end products such as Montrachet, Chambertin, Romanée-Conti, Pétrus, Latour, Margaux, Haut-Brion, Chateau d'Yquem, Grange Hermitage etc, getting the 'wine side' of their charter right, from day one has now become one of the top priorities. It gives the owner, lead charterer etc the opportunity to impress his/her guests by providing them with the very best wines, which have been carefully selected to match to beautiful plates of food provided by your seven star chef. Rare wines do, of course come at a premium price, so it will come as no surprise that you will get requests for such rarities, which can be extremely difficult to source at short notice. Good forward planning is essential.

It is important to understand that (as noted above), wine offers the consumer incredible diversity. There are thousands upon thousands of different wines produced in countries across the world, each from a succession of vintages. So if your guests select a specific wine, which falls outside of the normal generic expectation, then it is unlikely that anywhere except the most well stocked supplier will be able to help you out. It is therefore important to build a network of Fine Wine provisioners in and around the ports of call, which your yacht normally visits. Selecting a supplier who holds a large range of stock, will obviously increase your chances of being able to supply your guests with what they have asked for.

By doing this, you will build up a working relationship and hopefully come to trust these suppliers, to provide you with products that will satisfy your most discerning customers. An example of such a provisioner is CORKERS Fine Wines & Provisions, who provision yachts in France, Italy and Croatia. Contact details page 286.

A little (or a lot) of wine knowledge, will also arm you with the ability to identify and suggest suitable alternatives to guests if necessary. So just bear this in mind that training, knowledge and experience are crucially important. Master of Wine – Rod Smith of Vins Sans Frontières (www.vsfgroup.com), one of the few Masters of Wine working in France, says this: *"Expertise – yours or your supplier's, is the key. Interpreting some obscure wine name into a set of flavours that can be replicated, or even improved upon, by another immediately available wine or vintage takes knowledge and experience"*.

The 'weighty' but invaluable Yachting Pages (www.yachting-pages.com) provides contact details for provisioners across the globe. However, be warned, many yacht suppliers and fine wine companies simply broker wine and will, as a rule, hardly hold any stock themselves. If it's sat on their shelves, the inventory is costing them money.

There is a lot of snobbery about wines, often from people who do not have a great deal of knowledge on the subject, but go with the flow and you will learn very quickly – it really is a fascinating subject. A little focused research, particularly on European wines will certainly help increase your knowledge. Hugh Johnson's annual Pocket Wine Book, is a must as an accurate and up-to-date quick reference that will only take up micro-room in your flight bag. Malcolm Gluck, also produces a good guide.

GRAPE VARIETIES

In recent years a mere handful of grape varietals have become known globally and names such as Shiraz and Chardonnay are purchased in the same breath as Jack and Coke.

As an introductory guide, I have listed below some grape varieties, which I hope will help you in selecting some good quality wines. At least some of these varieties – Cabernet Sauvignon, Pinot Noir, Syrah (Shiraz), Merlot, Riesling, Sauvignon Blanc, Chardonnay and Gewurztraminer have very distinctive tastes and smells. I will take look at food and wine combinations for you a little later.

RED WINE GRAPES

Cabernet Franc:-   Used a great deal in St Emilion (Bordeaux). This grape also produces the often high quality reds from Chinon and Bourgueil on opposite sides of the River Loire.

Cabernet Sauvignon:-   The global gladiator, always dependable, full of character with a blackcurrant aroma, spices, herbs and tannins. This is the premiere grape of the globally acclaimed Médoc red wines from Bordeaux, known as Claret. The grape benefits from aging and may also profit from blending with the likes of Merlot, Cabernet Franc or Syrah (Shiraz). 'Cab Sauv' also produces many of the outstanding reds in California, South America (Chile & Argentina) and Australia, although the Australians do love to blend it with Shiraz.

Merlot:-   Blended with 'Cab Sauv' to make the great wines of Pomerol like the prestigious and extremely expensive Château Pétrus and in St Emilion, producing such greats as: Cheval Blanc, Ausone and Canon.

Pinot Noir:-   Produces the great red wines of the Burgundy region in France, such as Gevrey Chambertin and Nuits St Georges. Not a grape variety that has produced fine wines elsewhere, however, there are now some interesting wines coming through from California, Australia and New Zealand. This is also one of the two black grape varietals (plus one white) which are used to produce Champagne.

Pinotage:- Is the red wine grape that is South Africa's signature varietal. It was created there in 1925 as a cross between Pinot Noir and Cinsaut. It typically produces deep red wines with smoky, bramble and earthy flavours, sometimes with notes of bananas and tropical fruit.

Syrah (Shiraz):- This well know red grape from the Rhône in France, has in more recent years gained global recognition through the production of some high quality wines in Australia, where it is known as Shiraz. It is now increasingly produced in California, South Africa and the Midi (Southern France), where there is an increasing influence on wine production from Australian vignerons (wine growers), who have been brought to Southern France to successfully rejuvenate what was a failing industry in that part of the Eurozone.

Tempranillo:- Is a widely grown, early ripening, black grape variety used to make full-bodied red wine in its native Spain. It is the main grape used in Rioja and is often referred to as Spain's "noble grape". In the last 100 years, it has been planted in South America, USA, South Africa, Australia and Canada. Tempranillo wines can be consumed young, but the most expensive ones are aged for several years in oak barrels. The wines are ruby red in colour, with aromas of berries, plum, tobacco, vanilla, leather and herb.

Zinfandel:- This black grape variety is planted in over 10% of California's wine vineyards. DNA fingerprinting has shown that it is genetically equivalent to two little known grape varietals from Croatia and Southern Italy. It was introduced to the USA in the mid-19th century, becoming known by variations of the name Zinfandel (Zin) – a name of uncertain origin. The grapes typically produce a robust red wine, although a semi-sweet rosé (blush-style) wine called White Zinfandel, has six times the sales of the red wine in the USA. The grape's high sugar content can be fermented into high levels of alcohol exceeding 15 percent.

FOOTNOTE

I cannot finish this section on black grapes, without making mention of two very fine Italian reds. Brunello di Montalcino and Barolo, are celebrated as Italy's finest. They are full-bodied, strong (high in alcohol), uniquely flavoured, tannic and tend towards longevity, therefore expensive. A good Barolo has the most remarkable "brick-red" colour and a unique flavour. Produced from the Nebbiolo grape, this fine wine has the ability to age for up to 20 and 25 years and should not really be opened until at least 5 years old. Both of these wines are well worth spending your extra 'euro-pennies' on, but need to be paired up with the right type of food. 'Slurping wines – they are not'.

WHITE WINE GRAPES (Can also be black grapes)

Chardonnay ('Chard'):- The Holy Grail, this is the white grape of the great Burgundy region and the white grape of Champagne (the other two are black) and the signature grape of many New World whites, because of its ability to grow and vinify in most wine growing countries of the world. It is often oak aged, or even better, fermented in oak to try to replicate the distinctive flavours of the classic white Burgundies. Australia and California produce some classics (Fetzer is a favorite of mine), however too much of the production is only of average quality. Keep an eye out for some of the 'new' countries producing this grape, which may make a dent in today's popular market i.e. wines from: New Zealand, South Africa, Italy, Spain, Chile, Argentina and the Midi (Southern France).

Chenin Blanc:- Is the great white grape variety from the Central Vineyards of the Loire. This grape has plenty of acidity and can produce both dry or sweet wines, so be careful and check out the label. It is very popular for production in South Africa, where it is known as Steen.

Gewurztraminer:-   This grape, produces characteristically spicy wine, with the most beautiful aromas of rose petals and tastes of grapefruit and lychees. There are some outstanding examples which are produced in the Alsace region of North East France. Be careful on food combinations with this wine – this is a wine of strong, powerful flavours and it is important that you make the right choices.

Muscadet (Melon de Bourgogne):-   This grape is grown in profusion in the Nantes region of the Loire, providing us with a light, refreshing dry wine, which is very popular with seafood in the coastal towns of Brittany and Normandy. The wine, Muscadet-sur-Lie, makes an interesting alternative; more full-bodied, with a yeasty nose and fuller flavour.

Pinot Grigio:-   This wine has become the 'in' white wine over the last couple of years. The grape is grown all over Italy with some of the better quality wines produced in the North East. Although the wine has a questionable pedigree, it is one of Italy's most popular and certainly the most popular imported white wine going into the USA.

Riesling:-   The equivalent in rankings to Chardonnay as the two global white grape greats, producing characteristically different styles of wine. This grape, still primarily grown on the sloping banks of the rivers Rhine and Mosel in Germany, producing a range of wines from steely to voluptuous, always beautifully perfumed, with the potential to age. Although producing some truly outstanding wines in Germany and Australia, these wines seem to have 'missed the boat' with the British public and are just not fashionable with the patriotic French.

Sauvignon Blanc:-   Produces a distinctive wine, characteristically linked to the smell of gooseberries. This classic white grape produces two of my favorite medium priced white wines. The outstanding Sancerre from the far eastern end of the Loire region and the amazing triumph from the Marlborough region, located in the northern extremes of the south island of New Zealand – Cloudy Bay, an outstanding wine from the Southern Hemisphere (Chard' also produced).

Semillon:-   This is the classic grape which contributes to the greatness of the best dessert wine in the world – Sauternes from the Bordeaux region of France. These late harvested grapes are subject to 'noble rot' (Botrytis Cyneria) which concentrates the sugar content of the grape, while reducing the volume – hence the high cost!

Viognier:-   I just had to include this little known grape variety in my list of recommendations – one that you can 'pull out of the hat' and surprise your charter guests with. It is not that well known at the moment, but watch out for this one. Condrieu is a good example from the northern Rhone, producing a wine of great character, with a price that reflects the relatively small 100 hectares of vineyards.

FOOTNOTE

As many of you will spend time in Palma, Barcelona and other Spanish ports, I had to include a couple of little Spanish gems, which compared with my 'red footnote', are relatively inexpensive. Both of these wines are made by the internationally famous Miguel Torres vineyards of Pènedes near Barcelona.

Vina Sol:-   made from the Parellada grape providing a fresh fruitiness. Excellent as an aperitif or served with cod dishes, salads, soft cheeses, trout and sea food in general.

Vina Esmerelda:-   made from a blend of Moscatel and Gewurztraminer, the seductive, well defined aromas of honeysuckle and ripe pear intermingle with sweet vanilla spice. Fresh and lively on the palate with an aromatic richness. Sublime served with seafood, fish and especially paté.

CHAMPAGNE

Champagne is a sparkling wine produced in a specific region of Northern France and made by the traditional method of inducing an in-bottle secondary fermentation of the wine to create carbonation – or as you know it – sparkles! No other wine produced or sold in the European Union (EU) can be called Champagne.

Other non-European countries, such as USA have also recognised the exclusive nature of the name, yet maintain a legal structure that allows long time producers of sparkling wine to continue to use the term "Champagne" under specific circumstances. However, the majority of US produced sparkling wines do not use the term Champagne. Remember – all the information you need to check the origin is on the label.

Champagne can only be made from three grape varietals:- Chardonnay, Pinot Noir and Pinot Meunier. Champagne known as Blanc de Blancs is made only from the Chardonnay grape, however many champagnes are made by blending two or more of the legally allowed varieties.

Working in the superyacht industry you won't get away with just knowing that the label on a bottle of Veauve Clicquot is bright orange. Often very expensive vintage Champagne is the norm and you will need to know how to open bottle after bottle, efficiently and with no fuss. You will be expected to serve and pour discretely without spilling a drop. Approval from guests, for topping their glasses, is often only prompted by observation, how much is left in their glass or their body language. Never over-fill – 2/3 full is the accepted max'. Your fastidious attention to the needs of your owner's guests should be noted by those who matter.

Make the effort to find out the names of the top Marques and Grande Marques. The owner will have his/her preferences, but it is still worth getting to know good vintages, appropriate storage methods, service temperature, effective methods of pouring and how to avoid excessive 'mousse' (foam) when you fill a glass. Here are a few high end brands (Grande Marques), to be aware of: Moet et Chandon, Bollinger, Krug, Lanson Père et Fils, Veauve Clicquot Ponsardin ('The widow'), Laurent Perrier, Taittinger, Louis Roederer, Piper Heidsieck (pronounced peeper hide-sec).

Louis Roederer Cristal tends to be an extremely expensive Champagne; however some observers say this is down to the limited quantity made available on the market at any given time. It is also the champagne of choice of Premiership Footballers, 'new money' and celebrities – therefore not necessarily a good recommendation for outstanding quality. Widespread awareness of its high price has given the wine an image of exclusivity that, in turn, has elevated demand. It is considered to be Veblen good i.e. it is often purchased by people whose preference for buying this champagne is directly linked to its high price, much in the same way as Rolls Royce cars.

Dom Pérignon is a brand of champagne produced by the Champagne House, Möet et Chandon and is recognised as the champagne house's prestige brand. It is named after Dom Pérignon (1638-1715), a Benedictine monk who was an important quality pioneer of champagne wine production. Contrary to popular myth, he did not discover the champagne method of making sparkling wines.

FYI:-   In just seven years, between 1992 and 1999, the UK increased its annual Champagne consumption from 14 million bottles to 32 million. However, the recession has had a big impact on the number of bottles leaving the cellars of producers in France. October 2008 saw a 23% drop in overall sales against the same period from the previous year.

CHAMPAGNE COCKTAILS

You can use Cava as a good substitute for Champagne, and the vast majority of your guests are unlikely to know the difference, although most will insist on the real thing.

SYRUPS

Check out which syrups or purées work well with Champagne/Cava.

Bellini

White Peach purée is used for the famous Bellini cocktail, which originated in Italy and is traditionally made with Prosecco. This is one of Italy's most popular cocktails, created by Giuseppe Cipriani, founder of Harry's Bar in Venice, the famous haunt of Ernest Hemingway and Orson Wells. Later becoming popular in its New York counterpart.

Bucks Fizz

The drink was named after Buck's Club in London in 1921, by one of its barmen, Mr McGarry. This drink is popularly served at weddings as a slightly less alcoholic alternative to champagne.

Kir Royale

Made with a measure of Cassis (blackcurrant liqueur) and topped up with Champagne, or pour the Champagne first, and then very slowly add the Crème de Cassis (Blackcurrant), to give a 'blush' effect.

CAVA

Data often suggests that champagne is the world's most drunk fizz; sorry to disappoint but that's way off mark. Cava, the original Spanish fizz, produced in San Sadurni de Noya, near Barcelona in the Catalan region, is made using the champagne method, individually sells more bottles world-wide.

To give you a better idea of volumes, there are usually around 250 million bottles of champagne produced annually. Looking at the global sparkling wine market, only one bottle in twelve consumed can call itself champagne, therefore there are approximately 2,750,000,000 alternative fizz bottles sold annually on the global market – that's 2.75 billion!

So what's the difference you will be asking yourself – *"very little to nothing"*, is how Malcolm Gluck, the accomplished wine writer and critic puts it. The main difference is, that they are not allowed by law to call themselves Champagne, although they use the same methods and often have finer grapes to select from.

Some of the outstanding sparkling wines from around the world come from Spain, California, Australia and New Zealand. The Italians have their often exquisite Prosecco. Try tasting champagne produced by Moët en Chandon, alongside their Chandon Australia Brut and Chandon Argentina Brut and tell me which one is best – you would be extremely surprised at the outcome. The same thing goes for Mumm Cuvée Napa from California, which I rate highly; a wine more persistent in flavour than its French counterpart. From New Zealand, Cloudy Bay's, Pelorus is a legend, as well as being the name of one of Roman Abramovich's fabulous superyachts.

FOOD & WINE COMBINATIONS

If wine is your owner's or charterer's choice for Sundowners, then you may consider a Riesling or Chenin Blanc, you can then move your guests on to something more conventional with their meal. Avoid serving peanuts, they just do not work and can spoil the flavour of wine. Olives can also be a little piquant for many wines, but go well with a nicely chilled sherry. A good quality Manzanilla from Sanlúcar de Barrameda in the Jerez region of Spain works well. Almonds and pistachios can work, but beware the potential impact of those with a nut allergy.

Below are some suggestions for you. They are not hard and fast rules, more of a guideline to help you take onboard the idea of food and wine combinations.

FISH & SHELLFISH

Bream:-   Full bodied white or rosé

Cod:-   Chablis, Mersault or a Cru Classsé Graves

Crab:-   (Cold) - Condrieu or a dry Californian white

Crab:-   (Soft shell) - Chardonnay or a Riesling Spätlese

Fish Pie:-   Pinot Grigio

Fruits de mer:-   Muscadet or Muscadet Sur Lie

Lobster salad:-   Champagne, Premier Cru Chablis,
Condrieu, Penedès Chardonnay or Cava

Lobster:-   (Cream sauce) - Champagne, good quality white burgundy,
Cru Classé Graves or Californian Chard'

Monkfish:-   Often a roasted dish, so go for a richer wine,
such as New Zealand Chardonnay, French
Pinot Noir or even Chilean Merlot

Mussels:-   Chardonnay, Premier Cru Chablis or
Muscadet sur Lie

Oysters:-   Chablis, Sancerre, Muscadet-sur-Lie or
Champagne

Salmon:-   (Pan fried or grilled) - White Burgundy:
Montrachet, Meursault or Chablis Grand Cru,
Condrieu or a south island New Zealand Chard'

Salmon:-   (Fish cakes) - Similar to above but less
expensive wines will suffice

Sardines:-   (BBQ):   Very dry white: Manzanilla (Sherry),
Vinho Verde (Portugal), Soave or Muscadet

Scallops:-	(Cream sauce) German Spätlese, Montrachet or quality Australian Chard'
Scallops:-	(Pan fried or grilled) – White Hermitage, Champagne or Entre-Deux-Mers
Sea Bass:-	Chablis or a white Châteauneuf-du-Pape
Skate:-	(Classic brown butter) Pungent white, such as Pinot Gris d'Alsace or a Muscadet
Swordfish:-	Full-bodied white – nothing too expensive
Trout:-	Delicate white: Mosel Saar or Mosel Ruwer
Tuna:-	(Pan fried or grilled) – Fruity white, red or rosé: St-Véran or white Hermitage or Côtes du Rhône. For red: Pinot Noir or Merlot. Rosé: try Buzet or one of the classic rosé wines from Provence
Turbot:-	Deserves nothing but the best: Meursault, Chablis, Chassagne-Montrachet or Condrieu

MEAT & POULTRY

BBQs:-	Shiraz, Chianti, Toulon from Provence or Buzet from SW France
Braised beef:- :-	Heavyweight red – Barolo, Cahors (Malbec grape) or Hermitage
Cajun food:-	This spicy food is complimented by a red Fleurie or Brouilly (Gamay grape from Beaujolais) or an intense Sauvignon Blanc. Alternatively a nicely chilled San Miguel (Spain), Peroni (Italy) also Corona or Sol beer from Mexico
Cassoulet:-	Only drink reds produced in the areas where this fabulous dish is king. Gaillac, Cahors from South West France or Corbières from the Midi (France)
Chicken:-	Because of the inexhaustible recipes – virtually any wine, including medium and dry whites and some of the quality reds from Burgundy go well
Cold meat:-	As a general rule of thumb, full flavoured whites go better than reds. Try a white Côte Chalonnaise or Rully from Burgundy. If it must be red, try a Fleurie; a top notch Beaujolais Cru
Coq au vin:-	The classic dish of Burgundy. Do a Keith Floyd; just serve a good red Burgundy

Duck breast:-	This gamey meat deserves a robust red or a rich white. For the red, try a Morey-St-Denis or Gevry Chambertin. White such as a Pflaz Spätlese from the region south of Rheinhessen (Germany) try Trocken (dry) or Halbtrocken (medium dry)
Lamb cutlets:-	Red: Cabernet Sauvignon from Bordeaux, New World, Rioja or Ribera del Duero
Moussaka:-	Red: Greek Naoussa, Italian red Chianti or Rosé from Provence
Paella:-	White: Macon Lugny works very well or Vina Esmeralda
Steak:-	Fillet or tournedos: good quality red. If served with Bearnaise sauce: a Fetzer Chard' goes well.

WINE with DESSERT & CHEESE

Here we go folks, with the old debate about when is the correct time to serve cheese during a formal dinner; before dessert or after dessert and also, what should you drink with your cheese or dessert. Over the years, I have been told many reasons why the French follow their main course with cheese, which is traditionally followed by dessert. Only one explanation really makes any deal of sense to me. If you have just been drinking *un peu de rouge* with your main course, then surely the only right and proper thing to do is to finish off that same wine with your cheese (savoury) course, rather than drinking it with your sweet course (dessert), that will totally destroy the flavour of your palate.

I am not going to tell you what wine you should or shouldn't drink with cheese, because the characteristics of different types of cheese varies so much, what with, soft, hard, blue, goats cheese etc., it can get quite confusing. The 'new thinking' is that white wines should be served with cheese, however, I am a traditionalist (well – sometimes!) and I still go with the idea that if you are drinking red with your main course you should then go straight onto the cheese and finish your bottle of red or even crack a second. Either that, or throw it away, because drinking it later with, or after your dessert, you certainly wouldn't want to touch another drop! Your owner or guests will have their own preferences, so go with the flow and offer advice if asked.

A good quality red can be ruined by the flavour of a strong cheese. However, this can be counteracted by serving one of the heavy reds, which are produced in South America – an Argentinian Merlot can be quite robust.

MCB tip: One basic rule of thumb, which usually works quite well - in your hour of uncertainty, I always say *"Local cheese, with local wine"*.

DESSERT WINES

It makes a lot of sense to drink a sweet white dessert wine with puddings. Many people are not too keen on sweet white wine, however, it should really only be drunk with the right food to get the best flavours out of it. If you want your guests to drink a wine that will compliment their dessert, you might consider a well chilled Sauternes from Bordeaux, or select from one of the somewhat less expensive sweet white wines from across the River Garonne: Loupiac, Ste-Croix-du-Mont or St Macaire. For French budget buys, with reasonable quality, try a Blanc Moelleux de Bordeaux or alternatively the popular Muscat Beaumes de Venise (Rhône) or Muscat de Rivesaltes (Rousillon).

The very finest and naturally most expensive sweet white wine is, without doubt, Chateau d'Yquem (dee – kem) from the Sauternes area of Bordeaux. This is the world's most famous sweet white wine producing estate of some 250 acres. Most vintages improve in the bottle for 15 years; some have been known to 'live' for up to 100 years, with prices very much to match. A 1784 vintage sold recently at auction for a record $56,588 US, making it the third most expensive bottle of wine ever sold.

Wine and chocolate: Not the easiest food to match with wine. A nicely chilled Asti Spumante goes well with a light fluffy chocolate mousse. Powerful flavours tend to work well with other chocolate dishes. Try Tokay Azsú from Hungary or Muscat de Rivesaltes. I love a Banyules from SW France or a nice tawny port. Alternatively why not experiment with a rich red, such as a new world Shiraz.

CHEESE BOARD

The Americans serve cheese as a starter, the French before the dessert and the English as a grand finale.

Your onboard cheeseboard can be as simple or as extravagant as you wish, or your guests require. However, preparing the perfect one can be somewhat of an art. These cheeseboard tips are designed to help you select and display, ready for your guests to enjoy all your cheese to the fullest. When you follow these guidelines, your perfect cheeseboard will impress and delight your guests with every bite.

Selecting
When preparing your cheese board, plan on serving from three to five cheeses; any more will overwhelm the palate. To make your selections, visit a good cheese counter (or provisioner) and aim for variety. You will want to temp the taste buds with cheese of distinctly different styles, tastes and textures.

For a simple, yet interesting cheese board, start with these three selections: one soft cheese i.e. Brie or Camembert, one firm cheese i.e. Manchego, Cantal or Monteray Jack and one blue vein cheese i.e. Roquefort or Stilton. To expand your offerings, add a spreadable cheese such as fresh Chevre (goat's cheese), or a 'surprise' local cheese from wherever you happen to be in the world.

For a more creative twist, build your cheese board around a theme. You might offer cheese from different milks i.e. cow's, sheep's and goat's milk.

Purchasing tips
Make your cheese board a memorable experience; avoid the common and go for artisan cheeses that will be new to your guests and always go for good quality cheese, rather than many lesser quality ones. If you are uncertain, seek advice from staff at the 'cheese counter' or your provisioner.

Temperature in the fridge
If your cheese is stored in the fridge, the danger is not that it is too cold, but that it will dry out. Storing near salad leaves can create a bit of humidity. In most cases, storing cheese in the fridge is the best option. If you need to keep cheese for a few days, the fridge will slow down its development and you can keep it for longer, provided it doesn't become dry. When it comes to pre-meal preparation, bring it out of the fridge a couple of hours early, so that it can warm through. This is very important for the flavour, as cold cheese will taste bland and inert.

Humidity
Humidity is actually more important than temperature. Most cheese should be kept at a relative humidity of 80% or more.

Wrapping
Cheese, wrapped in cling film will become soggy and smelly. Left uncovered, it will dry out. One of the best ways to store cheese is by wrapping in waxed paper, which seems to achieve the best balance between the two extremes. It is also easier to handle for rewrapping.

Presenting
Display your cheese board in a way that will inspire "oohs" and "ahs". To begin, choose a serving dish or platter large enough to keep cheeses of different shapes and sizes from touching. Cheese boards made of wood are traditional, while marble is more elegant, offering a cool surface and a contrasting background colour to make your cheeses "pop" off the platter.

When arranging your selection, be sure to display them in a manner what makes them most accessible to your guests. Put small cheeses in the middle and then place soft cheeses around them. Hard cheeses should be arranged around the outside of the cheeseboard, to make them easier to cut.

Accompaniments
To make your cheese board an edible piece of art, garnish it with natural ingredients such as: parsley, sweet, musky muscat grapes, apples, tomatoes, celery and dried berries; all add beautiful colour and flavour. In separate dishes, you might also offer olives, pickled vegetables such as cornichons (gherkins), artichoke hearts and peppers or lightly roasted nuts such as walnuts, macadamias or almonds. Balance your offerings with a variety of breads, biscuits and crackers, which are not too strong in flavour or too salty. Avoid the common and treat your guests to something special – maybe slices of tangy sourdough or biscuits flavoured with cracked black pepper.

In general, fresh cheeses pair well with Sauvignon Blanc or Pinot Noir (see Grape Varieties – page 254), blue cheeses with Sauternes and Port and aged cheeses with Zinfandel or Burgundy. If in doubt, a wine from the region of the cheese is often a good match.

Serving tips
- Remove the wrapping from your cheeses, but leave on the rinds
- Serve each cheese with its own knife to avoid mixing flavours
- Bring cheese up to room temperature for optimal flavour – take out of the fridge up to two hours before serving.

BRANDY
How long have you got? .... Ok, I will keep it fairly brief, but read and remember.

As a starting point and without sounding patronising and to keep it simple - there a two types of brandy that you need to be familiar with: Cognac and Armagnac, both from the South West of France. Although you can buy fruit brandies, the ones I am talking about are the ones which are generally consumed after dinner as a 'digestif' and are produced from the double distillation of wine produced from specific grape varietals.

Cognac is produced just north of Bordeaux in the Charente and Charente Maritime Departments and brandies bearing the words Grande Champagne or Petite Champagne on the label will denote a really good quality cognac. There are a number of internationally recognised producers of Cognac and they are: Hennessy (owned by LVMH - Luis Vuitton, Moët, and Hennessy), Remy Martin (owned by Remy Cointreau), Martell (owned by Pernod), and Courvoisier (owned by Beam Global).

Armagnac is to be found to the south of Bordeaux in the ancient province of Gascony and is the oldest type of brandy in France, with references going back as far as the 15th century.

Cognac and Armagnac are both legally protected names and can only be produced by defined methods in recognised areas of production for sale in the EU when made in the area of origin in France. Keep an eye open for the following terminology on the label. VS is usually the least expensive:

- VS –   Very Superior
- VSP –   Very Superior Pale
- VSOP –   Very Superior Old Pale
- XO –   Extra Old
- Napoleon –   High-end Courvoisier.

SHERRY & PORT
These are the only classic fortified wines that I have space to mention in this book. I include these because they are the globally recognised classic fortified wines of Spain (Sherry) and Portugal (Port). There have been endless studies and books written over the years on both, so space dictates that I only dedicate a few lines to give you a brief overview of these amazing wines.

SHERRY
Sherry is the most famous of Spanish wines, much in the same way, but for different reasons, that Champagne is the best known French wine. The name Sherry (like Champagne) is legally protected, as belonging to a specific area in southern Spain to the west of Gibraltar. There are a couple of iconic grape varieties, which are used in Sherry production: Palomino (dry) and Pedro Ximenez (pronounced him-en-eth), which is used to sweeten 'cream sherries'. Like other fortified wines, sherry has taken a big hit on the popularity front, but remains an excellent aperitif. The wine is blended over a number of years in an interconnecting stack of barrels, known as a solera system. 'New' wine is poured in at the top and works its way down through the barrels. It is for this reason that you will never see a vintage sherry, because the blended wine comes from more than one year. In my mind, there are five styles of sherry, which are worth mentioning:

Fino: The lightest, finest sherries. Matured in Jerez, you will expect these to be completely dry, very pale in colour and delicate, but pungent on the nose. You need to serve them lightly chilled, as it should be drunk cool and fresh. The wine will go 'off' quite quickly once opened. You will find half bottles easily accessible on the South coast of Spain.

Manzanilla: I have to declare now, that this is totally my favourite. Try this, nicely chilled, or even over some ice, with vine grilled boquerones or sardines. This pale, dry wine, often more delicate than a fino, is matured in the coastal region of Sanlucar de Barrameda. Folk say that its proximity to the sea gives the wine a slightly salty flavour. To me, this wine brings out the true flavour of the Palomino grape.

Amontillado: This fino wine is cask aged to become darker, more powerful and pungent. These wines are naturally dry.

Oloroso: Heavier and less brilliant than fino when they are young, they mature to great richness and pungency. They are naturally dry, but are often sweetened for sale.

Palo Cortado: This rare style of sherry, is close to the Oloroso with some of the nutty Amontillado characteristics.

Top quality sherry has to be one of the best value wines in the world. Supreme old dry sherries cost less than a bottle of Chardonnay. Drink it with prawns or smoked salmon, there is little to rival this amazing wine – sherry is underappreciated and a globally neglected wine treasure.

MCB tip: The Palomino grape produces a wine of rather bland and neutral characteristics. This neutrality is actually what makes Palomino an ideal grape because it is so easily enhanced by the Sherry winemaking process. Personally and I guess it's because I love the grape, if I get the opportunity to try a bottle a nicely chilled Palomino dry white table wine, I jump at the chance.

PORT

Port is made from red wine produced in the vineyards of the Douro Valley in Portugal, from grapes that you will most likely never have heard of before. The young wine is then fortified by the addition of a neutral grape spirit (brandy) known as Aguardente in order to stop the fermentation, leaving residual sugar in the wine, and to boost the alcohol content up to as much as 22% ABV. The wine is put into barrels, called Pipes, at Vila Nova de Gaia (Porto), where it is barrel matured for varying lengths of time by the Shippers (that is the producers, blenders and bottlers), before being bottled. Vintage Port is bottled at a fairly young age and matured in the bottle.

Ruby Port: is the least expensive and usually made from the lower quality wine, which is wood aged for around two years and bottled while still young, fruity and bright red (ruby) in colour.

Tawny Port: as you might expect, is tawny in colour and ready to drink when bottled. It is made from a blend of grapes from several different years and can be aged in wood for as long as 40 years. The label typically indicates the number of years.

Late Bottled Vintage (LBV):   does what is says on the label. This port is made from single vintage grapes, that aren't as high quality as those for vintage ports. LBVs are generally aged in wood from four to six years and are considered to be high quality ruby ports.

Vintage Port: This is the best and most expensive. It must be made from grapes of a single vintage (year) and only the best years, those considered superior, are "declared" vintages. Vintage ports are initially barrel aged and must be bottled with two years; the very best can age 50 years or more. Some of the best I have ever tasted were from the classic vintage years of the 1960s.

"Passing the Port"

The age old tradition of 'Passing the Port' is believed to come from British naval customs for serving the wine. The decanter of port is placed in front of the host who then serves the guest to his right, then passes the decanter to the guest on his left (port-side). The port is then passed to the left all the way back to the host.

SMOKING ON YACHTS

The general consensus is that no smoking is permitted inside at all on commercial yachts or superyachts. Guests who wish to smoke would normally be expected to do so, on the aft deck only and close attention must be paid to any lit cigarettes or cigars which are left lit, or partially lit in ash trays. This creates an extreme fire hazard.

On larger yachts it is important to advise guests not to throw any lit cigarettes or cigars over the side, as the item may be sucked back onto a lower deck, hence creating a fire hazard. It is a good idea to provide smokers with a deep ash tray, containing ice cubes, which will hold ash and therefore prevent it from flying about. It is also an effective way of extinguishing cigarettes and cigars as the ice melts. Owners generally do not encourage their guests to smoke and crew are normally not allowed to smoke onboard.

CIGARS

Havana (Cuba) cigars are regarded as being the best of all hand-made cigars. Cigars made in Jamaica are also very good and tend to be milder in flavour and considerably less expensive. It is critical, especially onboard a yacht, that cigars are stored between 18-19°C at a relative humidity of 55 to 60°, with as little variation as possible. To help achieve this, it is good practice to buy individual cigars in tubes, which are lined with a veneer of cedar wood and hermetically sealed. Cigars stored like this should remain in good condition for a long time.

Cigars may also be stored in a humidor (also lined with cedar wood) which has a pad on the inside of the lid, which is kept damp (not wet), which maintains the humidity – hence the name: humidor. The reason for the use of cedar wood is because the aroma of the cedar blends well with the cigars and because cedar wood is porous, it enables the cigars to 'breath'.

A cigar should be smooth and firm to the touch. It should not be dry or brittle. The open end should be smooth and even, the other end will usually require cutting with a cigar cutter. It is 'good form' to offer your guests the cigar cutter, so that they can do this themselves.

SHAPES & SIZES

Cigars come in a variety of shapes and sizes, however the three most important are:

- Coronas (5½ inch)
- Petit Coronas (5 inch)
- Très Petit Coronas (4¼ inch)

SMOKING CIGARS

There will be a band around the cigar and it is generally accepted that this will be removed before lighting. If not already cut, then a V-shaped cut or slice cut with a cigar cutter is required for the 'closed' end. This will allow the cigar to draw easily, which is essential to the good smoking.

Cigars should never be lit with a petrol lighter, as this will leave an unpleasant taste to the cigar. They must be lit with either a gas lighter or match.

CIGAR TERMS

These terms classify the wrapper (outer) leaf of the cigar, according to their colour:

- Claro (CCC) –   light coloured cigar
- Colorado Claro (CC) –   medium coloured cigar
- Colorado Maduro (CM) –   very dark coloured cigar
- Maduro (M) –   extremely dark coloured cigar

SAMPLE YACHT & SUPERYACHT MENUS
different styles

As much of the industry operates in the Mediterranean, a good place to start on researching weekly menu plans is often based around the diverse cuisine of the Med. The important thing for you to think about is identifying dishes that you are confident in preparing and cooking for your guests. Always try to incorporate some local dishes into your repertoire; practice them and become confident in their production and presentation. Many of the smaller yacht charters operate in the central and eastern Med and increasingly, marinas are appearing on the North African coast, providing chefs with new challenges of researching and cooking with some of the beautiful spices which are synonymous with North African cuisine. Other new and emerging destinations, such as Croatia, will require further investigation.

I have already briefly mentioned Pacific Rim and Fusion cookery. These days, as luxury yachts move from ocean to ocean, there are increasing numbers which visit the Pacific and Asian regions, where different foods are sometime sampled for the first time. A good chef will already have done some research before hand and will have drawn up some menus prior to their visit. Although I have not included many of this type of recipe, I offer you a short insight into both below.

Pacific Rim
This is truly a cuisine of medleys, combining Pacific Island foods, Asian cooking techniques, Californian freshness and a host of other cultural and culinary influences. You will find everything from seafood tacos and shitake mushroom quesadillas to Japanese 'potstickers' (Oriental dumplings) and seared fish with peanut sauce.

Pacific Rim cooking has been described as "ingredient driven", meaning that Pacific Rim cooks use a recipe's main ingredients, mainly wonderful fresh food, as the focus of each dish. Also "Asian fusion", "Euro-Pacific" or "Regional Hawaiin" cuisine are ways of cooking, which enhance a great diversity of beautiful fresh foods with healthy cooking methods i.e. grilling, steaming or wok stir-frying.

The ingredients that drive the recipes include exotic, tropical fruit, including fruit salsas, fresh vegetables, rocket, avocados, red onions, tomatoes, cucumbers, just-caught seafood, sesame seeds, nuts, and flavourful, tangy sauces. Herbs and spices are crucial to Pacific Rim seasoning, but they're used to gently enhance the main ingredients, not to disguise or overpower them.

A few ideas for Pacific Rim flavourings are: cardamom, basil, dried mushrooms, dried tomato flakes, sesame seeds, sprouting seeds and the fiery wasabi – to be used with care!

Fusion
Just ask yourself – what happens when North, South, East and West converge in the kitchen? Answer: Fusion cuisine.

Fusion cuisine is the general term for the combinations of various forms of cookery and ingredients; the concept can take several different forms. One approach is regional fusion, which combines the cuisine of a region or sub-region into a single eating experience. For example, Asian Fusion restaurants have become popular in many parts of the USA, often featuring Indian, East Asian and South-East Asian dishes alongside one-another.

Another manifestation of fusion is a more eclectic approach featuring original dishes using varieties of ingredients from various cuisines and regions, and then combining them. This type of restaurant may like to be identified as being 'en vogue' and have no singular thematic cohesion, other than innovative eclecticism in their menus. This type of restaurant may feature a broad variety of dishes, inspired by combinations of various regional cuisines with new ideas.

The third approach is to use foods which are based on one cuisine, but prepared using ingredients and flavours inherent to another cuisine or cuisines. For instance: pizza, made with cheddar and pepper jack cheese, salsa, refried beans and other common taco ingredients is often marketed as "Taco Pizza", which, in very basic terms is a fusion of Italian-American and American-Mexican cuisines.

Since fusion cuisine is a general term, it is legitimately applied to all three descriptions noted above. While many feature dishes from Greek, Italian and sometimes Asian cuisine side-by-side, the restaurants are generally not considered fusion, as they fail to combine any elements of the cooking styles and also have no over-arching fusion or eclectic theme.

I have been searching for a really good fusion cookery book for some time, but without success, or at least until last year, when I spent a day at Hotelympia, the Hospitality and Catering Exhibition at the Excel Centre in Docklands (London). I was wondering around the exhibition and came across a demonstration kitchen, which was in full swing; cameras, spotlights and a large attentive audience, hanging on every word. What I head was the familiar New Zealand accent of inspirational fusion chef Peter Gordon. I have to admit, that I had not heard of this guy before, but as soon as I got home, I checked out the website and found 'Fusion – a Culinary Journey' on the Amazon website. This book really is worth a shout and also makes a good semi Auto-B read, which I found quite entertaining. Peter is truly one of the original fusion pioneers and ground breakers, with his daring combinations of ingredients, which I would previously have been frightened of putting together. This has opened up a whole new world of cooking for me.

Sample charter menus below

You must take note, that in my menu examples below, I have written these in the style of the book, usually using capital letters for the intro' word only. However, when presenting your sample seven day menus along with a job application, you should incorporate capital letters utilising normal capitalisation conventions i.e.Champagne sorbet or Champagne Sorbet, Portabello mushrooms or Portabello Mushrooms, Basque style Montaditos etc; these should be acceptable.

My personal advice is this – use capitals in moderation. For instance – 'Key Lime Pie' may be acceptable, when 'Key lime pie' may look less attractive to some, although it can stand out more on a page full of capital letters. The problem is, I guess, that some folk would totally disagree with my thinking and say the exact opposite – that excessive capitalisation enhances the appearance of a menu.

Another way to script a sample menu, is to use capitals for the ingredient items and use non-capitalisation for words such as: and, with, served with, or, for …… etc.

So, my final word on this is that you play around with your sample menus until you feel that they visually represent what your cooking is trying to say to a potential employer.

BVIs (British Virgin Islands)
Menus by Elli Rea

7 Day Sample Menu Plan

Monday
Breakfast: Blueberry pancakes with crispy bacon and maple syrup
Lunch: Crunchy Keralan salad and blackened prawns
Hors d'oeuvres: Crudité vegetables and garlic bread sticks
served with homemade Mediterranean dips
Dinner: Pork tenderloin served with lemon garlic butterbeans
and balsamic glaze
Dessert: Coconut creams with caramelised pineapple

Tuesday
Breakfast: Feta cheese and spinach omelette
Lunch: Tomato and olive spaghetti
served with a green salad and garlic bread
Hors d'oeuvres: Mini asparagus and mascarpone tartlets
Dinner: Steak served with creamy mushroom sauce
with green bean and chorizo salad
Dessert: Frozen berry brandy snap baskets

Wednesday
Breakfast: Wholemeal raspberry and banana muffins
with fresh fruit smoothies
Lunch: Caesar salad with tiger prawns served with garlic bread sticks
Hors d'oeuvres: Chicken goujons served with sweet chilli dipping sauce
Dinner: Cod loin wrapped in Palma ham served with a herbed potato cake
Dessert: Classic key lime pie

Thursday
Breakfast: Warm banana bread with yoghurt and maple syrup
Lunch: Roasted squash and pearl barley salad
Hors d'oeuvres: Greek style cheese pies
Dinner: Chicken with feta and herb stuffing served with lemon potatoes
Dessert: Pear tarts with hot fudge sauce

Friday
Breakfast: Cinnamon and apple French toast
Lunch: Cajun spiced chicken wraps with oriental coleslaw
Hors d'oeuvres: Bruschetta with pesto and roasted tomatoes
Dinner: Teriyaki salmon with noodles and stir fried vegetables
Dessert: Dark chocolate and orange liqueur BBQ bananas

Saturday
Breakfast: Scrambled eggs and smoked salmon on a toasted bagel
Lunch: Tomato and mozzarella tartlets on a bed of rocket
Hors d'oeuvres: Mini lamb koftas with a cucumber and mint yoghurt
Dinner: Poached chicken breast with Palma ham and spinach
served with steamed vegetables
Dessert: Tiramisu

Sunday
Breakfast: Traditional full English breakfast:
Bacon, sausages, egg, mushrooms and grilled tomatoes
Lunch: Mediterranean couscous salad with freshly baked bread
Hors d'oeuvres: Satay chicken skewers with spicy peanut sauce
Dinner: Mushroom and tarragon strudel with Madeira sauce
and crushed new potatoes
Dessert: Grilled mango with ginger mascarpone cream and ginger caramel

BVIs (British Virgin Islands)
Menus by Carly Williams

7 Day Sample Menu Plan

Daily Breakfast Selection
Freshly baked pastries, croissants, breads & muffins
Fresh fruit platter, cold meats, cheeses
Selection of cereals & yoghurts
(Choice of alternative cooked breakfast items on request)

Day 1
Breakfast
Daily selection as above
+ Pineapple & cinnamon pancakes with warm maple syrup

Lunch
Freshly baked bread
Peach & avocado salad with a ginger and coriander dressing
Thai spiced, coconut steamed mussels
Key lime pie

Pre Dinner Canapés
Mini chicken satay skewers
Watermelon fan

Dinner
Vietnamese spring rolls
Pan roasted duck in a spicy citrus sauce with a green papaya & rice noodle salad
Caramelized bananas with coconut ice-cream

Day 2
Breakfast
Daily selection as above
+ Eggs Benedict

Lunch
Freshly baked bread
Pumpkin, feta and pancetta risotto
Rocket & parmesan salad
Lemon drizzle slice

Pre Dinner Canapés
Crab fritters
Grilled asparagus & prosciutto bundles

Dinner
Wild mushroom soup with garlic & parsley
Herb crusted rack of lamb with a spicy eggplant relish
served with a tomato, tarragon & bulgar wheat salad
Red wine poached pears with mascarpone

Day 3
Breakfast
Daily selection
+ Full English cooked breakfast

Lunch
Fresh baked bread
Salmon, mahi mahi and sweet potato cakes
Mango salad
Chocolate & chilli brownies with ice cream

Pre Dinner Canapés
Crudités with homemade dips
Spring rolls

Dinner
Garlic baked prawns
Homemade chicken Chu Chee curry with jasmine rice
Coconut milk pana cotta

Day 4
Breakfast
Daily selection
+ Smoked salmon & scrambled egg on multi grain toast

Lunch
Freshly baked bread
Beef Tataki with tempura onions
Asian slaw
Tuille basket filled with fresh berries and cream

Pre Dinner Canapés
Crunchy Zucchini flowers stuffed with haloumi, mint & ginger
Prawn & mango crostini

Dinner
Caramelized onion & goats cheese tart
Monkfish bake with cherry tomatoes & pesto butter
served with crushed new potatoes
Sticky Fig Pudding

Day 5
Breakfast
Daily selection
+ Blueberry pancakes

Lunch
Freshly baked bread
Butternut squash & sweet potato soup
Sundried tomato & chorizo frittata
Green olive, walnut and pomegranate salad
Tart Tatin

Pre Dinner Canapés
Calamari
Marinated olives

Dinner
Ceviche
Pork fillet wrapped in Parma ham, stuffed with leeks, dates & gorgonzola
on a bed of baby spinach & potato rosti
Chocolate banana cream

Day 6
Breakfast
Daily selection
+ Feta & spinach omelette

Lunch
Freshly baked bread
Seared scallop & bacon tagliatelle
Green salad
Pear & frangipani tart

Pre Dinner Canapés
Crispy skin mackerel on focaccia croutons
Red pepper, basil and cream cheese wheels

Dinner
Duck proscuitto & rocket salad with truffle honey
Baked sea bass on a bed of herbed greens & lentils
Passion fruit cheesecake

Day 7
Breakfast
Daily selection
+ Cinnamon French toast

Lunch
Freshly baked bread
Sesame seared tuna salad with wasabi dressing
Avocado Salad
Praline parfait

Pre Dinner Canapés
Sushi Nori rolls

Dinner
Goats cheese, beetroot and walnut stack
Peppered beef fillet with roasted baby carrots & creamed parsnip mash
Pomegranate and Vodka sorbet

Sample Menus
Virgin Yacht Charters
for the Mediterranean & Caribbean
Menus by Joanne Plowman

Providing food of the highest standard, delighting charterers with food from every corner of the globe, designed with preferences in mind. Special diets and children are always catered for.

Delectable tropical cuisine is paired with excellent wines for each meal.

Breakfast
All served with fresh fruit platter, chilled juices
& freshly brewed tea or coffee

Eggs Benedict with grilled asparagus
Spinach & goat's cheese frittata
Bacon & ricotta cake with roasted tomatoes
Freshly baked cranberry muffins
Fluffy omelette of choice
Traditional English, American or Continental breakfast

Lunch
All served with a basket of fresh bread

Seared Thai Chicken with tomato chilli jam
Brie & walnut quesadillas with fresh tropical salsa
Fettucine with a walnut and parsley pesto
Freshly grilled tuna niçoise salad
Goats cheese & leek tart
Asian beef and watercress salad
Spicy crab cakes on a bed of baby greens

Hors d'oeuvres

Jumbo shrimp with a sesame & ginger dip
Roasted cherry tomato bruschetta
Chicken satay with a peanut sauce
Sushi selection
Baked brie with strawberries and walnuts
Conch fritters with a dipping sauce

Starters
Mussels in a sweet basil sauce
Caribbean shrimp salad with lime vinaigrette
Crispy vegetable spring rolls with a sweet & sour sauce
Baked feta with onion & olive
Spicy Thai asparagus soup with lobster
Warm goats cheese salad with a balsamic reduction

Main course
Accompanied by a matched wine selection

Citrus marinated grilled swordfish
Roast lamb with garlic & thyme, served with creamed potatoes
Mojo marinated steaks with cilantro sauce and Chilean salsa
Crispy stir fry duck on sesame chow mein noodles
Coconut spinach red snapper
Roasted pork tenderloin with molasses & mustard
Vegetable curry with cucumber raita & homemade mango chutney

All served with a selection of fresh vegetables

Desserts
Toffee crunch caramel cheesecake with freshly whipped cream
Spiced apple pie with vanilla ice cream
Rum chocolate mousse
Blueberry crème brulée
Chocolate Kahlua cake with roasted pineapple
Hot rum and citrus salad
Sticky toffee pudding

*All served with freshly brewed tea, coffee
& a selection of liqueurs*

Reproduced with the kind permission of Chris & Joanne Plowman at Virgin Yacht Charters

www.virginsailing.com
info@virginsailing.com
sailthecat@hotmail.com

Raiza's Seven Day
Mediterranean Menu Plan

Raiza Rodriguez has over five years experience as a superyacht chef, working the Med, usually out of Antibes or Palma and has worked both permanent and freelance charter. She has sailing and racing experience and has cooked on both motor and sail, including Atlantic and Pacific crossings for charter and crew. I totally love the Spanish influence in her menus.

Canapes and Hors d'oeuvres
Smoked salmon and fresh dill spread
Herbed foie mousse served with water crackers
Varied cheese platter
Assorted Spanish tapas
Crab and spinach stuffed wontons
with hoisin sauce
Goat cheese and caramelized fig tarts
Fresh vegetable crudités served with roquefort dressing
Black bean & garlic or red pepper hummus
served with warm pita chips

Daily Breakfast
Fresh fruit salad
Assorted croissants, fresh baked muffins, scones & pastries
quiches, tortilla espanola, frittatas
Bacon and sausage
Hot breakfasts cooked to order daily:
Eggs, pancakes, waffles etc.

Day 1
Lunch
Smoked salmon and parsley-dill cheese with mixed greens
stuffed in a wrap & a side of creamy cucumber dipping sauce
served with pesto potato salad
Apple crisp with candied walnuts & cinnamon gelato

Dinner
Starter: Spicy melon and chilli gaspacho

Entrée: Filet mignon topped with seared foie gras
served with grilled asparagus in a port reduction

Dessert: Plate of 3 dark distinct chocolate truffles
With Kiwi, Chili & Ginger fillings
garnished with crushed hibiscus sea salt
& drizzled with Marqués de Griñon olive oil

Day 2
Lunch
Thai beef salad served with a mango chilli vinaigrette
Slow roasted peaches with caramel sauce

Dinner
Starter: Avocado mint soup
Entrée: Seared Ahi tuna served on wakame salad
Dessert: Green tea and azuki mochi

Day 3
Lunch
Grilled herby chicken, with avocado served on micro greens
topped with blue cheese crumbles & chocolate-balsamic vinaigrette
Fresh fig tart with crème anglaise

Dinner
Starter: Lobster and prawn cocktail served in a martini glass
& topped with tequila cilantro mayonnaise
Entrée: Lavender-crusted duck magret served with grilled vegetables
Dessert: A tower of Langue de Chat
filled with a vanilla-rum mascarpone cream
& wild berries drizzled with caramel

Day 4
Lunch
Cava seared sea scallops served with micro greens
& a light ginger mandarin dressing
Valrhona Chocolate Mousse

Dinner
Entrée: Grilled Lamb chops served with lemon potatoes
& madeira porcini sauce
Dessert: Tiramisu

Day 5
Lunch
Grilled Chinese spiced duck breast wrap
served with Jicama slaw
Citrus sorbet

Dinner
Starter: Crab stuffed portobello mushrooms
drizzled with a balsamic reduction
Entrée: Seared cod served over a cream sherry sauce
garnished with chorizo shavings and sautéed spinach
Dessert: Margarita key lime pie

Day 6
Lunch
Open faced roast beef sandwich with aged provolone
& parsley oil, served with steak fries and aioli on the side

Poached strawberries with champagne sabayon

Starter: Smoked duck spring rolls with sweet chilli sauce
Entrée: Grilled salmon, topped with green mango curry sauce
served with mint basmati rice
Dessert: Basil lemon sorbet

Day 7
Lunch
King prawn satay served with coconut ginger rice
Lemon thyme cheesecake

Dinner
Starter: Onion soup with sage brown butter
and grated lemon zest
Entrée: Roasted rosemary rabbit tenderloins served with sweet potato medallions
garnished with creamy field mushroom sauce
Dessert: Crepe filled with bananas foster and topped with walnuts & cream

Raiza's Sample 5 Course Menu Options

Appetizers include assorted canapés, such as mini spinach quiche, lobster cocktail, chorizo stuffed wild mushrooms, goat cheese and strawberry puffs, and Basque style Montaditos.
*All Meals include fresh crusty French bread or assorted rolls served with herbed butter and aioli.

Menu 1
Roasted red pepper soup

Mint beetroot salad with mandarin vinaigrette

Lemon basil sorbet

Seared foie gras topped filet mignon
served with lemon grilled asparagus and madeira reduction

Ginger chocolate truffles with sea salt and olive oil

Menu 2
Avocado mint soup

Mixed wild greens with green dijon vinaigrette

Crystallized pineapple ginger kisses

Violet and lavender crusted duck with roasted herb potatoes

Warm apple crisp in caramel sauce with crème anglaise

Menu 3
Vichyssoise

Maple smoked bacon and goats cheese salad
with strawberry-fig vinaigrette

Cucumber melon granita

Champagne seared sea bass in lemon tarragon cream
served with grilled haricots verts

Tahitian vanilla bean tarts
topped with wild berries & fresh cream

Sample Mediterranean/Greek
Charter Menu
S/Y ANTARA
Menus by Jana Kruta

This fabulous 46m Perini Navi sailing yacht was returned to "better than new" condition following an extensive refit at Perini Navi, Viareggio, Italy during the winter of 2006/07. Her guest spaces, both interior and exterior, were completely refurbished and she now boasts an Italian marble top bar in the Dining Salon and an exercise area in the Master Stateroom. She has an extended flying bridge, featuring a large Jacuzzi, spa pool and a swim platform, which extends from the transom to facilitate easy entry and exit to the sea. She has underwater lights, which create a soft glow in the blue seawater at night all around the yacht.

Jana has held the position of chef onboard Antara for well over two years. She has previously worked on a 40m sailing yacht Destination Fox Harbor. Jana completed a course at the New Zealand School of Food and Wine and apart from her culinary skills, has managed to sail across the Pacific region three times!

When asked about her favourite style of food, Jan is a touch unwilling to commit herself to any particular region. After much pleading and haranguing, she did mention enjoying the fresh, light, flavourful style of the Med and added that Asian ingredients get her creative juices flowing.

Lunches

Salad with fried haloumi cheese, orange & walnuts
Saffron risotto with langoustines
Vodka & watermelon sorbet

Marinated artichokes & tomatoes on salad greens
Grilled tuna with olive tapenade
Almond baklava with thyme honey

Green salad with cherry tomatoes, mozzarella & basil
Vittel Tonnato thinly sliced veal with creamy tuna sauce & capers
Fresh figs with Greek yoghurt & honey

Asparagus & rocket salad with parmesan
& herbed mayonnaise dressing
John Dory with a tomato & cardamom sauce
Lemon ricotta cake

White peaches with prosciutto salad
Fresh pasta with lobster in a light tomato & herb sauce
Limoncello sorbet

Greek salad with feta & kalamata olives
Braised marinated octopus
Almond & yoghurt cake with citrus syrup

S/Y ANTARA
Dinners

Starter: Chilled Avocado soup with toasted coconut & tomato topping
Entrée: Herb & Dijon crusted rack of lamb
with couscous & roasted Mediterranean vegetables
Dessert: Sticky date pudding with caramel sauce

Starter: Salad of avocado & crab with pink grapefruit dressing
Entrée: Roasted poussin with lemon crumbs,
baby potatoes and sauté of green & white beans
Dessert: White chocolate cheesecake with balsamic strawberries

Starter: Sweet pepper soup with chilli goat's cheese
Entrée: Slowly cooked beef fillet with soft polenta,
pecorino cheese & mushroom sauce
Dessert: Warm chocolate fondant with raspberry coulis

Starter: Rosemary kebabs of marinated mozzarella & bacon
on rocket leaves
Entrée: Braised veal chops with honey & red grapes
Dessert: Apple strudel with vanilla ice cream

Starter: Ricotta stuffed courgette flowers
with roast pepper sauce
Entrée: Whole roasted sea bass on a bed of herbs
with saffron scalloped potatoes & roasted fennel
Dessert: Strawberry crème brulée

Starter: Roasted beetroot & goats cheese salad
Entrée: Pan fried duck breast with red wine & fig sauce,
with wild rice apple salad & asparagus
Dessert: Chocolate mousse with chestnut cream

Gluten Free or other Speciality Menu Samples Available Upon Request

www/syantara.com

Two week Caribbean Menu Plan
"Fresh local produce prepared to taste daily"

Breakfasts
Guests may choose whatever they desire from an array of fresh fruit, croissants with butter and jam, smoothies, French toast with whipped cream and syrup, crêpes with a variety of fillings, homemade pancakes, cold cereals, smoked salmon with cream cheese on bagels, and of course the option of a full English or American style breakfast or any combination of the above will be available everyday for the guest's enjoyment.

Lunch: Spanish omelette
Dinner to start: Sautéed wild mushrooms in a white wine sauce
Main: BBQ Swordfish with capers & lemon butter sauce
with summer vegetables & wild rice

Lunch: Vermicelli Pescatore
Dinner to start: Spinach salad with feta cheese, black olives
& rainbow peppers in a creamy dressing
Main: Glazed balsamic chicken, carrots in a brown sugar & butter sauce,
served with spicy couscous
Dessert: Mixed berry cheese cake

Lunch: Pork pesto & mozzarella parcels
Dinner to start: Leek & potato soup
Main: Grilled Scallops and spinach with a creamy shrimp sauce
served over angel hair pasta
Dessert: Apple pie

Lunch: Trinidadian bacon & brown rice
Dinner to start: Chicken Caesar salad
Main: Beef kebabs with green veg served with lemon couscous
Dessert: Chocolate hazelnut pots

Lunch: Curried Tobago shrimp
Dinner to start: Cabbage with gruyere cheese & crème fraîche
Main: Korean style BBQ chicken served
with wild rice in a mushroom sauce
Dessert: Strawberry tarts

Lunch: Mango chicken salad
Dinner to start: Rich tomato soup with fresh cream & crusty bread
Main: Pork, snow pea & cashew stir fry served over honey garlic noodles
Dessert: Lemon custard sponge

Lunch: Creamy spiced mussels
Dinner to start: Mozzarella, white anchovies & beetroot salad
Main: Grilled chicken a la king served in buttery toast cups
Dessert: Blackberry & apple crumble topped with fresh cream

Lunch: Spicy meatball soup with crusty bread
Dinner to start: Chicken, green apple & tomato salad
Main: Local white fish in Jamaican white wine sauce
Dessert: Banoffee cheesecake

Lunch: Warm bacon, parmesan & avocado salad
Dinner to start: Parsley soup with crusty bread
Main: Penne pasta in a creamy sauce with ham and asparagus
Dessert: Lemon meringue pie

Lunch: Chicken & black bean stir fry served over noodles
Dinner to start: Cold meat tray with cheese & cracker variety
Main: Salmon steaks pan fried in a lemon mustard sauce,
served with fresh vegetables & long grain rice
Dessert: Vanilla ice cream

Lunch: Prawn salad served over a bed of curried shell pasta
Dinner to start: Miniature beef & vegetable skewers
Main: Black peppered lamb shanks with garlic butter mash
Dessert: Lemon & lime syllabubs

Lunch: Niçoise salad
Dinner to start: Ham & asparagus pastry roll
Main: Gnocchi with broccoli & wild mushrooms
in a parmesan & black pepper sauce
Dessert: White chocolate tarts

Lunch: Jamaican avocado & lime marinated shrimp
Dinner to start: Soft cheese tray with crunchy veg hummus and crackers
Main: Local white fish poached with lime & red onion
served with parsnip & potato mash
Dessert: Fresh fruit salad served with cream

Lunch: American style potato salad
Dinner to start: Cheesy black bean nachos with olives & sour cream
Main: Jerk chicken thighs with black eyed peas
& mixed summer vegetables
Dessert: Deep fried bananas with custard & powdered sugar

Vegetable & Vegetarian Ideas

Aubergine, kumara, & pepper bake
Beetroot, carrot & orange salad
Braised leeks
Broccoli with ginger
Courgettes with garlic
Creamy camembert potato
Cucumber salad
Fried diced courgette
Fried diced pumpkin
Gazpacho
Goats cheese salad
Greek salad
Hazelnut green salad
Herb pate
Herb stuffed tomatoes
Humous, tabouleh & pitta bread
Pasta & ratatouille sauce
Pasta salad with saffron
Roasted aubergine
Sweet potato gratin
Red pepper purée with okra
Roast carrots
Roast tomatoes with basil oil
Roasted vegetable couscous salad with harissa
Potato & rosemary cakes
Spinach soufflé with tomato sauce
Stir fry cabbage with lime & coconut
Tomato & olive tarts
Tomato & tarragon
Tomato mousse with roasted peppers
Turkish carrots
Twice baked potato
Tzatziki
Vegetable & almond black bean stir fry
Vegetable korma
Vegetable strudel

One Week Vegetarian Meal Plan
(Plan to be adjusted to guests' level of vegetarianism)

Lunch: Fucelli & fresh summer vegetables in a rich Parmesan dressing
Dinner to start: Parsley soup with chives & cream
Main: Fresh tuna steaks served with roasted Mediterranean vegetables
Dessert: Chocolate hazelnut pot

Lunch: Black bean nachos with cheese & black olives
Dinner to start: Thai style carrot & mango salad
Main: Baked egg plant gratin
Dessert: Lemon & lime syllabub

Lunch: Avocado & tomato salad with balsamic vinegar
Dinner to start: Spinach soup topped with cheese, served with crusty bread
Main: Homemade leek & mushroom quiche served with a fresh green salad
Dessert: Apple pie served with fresh cream

Lunch: Mozzarella salad
Dinner to start: Fresh hummus with crusty bread
& assortment of crunchy vegetables
Main: Mixed summer vegetables in a spicy creamed peanut sauce
served over wild rice or noodles
Dessert: Strawberry tarts

Lunch: Caesar salad with homemade dressing
Dinner to start: Mozzarella, white anchovies & pickled beetroot salad
Main: Baked potato with goats cheese & chipotle cream
Dessert: Berry cheese cake

Lunch: Greek salad with feta & fresh black olives
Dinner to start: Tomato soup with fresh cream & crusty bread
Main: Vegetarian lasagne with fresh spinach & asparagus
Dessert: Baked lemon sponge with fresh custard

Lunch: Pesto and mozzarella parcels
Dinner to start: Sautéed wild mushrooms in white wine sauce
Main: Fettuccini Alfredo with garlic & fresh broccoli
Dessert: Fresh fruit salad with lime & fresh cream

BVI Vegan Charter
(Vegan menu plan provided by Elli Rea)

Day 1
Lunch: Tomato & olive pasta with green salad & focaccia
Dinner to start: Mediterranean Vegetable Tart
Main: Mushroom & tarragon strudel with Madeira sauce
Dessert: Poached pears

Day 2
Brex: Granola berry smoothies. Fresh fruit platter
Lunch: Semolina cake & green salad
Dinner to start: Garlic mushrooms stuffed with green pea pesto
Main: Roasted tomato risotto with balsamic roasted beef tomatoes
Dessert: Tropical fruit crumble

Day 3
Brex: Blueberry pancakes. Fresh fruit platter
Lunch: Mediterranean couscous salad. Humus with pita bread
Dinner to start: Crostini with tomatoes, caper & thyme
Main: Jewelled pumpkin rice with roasted root vegetables
Dessert: Mango with ginger cream cheese

Day 4
Brex: Granola, honey & banana smoothies. Fresh fruit platter
Lunch: Caribbean roti with papaya salad
Dinner to start: Mini falafel pitas with mint yoghurt
Main: Ratatouille stuffed courgettes with salted baked new potatoes
Dessert: Cranberry and apple crunch

Day 5
Brex: Scrambled tofu with toast. Fresh fruit platter
Lunch: Kerelan salad with blackened tofu
Dinner to start: Meze platter of olives, roasted peppers
& artichokes with crackers
Main: Sweet potato, wild mushroom & chestnut cakes
with Greek baked beans and vegetable gravy
Dessert: Peach melba brulée

Day 6
Brex: Granola berry smoothies. Fresh fruit platter
Lunch: Squash & barley salad
Dinner to start: Poppadoms, onion chutney, mango chutney,
lime pickle & raita
Main: Thai sweet potato curry, lentil dahl with jasmine rice
Dessert: Raw blueberry cobbler

Day 7
Brex: Banana muffins, granola muesli. Fruit platter
Lunch: Spicy chickpea couscous
Dinner to start: Indian snacks
Main: Pineapple fried rice
Dessert: Rum soaked baked bananas

Departure brex: Granola & yoghurt compotes. Fruit platter

USEFUL LISTINGS
& WEBSITES

Allergy Action
www.actionallergy.org.uk
+44 (0) 1727 855294
info@allergyaction.org

Allergy UK
www.allergyfoundation.com
+44 (0) 1322 619898
info@allergyuk.org

Ashburton Cookery School
Ashburton, Devon
Tel: (01364) 652784
www.ashburtoncookeryschool.co.uk

Blue Water Training
Antibes
Tel: +33 (0)4 93 34 47 73

Cocktails
Xtreme cocktail info'
www.in-the-spirit.co.uk

Corkers
Tel: +33 (0)4 93 77 51 13
Fax: +33 (0) 4 93 36 78 03
www.corkersfinewines.com

Denys
Chefs uniforms & more
www.denys.co.uk
+44 (0)1372 377904

Dockwalk
Essential monthly magazine
www.dockwalk.com

Food Standards Agency (FSA)
Safer food, better business
www.food.gov.uk
www.eatwell.gove.uk

Leith's
London, W8
Tel: 020 7229 0177
e.mail: info@leiths.com

Nisbets
Catering uniform and equipment (UK)
www.nisbets.co.uk

Rick Stein
Padstow Seafood School, Cornwall
Tel: 01841 532700
e.mail: reservations@rickstein.com
www.rickstein.com/seafood-school

Tante Marie
Woking, Surrey
Tel: 01483 726957
email: info@tantemarie.co.uk
www.tantemarie.com

The Anaphylaxis Campaign
www.anaphylaxis.org.uk
+44 (0) 1252 542029
info@anaphylaxis.org.uk

The Crew Report
www.thecrewreport.com

The Gables Cookery School
Tel: 01454 260444
info@thegablesschoolofcookery.co.uk
www.thegablesschoolofcookery.co.uk

The Vegetarian Society
www.vegsoc.org

TheCrewReport.com
Essential monthly mag
www.thecrewreport.com

UKSA
Cowes, Isle of Wight
Tel: +44 (0)1983 294941
www.uksa.org

Vins sans Frantières
www.vsfgroup.com
Tel: +33 4 92 29 88 66

Yachting Pages
www.yachting-pages.com

Yotcru
www.yotcru.com

www.allservices.net
www.apinchofitaly.wordpress.com
www.asianfood-recipes.com
www.askachef.com
www.bbc.co.uk/food
www.bbc.co.uk.food/cuisines/turkish
www.bbcgoodfood.com
www.bcnyacht.com
www.caribbeancaterers.com
www.chefolder.com
www.chefpaul.com/seasonings
www.cooks.com
www.cooking.com
www.cordonbleu.net
www.crewconnected.com
www.crewdiscount.com
www.deliaonline.com
www.denys.co.uk
www.earthlysupplies.com
www.fleursdecourgette.fr
www.floatplan.com
www.floridakeystreasures.com
www.genoainternationalsupplies.com
www.ichef.com
www.jamieoliver.com/recipes
www.keithfloydrecipes.com
www.lifestylefood.com.au/chefs/neilperry
www.lifestylefood.com.au/chefs/billgranger
www.marinewaypoints.com
www.myrecipes.com
www.nigela.com/recipes
www.nisbets.co.uk
www.pamperedchef.com
www.pasta-recipes-made-easy.com
www.provisioning@palapamarina.com
www.raymondblanc.com/bbc
www.rickstein.com/recipes
www.salvogrima.com
www.shiptoshoreinc.com
www.smereldafood.it
www.synfo.com
www.thecrewreport.com
www.thejamaicans.com
www.turnaround-france.com
www.workonaboat.com
www.veganchef.com
www.vsfgroup.com
www.yachtcrew-cv.com/crewagents
www.yachtandcrew.com

MY FAVORITE COOK BOOKS

Arabesque – A taste of Morocco, Turkey & Lebanon
Claudia Roden, Penguin/Michael Joseph, ISBN 978-0-718-14581-1

Balance and Harmony: Asian Food
Neil Perry, Murdoch Books, ISBN 9781740459082

Breakfast. Lunch. Tea – Rose Bakery
Rose Carrarini, Phaidon Press, ISBN978-0-7148-4465-7

Caribbean Flavours
Wendy Rahamut, Macmillan Caribbean, ISBN 0-333-93743-0

Celia Brooks Brown's Entertaining Vegetarians
Celia Brooks Brown, Brown Pavilion, ISBN 1-86205-534-3

Cruising Cuisine
Kay Pastorius, McGraw-Hill, ISBN 007-048703-0

Dix-Neuf. Cuisine du Terroir Corrézienne
Malcolm Alder-Smith, Leonie press, ISBN 1-901253-43-0

English Seafood Cookery
Rick Stein, Penguin, ISBN 0-140-29975-0

Fire: A World of Flavour
Christine Manfield, Penguin Global, ISBN 1920989390

French Leave
John Burton Race, Ebury Press, ISBN 978-0091898304

French Odyssey
Rick Stein, BBC Books, ISBN 978-0-563-52213-3

Fusion – A Culinary Journey
Peter Gordon, Jacqui Small, ISBN 1906417369

Good Food
Neil Perry, Murdoch Books, ISBN 9781740459235

Gordon Ramsey – Humble Pie
Gordon Ramsey, Harper Collins, ISBN 978-0-00-722967-3

How to be a Domestic Goddess. Baking & the Art of Comfort Cooking
Nigella Lawson, Chatto & Windus, ISBN 0-701-16888-9

How to Eat. The Pleasures & Principles of Good Food
Nigella Lawson, Chatto & Windus, ISBN 0-7011-6911-7

Jamie's Dinners
Jamie Oliver, Penguin, ISBN 0-718-14686-7

Jamie's Kitchen
Jamie Oliver, Penguin, ISBN 0-141-01037-1

Jamie's Italy
Jamie Oliver, Penguin, ISBN 0-718-14770-7

Le Cordon Bleu Complete Cooking Techniques
Morrow, ISBN 0-688-15206-6

Le Répertoire de la Cuisine (French copy)
Louis Saulnier, ISBN-10: 095018750X

Leiths Cookery Bible
Prue Leith & Caroline Waldgrave, Bloomsbury, ISBN 0-7475-6602-X

Leiths Techniques Bible
Susan Spaull & Lucinda Bruce-Gardyne,
Bloomsbury, ISBN 0-7475-6046-3

Made in Italy – Food and Stories
Giorgio Locatelli - ISB 0061351490

Mediterranean Cookery
Claudia Roden, BBC Books, ISBN 0-563-21248-9

Mediterranean Food. French Country Cooking. Summer cooking
Elizabeth David Classics, Grub Street, ISBN 1-902304-27-6

Majorcan Food & Cookery
Elizabeth Carter, Prospect books, ISBN 0-907325-43-2

Momofuku
David Chang & Peter Meehan, Random House, ISBN 978-0307451958

My Gastronomy
Nico Landenis, Ebury Press, ISBN 0-85223-682-4

Ottolenghi: The Cookbook
Yotam Ottolenghi & Sammi Tamimi, ISBN 978-0-091-92234-4

Plenty
Yotam Ottolenghi, Edbury Publishing, ISBN 10:0091933684

Practical Cookery (10th Ed)
David Foskett, Victor Ceserani, Ronald Kinton, Hodder Arnold,
ISBN 978-0-340-81147-4

Professional Cooking (5th Ed)
Wayne Gisslen, Wiley, ISBN 0-471-43625-9

Recipes from Provence
Andrée Maureau, Edisud, ISBN 2-85744-667-5

Sea Fare: A Chef's Journey Across the Ocean
Victoria Allman, ISBN 978-1-935254-02-7

Simple Mediterranean Cookery
Claudia Roden, BBC Books, ISBN 0-563-49327-5

Stirred But Not Shaken
Keith Floyd, Sidgwick & Jackson, ISBN 978-0-283-07105-8

Sydney Food
Bill Granger, Murdoch Books, ISBN 0-86411-991-7

The Arab Table, Recipes & Culinary Traditions
May, S, Bsisu, Morrow Cookbooks, ISBN 978-0060586140

The Best of Bread Book
Patricia Jacobs, Pan Books, ISBN 0-330-25519-3

The Food I Love
Neil Perry, Murdoch Books, ISBN 9780743292450

The Book of Desserts
Sally Taylor, Salamander, ISBN 0-86101-285-2

The Book of Jewish Food
Claudia Roden, Barnes & Noble, ISBN 978-0-394-53258-5

The Complete Book of Sushi
Hideo Dekura, Brigid Treloar & Ryuichi Yoshii, Apple Press,
ISBN 1-86302-066-2

The Hummingbird Bakery Cookbook
Tarek Malouf, Ryland Peters & Small, ISBN 978-1-84597-830-3

The Moro Cookbook
Samantha Clark & Samuel Clark, Ebury Press, ISBN 978-0-091-88084-2

The Ultimate Book of Fish & Shellfish
Kate Whiteman, Hermes House, ISBN 978-1844001958

White Slave
Marco Pierre White, Orion Books, ISBN 978-0-75287-4630

What Einstein Told His Cook. Kitchen Science Explained
Robert. L. Wolke, W.W.Norton & Co, ISBN 978-0-393-01183-8

BIBLIOGRAPHY

Allman, V, 2009, Sea Fare

Burton Race, J, 2003, French Leave

Carrarini, R, 2008, "Rose Bakery – Breakfast Lunch & Tea"

Diamond, P, 1992, Covent Garden Fish Book

Errico, J, 2007, Working on Yachts and Superyachts (2nd Ed)

Floyd, K, 2009, Stirred But Not Shaken

Floyd, K, 1992, Floyd on Spain

Food Safety for Supervisors, Chartered Institute of Environmental Health

Foskett, D, Ceserani, V, Kinton, R, Arnold, R, Practical Cookery (10th Ed)

Gordon, P, 2010, Fusion a Culinary Journey

Granger, W, 2004, Sydney Food

Gluck, M, 2008, The Great Wine Swindle

Johnson, H, 2008, Hugh Johnson's Pocket Wine Book

Ladenis, N, 1987, My Gastronomy

Oliver, J, 2005, Jamie Oliver - Jamie's Italy

Ottolenghi, Y, & Tamimi, S, 2008, Ottolenghi the Cookbook

Perry Lang, A, 2009, Serious Barbecue

Roden, C, 2005, Arabesque - A taste of Morocco, Turkey & Lebanon

Ramsey, G, 2006, Gordon Ramsey Humble Pie

Roots, L, 2009, Caribbean Food Made Easy

Slater, N, 1998, Nigel Slater's Real Food

Stein, R, 2005, French Odyssey

Stein, R, 1997, Fruits of the Sea

Stein, R, 1995, Taste of the Sea

Treuille, E & Erath, B, 2000, Barbecue

White, M, 1994, Marco Pierre White, Wild Food from Land & Sea

Whiteman, K, 2006, Fish & Shellfish (2nd Ed)

RECIPE INDEX

MINI TRANSLATION GUIDE
Italian, Spanish & French
Reproduced by kind permission of Lola (Lorenza) Savigni & UKSA.

All the translations below run in the same order: Italian, Spanish then French

COMMON WORDS & PHRASES

English	Italian	Spanish	French
Can I have	Posso avere	Me puerd dar	Je voudrais
Excuse me	Mi scusi	Perdone	Excusez-moi
Good morning	B uonjiorno	Buenos dia	Bonjour
Good evening	Buonasera	Buenas tardes	Bonsoir
Goodbye	Arrivederci	Adios	Au revoir
How much	Quanto	Cuanto	Combien
Is there…	C'e…	Hay…	Il y a
Please	Per favore	Por favor	S'il vous plait
Thankyou v.much	Grazie mille	Muchas gracias	Merci
When	Quando	Cuando	Quand
Where	Dove	Donde	Ou
Where is it	Dov'e	Donde esta	Ou est
Which	Quale	Cual	Que
Who	Chi	Quien	Qui
Why	Perche	Porque	Pourquoi

NUMBERS

0.	zero/cero/zero	11.	undici/once/onze
1.	uno/uno/un	12.	dodici/doce/douze
2.	due/dos/deux	13.	tredici/trece/treize
3.	tre/tres/trois	14.	quattordici/catorce/quatorze
4.	quattro/cuatro/quatre	15.	quindici/quince/quinze
5.	cinque/cinqo/cinq	16.	sedici/dieci-seis/seize
6.	sei/seis/six	17.	decussate/dieci-siete/dix-sept
7.	sette/siete/sept	18.	diciotto/dieci-ocho/dix-huit
8.	otto/ocho/huit	19.	diciannove/dieci-nueve/dix neuf
9.	nove/nueve/neuf	20.	venti/veinte/vingt
10.	dieci/diex/dix		

30	trenta/treinta/trente
40	quaranta/cuarenta/quarante
50	cinquanta/cincuenta/cinquante
60	sessanta/sesenta/soixante
70	settanta/setenta/soixante-dix
80	ottanta/ochenta/quatre-vingts
90	novanta/noventa/quatre-vingt-dix
100	cento/cien/cent/
1000	mille/mil/mille/
Half	mezzo/metta/demi

USEFUL SHOPPING PHRASES

English	Italian	Spanish	French
How much is it	Quanti costa	Cuanto vale	Ca coute combine
I would like	Vorrei	Quisiera	Je voudrais
100g	un etto	cien gramos	cent grammes (demi-kilo)
500g	mezzo chilo	medio kilo	demi kilo (un livre)
1 litre	un litro	un litro	un litre
a box	una scatola	un caja	une boite
a pack	una confezione	un paquete	un paquet
a piece	un pezzo	un trozo	un morceau
a dozen	una dizzina	una decena	un douzaine

Can I have a piece of this and a bit of that please?
- Mi darebbe un po' di questo e un po' di quello der per favour?
- Deme en poco de esto y un poco de aquello por favor?
- Donnez-moi un peu de ceci et un peu de cela s'il vous plaît?

Do you have a bigger/smaller pack please?
- Ha una confezione piu' grande/mas pequeno per favor?
- Tiene un paquete mas grande/mas pequeno por favor?
- Est-ce-qu vous avez un paquet plus grand/plus petit s'il vous plaît?

I would like some fruit ….. ripe/riper ….. not ripe
- Vorrei della frutta ….. matura/piu' matura ….. acerba
- Quisiera trusta ….. madura/mas madura ….. un poco verde
- Je voudrais des fruits ….. bien mûr/plus mûr ….. un peu verts

Can I taste it?
- Posso assaggiarlo?
- Puedo provarlo?
- Est-ce que je peux gouter?

Can you clean it ….. slice it
- Puo' pulirol ….. tagliarlo a fette
- Puede limpiarlo ….. cortalo a trozos
- Vous pouvez le nettoyer ….. le couper en tranches s'il vous plaît

I'd like some thinner ….. thicker slices please
- Vorrei delle fetter piu' sottili ….. spesse per favor
- Quiero lonchas mas finas ….. mas gruesas
- Je voudrais des tranches plus fines ….. epaisses

Do you have more?
- Ne avete dell' altro?
- No tienen otro?
- Vous avez en plus?

What would you recommend
- Cosa mi consiglia
- Que me aconseja
- Qu' est-ce que vous me conseillez

I would like it for four persons
- Ne vorrei per quattro persone
- Quiero pare cuatro personas
- Je voudrais pour quatre personnes

Do you have a different brand
- A vete unaltra marc
- No tiene otra marca
- Est-ce que vous avez une autre marque

Is it fresh
- E' fresco
- Es fresco
- C'est frais

Where can I get .....?
- Dove posso trovare .....?
- Donde puedo encountra .....?
- Ou peux je trouver .....?

Can I have a bag/box?
- Puo' darmi un sacchetto / una scatola?
- Puede darme una bolsa / una caja?
- Pouvez-vous me donner un sac / une boite?

What sort of ..... do you have?
- Che tipo di ..... avete?
- Que tipo de ..... tienen?
- Quel genre de ..... avez vous?

How much is the total?
- Quant'e in tutto?
- Cuanto es todo?
- Combien vous voulez?

Can I have the bill please?
- Posso avere il conto per favor?
- La cuenta por favor?
- L'addition s'il vous plaît?

Can I order ..... ?
- Posso ordinare ..... ?
- Puedo pedir ..... ?
- Je voudrais commander ..... ?

Can I pay by credit card?
- Posso pagare con la carta di credito?
- Puedo pagar con la tarjeta de credito?
- Je peux payer par carte de credit?

Can I have a receipt please?
- Posso avera la ricevuta/fattura?

- Puede haver la facture por favor?
- Je voudrais un reçu s'il vous plaît?

FOOD WORDS

FISH

English	Italian	Spanish	French
Anchovy	Acciuga	Anchoa	Anchois
Blue fin tuna	Tonno	Atun	Thon
Cod	Merluzzo	Bacalao	Morue
Dolphin fish	Lampuga	Lampuga	Dorade tropicale
Haddock	Eglefino	Eglefino	Aiglefin
Hake	Nasello	Merluza	Merlu/Colin
Halibut	Halibut	Fletán	Flétan
Herring	Aringa	Arenque	Hareng
Mackerel	Sgombro	Caballa	Maquereau
Monkfish	Rana Pescatrice	Rape	Baudroie
Red Mullet	Triglia	Salmonete	Rouget
Salmon	Salmone	Salmón	Saumon
Sardine	Sardina	Sardina	Sardine
Sea Bass	Spigola	Lubina	Bar
Sea Bream	Orata	Pargo	Brème
Skate	Razza	Raya	Raie
Sole	Sogliola	Lenguado	Sole
Sword Fish	Pesce Spada	Pez Espada	Espandon
Trout	Trota	Trucha	Truite
Turbot	Rombo Chiodato	Rodaballo	Turbot
Whiting	Merlano	Merlán	Merlan

SHELLFISH

English	Italian	Spanish	French
Crab	Granchio	Cangrejo	Crabe
Clam	Vongola	Almeja	Palourde
D.Bay Prawn	Scampo	Langostino	Langoustine
Lobster	Aragosta	Langosta	Homard
Oyster	Ostrica	Bogavante	Huitre
Scallop	Canestrello	Vieira	Coquille
Mussel	Cozza	Mejillón	Moule
Octopus	Polpo	Pulpo	Pieuvre
Prawn	Gambero	Gamba	Crevette
Shrimp	Gamberetto	Camarón	Crevette
Squid	Calamaro	Calamar	Calmar

MEAT

English	Italian	Spanish	French
Bacon	Pancetta	Tocino	Lard (smoked-fumé)
Beef	Manzo	Ternera	Boeuf
Breast	Petto	Pecho	Poitrine
Chicken	Pollo	Pollo	Poulet
Ham	Prosciutto	Jamon	Jambon
Cutlet	Costoletta	Chuleta	Cotelette
Duck	Anatra	Pato	Canard
Filet	Filetto	Filete	Filet

English	Italian	Spanish	French
Game	Selvaggina	Caza	Gibier
Goat	Capretto	Cabrito	Chevreau
Lamb	Agnello	Cordero	Agneau
Leg	Coscia	Piema	Cuisse/gigot
Liver	Fegato	Higado	Foie
Pheasant	Fagiano	Faisán	Faisan
Pork	Maiale	Cerdo	Porc
Salami	Salame	Saichichon	Saucisson
Steak	Bistecca	Bistec	Steak
Thin slice	Scaloppini	Escalopa	Escalope
Veal	Vitello	Ternera	Veau
Wild boar	Cinghiale	Jabali	Sanglier

FRUIT & VEGETABLES

English	Italian	Spanish	French
Almond	Mandorla	Almendra	Amande
Apricot	Albicocca	Albaricoque	Abricot
Apple	Mela	Manzana	Pommes
Artichoke	Carciofo	Alcachofa	Artichaut
Asparagus	Asparagi	Esparrago	Asperge
Aubergine	Melanzana	Berenjena	Aubergine
Avocado	Avocado	Aguacate	Avocat
Banana	Banana	Platano	Banane
Bean	Fagiolo	Judia	Haricot
Carrot	Carota	Zanahoria	Carotte
Cabbage	Cavolo	Col	Chou
Cauliflower	Cavolfiore	Coliflor	Chou-fleur
Celery	Sedano	Apio	Céleri
Cherry	Ciliegia	Cereza	Cerise
Courgette	Zucchini	Calabacin	Courgette
Cucumber	Cetriolo	Pepino	Concombre
Fennel	Finocchio	Hinojo	Fenouil
French beans	Fagiolino	Judia verde	Haricot vert
Garlic	Aglio	Ajo	Ail
Grape	Uva	Uva	Raisin
Grapefruit	Pompelmo	Pomelo	Pamplemousse
Lemon	Limone	Limon	Citron
Lentil	Lenticchie	Lentegas	Lentilles
Lettuce	Insalata	Ensalada	Salade
Melon	Melone	Melón	Melon
Mushroom	Fungo	Seta	Champignon
Nut	Noce	Nuez	Noix
Olive	Oliva	Cceituna	Olive
Onion	Cipolla	Cebolla	Oignon
Orange	Arancia	Naranja	Orange
Pea	Pisello	Guisante	Petit pois
Peach	Pesca	Melocoton	Pêche
Pear	Pera	Pera	Poir
Pepper	Peperone	Pimiento	Poivron/piment (chilli)
Pineapple	Ananas	Pina	Ananas
Potato	Patata	Patata	Pomme de terre
Pumpkin	Zucca	Calabaza	Citrouille
Raspberry	Lampone	Frambuesa	Framboise

English	Italian	Spanish	French
Spinach	Spinaci	Espinaca	Épinard
Strawberry	Fragola	Fresa	Fraise
Tomato	Pomodoro	Tomate	Tomate

DRINKS

Coffee	Caffé	Café	Café
with milk	Macchiato	Con leche	Crème
Water	Acqua	Agua	Eau
with gas	Gasata	Con gas	Gazeuse
Still	Non gasata	Sin gas	Naturelle
Orange juice	Succo d'arancia	Zumo naranja	Jus d'orange
Beer	Birra	Cerveza	Bière
Wine	Vino	Vino	Vin
White (wine)	Bianco	Blanco	Blanc
Red(wine)	Rosso	Tinto	Rouge

CONTAINERS

Glass	Bicchire	Vaso	Verre
Bottle	Bottiglia	Botella	Bouteille
Can	Lattina	Lata	Boîte
Cup	Tasse	Taza	Tasse

TEMP' & TASTE

Hot	Caldo	Caliente	Chaud
Cold	Freddo	Frio	Froid
Tepid	Tiepido	Tibio	Tiède
Sweet	Dolce	Dulce	Sucré
Savoury	Solato	Salado	Savoureux

GENERAL PROVISIONS

Bread	Pane	Pan	Pain
Butter	Burro	Mantequilla	Beurre
Cheese	Formaggio	Queso	Fromage
Chocolate	Cioccolate	Chocolate	Chocolat
Coffee	Café	Café	Café
Cream	Panna	Nata	Crème
Egg	Uovo	Huevo	Oeuf
Flour	Farina	Farina	Farine
Honey	Miele	Miel	Miele
Ice cream	Gelato	Helado	Glace
Jam	Marmellata	Mermelada	Confiture
Milk	Latte	Leche	Lait
Oil	Olio	Aceite	Huille
Pepper	Pepe	Pimiento	Poivre
Rice	Riso	Arroz	Riz
Salt	Sale	Sal	Sel
Spices	Spezie	Especias	Epices
Sugar	Zucchero	Azucar	Sucre
Vinegar	Aceto	Vinagre	Vinaigre

That's all folks, nada mas, c'est tout ……………..…. Ciao!

Made in the USA
Lexington, KY
24 July 2013